# Perspectives on *Crazy Ex-Girlfriend*

*Television and Pop Culture*
Robert J. Thompson, *Series Editor*

For a full list of titles in this series,
visit https://press.syr.edu/supressbook-series
/television-and-popular-culture/.

# Perspectives on CRAZY EX GIRLFRIEND

## Nuanced Postnetwork Television

Edited by

## Amanda Konkle and Charles Burnetts

Syracuse University Press

For a listing of books published and distributed by Syracuse University Press,
visit https://press.syr.edu.

ISBN: 978-0-8156-3704-2 (hardcover)
978-0-8156-3713-4 (paperback)
978-0-8156-5518-3 (e-book)

**Library of Congress Cataloging-in-Publication Data**
Names: Konkle, Amanda, 1982– editor. | Burnetts, Charles, editor.
Title: Perspectives on Crazy ex-girlfriend : nuanced postnetwork television /
edited by Amanda Konkle and Charles Burnetts.
Description: First edition. | Syracuse, New York : Syracuse University Press, 2021. |
Series: Television and pop culture | Includes bibliographical references and index. | Summary:
"Created and helmed by female showrunners, featuring a diverse cast, and exploring mental
health, gender and sexual identities, as well as media's influence on how we understand ourselves,
"Crazy Ex-Girlfriend" is a prime example of quality post-network television. The essays in this
collection situate the show within the current television market, explore its genre-bending
musical numbers as self-reflexive parodies, and argue for the show's groundbreaking treatments
of mental health and sexual and gender identities"— Provided by publisher.
Identifiers: LCCN 2020050672 (print) | LCCN 2020050673 (ebook) | ISBN 9780815637042 (hardback) |
ISBN 9780815637134 (paperback) | ISBN 9780815655183 (ebook)
Subjects: LCSH: Crazy ex-girlfriend (Television program) | Television musicals—
United States—History and criticism. | Television comedies—United States—History
and criticism. | Mental illness on television.
Classification: LCC PN1992.77.C699 P47 2021 (print) | LCC PN1992.77.C699 (ebook) |
DDC 791.45/72—dc23
LC record available at https://lccn.loc.gov/2020050672
LC ebook record available at https://lccn.loc.gov/2020050673

# Contents

# Acknowledgments

This collection is the result of the labor of love of many fans of *Crazy Ex-Girlfriend*, with whom the editors and contributors had conversations, geeked out on social media, and delighted in the show and its songs.

The editors and contributors would like to thank Rachel Bloom and Aline Brosh McKenna for creating this show and the musical team of Adam Schlesinger (whom the world sadly lost in 2020), Jack Dolgen, and Rachel Bloom for inspiring the essays in this collection with their ground-breaking songs. We thank Rachel Bloom for sharing her insights with Lauren Boumaroun and for her permission to quote extensively from this interview as well as from the songs in *Crazy Ex-Girlfriend*. Rachel's assistant was also instrumental in communicating with Rachel, and we thank her for her help.

We would also like to thank those who conversed with us about our research on *Crazy Ex-Girlfriend*, including panelists and attendees at the 2017 Console-ing Passions Conference and the 2018 Conference of the Society for Cinema and Media Studies. This collection has benefited greatly from the insights of Amanda Konkle's students in Gender and TV and Introduction to Women's, Gender, and Sexuality Studies at Georgia Southern University.

Thanks also to our editor, Deb Manion, whose enthusiasm for this project ushered it to fruition, and the reviewers of the manuscript, whose insights helpfully developed our thinking on the ideas contained herein.

Finally, the editors extend our gratitude to the contributors of this volume. Your hard work and dedication have led to a volume of essays on this show that showcases all of our enjoyment of *Crazy Ex-Girlfriend* as well as its important cultural contributions.

Amanda Konkle
Charles Burnetts

# Perspectives on *Crazy Ex-Girlfriend*

# Introduction

## "The Situation Is a Lot More Nuanced Than That"— How Crazy Ex-Girlfriend Defies Peak TV

### Amanda Konkle

Musical number titles featured in *Crazy Ex-Girlfriend*, such as "Where Is the Bathroom?" (1.08), "Heavy Boobs" (1.16), and "Period Sex" (2.12), might be expected on a YouTube comedy channel, but they aren't typical network television fare. These songs not only rely on cringe comedy, body humor, and parody but also are part of a generic formula that is rarely successful on television: the television book musical (a musical with original songs), whose songs are not motivated by a "backstage" integration. These numbers appear on a television show that has been hailed as "the sharpest pop satire you're not watching (or hearing)": *Crazy Ex-Girlfriend* (The CW, 2015–19).[1] The show's title is off-putting, which explains why the advertising posted in New York City's F train for the debut season was defaced with comments such as "This oppresses women!" and "Stupid show makes women all look dumb."[2] *Crazy Ex-Girlfriend* (hereafter CXG) follows the exploits of Rebecca Bunch (played by creator Rachel Bloom), who turns down a promotion at a law firm in New York City to move to West Covina, a bland suburb of Los Angeles, where her teenage summer-camp romance, Josh Chan (played by Vincent Rodriguez III), lives. But as she insists in the show's first-season theme song, "That's Not Why I'm Here!" This premise seems decidedly retrograde—a Harvard-educated lawyer upends her life to chase a man who already has a girlfriend. But it soon becomes clear that CXG deconstructs ideologies of

1

romance and craziness, among others. The show's earnest effort at cultural critique through parody might explain its status as a critical darling: *Vulture* named it the best show of 2016,[3] *The Daily Beast* insisted that it's "still the most charming show on TV" in 2017,[4] and the *New Yorker's* Emily Nussbaum repeatedly lauded it as one of her favorite shows.[5] In the final analysis, the title *Crazy Ex-Girlfriend* perfectly suits the show's ethos, which will reward the viewer who is willing to work and interested in challenging stereotypes and deconstructing generic conventions. All aspects of CXG—from title, to network strategy, to creators, to genre, to content—ultimately deconstruct the term "crazy" and demonstrate that what might initially seem "crazy" is just what is needed to stand out within a saturated TV market.

This introduction will situate the series within a changing television landscape, first discussing how The CW network used the show as part of its brand strategy as it moved into the digital television universe. Drawing on strategies developed in "quality TV" of the late 1990s and early 2000s as well as some of the emerging trends in recent "peak TV," the show's creators and showrunners, including Aline Brosh McKenna and Bloom, offered the network innovative content with which to accomplish these strategies. While CXG's early accolades are often cited as evidence of the show's success—in 2016, CXG won two Primetime Emmy Awards, a Golden Globe Award, a Critics' Choice Television Award, and a Television Critics Association Award—the show continued to win awards throughout its run, including Primetime Emmy awards for Outstanding Choreography and Outstanding Original Music and Lyrics in 2019, as well as Gracie Awards for acting in 2017 and 2019. Along with the authors of the chapters in the rest of the book, this introduction will discuss how the show challenges conventional genre boundaries and thereby deconstructs such genres as the Hollywood musical, the romantic comedy, and the music video and resists stereotypes associated with several contentious areas of modern life—heterosexual romance, bisexuality, mental illness, parenthood, gender roles, and feminism—and instead challenges viewers to reconsider the causes of and impediments to happiness.

CXG is well poised to contribute to these conversations because of its female showrunners, Bloom and Brosh McKenna. As a screenwriter, Brosh

McKenna had been deconstructing romantic comedies for years but did so within the constraints of major Hollywood studios, which meant that she had to receive someone else's approval for how she brought the women's stories in *The Devil Wears Prada* (2006, dir. David Frankel), *27 Dresses* (2008, dir. Anne Fletcher), and *Morning Glory* (2010, dir. Roger Michell), as well as more traditional romantic comedies, to screens. CXG was a passion project for both creators, an opportunity that Brosh McKenna embraced because of the security of her career and a risk that Bloom could take at the beginning of her career. According to Brosh McKenna, both women's security meant "we just never did anything to it that we didn't want to do. There's not one thing in there that anybody made us do, and I kind of think you can tell."[6] Bloom's training as a musical theater major at New York University and a sketch comic with the Upright Citizens Brigade prepared her to make original comedy with a musical element.[7] Her first comedy music video, "Fuck Me, Ray Bradbury," went viral in 2010, and Bloom began curating an audience for her blend of what she calls "ballsy and honest and vulgar" comedy.[8] Bloom's comedy joins the ranks of that of Lena Dunham in *Girls* (HBO, 2011–17) and Ilana Glazer (Bloom's former roommate) on *Broad City* (Comedy Central, 2014–19).[9] Bloom, according to Brosh McKenna, was a self-made YouTube star accustomed to making her own way without answering to anyone else: "She hasn't internalized all the rules and governors."[10]

While CXG was not initially intended for The CW, it found a fitting home at a network that has also not internalized all the rules and was willing to gamble on innovative content. The CW, formed in 2006 through the partnership of CBS, former owners of UPN, and Warner Bros., former owners of The WB, is arguably the most innovative broadcast television network, one uniquely equipped to navigate the rapidly changing television landscape and the transition to streaming video on demand (SVOD). Bloom and Brosh McKenna initially pitched CXG to Showtime as a half-hour show, but the series ended up on The CW as an expanded broadcast series, with each episode running 40 to 42 minutes. As a broadcast network, The CW is subject to pressure from both advertisers and FCC regulations. While a Showtime series would more likely feature sex and nudity, The CW network's home for the series has led to an expanded audience and increased opportunities for engaging in the cultural work of advancing conversations about sexuality, mental health, and gender roles. As Bloom pointed out in an interview with GQ's Scott Meslow: "Because we're on a network, and have to abide by FCC guidelines, mothers and daughters can watch this show together. . . . And that's really cool to me, because we talk about a lot of stuff that wasn't talked about when I was that age. And that's really special, as opposed to an edgy Showtime show that would just be watched by the hipsters who are similar to the people *making* the show."[11] The show's network and streaming presence give it the opportunity to speak to a broader audience than premium cable subscribers, and diversity within the cast and storylines appeals to that audience. Such an appeal continues the branding established by the network's precursor, The WB, which innovated in targeting the teen and young adult audience with genre-bending programming such as *Buffy the Vampire Slayer* (The WB, UPN, 1997–2003), *Dawson's Creek* (The WB, 1998–2003), and *Veronica Mars* (UPN, The CW, 2004–7).

Following years in which The CW had moved away from this legacy toward programming dominated by male-centered dramas, such as *Supernatural* (2005–20), *Arrow* (2012–20), and *The Flash* (2014–), The CW renewed its attention to women viewers as well as their established male audience. A 2014 article noted that the network was "up substantially with men, [but] it's drawing fewer female viewers," calling that "a potential problem for some current advertisers."[12] By 2016, after debuting *Jane the Virgin* (2014–19) and CXG, Maureen Ryan of *Variety* praised The CW as "the Gold Standard" for female audiences: "The network's shows celebrate female competency and complexity, and manage to be funny, imaginative, and poignant while doing so."[13] As noted by Amanda Lotz, around the mid-2010s, the majority of so-called quality TV programs on premium networks targeted male and well-educated audiences, making it less risky for broadcast networks to target female viewers with shows such as *Grey's Anatomy* (ABC, 2005–) and *The Good Wife* (CBS, 2009–16).[14] Michael Z. Newman and Elana Levine have pointed out that male-centered TV tends to be deemed worthwhile programming, while female-centered TV is delegitimated as what is watched by "less valued audiences . . . women, children, the elderly, those of lesser class status, people who spend their days at home."[15] The CW refused to be limited by these gendered distinctions and targeted the women's market with innovative programming.

It is no coincidence that the network's "Dare to Defy" advertising campaign, which calls attention to the unexpected characters, gender identities, and storylines of CW programming, was rolled out with the final season of CXG. The campaign even entered the series self-reflexively: after Rebecca's nemesis, Audra Levine (Rachel Grate), abandons her family and career for a gambler she meets in Las Vegas, Rebecca, Heather (Vella Lovell), Paula (Donna Lynne Champlin), and Valencia (Gabrielle Ruiz) fly to Vegas to convince her to return to her family. Describing their efforts to "rescue" Audra from her questionable decisions, Heather says, "We're basically heroes. Dare to defy" (4.15). This circularity of network branding and series content intentionally reminds viewers that the show is part of how The CW has defied standards for network television content with its "crazy" series.

The CW is able to defy conventions of network television programming because it has been quick to adopt new strategies for financing and distributing programming occasioned by digital streaming. Indeed, the network is known for its adaptability. As Jennifer Gillan points out, "From its inception the CW planned to 'strike alternative deals to deliver its content' to its tech-savvy demographic comfortable with the 'increasingly time-shifted, multiplatform media world.'"[16] In 2011, The CW and Netflix signed a $1 billion deal for Netflix to receive exclusive streaming rights of its scripted content; this deal was renewed in 2016.[17] Deals with streaming portals, as well as streaming their own series on their website, make it financially advantageous for the network to own its own programming (and for CBS and Warner Bros. to coproduce series).[18] CXG aired on The CW and streamed on Netflix (eight days after the season's end for viewers in the United States, next day for viewers in the United Kingdom), demonstrating the network's ability to take advantage of the postnetwork industrial transition in ways that other networks are just beginning to consider, for example, with CBS All Access or NBC's Peacock service.

The network model that originated in the 1950s is based on viewers simply watching what is on, but today's viewers expect choice and control. Those networks capitalizing on the changing times recognize that financial success depends upon giving viewers, as Netflix's Chief Content Officer Ted Sarandos said upon the renewal of this exclusive licensing deal, "exactly what they want, when and how they want it."[19] The CW's president, Mark Pedowitz, argues that such a deal also benefits the network: "The CW's programming has enjoyed tremendous success and increased exposure through Netflix. . . . The CW has positioned itself for the future by transforming into a true hybrid network, rooted in broadcast while fully embracing the digital and streaming habits of the viewers."[20] In 2014, Pedowitz said that "roughly 15% to 20%" of the network's audience consisted of streaming viewers.[21] The CW strives to attract interest via streaming services and then to direct viewers back to broadcast and to the network's website to catch new episodes, a strategy Pedowitz suggested in a 2020 interview was working.[22]

But striking streaming deals does not alleviate pressure to produce innovative and rewarding content that viewers will watch—and, in keeping with the library of legacy content model of streaming services, rewatch. According to Lotz, with SVOD came the "nee[d] to make not simply television shows people would watch on a Sunday night, but television shows people would watch and talk about ten years later. Such an endeavor didn't suggest a change from the pursuit of 'distinction,' but it explained how and why series were changing."[23] Netflix divides its viewership into specific "taste communit[ies],"[24] indicating that viewer interests now shape television content—and those viewer interests often require elements of quality and distinction, aspects that will distinguish the program from others for critics and viewers alike, thereby giving the show an immediate audience as well as longevity. The CW's financial model allows the network to be "slower to cancel low-rated shows, and [The CW] has a reputation for allowing programming time to develop . . . [and] is further driven by a desire to measure program success as a cable channel might in terms other than Nielsen ratings."[25] The hybrid model allows the network to cultivate a loyal niche audience.

CXG has benefited from these network strategies. The CW's president Mark Pedowitz insists, "Critically acclaimed, great programming, sometimes you just leave it on the air and hopefully it finds an audience."[26] CXG found an audience. For example, fans of the show on the Facebook group "Crazy Ex-Girlfriend Fans" report watching the series in its entirety two, three, four, or even eight times, as well as frequently playing the songs, which have hundreds of thousands of views each on YouTube and Spotify, and fans turned out to see the cast perform in a live tour after the series wrapped. Thus, while viewership for the series has remained relatively low by conventional Nielsen standards (for example, the third season of the show tied for ninety-fifth place out of ninety-six network series, with a rating of .3 of the 18–49 demographic),[27] these ratings do not account for Netflix streaming numbers, which have been integral to the series' financial viability.

Fans respect the network's attention to the integrity of the show's narrative arc. The series partakes in a degree of narrative complexity that depends upon character development over time. Bloom and Brosh McKenna designed the series in a four-season arc, with each season interrogating what Bloom has called "the cycles of being a quote-unquote 'crazy ex'": "falling in love with someone, being obsessed with them, getting over them, and the path to recovery."[28] The narrative is structured, as pointed out self-reflexively in the number "The End of the Movie" (3.04), sung by Josh Groban, like life: "a gradual series of revelations that occur over a period of time. . . . Life doesn't make narrative sense." CXG partakes in narrative strategies associated with complex TV. In contrast to previous decades, in which series aired until the network decided to cancel, leading to sometimes haphazard storylines and conclusions,[29] Jason Mittell points out that, since about 2005, "more series have planned their conclusions, creating a set of precedents for serial endings that variously embrace ambiguity, circularity, reflexivity, and finality."[30] For Rebecca Bunch's story to make narrative sense, viewers need all four seasons of carefully planned, self-reflexive content.

The beginnings and endings of each of CXG's four seasons are structured to "embrace ambiguity, circularity, [and] reflexivity."[31] For example, the recap for the season two finale features scenes of Rebecca and Josh at summer camp from the exposition of the first episode of season one. The season ends with a flashback showing Rebecca attempting to burn down her former professor's and lover's apartment, stating to the judge who tells her to seek mental help, "but I have no underlying issues to address," lyrics familiar to viewers from the second season theme song. Season two shows how Rebecca has both remained the same and developed over time, while also alluding to the revelations that will explain her "underlying issues" in season three, most notably with her eventual diagnosis with Borderline Personality Disorder. Season four's theme song asks viewers to "Meet Rebecca," contrasting the show's protagonist, Rebecca Bunch, with a seemingly perfect "Fabulous Girl" (Siri Miller) who nevertheless reveals some bizarre quirk at the end of each credit sequence, such as "I eat my own eyelashes" (4.05), "I'm dating my uncle" (4.08), and, to make the point of this series-long gag clear, "See? Perfection isn't real! Oh, did I have a thing? I could feel it right there" (4.15). Throughout the fourth season, Rebecca strives to establish her own identity; she wants to meet Rebecca. The finale ends with Rebecca revealing her desire to write the songs she has heard in her head in an effort to learn about who she is, effectively circling viewers back to the beginning of the series, as the songs in the series have already been identified as songs Rebecca hears in her head.

These circularities appeal to many viewers who choose to watch or rewatch the series despite the seemingly endless options made available by streaming platforms. In 2015, when "nearly 400 original series aired," including the premiere of CXG, FX CEO John Landgraf lamented an era of "peak TV" that he feared was unsustainable from a network's perspective and that made it difficult for viewers to find and keep up with good shows.[32] Landgraf intended the phrase "peak TV" as a warning, but it is now more commonly used to describe the current television landscape, in which, as Willa Paskin points out, "there is an insane amount of good television out there, and like Everest (and far lesser climbs), it can be genuinely overwhelming," not only because of "the sheer number of decent shows" but also because of "the wide variety of forms good TV now takes and the vast profusion of places it can be found."[33] Yet Landgraf's initial prediction that fewer original series would be developed in future years has not come to fruition—in December 2018, the number of scripted originals reached 495, with those fairly evenly divided between broadcast, basic cable, and online series,[34] and the number for 2019 was at about 520 in October, prior to the launches of the Apple TV Plus and Disney Plus streaming services.[35]

Television viewers have more options than time, so creators of original programming face distinctive challenges in developing that programming. The CW gambled on CXG's distinctiveness as a genre-bending and -blending series that deconstructs the romantic comedy, the musical, and the idea of "crazy." And critics have continually alluded to their "crazy" love for this "crazy" show. This collection's first chapter, David Scott Diffrient's "'Crazy for *Crazy Ex-Girlfriend*': TV Fandom and the Critical Reception of a 'Nutty' Network Series," discusses "the reciprocal interplay between text and paratext—between the show's depiction of obsessive behavior and the critical community's rhetorical accommodation of that trait in their own writing"—to acknowledge how the "crazy" in CXG remains a troubling term, despite the show's attention to the various symptoms of twenty-first-century American neuroses. Diffrient ultimately argues that the show has begun a conversation about neurodivergence and about productive aspects of fandom that must be continued. And the series' complete run has demonstrated that, as James Poniewozik concluded his review of CXG's pilot for the *New York Times*: "it could just be crazy enough to work."[36]

## Musical Television

Part of what makes the show seem "crazy," and equally what brings viewers happiness, are the show's musical numbers. While many of the series' most memorable musical numbers resemble YouTube music videos and can be widely shared out of context, the series also features several numbers that are more decidedly musical theater, often drawing on classical Hollywood musical stylings and incorporating several genres of music, including hair metal, musical theater, boy/girl bands, 1980s pop, and so on. From its inception, critics marveled at the show's successful use of the musical format. But, as *Vox*'s Constance Grady explains, CXG "succeeds where most TV musicals fail" because "its songs are overwhelmingly character-driven."[37] A closer look at previous musical television failures and successes will illuminate exactly how CXG defied the odds and became a successful television musical.

CXG has succeeded as an unashamed musical hybrid right from the start, but musical television shows, and especially those in which the characters are not performers, are still comparatively rare entities. Ron Rodman notes that musical numbers were common on sketch comedy shows, variety shows, and sitcoms of the 1950s, 1960s, and 1970s, but the musical numbers on these shows did not constitute the premise of the shows.[38] Prior musical series that were not integrated backstage musicals, like *Cop Rock* (ABC, 1990), which fused the musical and police drama, and *Viva Laughlin* (CBS, 2007), which aired only two episodes, have become jokes if they are remembered or commented on at all. According to Rodman, *Cop Rock* failed because "television-cop-show drama viewers were not ready to accept the hybridization of musical and cop show. However, the musical cop show did exist in the guise of *The Singing Detective*, which was a show quite different in its 'repertoire of elements,' featuring a fantasy world of an invalid rather than trying to pass itself off as a realistic rendition of a police procedural."[39] The "fantasy world" is also central to CXG's success.

In contrast to the failed musical episodes of the past, those television musicals that have been successful have centered around performers. Recent successful musical television shows include *Flight of the Conchords* (HBO, 2007–9), which used the music video parody aesthetic in a comedy about a two-man band from New Zealand. *Glee* (Fox, 2009–15) premiered with an audience of over nine million viewers and maintained a substantial audience, averaging over three million viewers in its final season.[40] *Glee* succeeded because the series as a whole is a backstage musical focused on a high school glee club, for whom bursting into song and dance are accepted, and even expected, behaviors. Since then, *Smash* (NBC, 2012–13), *Nashville* (ABC, CMT, 2012–18), and *Empire* (Fox, 2015–20) have joined the ranks of integrated, backstage musicals appearing on network television. CXG seems, at first glance, to have more in common with previous failures, which imposed musical theater onto nonmusical settings, than the more integrated network successes—none of the characters work in the music industry, and a lawyer in her late twenties isn't typically expected to burst into song.

Musical episodes of not otherwise musical shows are also relevant to the discussion of CXG's success as a musical series that does not feature musical performers. For example, musical episodes of *Xena: Warrior Princess* ("The Bitter Suite," 3.12, 1998, syndication), *Buffy the Vampire Slayer* ("Once More with Feeling," 6.7, 2001, UPN), and *Scrubs* ("My Musical," 6.6, 2007, NBC) have garnered acclaim. Mary Jo Lodge argues that "the book musical structure," featuring original songs written for the characters and narrative, rather than integrating preexisting songs into the show (such as in *Viva Laughlin* or, in an example more likely familiar to readers, *Moulin Rouge* [2001, dir. Baz Luhrmann]), might be one of the keys to the success of musical television shows.[41] Lodge also insists that an integrated book musical structure only works within a narrative that already consists of "a heightened reality and fantasy sequences."[42] Because CXG's credits and opening scenes introduce viewers to the workings of Rebecca Bunch's psyche, viewers are primed to read the musical numbers as Rebecca's fantasies.

CXG's storylines are largely realist, but the overdramatic or perhaps fantastic characters associated with them are made sympathetic through their corresponding musical numbers, which disarm our critiques of the characters and instead encourage us to sympathize with them. In films, musical numbers are thought of as ruptures in the narrative—moments of excess and spectacle, perhaps utopian spaces where solutions to the narrative's problems arise.[43] In CXG, the musical numbers are not always utopic—in fact, they often call attention to the dystopic situations in which Rebecca Bunch and other characters find themselves. Janet Halfyard transforms the utopic possibilities of musical numbers in film musicals (as outlined by Richard Dyer) into dystopic possibilities in television musicals—"abundance" becomes "excess," "energy" becomes "inappropriate playfulness or cheerfulness," "transparency" becomes "excessive honesty, involuntary spontaneity, [or] incomprehensibility," and "community" becomes "isolation, illusion of community, insincerity."[44] CXG makes viewers laugh out loud, but it does so through exposing its characters' vulnerabilities in ways that would be deemed excessive or inappropriate if not done in song; Rebecca and her friends are "excessive[ly] hones[t]" and "insincer[e]" in turn. Through the musical numbers, the characters comment on the causes of their isolation, causes explored in this collection: previous traumas, pressures to conform to unrealistic romantic ideals, and stigmas surrounding mental illness. Its engagement with these and other topics makes the show content that viewers seek out.

The example of the series' theme songs may serve to illustrate the crucial role music plays in defying expectations within the peak TV landscape. Each season has a unique theme song, and these theme songs contribute in multiple ways to the narrative overall. First, they provide variety in a postnetwork viewing situation in which viewers are likely to binge-watch the series. Second, they establish the show as a musical, so that viewers are not taken aback by the format but begin suspending their disbelief from the initial extravagant title production numbers. Third, they contribute to the overall narrative arc, providing narrative information about the titular character and also demonstrating that the character has developed and is developing over time. Finally, the theme songs participate in the show's deconstruction of the term "crazy." For example, Bloom says the season three theme song, in which Rebecca encounters several music-video versions of attitudes toward "crazy" women, was the most difficult song to write, "because [the] theme songs are the story Rebecca is telling herself," and Rebecca "was telling herself different stories, and she didn't know which story to tell herself. And she was running out of stories."[45] Following this, the season four theme song asks viewers to "Meet Rebecca," with a montage of her seemingly incongruous past actions placing viewers in a situation akin to Rebecca's efforts to make sense of herself.

Musical television also provides a way of stepping outside of and beyond accepted norms for self-expression. Through song, Lodge insists, "deeply locked away and painful secrets can be more easily revealed."[46] The series resulted in an eventual total of 157 original songs by Bloom, Jack Dolgen, and Adam Schlesinger, revealing a number of secrets related to mental health, to overcoming trauma, to resisting confining gender norms, to uncertain and shifting sexual identities, and to finding one's happiness. This applies not only to the characters within the narrative but also to the viewers, who use the songs outside the narrative for their own ends. Raymond Knapp has pointed out that musicals and gender/sexual identities are often seamlessly interwoven because of the performative nature of both; "musicals provide material for *performance*" and "gender roles and sexuality are, above all, *performed* attributes of personal identity and so constitute a central dimension of how people are defined, both onstage and off."[47] Thus, it is not surprising that, for example, viewers of CXG have used Darryl Whitefeather's song, "Gettin' Bi" (1.14), about his newly discovered bisexuality, to come out.[48] As Kathleen W. Taylor Kollman discusses in chapter 7, "'Gettin' Bi': Darryl Whitefeather as Bisexual Bellwether," the show's treatment of Darryl's bisexuality contradicts bisexual marginalization in both queer theory and other queer media. In contrast to media stories that erase bisexual identity as either "really" gay or "really" straight, CXG, Kollman argues, provides a character who is attracted to both men and women and normalizes that identity as an identity. CXG does this through song.

And yet the show's musical numbers are not only capable of appealing to those viewers who accept the fantasy elements uncomplainingly. Bloom is the master of parody, and she uses the dark musical comedy and the music video aesthetic to, as she says, "d[o] the genre so hard that you're parodying the genre."[49] CXG parodies the musical with its comedic takes on standards (e.g., "Settle for Me" [1.04], a riff on a Ginger Rogers and Fred Astaire waltz, or "Cold Showers" [1.12], which situates a legal suit against an apartment manager as a take on "Trouble" from Music Man), as well as its comedic take on pop music (see, for example, Bibi Burger and Carel van Rooyen's discussion of the pop-influenced "Sexy Getting Ready Song" in chapter 13). The show's self-conscious reflexivity becomes apparent in musical numbers in which the characters question why they are singing. For example, when Paula sings "Face Your Fears" (1.03), she transitions into a presentational mode of performance, in response to which Rebecca asks, "Who are you singing to?" Season two is even more self-reflexive; for example, in the song "Who's the New Guy?" (2.09), about Rebecca's new boss, Nathaniel (Scott Michael Foster), George (Danny Jolles), a coworker, sing-asks, "Do we really need a new guy this far into the season, and by far into the season, I mean it's almost fall?" The show explains its status as a musical only at the end of the second season, in a flashback of Rebecca at a psychiatric facility. The nurse explains, "She sings to herself all day. No one knows why." And in the final episode of the series, the songs are definitively motivated as Rebecca explains to Paula, "When I stare off into space, I'm imagining myself in a musical number.

That's how I sometimes see big moments in my life . . . as musical numbers. And because I do that, so does the show" (4.17). (Rebecca quickly goes on, "And by show I mean the very popular BPD workbook acronym 'simply having omniscient wishes'" [4.17].)

Such self-reflexivity works to bring viewers in on the joke rather than mock their acceptance of the show's fantasy format. In chapter 2, "Musicals Have a Place: Navigating the Television Market with a Crazy Cult Show," Chelsea McCracken discusses how CXG participates in what some warned were risky, or "crazy," forms of content and distribution for a network show: a television musical featuring exportable music-video style numbers. Nevertheless, as McCracken explains, the show integrates the musical numbers in a way that appeals to both fans of the musical, by alluding to a variety of musical genres from the classical to the contemporary, as well as skeptics, through its knowing self-reflexivity. And this format also primes the show for distribution through music videos on YouTube and through digital streaming services, demonstrating The CW's savvy in navigating the increasingly digital television market. The show's content, which the next section discusses, appeals to viewers with endless programming options in this market.

### "When Was the Last Time You Were Truly Happy?"

Throughout its four seasons, CXG asks hard questions about what makes us happy and what impedes our happiness—and this, approached as it is through humor and diverse, unconventional stories, is a big part of what draws viewers to watch and rewatch the show. Rebecca Bunch's life changes are initially inspired by a butter advertisement that asks, "When was the last time you were truly happy?," and, as the series progresses, all its characters confront their own unhappiness as well. CXG views happiness, much as Sara Ahmed does, as a "path" rather than an "end point."[50] CXG addresses pathways to happiness in a number of ways: it interrogates ideologies of love and romance, challenges "the patriarchy" with real women's bodies and real women's body humor, investigates alternatives to heteronormativity and the kinds of success associated with the American Dream, depicts mental illness and the slow process of recovery, and ultimately redeems its cringeworthy antiheroine through her discovery of what makes her truly happy.

CXG is ostensibly driven by ideologies of love and romance. Rebecca moves to West Covina because her job, which would have paid $545,000 a year, "made [her] blue" despite being "objectively fantastic" (1.01). Her choice of where to relocate, however, is the result of running into her teenage summer camp boyfriend, Josh Chan, in New York. She thinks, because of the fortuitous timing of an arrow on the bottom of the very same butter billboard asking, "When was the last time you were truly happy?," falling and pointing directly at Josh, that a renewed relationship with Josh would make her happy. Season two's theme song warns, "You can't call her crazy, 'cause when you call her crazy, you're just calling her in love," effectively equating love and insanity.

Rebecca and other women within the show recognize the workings of what they refer to as "the patriarchy," but they are nevertheless compelled to conform to hegemonic femininity, perhaps by the dictates of postfeminism, which suggest that unhappy career women could be happy if only they sought love. In chapter 13, "'Put Yourself First in a Sexy Way': Metamodernist Feminism in *Crazy Ex-Girlfriend*," Bibi Burger and Carel van Rooyen use the concept of metamodernism to analyze the tensions between second-wave feminist and postfeminist ideas in CXG, in particular in the first season songs "The Sexy Getting Ready Song" (1.01) and "Put Yourself First" (1.10). Ultimately, they argue that the show skirts rather than answers questions regarding the empowering nature of a woman's beauty, finding evidence of the show's oscillation between feminist ideologies in "sincere feminist statements that are relativized, simultaneously, by irony and humor." Burger and van Rooyen are careful to point out that the show does not invalidate any of its characters' postfeminist longings, but rather shows them to be dictated by men's desires and consumer capitalism. This is, Burger and van Rooyen argue, how the show navigates between modernist hopefulness and postmodern distancing and cynicism in favor of a renewed sincerity—we see the flaws of Rebecca and the other characters, but these characters are ultimately sympathetic figures.

CXG also garners audience sympathy when it refuses to pit women against each other as rivals. While Valencia is initially frustrated that

Rebecca is trying to get close to Josh rather than win her friendship, Valencia eventually ends up helping Rebecca plan her wedding to Josh. Similarly, when Heather realizes that Greg (Santino Fontana) is still in love with Rebecca, she breaks off her relationship with Greg but remains friends with Rebecca. Marija Laugalyte, in chapter 12, "Crazy Ex-Girlfriend's Female Networks: From Hacking and Selfies to Taking Responsibility," examines the "female networks" that are created and maintained through the use of technology within CXG, arguing that these networks help women both negotiate and resist heteronormativity. While Laugalyte acknowledges that these female networks allow the women to create their own narratives that do not rely on heteronormative romance, she also recognizes that technology keeps the narratives of heteronormativity in the forefront of the women's experience, reminding them of their "failures" in self-promotion and desirability. Ultimately, the women have to learn to live without the mediating technology and to focus on their own happiness, even if that happiness falls outside of heteronormativity.

Ultimately, then, although romantic comedy tropes initiate CXG's narrative, the show insists that buying into these tropes can impede happiness. As Charles Burnetts argues in chapter 3, "Deconstructing Crazy: Jewishness, Neuroticism, and the Stylized Rom-Com in *Crazy Ex-Girlfriend*," CXG plays with the conventions of the romantic comedy "to foreground the contradictions" of gendered, and raced, identity categories. Rebecca's Jewishness thus informs the show's romantic comedy. The "JAP Battle" (1.13) and its reprise (4.15) acknowledge the trope of the Jewish American Princess (JAP) and the stereotypes that accompany it. As Bloom told Whitney Friedlander, "I don't associate being JAP-y with not having a job and wanting your husband to do everything. It's the entire package. The princess aspect of it, to me, is kind of white privilege . . . that's true of anyone upper middle class in this country, especially if they're not of color."[51] That is, at times, the show acknowledges its characters' privilege as well as the stereotypes that shape their expectations for themselves. Perceptively, by discussing Rebecca's Jewishness within the rom-com genre, Burnetts argues that the embrace of the American Dream, which involves heterosexual coupling and the formation of the family unit, is what is crazy. Ultimately, Burnetts argues, the show resists the white heterosexual coupling associated with the rom-com in favor of mixed-race and queer relationships, as well as queered forms of desire.

One way this queered desire manifests itself in CXG is through the love triangle. Hazel Mackenzie, in chapter 6, "'Lady, We're All Gay!': The Math of Homosocial Triangles," insightfully contextualizes CXG's deployment of the love triangle, both male-dominated (Josh-Rebecca-Greg; Josh-Rebecca-Nathaniel) and female-dominated (Rebecca-Josh-Paula; Rebecca-Josh-Valencia) within The CW's brand, including both past and present shows built around the conventional use of the love triangle for dramatic tension, including The WB's *Dawson's Creek* (1998–2003) and *Felicity* (1998–2002) and current series *The Flash, Supergirl, Arrow,* and *The Vampire Diaries*. But Mackenzie argues that CXG differentiates itself from these other shows on the same network, and from other peak TV shows, by calling attention to the possibility of homosocial bonding implied in the love triangle. As Mackenzie argues, "'The Math of Love Triangles' both successfully undercuts the validity of the love triangle as portrayed by popular culture as a useful metaphor for human relationships and simultaneously points to more productive meanings buried within the metaphor: the love triangle as a means of constructing and expressing homosocial relationships." Each character in the show's various triangles achieves selfhood and agency only after they resist the triangulation in favor of genuine self-knowledge and relationships.

CXG also acknowledges that women within heterosexual relationships are entitled to desire and pleasure. CXG uses body humor and the "defamiliarization" that accompanies comedy to, paradoxically, familiarize viewers with the particularities of the female body that are rarely depicted on (broadcast network) television.[52] CXG's comedy functions as much women's humor has, to expose and critique the structures of oppression. According to Linda Mizejewski, "women's comedy has become a primary site in mainstream pop culture where feminism speaks, talks back, and is contested."[53] CXG has worked hard to demystify women's bodies, frankly discussing period sex (2.12) and women's orgasms (3.02) in an attempt to render the female body less intimidating. In season three, the series made television history by using the word "clitoris" on broadcast TV. When Tim (Michael McMillian) denies the existence of the "orgasm gap," Maya (Esther Povitsky) takes it upon herself to educate him. Tim argues that the G-spot is the locus of orgasm, but Maya insists, citing a "scientific study," that "70 to 80 percent of women only achieve orgasm from direct stimulation of the clitoris" (3.02). As Linda Mizejewski and Victoria Sturtevant note, "unless and until women's full range of experiences, including medical, scatological, and gynecological ones, are represented in popular entertainment—as male equivalents have been—then their bodies will remain fertile terrain for projected anxieties."[54] In an earlier effort to dispel the mysteries surrounding women's bodies, "The Sexy Getting Ready Song," in which Rebecca sings about dressing for a night out, calls attention to the labor that shapes emphasized femininity. Of the song, Susan Dominus writes, "Quietly and without much notice, last fall the CW network aired what was most likely broadcast television's first-ever depiction of anal waxing."[55] While the lyrics and musical style are sensuous, the words "I'm going to make this night one you'll never forget" juxtaposed with the splattering blood and hair-covered waxing strips are decidedly un-sexy, and as the verse rapped by Nipsey Hussle asserts, in fact "some nasty-ass patriarchal bullshit." Patriarchy, throughout CXG, is depicted as relatively mundane oppressions and inconveniences associated with the beauty industry and heterosexual romance rather than systemic inequality, but this aspect of the show also parodies the way patriarchy is figured in postfeminist discourse.

CXG also acknowledges that women's bodies have appetites. In chapter 14, "'I'm Ravenous': Hunger for Food, Sex, and Power in *Crazy Ex-Girlfriend*," Christi Cook explores women's hunger, arguing, "Where society's hunger for young women and simultaneous insistence that they not have their own hunger intersects with ambivalent expressions about appetite from the young women themselves is where those young women are able to find resistance and agency." Through the metaphor of the hungry, toothed *vagina dentata*, Cook alerts us to the ways in which CXG depicts women's appetites, both of their "horizontal and vertical lips," and gives "vaginas . . . a voice." Ultimately, the show embraces Rebecca's appetites but resists their satisfaction in traditional heterosexual romance, making the end of its story the beginning of Rebecca's finding her voice.

In addition to the realities of women's bodies and sexual desires, CXG also considers how heteronormativity and the very idea of the American Dream affect happiness by attending to other characters' stories. Viewers see not only Rebecca but also other characters develop self-awareness and contemplate their own happiness paths. Darryl recognizes both that he is bisexual and that he wants another child, Paula acknowledges that her happiness does not consist in her family alone and goes to law school, and Valencia begins a relationship with Beth (Emma Willmann) and moves to New York City. Billy Stevenson, in chapter 4, "Television after Complexity: *Crazy Ex-Girlfriend* and the Late 2010s," explains how the show deviates from the male-auteured "complex TV" of the 1990s and early 2000s by virtue of being created by two women and, because of the show's musical format, necessarily the creative vision of a team. Stevenson analyzes the same multiplicity of perspectives as they appear in the show's credit sequences, which continually play with both narrative tropes and self-reflexivity. Ultimately, the show's focus is not only on the titular crazy ex-girlfriend but also on the community that surrounds her, and Stevenson argues, drawing on Lili Loofbourow's phrase, that the show's "promiscuous protagonism" mirrors its promiscuous creation.

CXG also reconceives the workings of narrative to interrogate what impedes happiness. In chapter 5, "'This Is What Happy Feels Like': The Cripped Narrative of *Crazy Ex-Girlfriend*," Caitlin E. Ray reads the show through the lens of crip theory and argues that the show's musical numbers stop and bend time to tell a new, nonlinear story about the experience of living with mental illness. According to Ray, "the show also subverts typical representations of disability through its musical numbers," which tell a "nonlinear narrative through the *cripped* perspective of Rebecca." This cripped perspective can be the result of childhood traumas as well as diagnosable mental illness, as Stephanie Salerno explains in chapter 10, "'Let Us Ugly Cry': Spoofing Emotional Vulnerability in Season Three of *Crazy Ex-Girlfriend*." Echoing Ray's discussion of cripped time in chapter 5, Salerno analyzes "how nonnormative (traumatized, ill, and/or Othered) bodies express vulnerability along a flexible temporal spectrum that shifts between fantasy and reality." Through musical parody, Salerno argues, multiple characters within the series, including Rebecca, Nathaniel, Josh, and White Josh (David Hull), surrender to their own personal vulnerabilities, occasioned by childhood traumas and fears of abandonment.

The ideologies of success and the American Dream are often shown to be responsible for the characters' unhappiness. Salerno specifically analyzes musical numbers that challenge toxic masculinity, the stigmatizing of mental illness, and so-called adult responsibility as societal norms that cause individuals to be unable to express their emotions and accept themselves. None of these characters are "normal," and that is what makes their queered timelines and decisions relatable to audiences. Christine Prevas then takes on the idea that, as the song says, "Nothing Is Ever Anyone's Fault" (3.13), by examining the representation of familial trauma both within the show and within our culture in chapter 11, "Failure and the Family in *Crazy Ex-Girlfriend*." Prevas argues, "Through its examination of families and familial pressures, CXG condemns nostalgia for monogamy, domesticity, and traditional success as an impossible way of life." As opposed to an embrace of the American Dream of success, CXG, Prevas posits, might laud the merits of failure. Failure, after all, is outside the norms of American society, and thus embracing it frees one from striving to satisfy others' expectations. Prevas argues that the many failed families in the show act as a challenge to norms of domesticity, heterosexuality, reproduction, and capitalist success and the pressures these norms exert upon individuals to engage in self-surveillance. Prevas characterizes the show as a "post–'happy family'" embrace of the ways happiness is shaped outside of the heteronormative family, not only for Rebecca but also for all of the show's characters.

Rebecca's progress toward happiness is slower than that of the other characters because of her mental illness, but the show's engagement with mental illness acknowledges a frequently unacknowledged cause of unhappiness. And yet the show works deliberately to destigmatize mental illness and its treatment. In the season 4 number, "Anti-Depressants Are So Not a Big Deal," Dr. Akopian (Micheal Hyatt) tells Rebecca, "Honey, you're not special 'cause you're sad," and a crowd of other antidepressant takers sings, "Anti-depressants are so common that taking them is all we have in common" (4.13). In chapter 9, "'A Diagnosis!!': *Crazy Ex-Girlfriend* and the Destigmatization of Mental Illness in the Era of Postnetwork Television," Margaret Tally looks specifically at the show's third season, arguing that, although Rebecca is diagnosed with Borderline Personality Disorder, which is stigmatized as a woman's disorder, the show also destigmatizes the therapy and work that accompany any mental health diagnosis. As Tally argues, in contrast to other television series featuring women with complicated mental health, including *Broad City* (Comedy Central, 2014–), *Jessica Jones* (Netflix, 2015–19), *Shameless* (Showtime, 2011–), and *UnReal* (Lifetime/Hulu, 2015–18), CXG depicts a character whose life is improved with a diagnosis and treatment, and whose romantic exploits are jettisoned in favor of self-care.

CXG's depiction of diagnosis and recovery has been therapeutic for many viewers. Lauren Boumaroun spoke with Bloom in the interval between seasons one and two. In chapter 8, "'I'm the Villain in My Own Story': Representations of Depression and the Spectatorial Experience," Boumaroun argues, using paratextual information about the show and its creators, as well as the formal characteristics of significant songs such as "You Stupid Bitch," that the show, through its use of lyrics that accurately represent how one speaks to oneself when depressed, can provide a "therapeutic viewing experience." "Although Rebecca's obsessive and problematic behavior could have easily fallen into the realm of stereotype," Boumaroun concludes, "CXG's formal characteristics and comedic style work together to destigmatize mental illness and humanize the characters."

Even following Rebecca's diagnosis in 3.06, she struggles to find happiness and change her behaviors. Over the course of CXG's first three seasons, Rebecca sleeps with Greg's dad, puts a hit on Nathaniel's girlfriend, mails Josh poop, and tries to kill Josh's lolo, among other misdeeds to which she confesses (3.13). Rebecca's coworker, George, warns her, "You're a loose cannon, Bunch. You hurt everyone around you." Rebecca is an antihero at best and a villain at worst. Rebecca identifies this position for herself when she sings, "I'm the Villain in My Own Story" (1.14). She croons: "Though I insist I'm the protagonist, it's clear that my soul is up for sale" as she looks at a green-faced and pointy fingernailed version of herself in the mirror. A central antihero has long been a valued characteristic of male-centered serial drama, such as *Breaking Bad* (AMC, 2008–13) or *The Sopranos* (HBO, 1999–2007), but Rebecca's song indicates that antiheroines are often aligned with witches (or another, rhyming word). Shweta Khilnani explains, "a female anti-hero is often unapologetically ambitious and is willing to transcend moral boundaries to achieve her goals. Ultimately, this unbridled ambition becomes her redeeming quality."[56] CXG increasingly acknowledges the absurdity and harmfulness of Rebecca's selfish behaviors, until Rebecca pleads "responsible" to pushing Trent (Paul Welsh) off a roof when she thought he was going to hurt Nathaniel.

Doing time as the result of this plea of "responsible," Rebecca thinks she can punish herself into happiness—but the show reveals that it takes more than that to be happy. Nevertheless, Rebecca learns some important lessons from her time in prison, as indicated by the number "What's Your Story?" (4.01), which parodies *Chicago*'s "Cell Block Tango." When Rebecca finds out there's a theater class at the prison, she is elated, but when the inmates don't like singing "A Wonderful Guy" from *South Pacific*, with Rebecca in the lead, she comes up with a number more relevant to their experiences and begs them to tell their stories. Rebecca expects the sexy tales of revenge against the men who did them wrong that form the backbone of "Cell Block Tango," as is evident when she croons, "What does your story say about the patriarchy?" The inmates lounge in chairs wearing sexy lingerie over their orange jumpsuits, calling to mind not only *Chicago*'s sexualization of women inmates but also the recent success of *Orange Is the New Black* (Netflix, 2013–19) and its depiction of a white-collar criminal's experience in the prison system. But the simultaneous wearing of the lingerie and the jumpsuits indicates that Rebecca's fantasy can't overcome the reality of their imprisonment.

Rather than sexualized tales of woe, Rebecca hears the story of a woman who did the time when she was pulled over with her boyfriend's stashed meth in her glove compartment so that her son wouldn't have both parents in jail. Or a woman who stole a sweater, not "as the culmination of a lifetime of kleptomania" or "to stick it to the problematic fashion industry," as Rebecca assumes, but because the woman's heat went out and she didn't have money for a sweater. When a white prisoner enters the frame and says that she got two months for the same crime, this black inmate says she got three years. The woman apologizes profusely, but of course her apologies don't resolve the injustice. Nevertheless, Rebecca remains focused on her fantasy narrative of musical theater in a women's prison garnering the attention of NPR and Lin-Manuel Miranda, and recounts her story to show the women how to spice up these "bleak anecdotes." When she concludes her story, "And then when I plead guilty, just for like metaphorical symbolism, the judge knew I was innocent, so she didn't accept my plea but I wanted to go to jail anyway," the inmates walk away from Rebecca's game, disgusted.

This song is an example of how the show's cringe aesthetic is essential to its parody. Julia Havas and Maria Sulimma argue that "cringeworthy moments . . . expos[e] central characters' personal faults or their social environments' shortcomings as political issues" and thereby develop "'complex' central characters, a term often used in critical commentary interchangeably with 'antihero' protagonists."[57] When these antihero protagonists are women, however, "These female-centered cringe dramedies frequently explore their characters' violations of social and cultural taboos, many of which are particularly constituted as gendered expectations about appropriate enactments of femininity."[58] Rebecca is so out of touch with the criminal justice system and the real, heartbreaking stories of her fellow inmates that she has trouble recognizing that issues of socioeconomic status and race inform their crimes and sentences, and that her choice to spend time in prison as a metaphorical penance only reveals the extent of her privilege. Rebecca's privilege is a social issue, and it seems undeniable that the show intends viewers to cringe at her tone-deafness.[59]

Within this tradition, Rebecca (and perhaps Paula), might be considered what Jorie Lagerwey and Taylor Nygaard refer to as "Horrible White People" on "Horrible White People shows." According to Lagerwey and Nygaard, these shows feature "white women in emotional distress or facing mental illness—women who distract viewers from the plight of minorities most impacted by Trump's policies and broader political agenda."[60]

Certainly the ease with which Rebecca can write checks to get the things she wants, the ease with which she can move across the country and begin a new life, and the lack of financial difficulties when she quits her job as a lawyer and opens a not-that-successful pretzel stand in season four all suggest that she is somewhat out of touch with the concerns of many working women. Instead, as Lagerwey and Nygaard assert, "Horrible White People" characters like Rebecca force viewers to acknowledge "the failure of their white middle-class identity to grant them the privilege of stable or easy-to-find jobs, accessible home ownership, and long-term relationships."[61] Rebecca's mental illness damages her relationships, but the series' four-season arc is essential to understanding how it portrays Rebecca's attempts to be a little less horrible.

Rebecca is not always a likeable character. For example, she admits as she sits across a prison visiting room table from Paula, Valencia, and Heather, "I figured out something huge. I am privileged" (4.01). Heather, serving as a surrogate for the viewer, who has experienced demonstrations of Rebecca's privilege and tone-deafness throughout the series, calls her on this, asking, "That just occurred to you just right now?" Despite her failings, Rebecca learns and grows as a result of her experiences. Episode titles shift from being centered on others' actions (e.g., "Josh and I Are Good People!" [1.05], "Josh Is the Man of My Dreams, Right?" [2.11], and "Nathaniel and I Are Just Friends!" [3.11]), suggesting that others are responsible for Rebecca's happiness and unhappiness, to being centered on Rebecca's ownership of her own choices and feelings in season four (e.g., "I Am Ashamed" [4.02] or "I Have to Get Out" [4.13]), demonstrating Rebecca's slow process of stepping outside of herself.

This is not to say that Rebecca's whole character ultimately changes. In the series finale, she goes on dates with Josh, Greg, and Nathaniel, respectively, and asks all her friends to attend a self-aggrandizing open-mic night where she plans to dramatically announce her decision regarding which man she will continue to date and which man will make her happy. Even in the finale, when many fans clamored for Rebecca to choose one man and get her final, romantic, happy ending, the show "dared to defy" conventions. Demonstrating her growth in a very Rebecca fashion, in a stage show, Rebecca declaims, "Romantic love is not an ending. Not for me and not for anyone else here. It's just a part of your story" (4.17). And this show has inspired thousands of fans to also ask themselves when they were last truly happy, and to understand that asking that question, and answering it from one's own inclinations, rather than from society's pressures, is the greatest gift CXG gave to its audience.

# Part One

# Critics, Genre, and "Quality TV"

# 1

# "Crazy for *Crazy Ex-Girlfriend*"

*TV Fandom and the Critical Reception of a "Nutty" Network Series*

## David Scott Diffrient

A few days prior to and immediately following the October 12, 2015 premiere of *Crazy Ex-Girlfriend* (2015–19), dozens of American television critics weighed in on this latest addition to The CW's youth-skewing Monday night programming block. Created by Aline Brosh McKenna and the show's star, Rachel Bloom, this "most unusual" amalgam of comedy, melodrama, musical, and romance was greeted as "an out-of-the-blue surprise and an out-of-the-box treasure" by those who, already fatigued by a "fairly dismal fall TV season," found it to be a refreshing break from "normality."[1] Paired with another of the network's critically praised series, *Jane the Virgin* (The CW, 2014–19), which mixes genres with equal aplomb and adopts a parodic stance toward tropes associated with the *telenovela*, *Crazy Ex-Girlfriend* (hereafter CXG) was described by several of the nation's top reviewers as "clever," "fresh," "inventive," "original," "quirky," "unfamiliar," and "unique."[2] Such discourse attests to the overwhelmingly positive reception of a program whose most distinguishing feature (aside from the lavishly designed, lyrically audacious musical numbers that pepper each episode) is its unconventional protagonist: a "wonderfully flawed, dementedly romantic" young woman who—even as early as the pilot episode ("Josh Just Happens to Live Here!")—was already being labeled as "totally insane" and "certifiably cracked" by many of the same critics who were

29

exhibiting their own titular mania, their own crazed fixation on this new object of their collective fascination.[3]

In this chapter, I provide a snapshot of *CXG*'s critical reception, weaving together some of the common threads that cut across those initial reviews of the pilot episode and highlighting in the process the reciprocal interplay between text and paratext—between the show's depiction of obsessive behavior and the critical community's rhetorical accommodation of that trait in their own writing. A few pop culture critics in particular— *Entertainment Weekly*'s Jeff Jensen; the *New Yorker*'s Emily Nussbaum; the *New York Times*'s James Poniewozik; and Matt Zoller Seitz, the editor at large of the film review website RogerEbert.com who contributes TV reviews to *New York Magazine* and *Vulture*—have risen to prominence as purveyors of the *CXG* "gospel," spreading their unabashed love for the program in a way that is oddly consistent with heroine Rebecca Bunch's uninhibited romantic desires. These writers have spoken (and tweeted) about their own personal attachment to the program, the deep emotional investment that provides demonstrable evidence of its cultish appeals and that is shared not only by *CXG* fans but also by other individuals in their profession (i.e., the larger community of reviewers who are often tasked with objectivity and sometimes asked to keep their biases and fannish fawning to a minimum). And though they might share Nussbaum's contention that the show is "just too juicy, and too bold, to nitpick,"[4] these and other online reviewers adopt a sometimes-quibbling critical language that will be familiar to many academics and reveal a capacity to "go deep," below the surface of the text, in pursuit of symptomatic meanings that are only just now (in this book) being broached by media scholars.

Besides considering the reciprocal interplay between text and paratext, I also seek to contribute to ongoing conversations about the once clearly demarcated but increasingly blurred line between the vernacular writing style associated with pop culture journalism and the (presumably) more theoretically rigorous but sometimes off-putting approach of media scholars and other academics. Trained in the use of "specialized vocabulary," the latter group has long been counseled against the kind of emotionally "unhinged" rhetoric that is so apparent in the rapturous reception of *CXG*. Thankfully, though, forward-thinking members of that group, including

Henry Jenkins, Jane Shattuc, and Tara McPherson, have cleared a path out of the proverbial forest, pointing out that, within the porous arena of cultural studies, theory is beginning to look more and more like journalism.[5] Likewise, a new generation of nonacademic writers with large fan bases of their own (including Jensen, Nussbaum, Poniewozik, and Seitz) are bringing a keen eye for detail and an encyclopedic knowledge of the medium's history to bear on TV shows that, without these and other popular critics' efforts, might otherwise never receive the shrewd interpretative commentary or consideration that they deserve. As Jenkins, Shattuc, and McPherson argue in their 2002 "Manifesto for a New Cultural Studies," academics need not retreat from, or be ashamed of, their "passionate engagement" with media texts. Instead, they should embrace their "multiple (and often contradictory) involvements, participations . . . and identifications with popular culture—without denying, rationalizing, and distorting them."[6] In doing so, "aca-fans" with access to traditional educational capital as well as to interpretative communities outside the university are starting to occupy the amorphous space of public intellectuals, or what the authors of the previously mentioned manifesto refer to as "organic intellectuals" (whose words and ideas might reach "wider social and political fields").[7] Because fandom and academia each "rely on dialogue," as Karen Hellekson and Kristina Busse remind us, the discursive entanglements of one can be seen reflected in those of the other.[8] How that dialogue both constitutes and is constituted by a program like CXG is a question that I will take up toward the end of this chapter.

Before returning to CXG and to the gushing reviews that attended its 2015 debut, it will be helpful to first conceptually frame fandom from the perspective of someone who has tracked its recent shifts but also noted its consistencies over the years as a much-debated touchstone in media and cultural studies. As a self-described aca-fan whose scholarly output (in the form of published articles and book chapters) is at least partially fueled by an intensely felt emotional connection to the objects of my own fascination (e.g., television series such as *Northern Exposure* [CBS, 1990–95], *My So-Called Life* [ABC, 1994–95], *South Park* [Comedy Central, 1997–], *Strangers with Candy* [Comedy Central, 1999–2000], *Gilmore Girls* [The WB, 2000–2006; The CW, 2006–7], *Veronica Mars* [UPN, 2004–6; The

CW, 2006–7], *Deadwood* [HBO, 2004–6], *Mad Men* [AMC, 2007–15], etc.), I have heeded the advice of the abovementioned media scholars and taken professional pride in my so-called addictions. But I have also grown circumspect about the too-casual way that certain terms (like "addiction") creep into the proceedings, with media scholars and popular journalists alike resorting to expressions that feed into the conventional wisdom surrounding fandom. My interest in—nay, my *love of*—CXG is likewise troubled by the itching sensation that the show's spirit-lifting messages about community and inclusion (themes that resonate with many fans) might be counteracted by its questionable representations of the title character's "obsessive" behavior—the very thing that has led countless critics around the country to call her, and the show itself, "nutty" (both before and after Rebecca was diagnosed with Borderline Personality Disorder [BPD] in episode 3.06).

### "If You'll Excuse an Expression I Use": Obsessing Over "Obsession"

In the three decades that have elapsed since the first scholarly studies of media fandom were published in the English language, many of the deeply entrenched stereotypes of the "overly invested" TV fan have been subjected to critical scrutiny. In a similar manner, so have some of the formative theoretical frameworks for thinking through how the creative appropriation of material from a given program (e.g., *Doctor Who* [BBC, 1963–89; 2005–], *Star Trek* [NBC, 1966–69], *Buffy the Vampire Slayer* [The WB, 1997–2001; UPN, 2001–3]) might constitute a transcendent emancipation from the ideological strictures of mass entertainment more generally. From the first wave of pop culture fan studies (e.g., the work of Camille Bacon-Smith, John Fiske, and Henry Jenkins), which rightly sought to debunk negative views of the so-called crazed media consumer or pathologized social pariah stuck in arrested development,[9] to subsequent attempts by Matt Hills, Mark Jancovich, Nathan Hunt, Cornell Sandvoss, Rebecca Williams, Melissa Click, Suzanne Scott, and other scholars to unpack just what an "interpretative community" might be in an age of increased niche marketing, narrowcasting, and binge-watching,[10] the critical language that we use in this discipline has been calibrated over the years to reflect changes in the culture at large. In fact, as John Sullivan points out in *Media Audiences: Effects, Users, Institutions, and Power* (2012), the second and third waves of scholarship have consistently "questioned the normative conceptualization of fandom" and, to a certain extent, have challenged the more celebratory or recuperative approaches of their predecessors.[11] They have done this by suggesting that neither steadfast engagement nor resistant refashioning necessarily results in the kind of "escape"—from the confines of one's identity or from the social status quo—that was so strongly emphasized in the early 1990s. One's imaginative flight "into the world of popular media," Sullivan writes, does not necessarily mean "that individuals are escaping the systems of discrimination and power that define the society at large."[12] As such, he reminds us that fandom, while potentially freeing as a set of alternative reading protocols, might unwittingly reproduce "the same cultural, gender, and economic hierarchies" that characterize mainstream audiences' relationship to widely circulated forms of mass entertainment.[13]

Although discourses have shifted, both inside and outside academia, to account for the larger society's generally more accepting attitudes toward cultural activities once deemed "excessive," "odd," or even morally questionable (e.g., collecting toys and other merchandise, cosplaying, textual poaching, writing slash fiction), certain expressions and their associated meanings have persisted in ways that continue to stigmatize subordinated groups and their subcultural leanings. Take, for example, the word "crazy." Open any book about media fandom—or, indeed, about fandom in general (in discursively related areas, such as sports, fashion, the publishing industry, or critical theory itself)—and one is likely to encounter this term in discussions of individuals' unusually strong attachment to objects of their "obsession."[14] That latter term likewise problematically codifies fans' compulsive behaviors as being potentially dangerous or at the very least delusional in the sense of allowing one's infatuation with a given cultural production to influence one's actions vis-à-vis other members of society, which, to a certain degree, still looks upon that level of commitment suspiciously, if not scornfully. Indeed, "being committed" to something in that way carries a double meaning, as if one's emotional and material investment in a TV series, a football team, a rock band, a comic book character, or a literary property were a sign of deeper, less circumscribed or unsanctioned forms of social deviancy that, if taken "too far," might warrant psychiatric evaluation and even institutionalization. One need only to consider the titles of such made-for-TV documentaries as *Wacko about Jacko* (director Lucy Leveugle's 2005 film about misguided Michael Jackson followers) and *Crazy about One Direction* (Daisy Asquith's 2013 production about the titular boy band's "most angry and hysterical fans") to sense the pervasiveness of that attitude, which sees only the "dark side" of fandom—the presumed threat that it poses to others and to self—rather than its parasocially productive functions.[15]

The speciousness of that "slippery slope" thesis perhaps makes it undeserving of any further mention, and indeed the topic would hardly be worth exploring were it not for the persistent way that today's media outlets mark the obsessively "deranged" fan as a "potentially monstrous individual."[16] As Mark Duffett notes, media theorists themselves are partly to blame for this privileging of "extreme" fandom over more benign signs of a person's worshipful devotion to a cultural production. In tracing out the historical contours of what he calls the "pathological tradition" in fan studies, Duffett draws attention to many critics' insistent reliance on the word "obsession" when they describe behaviors and activities that, to outsiders, might seem abnormal but that insiders view as completely rational responses to the various objects that might elicit such adoration.[17] That rhetorical move has real consequences, insofar as fans are vulnerable to abuse (even within their own ranks) and precariously positioned between institutional thresholds—that of the entertainment industry and that of the academy—where their "value" is determined by their commercial exploitability and theoretical instrumentality. "Obsession," Duffett states, is a psychiatric term encompassing "a vast conceptual territory that extends between dedication, fascination, emotional connection and deviancy."[18] Peopling that vast conceptual territory are the cult TV fans and other pop-literate eccentrics whose "unhealthy" addictions and blinkered fixations are said to suggest a loosening grip on reality; a telltale sign—if one is to believe this alarmist rhetoric—that a different type of "institution" surely awaits those individuals should they ever fully embrace or give in to their inner "crazy."

Fans of The CW's CXG know that obsession is one of the central themes in this tellingly titled TV series, a much-loved critical darling that slyly comments on the social stigmatization of mental illness even as it solidifies some of the abovementioned cultural stereotypes surrounding fandom. As a densely intertextual mishmash of tones and genres (mixing everything from awkward cringe-comedy to parodic workplace/legal drama to genuinely sentimental, heartfelt romance), this small-scale yet ambitious production stands out from the primetime pack by liberally sprinkling each episode with elaborately choreographed musical numbers in which the main and supporting characters' innermost feelings—their frustrations, joys, longings, and, yes, obsessions—are externalized in gloriously campy fashion. Anyone who has delighted in the one-off musical episodes of nonmusical cult TV programs like Joss Whedon's *Buffy the Vampire Slayer* and Dan Harmon's *Community* (NBC, 2009–15) will appreciate the lyrical inventiveness and compositional care given to CXG, which devotes not just one but *every* weekly installment of its entire broadcast run—an impressive four-season stretch comprising 62 total hours of programming—to song-and-dance routines that somehow never really become "routine" in the sense of being predictable. Indeed, the *unpredictability* of the series' over-the-top musical numbers (which range from fierce rap battles to lilting Astaire-and-Rogers homages to intentionally cheesy riffs on 1980s MTV videos to Streisand-inspired showstoppers), like that of the protagonist's actions (as she endeavors to find true love and close the door on her painful past), is underscored by the very obsessiveness or "craziness" that compels this successful attorney to leave a high-paying if soul-deadening professional career in Manhattan behind in pursuit of an ex-boyfriend from West Covina who might (or might not) hold the key to her happiness.

The show's pilot episode directly engages the theme of obsession and hints at how one person's motives or actions might be perceived by others as irrational. Waving goodbye to a lucrative job promotion at a New York legal firm (where she was offered a partnership) and eventually settling down in California (where she will quickly make new friends while work-ing at a small law office run by Darryl Whitefeather [Pete Gardner]), Rebecca Bunch (Rachel Bloom) appears to be taking leave of her senses, and not because any such move—in this case, a coast-to-coast change of scenery—is unusual in itself. Rather, Rebecca's journey, which suggests a kind of cross-country fan pilgrimage, was prompted by her fixation on Josh Chan (Vincent Rodriguez III), a young man whom she once dated for two months in summer camp and recently bumped into on the streets of the Big Apple (where he had been living temporarily before his own return flight to West Covina). The mere sight of him, ten years after their teenage fling, coupled with a literal sign—specifically, a billboard advertising Truly Butter and bearing a crooked, downturned arrow, directing Rebecca's gaze toward Josh as he stands on the corner of West 56th Street—appears to her like a message from above. Like a fateful intervention on the part of a god that, ironically, she does not believe in, Josh's sudden appearance in the first few minutes of the episode opens this card-carrying atheist's eyes and heart to the prospect of happiness, something that has eluded her as a young professional. However, only after she follows him back to his hometown and ingratiates herself into the lives of others (including Josh's friends) does Rebecca come to see her behavior through *their* eyes.

In this episode's lengthy final scene, when her soon-to-be best friend Paula Proctor (Donna Lynne Champlin), a fortysomething office para-legal at Whitefeather & Associates, confronts her with the facts of her past actions, Rebecca initially refuses to admit that she is in love with Josh. "That's ridiculous, I barely know him," Rebecca tells her accusing colleague (who has been spying on her online activity). Paula knows that Rebecca has checked her ex-boyfriend's Facebook page 63 times and his Instagram page 18 times—clear signs that she is "obsessed" with him. The older woman in fact uses that word—*obsessed*—to describe Rebecca's state of mind before remarking, point blank, "You *love* him, you moved here for him, and you won't admit it." That rhetorical maneuver—Paula's spo-ken juxtaposition of *obsession* and *love*—is like the Truly Butter billboard arrow insofar as it points spectators in the direction of a dangerous, poten-tially "fatal" attraction. This is something that a few TV critics noted in their reviews of the pilot episode.

For example, writing for *Variety*, Brian Lowry suggests that CXG walks a tightrope and could just as easily tip over into the psychosexual territory of *Fatal Attraction* (1987, dir. Adrian Lyne) as it could into the more superficially comforting territory of dark comedy. Ultimately, Lowry correctly intuits, the series plays such material—Rebecca's "obsession with and social-media stalking of Josh"—for "laughs."[19] However, that response—that initial tendency to laugh off the main character's "craziness"—will become more measured or guarded over time as the episodes progress and the main character appears to *regress*, spiraling to a low point in her life that leads her (two years later, in episode 3.05) to overdose on her mother's antianxiety medication while seated on a plane.

Notably, after that pivotal episode from season three aired (on November 10, 2017), leaving fans with the bitter taste of Rebecca trying to commit suicide midflight, *IndieWire* contributor Hanh Nguyen called it the series' "darkest place yet." She begins her online review with a reminder that CXG "has never shied away from its title as a way to examine what issues . . . a person might have that other people might label as 'crazy.'"[20] Indeed, such labeling and the resistance that one might put up against it have been at the forefront of this show's rhetorical and representational modes, going all the way back to its first episode and to the titular heroine's defensive response to Paula's comment about obsession. Thunderstruck by her suspicious colleague's assertion, Rebecca paraphrases the entire premise of the series when she says, "So you're saying that I moved here from New York and I left behind a job that would have paid me $545,000 a year for a guy that still skateboards." "I *did not* do that," she exclaims, before telling Paula what (in her mind) *really* happened: "I was in New York, I ran into Josh, he made me feel warm inside, like glitter was exploding inside me. Then I moved here. I did not move here because of Josh, because that would be *crazy*, and I am not crazy." Then, hearing her own voice for the first time, her eyes widen in a moment of stunned realization and she repeats the phrase "I am not crazy" as if trying to convince herself of its truth. As Rebecca descends into visible neurosis, Paula—desperate to prevent her friend from sinking any deeper—quickly interjects and says, "You're *not* crazy, you're in love." Ironically, just as she had put the words "obsessed" and "love" together a few seconds earlier, now Paula is quick to emphasize that "crazy" and "love" are *not* synonymous. But she does so with the panicked desperation of someone who is likewise trying to convince herself of that statement's truth.

Rebecca's thrice-repeated declaration, "I am not crazy," would return in slightly different form in episode 3.03, which begins with a precredits scene in which she confronts her own gnawing anxiety, albeit manifested in the physical form of her younger self (played by Ava Acres). The usually cheery, adolescent version of Rebecca (who first appeared in a flashback of episode 1.03) casts a distressed, disapproving look at her older, bedridden self, telling her to take off the "stupid" wedding dress that she has been wearing ever since confronting Josh at the seminary he fled to weeks earlier (on the day of their abortive wedding). "You told Josh all the shady, lying, crazy things that you did, and *you did some crazy things*, bro. Even I'm surprised, *and I'm you*," preteen Rebecca stresses in a chiding voice, before running down an abbreviated list of what our miserable protagonist has done (and recently admitted) to him: "Tracking his car, breaking into his home, spying on him while he had sex with other girls." Incredulous, the girl asks, "Who does that stuff?" Then, after casually referencing Rebecca's time spent in a "loony bin" (a part of the protagonist's backstory that will be revealed as this third season progresses), she unloads a litany of dismissive terms, calling her an "obsessive, psycho, crazy" stalker.[21] Rebecca interjects twice during her younger self's spiel, informing her that her euphemism for a mental institution "is a derogatory term" and then defiantly repeating the phrase "I'm not crazy, I'm not crazy, I'm not crazy"—a virtual rehash or callback to the show's pilot episode that echoes her response to Paula's equally interrogative grilling.

It is telling that the pilot episode—and thus the entire series—begins with an apology of sorts. Set in the summer of 2005, the opening scene shows a much younger, pigtailed Rebecca, braces on her teeth and painted freckles on her face, on stage, performing the first of many song-and-dance numbers that will appear throughout CXG's run. She is a supporting player, not the lead vocalist, in a performance of Rodgers and Hammerstein's 1949 musical *South Pacific*. Specifically, the song that she and four other teenaged girls sing is "A Wonderful Guy," which includes the following lyrics: "If you'll excuse an expression I use / I'm in love with a wonderful guy!" Asking their audience to "excuse" that perhaps-cloying but heartfelt refrain, the singers metaphorically speak on behalf of this television series, which employs a questionable term in its title and will likewise reiterate the theme of being in love, again and again, over the course of its four seasons. In a way, the repetitiveness of those lyrics, as well as the fact that the Broadway hit's most telling stanzas—"I'm as normal as blueberry pie" and "A cliché coming true"—are not to be heard in this extracted rendition of the song, prepares us for the pilot episode's final scene, in which Rebecca similarly repeats "I am not crazy" (a rather clichéd way of emphasizing one's "normality"), as if singing a song that she has rehearsed a few *too many* times.

It bears remembering that the scene that immediately follows that theatrical performance of *South Pacific* is the first to show Rebecca and Josh together, walking side-by-side, hand-in-hand. Set on the last day of summer camp, just before he breaks up with her, it reveals how important it is for Rebecca to develop a "palpable connection with the audience," something that she says she experienced during the musical number (even though she was not the star). Like a metatextual nod to the viewers of CXG, especially those who have developed a strong emotional bond with the main character, that line of dialogue reflexively situates her as both object and subject of fannish adoration. For, just as she will cross the country and seek out her adolescent sweetheart as an older, but emotionally stunted, woman looking to fill a void, so too will we, the most devoted of audience members, see our own compulsive consumption of this series reflected in her actions. Moreover, fans are invited to adopt a cautiously adoring perspective like the one that Paula embodies, insofar as she exhibits a vicarious—some might say "obsessive"—interest in her best friend's "intoxicating" love life and admits to her husband, Scott (Steve Monroe), that she is "addicted" to the Rebecca-Josh storyline that she has helped to engineer. Notably, that admission, delivered by Paula in the eleventh episode of season one, comes after she and Scott have consulted local priest Father Brah (Rene Gube) about their failure to "connect" with one another in the way that married couples are supposed to do (and in the way that Rebecca apparently did with her audience years earlier). Furthermore, Paula's confession of sentimental addiction contains within it a theme that is at the heart of *CXG* and its fandom: namely, the *love of love*—something that many TV critics have likewise admitted to experiencing in their online reviews of the series.

## "Like Glitter Is Exploding Inside of You": Loving Love (a Bunch)

Judging from the critical reaction to the pilot episode and to the first season as a whole, Rebecca's longing for a "palpable connection" with her audience was achieved by creator-writer-star Rachel Bloom, a "talented multi-hyphenate" who had already gained a "cult following" thanks to her online music video "Fuck Me, Ray Bradbury."[22] Several reviewers noted Bloom's "braveness" in allowing herself to look "distinctly ridiculous and unglamorous," even during some of the show's musical numbers.[23] Jensen and others found her to be a "winning delight," blessed with a "distinctive voice" and "deep, deep wells of antic charisma."[24] Because Bloom "throws herself into the comedy, the music, the poignancy, [and] the madness" with no sign of debilitating self-consciousness, she exudes the manic energy of a "frazzled, soaring animated princess."[25] A few critics detected traces of the satirical stylings of other small-screen comedians, such as Tina Fey and Amy Schumer, in Bloom's performance of the "Sexy Getting Ready Song" (which has since generated more than 1.5 million views on YouTube). However, she and her series were held up as exemplars of originality, the likes of which have not been seen on broadcast TV for some time.[26]

Indeed, critics could not help themselves from piling up both the comparisons and the superlatives, describing *CXG* as an "ambitious, utterly singular show" that "gets its hands dirtier" than that other, more delicately plucked CW "camp-drama" with which it is sometimes equated: creator Jennie Snyder Urman's Peabody Award–winning *Jane the Virgin*.[27] Paradoxically, in their effort to distinguish *CXG* as a "wacky and whimsical" departure from the televisual "norm,"[28] reviewers habitually called upon earlier TV programs and other cultural productions as reference points, a hermeneutic maneuver that parallels this series' densely packed intertextuality. Although Urman's program is the one that is most frequently cited (not surprising, since *Jane the Virgin* and *CXG* have been joined at the hip as so-called sister shows on the same network for years),[29] additional productions, including the self-consciously "meta" legal-drama *Ally McBeal* (Fox, 1997–2002), the coming-of-age college drama *Felicity* (The WB, 1998–2002), the fish-out-of-water musical comedy *Flight of the Conchords* (HBO, 2007–9), and the indie sketch-comedy *Portlandia* (IFC, 2011–18), have also been referenced as stylistically, thematically, and/or tonally similar explorations of "unrequited love and workplace shenanigans."[30]

Other TV shows have been invoked less for any narrative content that they might share with *CXG* than for the way that their politically incorrect yet ironically knowing titles likewise give reviewers pause. For instance, writing for the *Hollywood Reporter*, Daniel Fienberg links the winking title of Brosh McKenna and Bloom's creation to those of recent network sitcoms such as *Trophy Wife* (ABC, 2013–14) and *Cougar Town* (ABC, 2009–12; TBS, 2013–15).[31] Predictably, within nearly every one of the two dozen reviews of the pilot episode that I have consulted are comments about this show's title, which—to borrow the words of *AV Club* contributor Molly Eichel—is not just distracting but also "immediately irksome."[32] Notably, Eichel begins her same-day review of "Josh Just Happens to Live Here!" with the reminder that "Women get enough shit in this world, especially on TV." "Do we need a show that explicitly points this out?" she asks, before reassuring her readers that "those initial annoyances" about *CXG* are "completely unfounded."[33] Similarly, Fienberg—only one episode in—seems to intuit Bloom and Brosh McKenna's long-game goal of deconstructing the titular archetype and, in his words, "reclaiming the pejorative."[34] "Previous attempts to reclaim rude terms about women in the titles of TV shows have not gone swimmingly," *Slate* critic Willa Paskin notes (a week before the pilot's airing), "but *Crazy Ex-Girlfriend* is not just how Josh Chan might see Rebecca . . . but how Rebecca occasionally sees herself."[35] This awareness on the part of both the main character and the intimately attuned reviewer is communicated via the show's first sustained musical number, "West Covina," the lyrics of which have her "persuading and unpersuading herself that what she is doing is insane."[36]

Why, then, is Rebecca doing those things? Because, as critics at the time of the premiere noted, she is an "in-love-with-love" woman who is ultimately less concerned with pursuing the "fantasy guy" than with chasing after "fantasy itself."[37]

Four years after the pilot episode's debut, one is struck by how perceptive many of those first reviews are in terms of predicting the eventual path that CXG would take during those intervening seasons. Indeed, Eichel was not alone in discerning, early on in the show's run, that its seemingly "demeaning and sexist" title is both "a bit of a red flag" and "a rallying cry" for the main character.[38] As James Poniewozik writes in his *New York Times* review of the pilot, "*Crazy Ex-Girlfriend* is playing with some tricky stereotypes of obsessive women. But it's also conscious that it's playing with them."[39] This, in addition to its risqué humor, is one reason why CXG might not be well-suited for broadcast network TV, he argues, alluding to the fact that the show was originally developed for Showtime in 2014 before the premium cable network passed on a slightly more "mature" version of the pilot.[40] Like her fellow CXG-defender on the East Coast, *Los Angeles Times* TV critic Mary McNamara believes that it tells a story "that is both a fairy tale and its deconstruction,"[41] something that would be only moderately apparent to anyone who has seen the pilot episode alone but that becomes more noticeable with each passing season.

The most insightful of those conjectural leaps during the week of October 15, 2015 was penned by Jeff Jensen, a TV critic for *Entertainment Weekly* who is perhaps best known for his meticulous episode-by-episode/scene-by-scene breakdown of *Twin Peaks: The Return* (Showtime, 2017), both online and in the pages of *EW* as well as on his cohosted podcast with fellow critic Darren Franich. Two years before crafting some of the most analytically elaborate theories about that David Lynch–directed cult phenomenon yet attempted, Jensen was busy speculating on the direction that Bloom and Brosh McKenna's show might take. Making his own nod to *South Pacific*, Jensen thinks that Rebecca will "eventually wash that man right out of her hair" and undertake a journey away from the romantic ideals associated with Hollywood musicals toward "authenticity and maturity."[42] With only that first episode under his belt, he is comfortable making the claim that *CXG* is not really about our heroine's obsession with Josh (or any other man for that matter), but instead is about her "recovering the aborted narrative of Summer Camp Rebecca and growing up anew, flailing and failing her way toward an authentic identity and her own definition of successful feminism."[43] He also senses the importance of Paula, the initially jealous paralegal at Whitefeather & Associates who is not only "the most interesting supporting character" on the show but also the most important in terms of sustaining, rather than shattering, the illusions that trap Rebecca's "errant, windmill-tilting idealist."[44] As Jensen states, Paula is an enabler whose mere presence in *CXG* "lays bare the pilot's best theme: how we turn people into idols, how we use and abuse their narratives for wish-fulfillment fantasy."[45]

Another of the show's most vocal supporters is Matt Zoller Seitz, who has similarly noted Paula's enabling tendencies, calling her "Vivian Vance to Bloom's nearly unhinged Lucy, getting a contact high from helping her bestie stalk an ex" (one of many references that Seitz makes to the classic sitcom *I Love Lucy* [CBS, 1951–57]).[46] Here, the critic anticipates various dialogue scenes between Paula and Scott, who tells his wife (in episode 3.07) that she tends to go through "phases" as someone who is always "obsessed" with people and things: "Before Rebecca, there were those vampire novels, Sudoku, and then there was the obsession with Amal Clooney's outfits." Interestingly, Seitz gleefully leans in to his own much-tweeted obsessions as a pop culture aficionado whose knowledge of films, television series, and other forms of mass entertainment runs deep and wide, and whose privileging of *CXG* as "the best show on TV" is made more significant by dint of that widely acknowledged knowledge. Like Jensen, this well-known writer for Vulture.com and other websites has a knack for teasing out the symptomatic meanings of texts that many academics tend to overlook, and in that sense his *CXG* commentary is no different from his astute analyses of quality TV shows like *The Sopranos* (HBO, 1999–2007) and *Mad Men* (AMC, 2007–15), both of which have been the subjects of numerous scholarly studies.[47] For Seitz, what sets Brosh McKenna and Bloom's consistently trailblazing series apart from those of David Chase, Matthew Weiner, and other male showrunners is not only its "casually multicultural" ensemble cast but, most importantly, its strong female lead—a "funny woman" who "jokes about her weight and her bust line, and who can and does hit the high notes."[48]

"We should take shows like this seriously as art," he defiantly argues, before favorably positioning CXG alongside other, more "respected" TV series such as *The Americans* (FX, 2013–18), *Orange Is the New Black* (Netfix, 2013–19), *BoJack Horseman* (Netflix, 2014–), and *Better Call Saul* (AMC, 2015–).[49] In doing so, we might eradicate the stigma around comedy (if not mental illness), "and along with it, the notion that a portrait of a neurotic suburban lawyer's romantic life is inherently less serious, and less worthy of scrutiny and praise, than a prison series about incarceration, power, and justice, a scathing animated Hollywood satire, a gut-wrenching Cold War spy potboiler, or a crime drama/legal thriller about one man's incremental corruption."[50] Just after Seitz emphasizes the seriousness with which CXG should be scrutinized, he slides into a decidedly "antiserious" rhetorical mode, employing language that would not be out of place in a fan blog. He rapturously proclaims it to be "an awesome show, soup to nuts, dialogue to music; a weekly beacon of delight that draws you in, then wrecks you. It's a comet passing through TV's solar system," the likes of which will not be seen again soon.[51] Such discourse on the part of a self-proclaimed CXG fan would be delivered, for months thereafter, in bite-sized nuggets via Twitter, which Seitz has used as a platform for spreading his unabashed love for the series in much the same way that Eichel, Jensen, Nussbaum, and Poniewozik have.

Although he incorrectly hypothesized that the series would settle into "case-of-the-week plots" revolving around Rebecca's employment at Darryl's small law firm (where she does, however, spend a lot of time developing strong relational ties that supersede her professional responsibilities), Jensen, like other critics, was able to pinpoint several relevant themes in CXG from a single viewing of a single episode. Acknowledging that "guestimating . . . is difficult" due to having only the pilot episode on which to base his thesis, Jensen nevertheless demonstrates journalists' and reviewers' capacity to actually develop a fairly sophisticated argument under the pressure of daily or weekly deadlines and amid the constant churn of pop culture commentary.[52] Of course, owing to the speed with which online critics are asked to complete their work, there is a tendency to fall back on blanket statements and hackneyed expressions when trying to summarize topics that need further elaboration or deeper thought before their complexities can be properly ascertained. Jensen himself is quick to state that Rebecca is "certifiably cracked" after watching that one episode, just as Eichel (who is likewise a professed "fan" of the series) feels the need to say that the protagonist is "totally [and] clearly insane."[53] Reductive though those comments are, we recognize them as first impressions, perhaps written quickly by individuals whose attitudes toward the main character and the series have changed over time.

It should be noted that the show's four-year path cuts across a rocky terrain of "highs" and "lows" leading up to a medical diagnosis, BPD, which forces a retroactive consideration of whether "crazy" and "obsessive" are appropriate or accurate terms in conveying Rebecca's relational challenges as well as some viewers' emphatic love of the series. Regardless, many critics have reacted—and continue to react—to the show as if there were "glitter exploding inside of them," to paraphrase the titular former girlfriend who eventually professes to being "in love with love" just as they have owned up to their own love for her. "I'm kind of in love with *Crazy Ex-Girlfriend*," Scott D. Pierce wrote four years ago in the *Salt Lake Tribune*, adding, "And with the woman who plays her, Rachel Bloom."[54] Not coincidentally, one line further into his review (which at times reads like the puppy-dog-slobbering blog of a longtime CXG enthusiast), Pierce remarks that this new series "is sort of nuts," reverting to the same problematic language that has been used to pathologize pop-culture fandom over the years. While part of me welcomes the incorporation of intense feeling—once "repressed in the sanctioned space of high culture"[55]—into the supposedly rarefied realm of media studies scholarship, another part of me recognizes how the "exaggeration of everyday emotions" might lead to pronouncements like the one above. Substituting it for any synonymous term—"cuckoo," "insane," "mad," "nuts"—does not lessen the effect that such "crazy" talk has on longstanding cultural and societal attitudes toward either clinical disorders or the kind of irrational, obsessive behavior that so many people, including TV critics and media scholars, still associate with fandom.

### Conclusion: "I Am Not Crazy"

Although done in a flippant manner, the persistent sprinkling of words such as "crazy" into fan discourse (as well as the sometimes-derisive commentary surrounding that discourse) has the cumulative effect of further trivializing many of the "unsanctioned" activities that have long been associated with women's engagement with media texts. Beyond CXG, one need only to consider the *Twilight* franchise, which includes (but is not limited to) the five feature-length fantasy films based on the novels of Stephenie Meyer, the motion picture soundtracks that topped Billboard charts and earned Grammy nominations, and the countless examples of online fan fiction written largely by women and nonbinary or genderqueer people, to see how both the "love of love" as well as the ridicule of that love (which is especially toxic among straight male antifans) conform to cultural and societal norms. As Matt Hills and Rebecca Williams have stressed in their respective studies of this franchise's distributed fan communities and "interfandoms," various motivating factors might compel someone to use a word like "crazy," which carries both positive and negative valences depending on the source and context of its utterance. For example, Hills notes that one of the Twilight Saga's lead actors, Taylor Lautner, employs that word when discussing his own followers during a Comic-Con documentary that is included as a paratextual supplement on the DVD release of *Twilight* (2008). However, "crazy" is invoked by Lautner in an affectionate rather than scornful way, just as other stars of the film series notably refer to themselves as devoted "fans" of Meyer's books (and are therefore not unlike their own admirers).[56] In contrast to this relatively benign evocation of obsessive or "nutty" behavior, a more troubling illustration of gendered devaluing is offered up in Williams's study of the interfandom that antagonistically links followers of the all-male rock band Muse (whose songs are featured in both the books and the films) with those of the female-driven *Twilight* franchise. As Williams notes, several longtime listeners of Muse react negatively toward *Twilight* (both the "awful movie" and the "piece of crap that some people like to call a book," to quote two such antifans) and tend to associate the franchise with "crazy fangirls" whose gender and youthfulness are perceived as signs of its frivolousness.[57]

Building on Williams's assessment of the ways in which *Twilight* fans are misogynistically "pathologized within the wider media via their association with the culturally devalued and feminized genre of romance," Dean Barnes Leetal furthermore points to the ableist undertones of such terms, which suggest a bigoted view of those whose neurodivergence from a constructed or imagined "norm" is frequently reduced to a state of "craziness" that remains deeply gendered even today.[58] Despite growing awareness of the "gender-specific risk factors for common mental disorders that disproportionately affect women,"[59] lingering stereotypes attest to the work that needs to be done in order to bring about the institutional changes Leetal and other disability rights activists are pursuing in their fan-based scholarship. With various mental health conditions and neurological disorders—from borderline personality to bipolar to clinical depression—becoming an increasingly conspicuous part of primetime programming (e.g., *United States of Tara* [Showtime, 2009–11], *Homeland* [Showtime, 2011–], *You're the Worst* [FX, 2014; FXX, 2015–19], *UnREAL* [Lifetime, 2015–18; Hulu, 2018], *Lady Dynamite* [Netflix, 2016–17], and other female-focalized shows), such scholarship serves an important bridging function by finding commonalities (rhetorical and otherwise) across different cultural arenas. *Crazy Ex-Girlfriend* and the critical discourses surrounding this remarkable program are doing much the same thing, albeit in sometimes-confrontational ways that challenge audiences to question their own complicity in the generic formulas—or, in one critic's words, the "zany clichés"—attending small-screen representations of "craziness."[60]

With the completion of its fourth and final season, capped by a live concert special (filmed at Los Angeles' Orpheum Theatre) that put actual CXG fans—including audiences in character-inspired costumes—front and center, Brosh McKenna and Bloom's "delightful and quirky musical comedy" stands as "one of the most genuinely compassionate shows on television, especially when it comes to looking at issues of mental health."[61] That assessment, part of Arielle Bernstein's 2018 review of CXG for the *Guardian*, echoes other pop culture journalists' appreciation of the program's exploration of BPD, a condition that affects women at a statistically higher rate than it does men in the United States. Notably, the series finale's "Greatest Hits" medley of songs culminates with full-cast performances of two numbers—"A Diagnosis" and "Anti-Depressants Are So Not a Big Deal"—that sum up the show's commitment to mental health care. That those performances serve as the creators' final word on the matter of Rebecca Bunch's so-called craziness—a topic that Paula weighed in on during the penultimate episode (4.17), when she happily informed her friend that she is "not weird or dumb or 'cray'" to imagine herself in musical numbers—further testify to this series' investment in fandom as a kind of "mind song" or "flight of fancy" (to borrow the protagonist's words) for women. As Lori Morimoto points out in her study of transcultural fandom, "being 'constantly dragged out to be laughed at' over 'our apparent inability to differentiate between reality and fiction' seems part and parcel of what makes women fans 'hysterical' and 'crazy' in both media creator and ancillary mass media discourse."[62] Now that CXG has reached its end with a literal showstopper about the positive consequences of fannish obsession and our ability to transform reality *through fiction*, one can only hope that its affirmative parting message reaches the hearts and minds of other cultural producers who, like Rebecca, might wish to turn a very private form of personal suffering into a very public form of popular art.

# 2

# Musicals Have a Place

*Navigating the Television Market*
*with a Crazy Cult Show*

## Chelsea McCracken

In an interview with *Bustle*, while in the early stages of producing the fourth and final season of *Crazy Ex-Girlfriend* (The CW, 2015–19, hereafter *CXG*), cocreator and star Rachel Bloom reflected that she hoped "we showed that musicals have a place."[1] Bloom's love of musical theater and her desire to create a musical television show were central in the formation of *CXG*'s musical premise.[2] The series uses a distinct combination of comedy, drama, and the incorporation of musical numbers in an integrated musical format. Musical television series have carved out a small niche in the last decade, with shows such as *Glee* (Fox, 2009–15), *Smash* (NBC, 2012–13), *Galavant* (ABC, 2015–16), *Nashville* (ABC 2012–present), and *Empire* (Fox, 2015–present). The 2010s also saw the airing of a number of live musical remakes, beginning with NBC's *The Sound of Music* in 2013, which held the attention of around twenty million viewers.[3] Despite this relative surge in the genre, however, there is still uncertainty about the commercial potential of musicals as well as an accompanying hesitancy within the industry to identify series as such. Some of this hesitation stems from famous failures, including *Cop Rock* (ABC, 1990), the musical crime show that failed to capture audiences, and more contemporary missteps, like *Viva Laughlin* (CBS, 2007) and the live production of *Rent* (Fox, 2019). The discourse surrounding musical series tends to emphasize their impracticality (musical numbers are challenging to prepare and film on

TV production schedules) as well as their lack of consistent quality and popular appeal. Some even go so far as to claim that the musical format is incompatible with television seriality.[4]

In contrast to the above flops, CXG is a fully integrated musical series that survived for its entire four-season arc. Each episode contains two to four original songs, complete with choreographed dancing and transitions into the supradiegetic, an idealized space that exists outside of both diegetic and nondiegetic classifications. The show follows the conventions of an integrated musical in which characters appear to break into song and dance spontaneously in order to express their emotional states. Through a careful examination of the series' formal qualities and published interviews with creative personnel, this chapter examines how CXG draws from the conventions of the integrated musical and uses this form to navigate the current television market. While the series foregrounds the musical in some ways, the creators also work to appeal to musical skeptics by narratively justifying the use of numbers and by shifting into the realm of parody. This chapter also explores the tension between numbers as "stand-alone" content that can be promoted as paratexts and numbers artfully and intricately integrated both within individual episodes and through the seasons in the form of refrains. I argue that, despite hesitation over the musical's appeal, it is the creative use of genre parody and the genre-specific qualities of the musical form that made CXG appealing to The CW and allowed the show to fit into the shifting, increasingly digital television landscape.

With few exceptions, recent musical series tend to revolve around narratives that allow for diegetically motivated musical numbers. In promoting Glee, for example, people were careful to note that songs were motivated through glee club practices and performances.[5] CXG likewise provides some justification for its elaborate musical interludes. Rather than focusing on narrative situations in which breaking into song and dance are socially acceptable practices, however, the series asserts that viewers are entering characters' minds, chiefly the central character, Rebecca Bunch (played by Bloom). The CW's press release before the initial airing of the first season focused on this rationalization, noting that the show follows "an unhappy lawyer who quits her job and moves across the country in search of love, with her inner monologue providing irreverent musical interludes."[6] The focus on motivation in musical series points to a concern that the musical is a risky genre and that audiences will not accept spontaneous bursts of song and dance. Correspondingly, integrated musical series are few and far between.

The premise that Rebecca imagines moments through musical numbers is explicitly stated. In season two, for example, Rebecca tells one of the dancers from the theme song that she is part of her (Rebecca's) imagination, and a flashback reveals Rebecca singing to herself while in a mental health facility. The series continues these references through the final season, when Rebecca tries to sing "One Indescribable Instant" (4.04) with her talented younger brother. She sings out of tune in the diegetic performance and comments that she only sings well in her head. The series finale takes this a step further, with Rebecca explaining to Paula (Donna Lynne Champlin) that she works through moments of her life by imagining them as musical numbers, even bringing Paula into her mind in order to show her this interior musical space. While season one established this basis for songs, the premise quickly shifted to include songs motivated from other characters' viewpoints, breaking the technical rationalization for these musical moments. After the first few episodes establish the formula for the show, viewers accept the shifts, which gives the showrunners freer rein to adjust the formula.

Despite the nominal motivation of coming from Rebecca's mind, CXG features characters breaking into song and dance within everyday, nonmotivated situations. The series earned praise and differentiated itself with this "willingness to celebrate, rather than explain away, the inherent ridiculousness of the genre."[7] Some numbers even play with this sudden entrance into the musical world by including characters or extras who appear to be observing the shift to song and dance with incredulity. In the first song of the series, "West Covina" (1.01), Rebecca removes her blazer and tosses it to a passerby on the streets of New York, who proceeds to turn and watch her sing, looking confused. In "Flooded with Justice" (1.13), as the crowd swells and sings together, White Josh (David Hull) looks around with a confused expression. Although he awkwardly joins the march, he continues to look around, uncertainly, and does not sing with the others. Even major characters can be hesitant to join in numbers, as when Heather (Vella Lovell) says, "Oh God, do I have to sing an inspirational musical theatre song right now? I just can't . . ." before breaking into an unenthusiastic rendition of "The Moment Is Me" (3.03). These moments add to the series' reflexivity, pointing out the oddity of breaking into song and dance, and give audience members who might be reluctant about the musical form a point of identification where they can see their hesitation mirrored on screen. The use of these points of identification, self-reflexivity, and parody help the show navigate the current television market by appealing to musical skeptics along with musical fans.

CXG continues the creation of ironic distance from musicals through twisting conventions of multiple musical forms and foregrounding a quirky, parodic sensibility. While songs often revolve around common musical themes such as love, they twist viewer expectations. Numbers might focus on topics such as urinary tract infections ("I Gave You a UTI," 1.17), vibrators ("The Buzzing from the Bathroom," 3.02), stalking an ex's new girlfriend ("Research Me Obsessively," 2.07), and heavy boobs ("Heavy Boobs," 1.16). Bloom stated in an interview with *Vulture* that whatever conventions they were drawing from, the songs should be "fighting that genre. It should be an 'opposite' or something that doesn't quite fit. Automatically, we're always looking for ways to subvert tropes in songs."[8] These antitheses contribute to the parodic and self-reflexive tone of the series. In genre parodies, comedy mixes with a "host genre," and "the resulting humor stems from ridiculing the textual conventions and cultural associations of the host genre."[9] In this case, the parody requires knowing and pushing against different musical conventions. The series likewise offers a reworking of the romantic comedy genre, as discussed by Charles Burnetts in chapter 3 of this volume.

To give a few examples of musical parody, "Settle for Me" (1.04) simulates a classic Fred Astaire and Ginger Rogers musical number, but it twists the content by having the character sing not about true love but about "settling" for someone who happens to be available. The "Sexy Getting Ready Song" (1.01) details, in a pop music video–inspired style, Rebecca's preparation routines before going out to a party. While the song purports to be "sexy," the images reveal decidedly unsexy details of beauty routines, such as tweezing body hair, wearing Spanx, and ass-waxing. A rap battle becomes a "JAP Rap Battle" (1.13), in which two Jewish American Princesses (JAPs) demonstrate their positions as "daughters of privilege" as they insult the other's scholastic and career accomplishments. Paula sings an ABBA-inspired number, "The First Penis I Saw" (3.07), about her high school boyfriend. And a ballad about starting a social movement, "This Is My Movement" (3.06), becomes a double entendre about bowel movements. The outlandish, parodic qualities of the numbers defuse the hesitation viewers may feel in watching a musical television show. Fans of musicals can enjoy the use of integrated numbers, and musical skeptics can enjoy the shifts into the supradiegetic while maintaining an ironic distance from musical conventions. By pointing out unrealistic aspects of the musical's form, the series acknowledges the constructed and artificial nature of the musical, creating an entertaining and pleasurable juxtaposition between form and content.

Parody does not imply that there are no conventionally emotional aspects to the series and its use of musical numbers. Programs that use parody "can also strategically draw upon elements from the genre and treat them seriously, eliciting pleasures and using defining elements of the genres being parodied."[10] Kyra Hunting and Amanda McQueen argue that Glee used musical numbers to both "heighten the dramatic tone" of a scene and "break the seriousness of the moment."[11] They see Glee's innovation, its position as a "mash-up," as connected with its use of genre elements to heighten both effects. Within the series,

> differences between dramatic and comedic components are not elided or blended, but rather emphasized, often through the use of musical numbers. . . . Rather than feeling disjointed, Glee's tonal variety allows it to moderate its own extremes, softening its humor with heart and tempering its sentimentality with snark, without diluting the individual components.[12]

In a similar vein, CXG contains tonal shifts and uses songs in both humorous and serious ways. "Face Your Fears" (1.03) is an early ballad sung by Paula (her first full solo song) in which she encourages Rebecca to face her fear of hosting a party. The situations she refers to in the song get increasingly ridiculous—including staring down a bear, staying in a burning building, running with scissors, and jumping out of a window. In the season three reprise of the song, Rebecca sings a pared-down somber version standing alone in the hallway outside of Nathaniel's (Scott Michael Foster) apartment. In this heartfelt rendition, Rebecca grapples with her fear of opening herself up to love again. This combination of comedy and heart is central to the series' appeal and demonstrates The CW's desire to connect with women in the highly sought-after 18–34 demographic. Industry discourse varies significantly over whether these prime younger audiences want distanced, ironic, and cynical media or whether they are drawn in by earnest sincerity.[13] CXG is able to appeal to both poles, however, by walking a tightrope between sincere emotion and playful irony.

While CXG songs are generally played for humor and parody musical structures, they are not simply novelties that halt narrative progression. Rather, they are fully integrated and essential components of the show's plot and character development. Broader arguments over the narrative integration of musical numbers can be broken into two camps: those who believe these scenes exist apart from the narratives, which they arrest and interrupt; and those who view scenes of spectacle as having the capacity to be integral to the narrative and overall structure of the film. Pierre-Emmanuel Jacques sees moments of song and dance as having a "purely aesthetic function. . . . These are moments of pure show given as such," in which characters "stop being active agents of the narrative to become pure visual pleasure."[14] Katherine Spring, on the other hand, argues that musical numbers, even those bracketed off in the form of performances within the diegesis, are in fact integrated and function within the narrative. Rather than interrupting narrative progression, musical performances can in fact "work to establish setting, reveal information about characters, and serve other kinds of dramatic purposes."[15] Songs can serve associative and structural functions, and theme songs in particular "tended to encapsulate a film's primary subject matter by summarizing or mirroring the dramatic theme of a picture with which the song was associated."[16]

In thinking about the integration of narrative and musical numbers within CXG episodes, Brosh McKenna noted that "we focus on the story-telling and the character stuff before the songs. The songs come out of that."[17] The creative team put a higher value on story content and used that to inspire songs, which in turn support the narrative and character development. In discussing her decision to tell Rebecca's story as a musical, Bloom remarked that "in Musical Theater Writing 101, they say, 'Only musicalize something if the piece demands to be a musical.' And I think the reason this is a musical is because music represents the last time she was happy. Music is her heart. It's her true happiness that she hasn't married with her external life yet."[18] Within CXG, individual songs disclose characters' thoughts, contribute to deeper understandings of character emotions, convey the evolution of relationships, and provide exposition. Musical numbers allow for a deeper connection with characters, which is one reason why fans feel so invested in the series.

The careful integration of numbers makes them feel less like novelty items and more like part of a cohesive whole. Each song opens up a complex intertwining of character emotions, development, and interactions. Some numbers explicitly connect with narrative developments. In "Oh My God I Think I Like You" (1.17), Rebecca relates her growing feelings for Greg (Santino Fontana). The contrast between the sexual basis of their relationship with the understated "I think I like you" marks the transition of their relationship in Rebecca's mind from purely physical to emotional. "Who's the New Guy?" (2.09) showcases personnel at the law firm (Paula, Tim [Michael McMillian], Maya [Esther Povitsky], Karen [Stephnie Weir], and George [Danny Jolles]); narrates the arrival of their new boss, Nathaniel; and conveys the group's hesitation and fear that the new addition might disrupt their lives in negative ways. The song offers tongue-in-cheek, self-reflexive references to the new character, episodes, and ratings, which are quickly justified as diegetically plausible references ("You mean our terrible ratings on LegalScores.com?"). The song is reprised as "He's the New Guy" (3.10) when Rebecca rallies her coworkers against Nathaniel, even though they have grown to like him. The use of a refrain calls back to their initial distrust and hesitation. Even songs that appear to be less connected to forward narrative progression, such as "We Tapped that Ass" (2.04), are connected to deeper understandings of the characters. Rebecca is being haunted by the ghosts of her former lovers who remind her of all the places in her apartment where they had sex. The number, while a lighthearted tap piece, demonstrates Rebecca's inner turmoil. This distress leads her to almost burn down her building, which prompts her to move into a new apartment with Heather and shift her relationship with this other central character.

Having a singing role suggests a kinship between characters. For example, numbers are, as mentioned earlier, initially motivated as occurring in Rebecca's mind. Gradually, other characters begin to have larger singing roles, and their entrance into the musical world suggests their ability to understand and connect with Rebecca. Paula is given the second-biggest singing role, followed by Rebecca's love interests, other friends (particularly Darryl [Pete Gardner]), and even her mother. If her escapes into a musical world are symptomatic of Rebecca's mental state, her "craziness," then the musical harmony she finds with friends and loved ones suggests that she is not so different from them. They (we) are all a little crazy. Paula is given particular prominence musically, and on a formal level this connects her with Rebecca and solidifies their bond. This is apparent in the song "West Covina" (1.01) and its reprise. "West Covina," the first number of the series, sets up Rebecca's tendency to break into song. At the end of the first episode, Paula joins Rebecca in a reprise. Rebecca sees Paula from a new perspective, having found someone who can share this inner song world. This is the start of their friendship, which is the most important structuring relationship of the series. In episode 1.09, Josh (Vincent Rodriguez III) joins Rebecca in a second reprise of "West Covina," signaling that he can also connect with Rebecca on a musical, and therefore mental and emotional, level. Soon after this moment, Rebecca admits her love for Josh. In the finale, it is Paula who is invited to share this musical world again by literally entering the space of Rebecca's mind. Paula sings an a cappella final reprise of "West Covina," changing the lyrics but keeping the melody.

Notably, the first song to be sung without Rebecca present is Greg's "What'll It Be" (1.06), which connects him with Rebecca in two ways.

Firstly, he is clearly a musical character in that he launches songs without the justification of Rebecca's imagination. The song's repeated lyrics of "Hey, West Covina" connect with Rebecca's first number and the repeated "West Covina" refrains. Greg (played in season four by Skylar Astin) reprises this song in the final season (4.14), and the lyrics reflect his personal growth. Rather than blaming the town for his frustrations in life, he admits that "the problem was me." Now that he is confident in his personhood, he no longer feels trapped. The final season contains numerous reprises and callbacks to earlier songs.[19] This rewards fans with echoes of past favorites, and it gives the series a sense of unity and completion. Although generally played for humor, songs help shape and structure the show's narrative arcs. Individual songs provide exposition, disclose characters' thoughts, contribute to deeper understandings of characters, and convey the evolution of relationships.

CXG has found a certain form of cult popularity, attracting a group of loyal, diehard fans. Bloom jokes that although the show is considered successful in some ways, it is also the "lowest rated show on network television."[20] Viewership for the first season tended to range from .8 million to just over a million viewers per episode, with that number falling to closer to half a million in season two, and rebounding slightly to a consistent .6–.66 million in season three.[21] To offer some comparison, The CW's most viewed series in 2016 was The Flash (The CW, 2014–), at an average of 3.5 million viewers.[22] Despite these low viewing numbers, The CW renewed the series for a fourth and final season, allowing the showrunners to end the series on their own terms. They even extended the order to a full eighteen-episode season, rather than the shorter length of seasons two and three.[23] Bloom herself noted, "It's amazing that it's on and that we've gotten to do four seasons of this weird fucking specific cult show. It's insane."[24] For a series that has brought in relatively low numbers, why has The CW supported it so consistently?

In part, this is due to CXG's critical success, which David Scott Diffrient unpacked in greater detail in chapter 1. The series has been nominated for and won Golden Globe Awards, Emmy Awards, Critics' Choice Television Awards, GLAAD Media Awards, and more. The show therefore provides a certain amount of prestige to The CW's lineup. In response to questions about why The CW supports underperforming shows like CXG and *Jane the Virgin*, The CW's president, Mark Pedowitz, stated:

> It has nothing to do with numbers. It has everything to do with [how] *Crazy Ex, Jane the Virgin* and the DC franchises have helped alter the perception of what The CW has become. . . . Critically acclaimed, great programming, sometimes you just leave it on the air and hopefully it finds an audience. . . . I am hoping that happens. If it doesn't, I will have no regrets of having continued the series. . . . It takes these very dark topics and puts a bright light [on them]. . . . To me it's something that should be on the air.[25]

Critical acclaim draws attention to the network and helps shape the image the network wants to present. The decision to support this programming has been applauded in, for example, *Vanity Fair*, which published an article remarking that, "by continuing to renew these shows, the CW has proven its commitment to innovative storytelling and complicated, deep narratives."[26]

Another factor to consider is the network's experimentation with different forms of distribution. The CW formed in 2006 as a result of a deal between the CBS Corporation and Warner Bros. Entertainment. This fifth broadcast network was introduced as one that would "serve the public with high-quality programming and maintain our ongoing commitment to our diverse audience. . . . With this move, we will be creating a viable entity, one well-equipped to compete, thrive and serve all our many publics in this multi-channel media universe."[27] This focus on new approaches to the market was reiterated during a drastic ratings slump in 2008, when the future of the network was at stake. The CW network's president of entertainment at the time, Dawn Ostroff, pushed to focus on the network's target demographics, stating that "we are playing to our strengths and programming to women 18–24," as well as emphasizing a cutting-edge, tech-savvy marketing campaign.[28] Ostroff remarked, "We knew the [TV] world was going to change," and she recalls discussions about "whether the new-model CW should be delivered from the start via the Internet as well as broadcast stations. YouTube at the time was a fledgling entity that was months away from being acquired by Google, but it was a harbinger of the upheaval to come."[29]

The CW has continued exploring evolving media platforms and where network television fits into the digital media landscape. In 2012, *Variety* reported that The CW was "doing its darndest across digital platforms to live up to its billing as the 'first fully converged network,'" and the network's executive vice president of marketing and digital programming, Rick Haskins, noted that "18% of all in-season consumption of CW series occurs on a combination of CWTV.com, Hulu Plus, which shares the next-day window with CW's website, and the free component of Hulu, which gets episodes one week after the TV airdate."[30] The network produces CXG for multiple audiences—those who watch on TV as it is broadcast is only one group to consider. Midway through the first season of CXG, "to garner new fans and promote the all new original episodes," the network streamed the entire first half of the season on their site and on Hulu.[31] Deals with Hulu and Netflix have been critical in maintaining the network's profitability.[32] In 2016, The CW negotiated a deal with Netflix for an estimated $1 billion for the next five years of CW content, as well as continued rights for several years after the end of each series.[33] The deal also pushes content to Netflix much faster, appearing in a few weeks versus the previous months-long wait. The CW encouraged watching via their website by eliminating the gap between broadcast airtime and streaming availability, introduced an app for mobile viewing, began creating exclusive online content, and factored in viewership across platforms, so that even series that had limited traditional viewing numbers might be renewed if their streaming numbers were solid.[34] Continuing in this trajectory, Pedowitz announced in the fall of 2019 that they would not be renewing their contract with Netflix, leaving future series to be accessed either on The CW network's website or on the streaming services provided by parent companies CBS and Warner Bros.[35] This allows the network to maintain more control over content and potentially leads to greater streaming revenue.

In this digital landscape, musical numbers have another function. Despite the formal and narrative integration of songs within CXG, they are also exportable and thus able to find distribution as preformed clips and audio files. The musical as a genre is uniquely designed to allow for the exporting of bite-sized segments of each episode. Musical numbers become stand-alone pieces, consumable and reconsumable on multiple platforms, including YouTube, streaming services like Spotify, and purchases through iTunes. The exportability of individual numbers makes the musical an ideal genre for ancillary distribution platforms. This possibility for supplementary musical marketing has proven highly effective for series like *Glee*. The series' connection to musical programming included a consideration of links between the television and recording industries. A substantial portion of *Glee*'s annual revenues were derived from profits from music sales. Songs from the series topped the Billboard Hot 100, and "*Glee*'s covers have also been known to outperform—and even lead to revivals in sales of—the original versions."[36] The series' uniqueness lay in its integration of television and music "into the form of the series explicitly, and how it significantly altered the use and meaning of ancillary music products to add diegetic significance. . . . *Glee* has fully integrated music into the storytelling itself, making music essential rather than supplemental."[37] In part because of the success of *Glee*, the rhetoric surrounding musicals changed in the first decade-and-a-half of the 2000s. Trade press reports shifted their tone in conjunction with a growing audience that were raised on musicals and accepted the conventions of the genre.[38]

The catchiness of *CXG*'s songs often inspires repeat listening, and these video excerpts are available to fulfill the demand. YouTube clips can be watched and shared through multiple online platforms, including social media, blogs, and direct messages, thereby increasing the show's reach beyond traditional viewing numbers. One of the series' initial selling points was the notoriety and cult following that Bloom generated through her short-form works, specifically her offbeat, funny music videos. Released through YouTube, these videos contain explicit language and sexual content. Examples of this earlier work include "Fuck Me, Ray Bradbury" (2010) and "You Can Touch My Boobies" (2012). Releasing *CXG* songs on YouTube corresponds with the release strategy of Bloom's earlier work and her star persona/brand and also connects with her role as auteur as discussed in chapter 4. Through this release tactic, the series reaches a larger audience. The most-watched CXG videos uploaded to YouTube by The CW (as of April 2019) are "Sexy Getting Ready Song" with around 1.7 million views, and "Let's Generalize about Men" (3.01), with around 1.2 million views. These two videos were both in the top 5 most-watched videos on The CW's YouTube channel, and 50 of their top 68 most-watched videos were CXG songs. This dominance of CXG videos demonstrates the series' importance to The CW's online presence.

The eventual packaging of songs on YouTube is a key component of the show. As evidence of this, the creators will often produce two versions of a song—one for the show's airing on network TV and an "explicit" version solely for online distribution. As producer Brosh McKenna has noted, being on a network show "reins us in, in I think, in an interesting way. They've done things I don't think they ever, ever thought they would do. And it's been hilarious, like fighting to say 'clitoris' on the air."[39] Despite their success in pushing the bounds of allowable content, there are still limitations, and this is where the access to other modes of distribution comes into play. Bloom maintains her YouTube channel, RachelDoes-Stuff, which she uses to host CXG content, including explicit versions of songs. The explicit version might have minimal differences from the original, perhaps even a single lyric or two, or it might be substantially different. The song "Buttload of Cats" (3.12), for instance, was also filmed as "Fuckton of Cats." Throughout the seasons, the show has also included brief teasers for a song about period sex, which would not make it through FCC content regulations. They decided to create a full version of the song, however, to release online. Viewing numbers for the videos on Bloom's channel, including explicit song versions, are significantly higher than for The CW uploads: 6 million for "Sexy Getting Ready Song," 4 million for "Heavy Boobs," and around just under 1.6 million each for "It Was a Shit Show" and "Settle for Me."[40] While these numbers are not as high as Bloom's "You Can Touch My Boobies" (6.7 million), and only "Sexy Getting Ready Song" tops "Fuck Me, Ray Bradbury" (5.4 million), the majority of the content on RachelDoesStuff consists of CXG songs.

The musical format of the show also opens up the possibility of live concert tours. Members of the cast came together for a limited, ten-city run in March and April 2018, and lined up select performances in New

York City and London in 2019. Tickets for the initial shows sold out rapidly, which suggests that this could be another lucrative market to continue pursuing.[41] Bloom has said that "we're probably going to do more touring after the show ends. Especially because it's a musical. . . . I could see a world where we could revive and keep doing performances for the next 50 years."[42] Although some general audiences are hesitant about musicals, this genre actually fits well in a world of multiple distribution platforms and ancillary markets.

Bloom and her team's risk-taking approach to creating a comic musical puts a new spin on music genre conventions. The show's critical and cult success is based on quirky, unexpected dichotomies that create unlikely, antithetical combinations of style and content. These numbers would be one-off, parodic novelties that detracted from the emotional core of the series, if not for the careful way that they are formally integrated, contributing to narrative and character development and building through reprises and internal references that occur over multiple seasons. This thoughtful approach to playfulness contributed to the series' critical acclaim, and emerging distribution tactics aligned perfectly with the musical's ability to supply preformed short videos. Musical numbers can easily be excerpted to stand alone, consumed and shared over and over by fans, with new numbers appearing every week. The musical lends itself to multiple avenues of distribution, and the tongue-in-cheek, comic approach has found great appeal among certain audiences. Perhaps this will, as Bloom hoped, show that musicals have a place in the contemporary television market and create space for another renewal of the television musical.

# 3

# Deconstructing Crazy

*Jewishness, Neuroticism, and the Stylized*
*Rom-Com in* Crazy Ex-Girlfriend

## Charles Burnetts

This chapter examines the way *Crazy Ex-Girlfriend* (CXG onward) re-hearses the conventions and contradictions of Hollywood's romantic comedy ("rom-com") and how it uses "crazy" in particular as a metaphor for its play with genre and identity. The show's postmodernism represents more than just a superficial intertextuality, a charge quite often leveled at excessively *smart* or knowing TV shows and films. Self-consciousness in CXG serves rather to foreground the contradictions of various gendered categories reproduced by the show in its negotiation of genres like the musical and the rom-com in an era of rapid media convergence. To demonstrate this, the discussion will focus initially on the show's first season and the way it introduced its main women characters: Rebecca (the show's main protagonist, played by Rachel Bloom), Valencia (the fiancée of Rebecca's main love interest Josh, played by Gabrielle Ruiz), and Paula (her newly adopted best friend, played by Donna Lynne Champlin). In particular the discussion will highlight how each character is shown to be caught up in gendered codes of romantic coupling, competition, and deception. The discussion will then turn to Rebecca and, in particular, her Jewishness to demonstrate and shed light on the show's weaving of ethnic, cinematic, and psychological categories alongside its play with various symptoms.

Although the show has been very innovative in its blending of genres and forms, it's important first to note, as shown by much scholarship examining postclassical cinema and television, that CXG is hardly the first televised or filmed rom-com to be self-conscious and playful in relation to genre. As many scholars have noted, we live in an era of the "smart film," a postclassical Hollywood genre that is highly *knowing* about its audiences in its reproduction of, and departure from, received formulae and codes.[1] The rationale for such shifts is economic as much as aesthetic. Various Hollywood rom-coms of the last forty years, for instance, have expanded their audiences through cross-fertilization with traditionally male genres. Examples include the adventure genre (*Romancing the Stone*, 1984, dir. Robert Zemeckis) or crime thriller (*Desperately Seeking Susan*, 1985, dir. Susan Seidelman; *Bird on a Wire*, 1990, dir. John Badham), which splice a usually heterosexual romance narrative with the compulsory "quest" or "mission" of classical Hollywood narrative.[2] Such decisions often work on the principle of attracting wider audiences than the traditional rom-com's female core audience, while reproducing norms of white, heterosexual coupling. Even *Bridget Jones's Diary* (2001, dir. Sharon Maguire), despite its foregrounding of intertextuality and its key protagonist's neuroses, ends with the reaffirmation of the central couple's union.

CXG's particular deployment of the musical and the music video as key intertexts results, however, in a rendering of romantic comedy that somewhat destabilizes the genre's usual dependence on dialogue and theatrical naturalism. While the show certainly works off the recent successes of such TV shows as *Glee* (Fox, 2009–15) and *American Idol* (Fox/ABC, 2002–), and to a lesser extent *Smash* (NBC, 2012–13), the show's playfulness surrounding issues of genre and race signals an *edge* that is rarer on network television and in Hollywood. The casting, for instance, of Filipino American actor Vincent Rodriguez III as Rebecca's main love interest, Josh Chan, sets the show apart from the traditional rom-com and its obsession with white coupledom, signaling from the outset an attention to issues of identity and diversity. Alongside its foregrounding of same-gender relationships between supporting characters (White Josh [David Hull] and Darryl [Pete Gardner]; Valencia and Beth [Emma Willmann]), the show indeed has gone some way to expand the scope of both rom-coms and musicals in terms of race and sexuality.

Bearing out this sense of CXG's less than conventional mode of address, the show indeed struggled to get commissioned. It began as a half-hour pilot for Showtime that the channel chose not to go ahead with. Once the show had cleaned up its language, it was picked up by The CW channel in 2015. The show's approach to love and romance nevertheless remained somewhat schizophrenic in relation to the rom-com's traditional character categories, none more so than in its delusional central character, Rebecca Bunch. As noted in Frank Krutnik's analysis of Hollywood rom-coms, self-deception and fantasy play important roles in the genre's working through themes of love and courtship. Discussing a replay of Edmond Rostand's *Cyrano de Bergerac* in the 1995 film *The Truth about Cats and Dogs* (dir. Michael Lehmann), Krutnik focuses on the genre's highlighting of tensions between physical attractiveness and personality. Thus the character Abby (played by Janeane Garofalo), who lacks confidence in her own physical appearance, uses her friend Noelle (played by Uma Thurman) as a physical surrogate for her relationship with Brian (played by Ben Chaplin), who's fallen in love with Abby on the phone and through her radio show. In one scene, Brian's visualization of Noelle while he masturbates, seduced nonetheless by Abby's words, serves for Krutnik as a paradigm of the contemporary rom-com's increased attention to the constructedness of romantic love, wherein the ideal partner is conceived of, and maintained, as a fantasy that cannot be contained in one actual living person.

CXG can be seen as a direct corollary of such forms in its analogous attention to the looks-versus-personality binary. As a Type-A former high-flying lawyer from New York City, Rebecca applies her skills of strategy and manipulation to negotiate Josh's current relationship with his fiancée Valencia, aided and abetted by her newfound bestie and colleague, Paula, a jaded wife and mother of two who latches onto Rebecca and her romantic ambitions as an escape route from her own suburban tedium. If Valencia represents "looks," and Rebecca "personality," the entire season serves as a problematic defense, and eventual victory, of mind and internality over body and surface appearance. This resolution is nevertheless "crazy" in its analogous dependence on fantasy and orchestration, wherein Josh becomes the mere trophy partner that Valencia seemed initially to embody. Female agency is certainly foregrounded here, both in Rebecca's own emphatic bids to transform her life (ostensibly all for Josh) as well as Paula's somewhat unhealthy deployment of IT and social media skills to engineer Rebecca's and Josh's romance (see Marija Laugalyte's chapter in this volume for a more thorough discussion of the intersections of technology and gender in the show). Deception and self-deception nevertheless persist beyond Josh and Rebecca's coupling, thus pushing the rom-com's usual attention to neurosis into new territories, tackling issues of sexuality, body dysmorphia, stalking, and rape culture.

## Queer Eye

The show's dysfunctionalisms and boundary-crossing are played out most revealingly in its frequent foregrounding of looking and desire, where the audience is frequently invited to share Rebecca's distorted and stylized perspective on characters and events. The sequence that introduced the character of Valencia (in episode 1.02) epitomized the intensely mediatized nature of Rebecca's gaze, wherein Rebecca's apparent plainness is counterposed to both Josh's and Valencia's embodiment of eroticized fantasy. The sequence gazes initially at Josh in a highly stylized slow-motion shot of his profiled body, as he opens a supermarket refrigerator, and then the soundtrack jolts with a reality TV–style kick-bass thud as Valencia joins him in a steamy embrace and kiss. Unusually here, Josh and Valencia are gazed upon specifically by Rebecca, who stands in for the male of Laura Mulvey's seminal formulation of the voyeuristic gaze. Rebecca is coded male not only owing to these looking relations but also to her attire, having seemingly thrown on frumpy clothes with no makeup after a previous night of drinking and snacking. Rebecca's initial voyeurism at a male object abruptly shifts register with the arrival of Valencia into the shot. Valencia's initiation of a hip hop–style erotics is coded as the reality Rebecca must now contend with, having initially beheld Josh in the classic orientation of cinematic "to-be-looked-at-ness," replete with Hollywoodian nondiegetic orchestral strings.[3] As she looks on at their embrace, Rebecca's dreams of being with Josh (a fantasy that has motivated her move to West Covina) are shattered, not by any return of the look that conventionally ends the voyeuristic encounter but by the abrupt insertion of a queered erotics, wherein Josh is supplemented, if not supplanted, by Valencia. When Rebecca comes to remark to a shelf-stacker that she's just "watching her ex-boyfriend make out with the hottest woman I've ever seen," the sequence is marked by the emergence not just of a rival but also by a more sexually ambiguous mode of looking entirely.

The sequence exemplifies the way *CXG* frequently aligns audience perspective with Rebecca's unstable coloring of events, filtered through the lens of television, the musical, and the music video. On one hand, it promotes our sense of Rebecca's remove from reality through the alignment of her POV with the stagey artifices of dry ice and the heavy stylization of Josh and Valencia making out—excesses that we know to be false and colored by the subjectivity of the beholder. The sequence invokes the overt sexuality of a hip-hop music video and the intrusive feel of reality television in its focus on Rebecca's gaze, wherein the feelings of physical inadequacy imposed on her by media are projected onto the mise-en-scène. Her unmade-up appearance adds comic irony to the sequence in its dramatic contrasting of Valencia as object of erotic fantasy with Rebecca, whose appearance just shortly after this sequence is referred to by a group of her male friends as being like that of a "homeless" person. Meanwhile, the second opinion of Valencia we get from the supermarket's shelf-stacker, Marty (Hunter Stiebel), adds to the overdetermined categories informing the sequence in his use of the terms "smokin'" and "booty" about her. The smokin' Valencia is both absent and present in the above sequence, the shelf-stacker's point-of-view acting merely as a doubling of Rebecca's own insecurities and uncertainties.

Through such sequences, the show introduced the audience very early on to an approach to genre that foregrounded spectatorship and the rom-com's erotics, adding a critical dimension to the genre's focus on the heterosexual couple's torpid courtship. Krutnik argues succinctly, for instance, that:

> Although the contemporary romances continue to value love as a source
> of creative inspiration, their aesthetic emphasis shifts from the inter-
> nal interpersonal dialectic of the film to the ludic relationship the film

builds with its audience. The credibility of the relationship is often sustained not by the couple themselves so much as by a highly self-conscious mode of amorous signification that blatantly manipulates conventions and discourses to generate an expressly stylized rendition of the mating game.[4]

The many deceptions and manipulations on Rebecca's part as to her true intentions for moving to West Covina can be understood in turn, then, as actions taken on in the name of a playful spirit of self-conscious performance. Playing with the audience's familiarity with the genre and its ideology, CXG shows Rebecca continuously acting in awareness of received positions she too inherits from these overdetermined codes of "amorous signification," self-consciously going against type and cliché as much as she also enslaves herself to the hypertraditional aim of initiating a romance with Josh at any cost.

### Unorthodox Satisfactions

Specifically feminist and queer positions come under close scrutiny therefore amid the show's intense focus on female and male bodies, particularly at the level of friendship and loyalty. While Valencia is coded, as discussed in the sequence analyzed, as every woman's worst nightmare, Rebecca's impetus is both to desire and to befriend her, going against the traditional rom-com's setup of the inevitable catfight between women for a man, and signaling ideals, specifically feminist, that fall outside the scope of the romantic coupling narrative.

Acknowledged indeed as an (excessively?) feminist development for the show to take, such friendship becomes regulated and curtailed in much of the first season by Paula, Rebecca's closest confidante and confederate in numerous plots to ensnare Josh. It is she, for instance, who insists that Rebecca "hate" her rival Valencia, while Rebecca defends this potential friendship with recourse to a feminist discourse immediately dismissed by Paula as "boring" because of its politically correct jargon.

Feminist discourse becomes equated in such sequences indeed with Rebecca's craziness, owing to her contradictory impulses to both compete with and befriend Valencia. This approach is framed (ironically) as a fan-ciful flight from reality that goes against the apparently self-evident his-torical norms of perpetual competition and mutual contempt between women for a man. Bracketing Paula's opinions as equally delusory in her obsessive adherence to, and imposition of, mating game rituals and rules becomes thus for the show a vital counterpoint to such mores. As Rebec-ca's older friend-cum-surrogate mom, Paula's resistance to Rebecca's femi-nist counterdiscourse is continuously shown to lead back into her comical dissatisfactions with a husband and suburban family, wherein her own desperate needs for self-fulfillment outside of the domestic sphere become merely the recto to the verso of Rebecca's need for close friends and a soul-mate. Rebecca and Paula's relationship becomes dysfunctional toward the end of the first season not because they are women, the show eventually intimates, but because both *enable* each other's dysfunctional fantasies: Paula's for a best friend and surrogate daughter she can control, Rebecca's for a devoted friend that selflessly feeds her narcissism.

This foregrounding of the mating game as a highly conventionalized, yet morally deregulated, code continuously undercuts the sense of CXG as a simple homage to the genre. The modified rom-com setup serves indeed as a quite complex terrain for enjoyments and subject-positions that fall out-side the usual scope of heterosexual couple formation. Using Krutnik's ex-planation, the show sits in continuity with other new romances in the way

> the man-woman story seems to operate as an alibi for other less ortho-dox, satisfactions—suggesting that quite diverse projects may actually be working in the name of love.[5]

Female friendship becomes in CXG, I suggest, the key example of such unorthodox satisfactions, a counterforce to the ideal of the "one true pairing" represented by Rebecca's quest for Josh. Women certainly talk about men in this show, indeed sometimes obsessively so, but they also speculate at length about things like Vampire Weekend, the sadness of leaving college, and the feasibility of having sex during menstruation. In an almost perverse inversion of *Cyrano de Bergerac* and its hero's linguis-tic mastery of courtship and romance, Rebecca is shown to be a master of "killing the mood," never more so than in the many "epic fails" that predominate in her encounters with Josh. The taboo-breaking number "Period Sex" (first alluded to in episode 2.03), for instance, exemplifies this tendency of the show. The number was disallowed from being aired in full owing to its stylized celebration of sex during menstruation.

In accordance then with the way rom-coms have come to reflect the sexual liberation of the 1960s, for example in such movies as *When Harry Met Sally* (1989, dir. Rob Reiner, particularly the famous fake orgasm sequence), CXG highlights Rebecca's sexuality in her various sexual encounters with other men once she's moved to West Covina, such as with Josh's best friend Greg. If it were limited to the formation and resolution of love triangles like this, we'd have a more conventional rom-com narrative that often, as we see, serves to compound the romantic couple's rightness as its final conclusion. In accordance, however, with the show's "ludic relationship" with its audience,[6] as discussed above by Krutnik in relation to rom-coms more broadly, Rebecca's body is foregrounded by such sequences in ways less presaged by the rom-com, where the playful juxtaposition of pregnancy, menstruation, and sex clashes with codes that mandate a time and place for these usually distinct regimes. Doubling-down on the rom-com's nods to sexual liberation, the female body is shown to be more than fully amenable to "less orthodox satisfactions" and a concomitant decentering of heterosexual romance. Rebecca's studied inappropriateness entails a supplanting of *Cyrano de Bergerac*'s linguistic dexterity through a uniquely female insistence on the body and its possibilities.

### Rebecca the Jew

The show is indeed quintessentially postmodern in its continuous allusions and play with genre, most particularly, as noted above, in its play with audience literacies concerning gender and representation. Another dimension that problematizes these regimes, however, is Rebecca's Jewishness, which becomes a cipher of sorts for the show's complex negotiation of genre, identity, and the body. CXG follows on from a number of US TV shows of the last two decades that have foregrounded nonclassical female central characters in positions of traditionally male authority (Dana Scully in *The X-Files* [Fox, 1993–2018], Liz Lemon in *30 Rock* [NBC, 2006–13], Jessica Day from *New Girl* [Fox, 2011–18]), but rather less characteristically foregrounds Jewishness as both an important determinant and constraint to female empowerment. Bloom's character thus also rehearses the "nebbish" character of films encompassing Woody Allen's comedies, the *Revenge of the Nerds* films of the 1980s, and Seth Rogen comedies, all of which are unified by their articulation of problems concerning belongingness in America, internalized antisemitism, and desire for the gentile.[7] If CXG's intervention is to transpose such problems to a woman, it nevertheless stays faithful to the form's adherence to self-mockery and the fundamental ambiguities surrounding ethnicity in US culture. Just as the many semiautobiographical characters of Woody Allen's films of the 1970s and 1980s articulated Portnoy-esque desires for the gentile (woman) as symptoms of anxieties surrounding assimilation in America, so CXG continuously foregrounds Rebecca as quintessentially "East Coast" in her self-sabotaging quest for the Other, both in terms of her ideal partner and her existential quest for self-fulfillment and happiness.

Propelled by the show's "fish out of water" premise, Rebecca's fresh start in West Covina is thus continuously challenged by various Jewish characters emerging from the Tri-State Area she grew up in, from her stereotypically demanding mother, Naomi (Tovah Feldshuh), to her childhood nemesis, now a high-flying lawyer, Audra Levine (Rachel Grate), all of whom stand as models for the urbane conformity she rejects at the outset of the show. Audra, in particular, not only represents the life Rebecca could have had but also speaks very self-consciously to second- or third-generation immigrant aspirations for making it in America through focused graft and ruthless gamesmanship. While Rebecca seems to have gone native in her embrace of a laid-back West Coast fatalism concerning her court case for the townspeople of West Covina, Audra reminds her at various points of the cutthroat pragmatism with which success, and victory, must be pursued at the cost of failure, poverty, and loss of social standing. Rocked momentarily by Rebecca's choice of forfeiting her court case for Josh's affectionate approval of her goodwill, as manifest by a neurotic tick that mars her facial composure, Audra quickly pulls herself together to remind Rebecca that both he and she are "losers."

Compounded by Rebecca's mother's extreme disapproval and barbed comments as to her daughter's life choices, it became clear early on in the show's run that immigrant upward mobility and obedience to parents/authority figures would be vital to comprehending Rebecca's unhappiness and *mishegas* (the well-known Yiddish term for craziness). Audra's appearances throughout the show's four seasons serve in turn as continuous reminders of Rebecca's failure to live up to her mother's upwardly mobile values, as epitomized by the scene where Naomi goes up against Audra's mother in a comparison of their respective child's accomplishments in season four (4.07). With Audra now pregnant with triplets in this scene, a high-flying career is now supplemented by marriage and children ("all boys") as signs of *having it all*, values upheld as sacrosanct irrespective of whether their children (epitomized by Audra with her uncomfortably pregnant belly) are "happy." Happiness indeed sits at a very low rank of priorities in this particular world, deemed futile by a group consigned to perpetual victimhood and suffering by long histories of persecution and trauma.

The musical number "Remember That We Suffered" (2.10), which Rebecca performs alongside her mother and other family members at an East Coast bar mitzvah she attends in season two, is perhaps the furthest the show goes in conveying this sense of Jewish doubt and self-enforced misery. Choreographed as many a Jewish occasion's traditional "hora" dance, the number here substitutes Hebrew or Yiddish for English, as Naomi imparts a prescriptive lesson that foregrounds the Holocaust's dominance in contemporary Jewish pedagogy. Undercutting the usually Utopian dimensions of both the musical number and the hora itself, the lyrical refrain of "but remember that we suffered" serves to set limits on any inclinations toward an (escapist) joy, while carefully highlighting its self-regulating dogmatism as a quintessentially Jewish mode of ironic detachment. While, for instance, the Jewish wedding is noted by the culture for its "noshing, dancing, singing," Naomi reminds Rebecca in the following line that Jewish song is sung most often "in a minor key" and thus that they should always "remember that we suffered."

Jewishness becomes thus a particularly vexed strand of CXG. Filtered through the playfulness of the contemporary rom-com and musical, it serves, like the other ethnicities foregrounded by the show, as an identity that both liberates and limits agency. Rebecca's performance in the number described above, signified most visibly by her "eye-roll" reactions to Naomi's admonishments, is unusually passive compared to her typically manic self-possession in most of her own numbers. As with Josh and his disinclination to ever leave his Filipino mother and the comfortable family home, Jewish parental expectations hang over Rebecca's bid for the American Dream and its ideology of individual freedom and unfettered choice. Just as the young Joe of Woody Allen's *Radio Days* (1987) is physically hit by his rabbi for quoting the "Lone Ranger" at him, Jewishness always seems to be of the "old country," whether with respect to the shtetl of Yiddish theater and film or the usually offscreen New York City (or, more acutely, Scarsdale) of *CXG*. If Josh's nirvana is to sell TVs at his favorite Hawaiian-themed electronics retailer in the show's first season, and Rebecca's to go west and seek fulfilment with him, a very ethnic attachment to parental approval and security prefigures the inevitable failure of such choices.

It is this problematic embrace of the American Dream on the part of *CXG*'s ethnic characters that in many ways serves as the master "crazy" to rule them all, arguably undergirding the show's skepticism of American idealism and choice. Through its glossing of Rebecca's experience as a Jewish quest for belonging and acceptance, the show frames both coasts of the United States as equally inimical to minority identities. It quickly becomes clear, for instance, that West Covina presents its own inherent problems, whether with respect to Darryl's repression of his bisexuality; the unreflective "dude-bro" culture of Josh, White Josh, Hector, and Greg in season one; or Valencia's distinctly unspiritual brand of yoga instruction with which she makes a living. Within this context, Rebecca's Jewishness comes to serve a different set of functions to those outlined thus far, symbolized equally for instance in her introduction of legalistic rigor and professionalism to Whitefeather & Associates, or by her Utopian glossing of West Covina with the conventions of Broadway and the Hollywood musical. Jewishness serves here not simply as a throwback to the demands of gender normativity and worker conformity but also as a catalyst of sorts to changes Rebecca effectuates in this small California town.

If West Covina is misrecognized by Rebecca, then, as a place of opportunity and freedom, the show is at pains to underscore Jewishness as a "crazy" response that may nevertheless have self-preserving functions, aligned with a condition Thomas Elsaesser has described, albeit in a different context (the "mind-game" film), as the "symptom of the disease for which it also hopes to be a cure."[8] Although CXG is not a "mind-game" narrative per se, it nevertheless shares attributes with the subgenre Elsaesser describes in the way it is formally shaped by Rebecca's games and imaginings and, by extension, the musical genre's play with space and cultural memory. Jewishness, in other words, becomes an ambiguous mode of resistance to the various cultures vying for dominance in the show, where West Coast anti-intellectualism and superficiality is pitted against East Coast cynicism and hierarchy. For Rebecca, this opposition is unstable, with Jewishness continuously serving as an engine of doubt with respect to her pursuit of happiness.

## Dollar-Book *DSM*

Although much of season three is taken up with the psychologization of Rebecca's craziness (through her officially being diagnosed and treated for borderline personality disorder), it is important in light of the discussion above to examine how the show draws attention from the outset to mental illness as a culturally constructed field of meaning. Just as Orson Welles quipped self-disparagingly that the famous "Rosebud" denouement of *Citizen Kane* felt to him in retrospect like "dollar-book Freud,"[9] so CXG's recourse to psychological discourse serves as a symptom of the show's persistent contradictions as much as a conclusive explanation of Rebecca's problems. The segmentation of *Kane* into accounts of the protagonist's story from multiple narrators gave the film a notoriously nonunifying and open structure that resisted any easy attempts at explanatory closure, on the part of either its key characters or the spectator. CXG equally resists a classicist impulse, albeit through a less narratological approach, focusing rather more on fragmented, self-destructive characters who seek answers from various received forms. While the rom-com and its notoriously neurotic characters have always harvested comic capital from the foregrounding of contradiction, *CXG* leavens its cynicism with the Utopian earnestness of the musical and audiovisual impact of the music video, resulting in a detached performativity that simulates the borderline condition.

This ludic approach to our expectations remains of key importance indeed to understanding the various breakdowns that occur on the part of *CXG*'s characters, perhaps most particularly Rebecca's suicide attempt in season three (3.05). If this plot turn seemed to take the show into unprecedented, and apparently sobering, territory for a rom-com (with various episodes focused on Rebecca's treatment, relapses, and recoveries), it is important to note the extent to which Rebecca's and *CXG*'s deconstructive tendencies (and its comedy) persisted as an important adjunct to the drama and catharsis of the show's last season. Season four's (non)resolution of Rebecca's love-life, deploying conventions adopted from reality shows like *The Bachelor*, served in particular to foreground the critical approach of the show toward all its romantic male leads. As Rebecca decides to make a final definitive choice among Nathaniel, Greg, and Josh, popular culture and its stereotyping tendencies is underlined once more as Rebecca's key filter: the cutthroat corporate/legal world represented by upper-crusty Nathaniel, and Josh standing in for the easygoing West Coast bro-culture. Finally, there's Greg, who served from the outset as the "Settle For Me" boy-next-door character, on whom Rebecca could always fall back.

Rebecca's final decision to abandon romance with any of these characters serves in such respects as a final grand maneuver on the part of the show to shut down the romantic mating game. Alongside Rebecca's uncharacteristically well-considered resolve to pursue her own destiny and desire in music and theater before entangling herself in another relationship, her prior "crazy" is contextualized as a set of understandable, and even necessary, responses to the dysfunctional cultures she's encountered throughout the show and their particular foundation in variants of patriarchal subjectivity. Although Rebecca's self-sabotaging acts presaged each of her breakups (e.g., stalking Josh, obsessively trying to resolve Nathaniel's relationship with his parents, sleeping with Greg's father), in each case such failures emerge also as fail-safes to her subsumption to whichever code is made salient by the male character in question. Craziness emerges here not merely as resistance, although it precipitates such effects, but rather more as a mode of what Steven Shaviro terms "aesthetic disinterest" in relation to postmodern culture's litany of choices.[10] If Rebecca's relationships are framed ultimately as instances of misrecognition and self-escape, catalyzed in each case by dictates of romance and lifestyle choice, the affective intensities of the borderline sensibility seemed to have shielded her too from longer-term misery.

It is revealing, indeed, that the male character with whom Rebecca shares the most pathological baggage is one of the only men with whom she refuses to engage romantically. A former Harvard acquaintance who serves in many ways as her alter ego, Trent Maddock pursues Rebecca once she uses him as a faux boyfriend in one of the show's many farcical cover-ups, and quickly makes plain his intentions to possess her romantically through incessant pursuit, bribery, and blackmail. Matching Rebecca's pathologically obsessive attachment to romantic others, Trent resists the easy categorization of other male characters of the show. Sexually ambiguous, not classically handsome, and socially awkward with both men and women, he serves as a continuous threat to Rebecca, but more than simply in terms of his predatory behavior. Unmoored to any particular ideology, Trent's obsession with Rebecca lends him connotations of the queered "monster" rehearsed in such characters as Norman Bates of *Psycho* (1960, dir. Alfred Hitchcock), Buffalo Bill in *The Silence of the Lambs* (1991, dir. Jonathan Demme), or the villains of various Bond films. By this reading, Trent serves not as Rebecca's archenemy (Valencia in season one) or her nemesis (Audra) but as a cryptic confederate who is woven in and out of Rebecca's encounters for the purpose of liberating/ trapping her from forces about which she can only be partially cognizant. Compared to Rebecca's more intentional allies, like Paula, Heather, and eventually Valencia, Trent's presence in the show is partial and spectral, a demon or angel depending on perspective, whose inhuman power to manipulate and conspire is matched by an inverse incompetence at the level of human discourse (exemplified in his hopeless attempt to "hang" with the guys in season three).

A character like Trent amplifies, then, certain feminist tendencies in the show with regards to its deconstruction of masculine categories and its foregrounding of queer identities. If Rebecca is seen to be in continuous negotiation with problems relating to image and body in a postfeminist world, Trent is curiously inhuman, or disembodied, in his hyperefficient pursuit, or what in Slavoj Žižek's Neo-Lacanian terms may be considered an "obscene enjoyment" of his fantasies.[11] It is noteworthy, for instance, that Trent's only musical number in the show came in the form of a copy-cat remake of season two's intro sequence, where Trent merely substitutes for Rebecca as lead singer (3.12). Both Trent and Rebecca are in many ways monsters, in each case owing to the radicalism of their respective fluidities, his in relation to space (his many unexpected appearances), hers in relation to identity (as epitomized by season three's intro sequence that showcases various fictional incarnations of Rebecca).

Like other crazy characters on US television (*Seinfeld*'s Kramer comes most readily to mind), Rebecca Bunch is driven ultimately by an aestheticism, a pursuit of beauty in a deregulated, consumer-driven world where normative gender categories persist dysfunctionally. While eccentricity of this kind may often be confined to minor characters in the sitcom, or somewhat tamed by heterosexual coupling in the rom-com, CXG allows it to dictate the form via the deployment of the more sensually fertile medium of music video (see Chelsea McCracken, chapter 2 in this volume, for more on how the music video format functions within the show). Echoing the neuroticisms of Jewish American comedy and the Utopian dimensions of the musical, the show's play with craziness is very much of its time in its hyperactive confluence of cinema, television, and new media. Just as these media speak to different histories and modes of spectatorship, so characters like Rebecca are subject to a disorienting and impermanent field of self-knowledge, where choice and self-fashioning stand in for freedom or liberation as such. If Rebecca defensively asserts in her intro number of season two that she's "just a girl in love," the show seems dictated by the problematics of pathologizing this claim given its rhetorical force in the culture.

# 4

# Television after Complexity

## Crazy Ex-Girlfriend *and the Late 2010s*

### Billy Stevenson

### Postcomplex Television

*Crazy Ex-Girlfriend* (hereafter CXG) exemplifies a series of formal and cultural shifts in television that have occurred over the last five years. Taken collectively, these shifts constitute a move toward what I label "postcomplex television." By "postcomplex," I don't mean that this form of television lacks complexity. Rather, it departs from a model of televisual complexity that has been dominant in American television over the last two decades. As a result, CXG indicates that we might be experiencing a new era of televisual innovation.

In *Complex TV*, Jason Mittell notes that a new form of televisual complexity became common during the 1990s and peaked during the 2000s. This was primarily a narrative complexity that involved writers and showrunners blending episodic and serial imperatives in new and innovative ways. In Amanda Lotz's study of the periodization of television, *The Television Will Be Revolutionized*, this formal evolution coincides with a shift from the multichannel transition, which she situates between the mid-1980s and the mid-2000s, to the postnetwork period, which she situates between the mid-2000s and the present.[1] This "drive towards unity and complexity" of serial and episodic forms was "fulfilled by bound volumes such as DVD sets as a *boxed* aesthetic, tied together and treated as a complete whole comparable to similarly unified forms such as novels and

78

films."[2] When television series could be bound and displayed like books, their complexity was complete, since they could now be experienced both as a series of episodes and as a seamless whole.

However, Mittell notes, this boxed aesthetic also meant that a crucial element of television was lost. Since television series could now be consumed as a single entity, at the pace that the viewer demanded, there was no necessary gap between episodes. This not only offset the episodic quality of television but also offset the serial quality, since seriality depends upon a regular delivery of content. Rather than balancing serial and episodic imperatives in the manner of earlier complex television, boxed television could be seen to remove seriality and episodicity altogether in favor of a more streamlined experience that was often perceived as cinematic.

The boxed aesthetic was therefore the start of the postnetwork era because it dismantled the serial and episodic vocabulary of the network era. This also meant dismantling the experience of broadcast television, since "the broader experience of communal serialized viewing is tied to the original broadcast moment."[3] Identifying the release of *Lost* as a key moment in this final transition from broadcast to boxed television, Mittell argues that "the truly ephemeral aspect of the series was not the initial textual broadcast, but the experience of serialized spectatorship."[4] While the structure of broadcast flow might be replaced by the control of boxed "publication," there was an experiential loss that could not be artificially retained. Although the "broadcast schedule is ultimately arbitrary and artificial," it provided "the structure for collective synchronous consumption" impossible with the boxed model.[5]

What I am describing as postcomplex television largely resists this process, combining serial and episodic experiences in provisional and messy ways. This project is encapsulated in the opening credit sequences of *CXG*, which embed this formal gesture within the gender politics of the postcomplex period. These credit sequences increasingly reject the "operational aesthetic" that Mittell identifies as crucial to complex television, which posits narrative ingenuity as the televisual form of special effects.[6] While these postcomplex credit sequences deploy many of the narrative special effects that Mittell identifies, such as analepses, dream sequences, multiple perspectives, and self-conscious voiceovers, these are rarely presented as exceptional or avant-garde. Instead they are folded into more conventional effects and used to disrupt the relation between serial and episodic experiences, rather than converging these elements into a narratively spectacular and seamless whole.

## Credit Sequences

The credits for the first season of CXG initially present as a narrative special effect, as the main character, Rebecca Bunch, condenses the entire premise of the series into a brief musical number, not unlike the ironic plot summary of Ron Howard's narration. This musical number explicitly presents Rebecca as protagonist and Rachel as showrunner, shrouding them both in a stark spotlight that is the first image that we see of the series' world. Thereafter, the credit sequence seeks to introduce a televisual experience that still feels elliptical, discontinuous, and incomplete when watched in a boxed or published form. Rather than erasing the original moment of broadcast in the act of boxing (as occurs with DVD sets), or collapsing the original moment of broadcast into the act of boxing (as occurs with simultaneous release), the credit sequence here opts for a postcontinuous aesthetic that embeds the contingencies of the original broadcast into the final, published form of the televisual text. I take my definition of postcontinuity here from Steven Shaviro, who notes that "postcontinuity" doesn't simply designate a lack of continuity, serial or episodic, but rather an aesthetic milieu in which "the violation of continuity rules isn't foregrounded, and isn't in itself significant."[7]

This process starts with a slippage between the name of the series and the thematic tune of this opening season. After her initial appearance, Rebecca is surrounded with an animated cast of characters who provide a brief overview of her backstory and then repeatedly refer to her as "crazy." For a moment, she seems poised to go along with them, before complaining to them that it's "a sexist term." The balance between singer and chorus, so critical to musical theater, is unbalanced, as the rhythm and lyrics of this opening musical performance become compressed, convoluted, and increasingly difficult to deliver coherently. Finally, this opening musical number doesn't "conclude" per se but instead exhausts itself, creating the impression that the credit sequence has ended prematurely. The conflict between Rebecca and the chorus, and the contrast between the real and animated footage, further disrupts the relationship between the nondiegetic world of the showrunner and the diegetic world of the protagonist. Bloom as showrunner can't fully fuse herself with Bunch as protagonist, while the "craziness" that initially defines her becomes a point of conflict, contention, and comedy.

This focus on gendered craziness, and the formal restlessness that it suggests, corresponds to dramatic cultural changes that started to reshape the American television industry in the mid-2010s. In her landmark study of female television auteurism, Joy Press identifies 2015 as a watershed moment in the industry for the recognition of female talent, labor, and vision:

> The idea for this book started clattering around in my brain in the spring of 2015. If you had to pick a triumphant moment for the twenty-first-century surge of revolutionary TV made by and about women, that would be it. More than a dozen new female-centric series created by women premiered in 2015—as many as had emerged in the three previous years combined. At the 2015 Emmys, *Inside Amy Schumer* won Best Variety Show and Jill Soloway accepted an award for directing the series she'd created, *Transparent*. The same year, at the Golden Globes, four of the five nominated comedies, *Orange Is the New Black*, *Girls*, *Jane the Virgin* and *Transparent* (which won), were made by women. On the drama front, Shonda Rhimes reigned over ABC's Thursday-night lineup with three hit series, making her one of the most powerful producers in Hollywood.[8]

While Press identifies these series broadly as "female-centric," they are notable for focusing on black women, trans women, Hispanic women, and women such as Amy Schumer and Lena Dunham who have resisted the idea of how normative femininity should play out on television. In an article written at the start of 2015, Lili Loofbourow argued that these series mark the dawn of "promiscuous protagonism: a style of television that, rather than relying on the perspective of one (usually twisted) character, adopt a wild, roving narrative sympathy."[9] While Press and Loofbourow don't use the term "complex television," they periodize the evolution of television in a similar way to both Lotz and Mittell. However, they focus as much on cultural representation as on textual form, associating the period between the mid-1990s and the early twenty-first century—what Lotz calls the "multichannel transition" and Mittell associates with the complex era—with the rise of a form of televisual auteurism that was helmed by men and was particularly preoccupied with masculine representation and identity politics.

Loofbourow describes this period, which has also been identified as the third wave of quality television, as invested in "stories of threatened male power that were also commentaries on American dysphoria." She notes that the complex series that emerged during this time were often allegories of their own conditions of production, featuring protagonists who frequently adopted an auteurist approach to the narratives they commanded. Since "many of the male show runners replicated the dynamics of their shows in their crew,"[10] complex television played as a sustained argument for the concessions that needed to be made to televisual genius, such that "the abuse doled out by an auteur becomes a guarantor of quality through a kind of backward reasoning: if he weren't truly great, who would put up with him?"[11] This resulted in male protagonists whose craziness was often self-consuming, leading Naja Later to identify *Hannibal* as emblematic of complex characterization.[12] This eventually produced what Caetlin Benson-Allott has described as a broader "masculinist bias" to how complexity was configured, since "shows celebrated . . . tend to be about men and for men."[13]

The credit sequences to the second season of *CXG* continue Bloom's dialogue with this more cultural and identity-driven dimension of what I am calling "postcomplex television." These are the last credits to focus specifically on musical theater as the basis for the series' aesthetic outlook. Virtually all the episodes in *CXG* feature musical numbers that translate the events of the narrative into song. To some extent, these musical numbers play as narrative special effects, compressing the storyline into ingenious bursts of theater. However, they often end prematurely, deteriorate as they proceed, or else undercut the cohesion of the narrative they are supposed to be supporting. When they *are* coherent and self-contained, this very self-containment is often presented as a parody effect. In all of these cases, there is a threshold between the musical numbers and the narrative that they are supposed to condense into narrative special effects, which becomes the real subject matter of Bloom's vision.

The musical number that opens the second season is more seamless than that which opens the first season. It is also presented more consciously as a special effect, as Bloom mirrors the geometric creations of Busby Berkeley in a 1930s-styled dance sequence. Once again, the lyrics challenge the way in which craziness is gendered in contemporary complex television: "I'm just a girl in love / I can't be held responsible for my actions." Unlike the musical number of the first credit sequence, however, this dance sequence shows no sign of accelerating into chaos or collapsing under the weight of its own artistic ambitions. In fact, despite the lyrics, this opening sequence could quite plausibly function as a complex television trope, since the self-referentiality is more seamless and fluid than in the first credit sequence, and not unlike the metatelevisual register of *Arrested Development* (Fox, 2003–6; Netflix, 2013–19) in its assurance of ironic detachment. At no point does it feel as if these self-aware lyrics are going to impede the musical performance that has been erected around them, while Bloom—and Bunch—don't seem to be struggling with the notion of craziness as viscerally or as directly as in the initial credits.

Instead, the postcomplex gesture of this opening sequence depends precisely upon its seamless appearance of traditional complexity. After the dance has finished, the credit sequence moves to an aerial shot before Bunch's face bursts through the image, inviting us to admire its narrative complexity with a plosive "Blam!" This in itself undercuts the complexity of the image, or at least the originality of its complexity, suggesting that complex television cues us to admire narrative special effects with the same mechanical regularity as canned laugher cues us to laugh at prerecorded sitcoms. In addition, this cued admiration is followed by an uncomfortably long pause, in which the camera simply lingers on Bunch's face, frozen awkwardly in the posture of an appreciative complex-television viewer. The pause during which we're supposed to be appreciating the narrative special effect of this musical sequence is distended too far, as our presumed appreciation, and our presumed complexity, becomes a contrivance and then a source of awkwardness, discomfort, and displaced comedy. Once again, the narrative special effects of complex television are unsustainable—not because the credit sequence is internally schismatic, as occurs in the first season, but because the space we are given to appreciate it stretches on for such an interminable time.

This temporal lapse corresponds to the critical veneration reserved for the showrunner in complex television. Press describes the canonical complex showrunners as "visionary in chiefs," centered on "HBO's flock of Davids: *The Sopranos'* showrunner David Chase, *The Wire*'s David Simon, and *Deadwood*'s David Milch."[14] For Press, the narrative special effects of complex television were not a free-floating experience but testified to the genius of individual showrunners, whose behavior often "mirrored that of the male antiheroes in their dramas, as if the set were a stage for them to play out their own psychodramas."[15] By contrast, Loofbourow argues, promiscuous protagonism, or what I am calling postcomplex television, is interested in truths that are "collectively produced," opting for a "collaborative, egalitarian ethic that prioritizes community and caretaking" over self-conscious displays of narrative and auteurist virtuosity.[16] Both Loofborouw and Press thus identify a parallel between the production conditions and character typology of postcomplex dramas, since in both arenas "the spotlight is shared among characters in a way that avoids heroes, antiheroes or other familiar devices for generating dramatic crisis."[17] This production ethic impacts the camera itself, whose "roving inattention" casually "slides from one perspective to the next."[18]

This roving, sliding perspective is explored and intensified in the credit sequences for the third and fourth seasons of CXG, whose credits move away from musical theater to encompass a broader audiovisual field. In the third season credits, Bloom plays four musical figures—country star, diva, punk rocker, rapper—presenting each of them in an artificial soundstage before they are united for a live concert at the end of the credit sequence. Each persona reflects upon the nature of female craziness, presenting it as a source of gutsy eroticism (country), smooth eroticism (diva), angry objectification (punk rock), and frank misogyny (rap). The first two singers are female and the second two singers are male, allowing Bloom to move from female embodiments of craziness to male projections of female craziness. As Bloom transitions from female to male, images of mirrors and multiplicity abound, especially in the case of the diva (the last female singer), who we see looking at her reflection in a mirror on an endless beach, and the punk rocker (the first male singer), who is situated in a mirror-walled room that reflects him endlessly in every conceivable direction.

This transition from female to male craziness suggests that craziness is only acceptable for women in complex television when it is directly addressing a male gaze—when it is framed as a form of seduction, whether aggressive or passive. Conversely, female craziness becomes a necessary muse for the masculine craziness of complex television. Between these two poles, a vision of television authorship emerges in which craziness is an appropriate trait for a male auteur and a female protagonist, but not for a female auteur or a male protagonist helmed by a female auteur. This schismatic ideology of televisual authorship culminates with the penultimate scene in this credit sequence, which gathers all four of these embodiments of craziness for a live concert, where their shared performances all start to deteriorate as they grow increasingly confused about what form of craziness, exactly, they are actually espousing.

At this point, the third credit sequence reflects elements of both the first and second season credits. As in the first season, this musical number starts to decay under the weight of its own contradictory approaches to craziness. Like the second season, however, this musical number still has enough cohesion—just—to play as a narrative special effect. However, the last part of the credit sequence ruptures any seamless display of complexity. Once again, we are presented with a sustained pause during which we are meant to admire the complexity of the sequence we have just watched. In this case, however, the pause encompasses a shift from nondiegetic to diegetic space, as the sequence now reveals that the entire musical number we have just watched has been playing out on an iPhone. We have, in effect, been watching someone else watching this credit sequence. Yet this produces another confusion of diegetic and nondiegetic space, since the person watching the sequence is Rebecca herself—or Rachel herself. Rebecca/Rachel is watching the clip on the toilet, a situation that is at once interstitial and abject, making it impossible for us to situate ourselves at the critical distance required to appreciate complexity or to adopt the highbrow approach implied by complexity.

This indeterminate space therefore ruptures the critical posture of complexity at the very moment we are invited to indulge in it. Yet even this indeterminacy cannot become a critical vantage point, since this toilet cameo does indeed turn out to be a scene from later in the third season, although the original viewers of the season would have had no way of knowing this. Even when this scene arrives, however, its emotional import, and its link to the clip on Rebecca's phone, is ambiguous—an ambiguity that is foreshadowed here by the title card prematurely and dramatically drowning out Rebecca's half-formed "What?" As in the second season credits, the appreciation of televisual complexity becomes an open question, rather than a foregone conclusion, in the most disorienting and dramatic credit sequence of the first three seasons.

### From Precomplex to Postcomplex

The credit sequence for the fourth season moves even further in this direction. However, before concluding with it, I will now turn to a sequence in the third season that continues the momentum of the third credit sequence, forming a blueprint for the series' postcomplex ambitions as a whole. This occurs midway through "Nathaniel and I Are Just Friends!" (3.11) and takes place at Home Base, a sports bar where many of the characters work and socialize.[19] Home Base often exhibits a postcomplex sensibility in the sheer proliferation of bodies, experiences, and tonalities that are situated inside it—a diversity that culminates with this episode, in which the camera drifts around the space, taking us through a series of familial and romantic situations, while never settling on a single point of focus. Even Rebecca's relationship with Nathaniel (Scott Michael Foster), which gives the episode its name, is subsumed into this broader sense of provisionality, incorporating nearly all the major characters of the series but also refusing to correlate the series with any one character either.

Rebecca is one of these characters, but she is keeping her relationship with Nathaniel, her boss, secret, meaning that they are always sequestering themselves from the rest of the bar or sneaking off into parts of the bar where they can't be seen or heard. Meanwhile, Rebecca's best friend Paula (Donna Lynne Champlin) is also present, but she's jettisoned from the relation with Rebecca that initially defined her. Instead, she's spending time with her new friend Sunil (Parvesh Cheena), leading Rebecca to observe that "the sidekick has a sidekick." Rebecca's old flame, Josh (Vincent Rodriguez III), is also at the bar, as is his best friend, White Josh (David Hull). White Josh, too, has been dissociated from Josh ever since he came out as bisexual in the second season and unexpectedly started an affair with Darryl (Pete Gardner), Rebecca's boss. By this point, White Josh and Darryl have broken up, but they're still friends. Meanwhile, Heather (Vella Lovell), Rebecca's flatmate, and the manager of Home Base, is dating Hector (Erick Lopez), Josh's friend from high school. However, she is also carrying Darryl's baby, while Darryl is considering how fatherhood will appear now that he has also recently come out as bisexual.

These plot strands indicate that all of the characters have been abstracted from the romance between Rebecca and Josh that originally shaped the series. While there are other characters and stories at play in this scene, these few examples illustrate the "promiscuous protagonism" that Loofbourow identifies as a hallmark of recent television. Here, as Loofbourow argues, "gender is treated as a curiosity rather than a constraint."[20] In fact, Loofbourow sees small-scale service industries like Home Base as a prototype for this new televisual workplace, noting that "Liz Meriwether once said that the best job preparation for her work on 'New Girl' was waitressing."[21] More than any scene in CXG, this sequence in Home Base articulates the conditions of postcomplex production—not as a complex "deconstruction" of the conditions of production, nor as a static lesson in the ethics of community, but a *process* in which the camera simply "slides from one perspective to the next," discarding the "entire moral vocabulary" of complex television in favor of "truths that are collectively produced."[22]

However, CXG extends Loofbourow's model by suggesting this postcomplex orientation is, in part, a return to *prequality* modes of televisual enjoyment and attachment. While the interpersonal arrangements in Home Base might be every bit as fluid as those of the series that Loofbourow invokes, the sports bar is also anchored in the hokiness, hominess, and endearing domesticity of an older form of the three-camera sitcom. If the sexual and interpersonal politics of this space are radical, then part of their radicality consists in never exactly advertising themselves as such, but instead displacing the auteurist aspirations of complex television with the mildness that Brenda Weber and Joselyn Leimbach attribute to Ellen DeGeneres. Ellen, they suggest, functions as a prototype for postcomplex community precisely because her own sociability is anchored in the classic sitcom model.[23] In CXG, Home Base operates as a repository of both these postcomplex interpersonal connections and precomplex affects of comfort and security in what amounts to an alternative timeline in which the artistic ambitions of complex television simply never existed.

As a tableau, this sequence would therefore function as an emblem of postcomplex television. However, this postcomplex gesture is further compounded by a striking time lapse. After a pan that encompasses Home Base, Heather passes behind the bar and returns eight months later. This is the only time in CXG that there has been a time lapse of this length up to this point (the series' final episode does feature a time lapse of a year, but moves back and forth between present and past), and it doesn't occur in an episode that is otherwise distinguished as a flagship episode, experimental episode, or bottleneck episode as often occurs in complex television. Moreover, the episode could conceivably function without the time lapse, since most of the characters are in the same position where we last left them, with one dramatic exception. Valencia (Gabrielle Ruiz), Josh's ex-girlfriend and Rebecca's onetime rival, is now in a long-term relationship with a woman, despite never having been signaled or outed as bisexual earlier in the series.

The surprise of the time lapse corresponds largely to the surprise of Valencia's sexual orientation, since everything else in the series' world remains business as normal. Yet by refusing to dwell on Valencia's sexuality, the episode also prevents this operating as a coming-out moment in the traditional sense. Rather than Valencia announcing herself as bisexual, her relationship with Beth (Emma Willmann), a party planner, feels like a natural outgrowth of the series' fluidity around gender, sexuality, and identity. By refusing to frame Valencia's new relationship as a revelation, the episode also refrains from presenting the eight-month ellipsis as a revelation or as conducive to revelation. As with the opening credits of the first three seasons, we are presented with a narrative innovation that nevertheless falls short of the narrative special effects so precious to complex television. In this particular case, the benefits of resisting that fetish for narrative special effects turn out to be a broader lifeworld and more relaxed attitude to identity—exactly the promiscuous protagonism that Loofbourow suggests is so liberating.

There is, of course, another rationale for the eight-month shift—Heather's pregnancy. Yet the resulting narrative gestation is quite different from the normative narratives that complex television typically generates around family life. Heather has very little interest in having a baby of her own, and is carrying the child for Darryl, a bisexual man, who decides to become a single father after his ex-partner, White Josh, decides that he does not want to become a father. Within the series as a whole, Heather and Darryl have very little contact with each other, while her decision to carry his child is as incidental and as off-the-cuff as any other that is made over the course of the narrative. As a result, Heather's pregnancy never takes on an oppositional quality or plays out like a study in a nonmaternal woman carrying a child that she has no personal interest or investment in raising. Instead, Heather's pregnancy is displaced from the dichotomy between maternal and nonmaternal women, and parental and nonparental labor, that drives the complex model and is deflected into a more collective and collaborative model of caregiving that transforms the crowd at Home Base into a new family.

This expansive notion of family might be inflected through postcomplex aspirations, but it also recalls the precomplex sitcom, which often focused on families that were elasticized and improvised. Indeed, this scene, and CXG itself, rehabilitates the reparative visions of family present in the classic sitcom, but contours them with a more contemporary awareness of identity and inclusion. The final twist in the Home Base scene is that this ellipsis, which initially seems so promising as a narrative special effect, ends up recalling the notional temporality of the classic symptom, as a feel-good piano refrain eases over the eight months of Heather's pregnancy as if we're just switching from one season to the next similar season. By squaring the circle between precomplex and postcomplex television,

CXG is able to incorporate the narrative innovations of complex television, but also to stop short of presenting them as special effects, in the name of a more collective, generous perspective.

## "Meet Rebecca"

With the Home Base sequence articulating this project at the close of the third season, the credit sequences for the fourth season take on a new quality. Once again, we are presented with a musical refrain, but this time the focus has shifted away from musical theater and musical performance. Instead, we're treated to a sitcom refrain, which also happens to be the longest opening number yet, in which we're invited to "Meet Rebecca." The jingle then takes us through a series of Rebecca's qualities, accompanied by a montage sequence from the first three seasons, as Rebecca sits on a bench in a sunny park. As in the first three seasons, however, the music starts to dissociate from Rebecca, and from the auteurist claims of complex television, gradually shifting to "another Rebecca" (Siri Miller)—a woman we've never seen before, on a bike—who's apparently standing in for Rebecca, who is ultimately "too hard to summarize." In a final act of displacement, this Rebecca doesn't even turn out to be a Rebecca, telling the camera bemusedly that "my name is Deborah," before the title card abruptly flashes up. Yet even this final gesture is further displaced after the first episode of the fourth season, as Deborah comes up with a new quip each opening sequence, effectively turning her into a character in the series, albeit one who only comes on for the odd one-liner.

The final credit sequence for the series therefore exemplifies both the formal and cultural properties of postcomplex television. Formally, the credit sequence presents a series of narrative reconfigurations but refuses to allow us to enjoy them as a narrative special effect, due to the precomplex, sitcom atmosphere of the clip. Culturally, the credit sequence punctures a television milieu in which feminine complexity has traditionally been subordinate to male complexity and used to serve the masculine auteurist model of complex television. Like the series as a whole, the clip displaces this complex gesture, neither affirming it nor subverting it, but instead imagining an alternative timeline in which complex television didn't occur—a timeline encapsulated in the continual temporal revisions of the credit sequence itself. These temporal reconfigurations, which have become common in postcomplex television, finally speak to a televisual milieu that, in some sectors, is restless to escape from the hegemony of complex television and to envisage a more provisional and open futurity.

# Part Two

# Queering Television

# 5

# "This Is What Happy Feels Like"

## *The Cripped Narrative of* Crazy Ex-Girlfriend

## Caitlin E. Ray

*Crazy Ex-Girlfriend* (hereafter *CXG*) is critically praised for challenging narrative tropes of mental illness, particularly the stereotype of the "crazy ex-girlfriend," and engaging in feminist and queer criticism of social issues (many of which are highlighted in other chapters in this collection). In addition to feminist and queer criticism, the show also subverts typical representations of disability through its musical numbers. The musical numbers and surrealist moments in the show allow *CXG* to tell a nonlinear narrative through the *cripped* perspective of Rebecca.

Crip theory—a critical lens that incorporates ideas from disability and queer theory—is a useful way to examine *CXG*. Musicals already are considered queer forms of storytelling that allow marginal voices to connect to the medium.[1] This connection to marginal identities also includes people with disabilities. Alison Kafer writes about the way that disability and queer theory come together to challenge normative notions about illness, narrative, and temporality. One specific way this happens is through the use of "crip time," wherein time, linearity, and futurity are reconfigured by disability. *CXG* is an example of a narrative that utilizes crip time to challenge more familiar, linear illness narratives by breaking up the story with musical interludes that render time bent—and thus crip it.

In this chapter, I will detail how *CXG*, as an illness narrative, challenges normative storytelling in typical broadcast television shows. I will do so by examining how crip theory challenges conceptions of time and emphasizes the importance of perspective. Then, I will focus on specific musical examples throughout the run of CXG that engage in atemporality and nonlinearity in Rebecca's (Rachel Bloom) perspective, including "You Stupid Bitch" (1.11), "I'm Just a Girl in Love" (2.01), "The End of the Movie" (3.04), and "No One Else Is Singing My Song" (4.01). By using crip theory as a lens through which to examine CXG, I hope to demonstrate how normative assumptions of temporality and perspective are challenged through music, creating an authentic representation of mental illness in a major television network broadcast comedy.

## Crip Theory, Disability Studies, and Temporality

*Crazy Ex-Girlfriend*, at its core, is an illness narrative created by Rebecca Bunch's romantic fantasies, produced by a "bodymind"[2] that experiences life nonnormatively. Through the medium of a musical comedy television show, the creators depict Rebecca's experiences in ways that challenge typical narrative tropes surrounding mental illness. In doing so, the show challenges the temporality and perspective of typical narratives through musical interludes and surrealist details that allow for a new type of storytelling. CXG might, for instance, utilize simple stock characters (like the wacky neighbor, the best friend, the evil girlfriend), but the show takes pains to ensure that those "simple" characters are challenged and made complex—including Rebecca's role as the "crazy ex-girlfriend."[3]

CXG depicts the symptoms, diagnosis, and treatment of mental illness, making it an illness narrative. *Illness narratives* primarily focus on the experience of illness from the perspective of the person *with* illness. Illness narratives are about the diagnosis, treatment, and acceptance of illness.[4] These narratives are important in both making illness visible to a public audience and being key representations that people with illness can turn to in order to recognize and make sense of their experience.[5] Sociologist Arthur Frank writes about narrative and illness, arguing that the role of the illness narrative is to allow someone who is ill, whose world has been made chaotic by illness, to regain control over that world by fitting their own chaotic narrative into culturally ascribed narrative structures.[6] Narratives shape an unfamiliar world into one that makes sense again, and illness narratives work to shape an "unfamiliar," sick body into something recognizable through story.[7] Examples of such narratives include *Autobiography of a Face* by Lucy Grealy, *The Diving Bell and the Butterfly* by Jean-Dominique Bauby, and *Anatomy of an Illness* by Norman Cousins. Disability and illness are also topics of many films and television shows, including *The King's Speech*, *The Shape of Water*, or *Friday Night Lights*. However, one critique of narratives of illness, especially in film and television, is that they offer limited, individualized experiences that often focus on the people around the person with illness, rather than the person with illness themselves. By allowing disability to become a "narrative prosthesis," or a character's only defining characteristic, these narratives erase the nuanced experience of disability and instead focus on how disability impacts others.[8] The perspectives in many depictions of disability are limited in this way, and so it is important to always ask: Is this story told by the person with a disability? Does that character have agency in the story? Are they used to make meaning for other, abled characters? If a narrative challenges normative expectations of time (that it is linear) and perspective (the story is told by a disabled body), then it is a *cripped* illness narrative.

Crip theory, a theoretical frame at the intersection between disability studies and queer theory, can help analyze narratives from a disabled perspective. Queer theory and disability studies have a close relationship, as the ideas that queer theory challenges, disability theory also seeks to disrupt.[9] Crip theory is named in order to reclaim the slur "cripple"—much like how queer scholarship reclaims the word "queer."[10] Originally articulated and developed by disabled queer theorists such as Robert McRuer, Merri Lisa Johnson, and Alison Kafer, crip theory argues that abledness is aligned with heterosexuality and deviations from abledness can be paralleled to queerness.[11] The term "crip" also embraces an activist stance that accepts that people with disabilities, as a collective, are oppressed and subject to a higher rate of physical, emotional, and medical abuse than those without disabilities.[12] Further, crip scholarship considers questions pertaining to mental illness and disability, including forced surveillance (like involuntary commitment) and attempts to normalize psychiatric difference.[13]

In order to understand how *CXG* "crips" linear storytelling, one must also agree that disability is an identity much like queer or feminist.

Identifying as disabled means embracing physical and mental difference as a fundamental part of the human experience and not as a "deviance" from culturally ascribed norms.[14] Although people with disabilities are the largest minority group in the United States (approximately 20 percent of the population in the United States has a disability), the idea of "disability" as an identity category and a space for theoretical and critical work remains surprisingly controversial.[15] However, theories of disability can provide valuable cultural critiques, allowing texts to be claimed and shaped by the disabled experience. Disability scholar Lennard J. Davis, for example, argues that scholarship within disability studies lets disability "[gain] a new, nonmedicalized, and positive legitimacy both as an academic discipline and as an area of political struggle."[16] Davis also works to "[place] disability in a political, social, and cultural context that theorizes and historicizes deafness or blindness or disability in similarly complex ways to the way race, class, and gender have been theorized."[17] Disability studies finds new and important ways to engage with questions of interest to feminist and queer scholars, like perspective, temporality, and normativity.

Just as queer theory challenges "normative narratives of time" (which assume time is linear), crip theory articulates how illness can also render time *nonlinear* and atemporal. Kafer, for instance, highlights how disability challenges a typical understanding of time by saying that "crip time bends the clock to meet disabled bodies and minds."[18] Crip time, in her view, might mean that disability might cause someone with a chronic illness diagnosis to "live in 'prognosis time,'" which is a "liminal temporality, a casting out of time; rather than a stable, steady progression through the stages of life, time is arrested, stopped."[19] Crip time is therefore a way to understand how disability can speed up time (while under anesthesia or in a manic state, for example) or slow it down (finding accessible entrances and transportation, the way that pain causes time to be agonizingly slow, and the ways that anxiety can loop thoughts in a never-ending circle).

I argue that *cripped* illness narratives "bend" certain narrative elements like time and perspective. Physical, psychological, and developmental disabilities challenge traditional notions of time and space, as those with disabilities often experience time and space differently than those who are able-bodied. Temporality is a key theme in these narratives, as disability bends and challenges normal constructs and perceptions of time. Another key theme is perspective and whether there is a fully realized character with illness and/or disability at the center of the narrative. Illness narratives that push against temporality and perspective, that bend and disrupt time, and that tell stories from perspectives of characters with disabilities (rather than *about* them), are cripped.

CXG is an example of a cripped illness narrative that "bends" temporality and Rebecca's cripped perspective through musical interludes. These moments of musicality are ways that Rebecca engages with the events around her—even if she is not the one singing, the songs are still rendered through her perspective. For example, songs comment on Rebecca's view of her role in the story she has constructed ("I'm the Villain in My Own Story" [1.14] and "The End of the Movie" [3.04]), her opinion of other characters ("Settle for Me" [1.04] and "After Everything I've Done for You" [1.17]), and ways to interpret events in her life ("Oh My God I Think I Like You" [1.17] and "A Diagnosis" [3.06]).[20] CXG disrupts the expected narratives with the chaotic temporality of illness articulated by Kafer, while telling the story of illness from an embodied perspective that allows for new ways of understanding illness narrative tropes.

## Musical Numbers Bending Time

CXG utilizes musical numbers to tell nonlinear stories through Rebecca's perspective. Seasons one and two of the series focus on Rebecca and her relationships, centering on how she experiences the world around her—through manic highs and depressive lows. The show's storytelling arc begins with Rebecca having a panic attack as she runs into her old camp boyfriend, Josh (Vincent Rodriguez III), in New York City. She subsequently moves to West Covina, convinced she will be happy now because she is near Josh. Season two ends with what should be Rebecca's happiest moment, her wedding to Josh, but instead she is left at the altar as she experiences flashbacks to other moments in her life. The musical numbers in seasons one and two highlight a sense of immediacy and atemporality that lends itself to a crip reading. The musical numbers allow for

Rebecca's story to be told "sideways," engaging with felt-sense and experiential knowledge of illness to pause, halt, or speed up the narrative. There are several examples of this bending time in seasons one and two, particularly through season one's "You Stupid Bitch" (1.11) and season two's "I'm Just a Girl in Love" (2.01).

Seasons one and two use song to render time fast or slow, as needed for Rebecca to reflect on her experiences. Many songs in CXG are sung during what is most likely a short moment in Rebecca's life, but by stopping time for the duration of these songs, specific moments in Rebecca's perspective are drawn out. Additionally, musical scores used in the show allow for themes from earlier songs to be called forth in later seasons. One early example of how the show challenges temporality by slowing/stopping time and presenting Rebecca's perspective is in the song "You Stupid Bitch" (1.11). After a fight with Josh, Rebecca sits next to broken sliding door glass and sings about being "a stupid bitch"—an example of the negative self-talk that Rebecca often engages in during moments of depression. This song is set up as a Bernadette Peters–style ballad to "sing a song about self-indulgent self-loathing" while Rebecca's imagined self sings in the footlights.[21] The chandelier in her imagined scene is made of the shards of glass of her broken sliding glass door, connecting even more strongly to Rebecca's shame and doubt. As the imagined audience cheers along in recognition of the song that Rebecca sings "a lot," she asks everyone to "sing with me." The lyrics point to deeper hatred of herself than perhaps any other song in the series as she sings, "Yes, Josh completes me / but how can that be / When there's no me left to complete." This passage in particular points to Rebecca's struggles throughout the rest of the series and how she tries to find happiness through other people, rather than within herself. Additionally, the song's repetition of phrases like "you stupid bitch" and "you ruined everything" heighten her negative and looping self-talk. In fact, the phrase "you stupid bitch" is recurring throughout the show, appearing in one of the "Santa Ana Winds" reprises (2.11) (after she kisses Nathaniel [Scott Michael Foster] in the elevator) and when she sees her new therapist (3.07). The callbacks not only humorously recall the song but also connect the audience to other moments in Rebecca's life—another way temporality is "bent" throughout this show.

The opening theme songs, which change with each season, also demonstrate how musical numbers can challenge narrative temporality. In each of the four seasons, the theme song lyrics (each unique to the season) become dialogue in the show, again bending time and challenging the audience's perception of the songs and characters performing them. Perhaps the most effective is the season two theme song, titled "I'm Just a Girl in Love" (2.01). Over the course of the second season, Rebecca and Josh fall into the romantic narrative that they think they both want. Rebecca describes "I'm Just a Girl in Love" as an "emotional thesis statement" for herself, and the lyrics include:

> I'm just a girl in love
> I can't be held responsible for my actions
> I have no underlying issues to address
> I'm certifiably cute and adorably obsessed
> They say love makes you crazy
> Therefore, you can't call her crazy
> 'Cause when you call her crazy
> You're just calling her in love.[22]

This song, presented as a Busby Berkeley 1930s-style musical number, features Rebecca and a group of chorus girls dancing with red hearts, which, when put together, make up Josh's face. At the end of the number, Rebecca's face bursts out of the grouped red hearts, shouting "Blam!" and staring at the camera a moment too long as the last chord of the number plays. In an interview, Rachel Bloom and Aline Brosh McKenna (the cocreators of the series) describe the significance of this theme song: "This season we're dealing with the socially sanctioned way that courtship allows people to behave in ways that are *crazy*" and that "anything you do for love is justifiable."[23] This song establishes the tension of season two, where Rebecca uses romantic fantasies to excuse otherwise problematic behavior. This is a cycle she continually returns to throughout the run of the series, but in the season two finale (2.13), "I'm Just a Girl in Love" is used to emphasize Rebecca's issues when the song breaks out of its typical placement in the opening credits and enters into the plot of the episode.

The season two finale depicts Rebecca experiencing flashbacks (another way that time is rendered both past and immediate, bent and circular) about a relationship she had in college, after attempting to burn down her ex's apartment. When Rebecca is sentenced and committed to a hospital, she repeats lines from "I'm Just a Girl in Love" (2.13). However, instead of the heightened color and choreography of the Busby Berkeley style dance number, the color on screen is drab as she and her mother, Naomi (Tovah Feldshuh), defend her to the judge:

> NAOMI: She's just a girl in love; she can't be held responsible for her actions.
> REBECCA: I have no underlying issues to address. (2.13)

The show both slows down and extends the musical callback in a way that allows it to resonate with the audience. It also essentially flattens time by calling back events earlier in the show. However, instead of just recalling a line from the song (like "You Stupid Bitch" [1.11] is typically reiterated), this changes the context of the song entirely and raises the stakes of Rebecca's mental illness.

Seasons one and two utilize music to explore Rebecca's perspective, challenging the temporality of typical illness narratives. Through recalls to "You Stupid Bitch" (1.11) and "I'm Just a Girl in Love" (2.01), the audience experiences Rebecca's interiority. These songs set the stage for Rebecca's recovery in seasons three and four.

## The Antinarrative of Season Three

In season three, Rebecca finds herself at her lowest moment and ultimately is diagnosed with Borderline Personality Disorder (BPD). The tone and perspective of the show change to follow her new diagnosis. The musical scenes in season three work to highlight the chaos Rebecca feels. Overall, critics praised the way that CXG handled mental health, suicide, and diagnosis in this season (GQ called it "one of the most unflinching, open-hearted depictions of mental illness on television").[24] It is also pivotal in how the show resists the typical resolution or linearity that the audience may want in a story and instead uses music to explore the chaotic ways that mental illness defies those expected narratives.

The three-episode arc (3.04–3.06) that leads up to Rebecca's suicide attempt is the most chaotic in both temporality and perspective, and is particularly resonant in the song, "At the End of the Movie" (3.04). In these episodes, Rebecca begins to lash out at her loved ones. Through her actions, she ends up spiraling to her lowest moment. As she walks through an empty, dark street, she does not imagine herself as the star of a musical number, but instead imagines Josh Groban singing "The End of the Movie" (3.04), which highlights the chaos Rebecca is experiencing.

"The End of the Movie" (3.04) is a shift for Rebecca as she starts to realize that she is not in a horror movie or romantic comedy. The lyrics highlight the chaos this realization causes for her:

> Because life is a gradual series of revelations
> that occur over a period of time.
> It's not some carefully crafted story
> it's a mess, and we're all gonna die.
> If you saw a movie that was like real life
> you'd be like, "What the hell was that movie about?
> It was really all over the place."
> Life doesn't make narrative sense . . . people aren't characters.
> They're complicated
> and their choices don't always make sense.

This song also works to connect Rebecca's story to those of the other characters in the show—widening the show's perspective to include Josh's attempts to find a job, Nathaniel's feelings about Rebecca, and Darryl (Pete Gardner) and White Josh's (David Hull) conversation about whether to have a baby.[25] "The End of the Movie" leads to 3.05, wherein Rebecca leaves West Covina and returns to her mother in New York. However, after discovering her mother is secretly drugging her with antianxiety medication, she leaves again. On the plane, Rebecca is at another crossroads. She is alone, and while looking out the window, she decides to take all of the antianxiety medication. She ultimately does ask for help from the flight attendant, but the episode cuts to silence—the first time there is no musi-cal score during the end credits in the series.

Episode 3.06 shows the aftermath of Rebecca's suicide attempt, and how she is hoping for answers from medical professionals to solve her problems. However, the depiction of mental illness here does not leave Rebecca with easy answers or solutions. When setting up therapy sessions for her discharge from the hospital, she is informed that she has been misdiagnosed and that she will receive a new diagnosis in therapy. As Rebecca digests this news, she sings "A Diagnosis" (3.06), expressing her hope that this new diagnosis will provide her with answers, appropriate care that will allow her to enter into a community where she belongs, and a narrative for her life. However, she is devastated to learn that it isn't as simple as she wants: she is diagnosed with Borderline Person-ality Disorder (BPD), and instead of being given medications to cope with symptoms, she is faced with talk and group therapy to address her issues, setting up the narrative arc for the rest of the series. The show depicts Rebecca's recovery as the slow, imperfect process it often is. This accurately represents the process of diagnosis, prognosis, and treatment as halting, full of stops and starts.

### Being "Off-Time": Season Four

Season four continues to explore Rebecca's diagnosis and how her mental illness impacts her life and perspective of the world. The show also com-ments on the stops, starts, and pitfalls of a chronic mental illness (like BPD) and how it affects daily life. Although Rebecca does stumble in her recovery, she also starts to find healthy ways to engage with her problems, rather than slipping into delusional thinking or external validation for her emotions. Through the support systems and relationships Rebecca devel-ops, she is able to find ways to healthily engage with the world. Rebecca slowly develops connections through season four, as her perspective wid-ens and her cripped temporality is welcomed by others.

Rebecca still struggles with connection and engagement with her peers through season four, despite the progress she makes. Episode 4.01 closes with a song that sets the theme of community and voice throughout season 4, "No One Else Is Singing My Song." Like "The End of the Movie" (3.04), this song starts with Rebecca's perspective alone. However, as she sings, other characters join in from different points in a split-screen. The screen is ultimately split into twelve boxes as the "entire company" sings along. By the end, the other characters around Rebecca see the others, wave, and greet one another—they end the song out of the isolation they may have felt at the beginning. Only Rebecca doesn't see anyone else, and ends the song singing "only I am." Here, "No One Else Is Singing My Song" highlights Rebecca's perspective and the loneliness she feels. As the audience, we are seeing how other characters are not so unlike Rebecca (further represented by Dr. Akopian [Michael Hyatt] in 4.13, "Antidepressants Are So Not a Big Deal"), and that she only needs to continue reaching out for connections with others. Through season four, Rebecca realizes these connections, particularly when Nathaniel very literally "sings her song" when he performs Rebecca's revised musical theater number in "I Am Finding My Voice" (4.14).

As a song representative of Rebecca's cripped perspective for season four, "No One Else Is Singing My Song" (4.01) is highlighted in multiple ways as Rebecca works toward recovery. However, as recovery often is, it is full of stops and starts and is an imperfect process. One particularly representative example of these stops and starts of Rebecca's day-to-day struggles with her mental illness occurs in episode 4.04, where Rebecca struggles with feeling "off-time" from her peers. The phenomena of being off-time is particularly resonant to young people who have a chronic physical and/or mental illness.[26] Young people with chronic illness experience more stress and stigma than peers and often do not meet what are considered age-appropriate milestones, like marriage, moving to a new place, or finding a new job.[27] This episode explores the realities of a diagnosis with a serious, lifelong illness. While Rebecca initially feels competitive with other friends who are succeeding in their careers, marrying, and moving, Dr. Akopian tries to assure her that feeling off-time is normal. She says, "You are in a sense a little behind. You have overcome challenges other people haven't faced. And you have wisely taken the time to do the hard work. It makes sense that some of your friends might hit some early adult milestones before you" (4.04). Instead of finding that comforting,

Rebecca instead attempts to connect with acquaintances who are younger than her but are perhaps more "in time" with where she is in her life. In doing so, Rebecca forgets that she is neither young nor old but is instead in an in-between place, with experiences that differ from those of her peer group. In Rebecca's final scene of the episode, she sits with her "girl group," shares how she is feeling, and they validate her and share that they, too, have feelings similar to hers. While Rebecca is not process-ing these feelings through a musical number, she realizes that Valencia (Gabrielle Ruiz), Paula (Donna Lynne Champlin), and Heather (Vella Lovell) are singing "the same song" as her, and that she can still depend on them as friends.

This is not to say that the show argues for Rebecca to move away from music as a way to process her world. The show instead emphasizes that she should be able to experience the world with others who understand and value her perspective. The series finale of the show demonstrates this. As she performs "The Eleven O'Clock Number" (4.17), which reprises many songs over the run of the series, she sings to the tune of "You Stupid Bitch": "Well Rebecca, you've done it now. / You've ruined everything, / you stu-pid bitch, / uprooted everything. / And said you'd made a switch, / but you're still a poopy little slut who lives in a dream / and doesn't know how to love." Recalling "You Stupid Bitch" to reemphasize Rebecca's looping self-talk is not new, but what is new is Paula interrupting to ask Rebecca what she is doing. And Rebecca tells her: she writes songs to make sense of her life and help her make decisions. Even as Rebecca doubts the useful-ness of her music, Paula encourages her and tells her how important and valuable her voice and experiences are. This sets the stage for Rebecca to spend time on her craft and to share her music (and within it her voice and experiences) with others. Her cripped perspective is valued and honored. She does not *have* to only work through her experiences through song (as she now has a valuable support system and people who love her), but she *should* because her voice in the world is valuable. The series finale thereby self-reflexively comments on how the cripped narrative offered by the show has resonated with many viewers who feel that they too are alone and off-time.

CXG moves from season one's story of a woman struggling to find happiness through external gratification to a more nuanced ability to self-reflect and find healthy strategies to connect with others in season four. Rebecca learns, grows, and makes mistakes through the run of the show, and is ultimately able to see how she is valued in her friend and support group, not in spite of her differences but because of her value as a person.

## Future of Cripped Narrative

The trope of the "crazy ex-girlfriend" is not just a comment on societal expectations of women but also carries with it the implication of serious mental illness. This trope is deeply embedded in our culture, made even more complex when considering the deep stigma mental illness continues to have (particularly true for certain mental illness conditions like BPD). CXG offers one way to consider the intersections of gender, sexuality, and disability. It resists the typical linear temporality of television shows through musical numbers.

But what is the future of cripped narratives? Rachel Bloom has been public about her own experiences with mental illness, particularly depression and anxiety.[28] However, her character's positionality as a white professional (Rebecca spends most of the show as a highly successful lawyer) demonstrates only one story and one point of view. More representations of "madder" women, people who aren't "high-achieving" or positioned as white, upper-middle class, and heterosexual, are needed to diversify these representations.[29] Additionally, there is criticism that the show was seemingly reluctant to really dive into mental illness until season three.[30] The show, especially in the early seasons before Rebecca got a diagnosis, could be read as pandering and playing off mental illness as a joke rather than really diving into the experience of mental illness. However, the show's commitment to telling a story through the perspective of Rebecca's cripped bodymind, the way temporality is subverted through musical numbers, and the overt turn to themes of mental illness in season three allow the show to dig deeply into these issues.

CXG is a high-profile depiction of mental illness, pushing against the tropes, time, and perspective mental illness renders. It provides the audience with a language and touchstones of psychiatric difference that can help people not feel "so alone" and find others who are "also singing along" (4.01). Through a cripped narrative, CXG allows for others, on screen and off, to "sing along" to Rebecca's perspective and potentially to write their own.

# 6

# "Lady, We're All Gay!"

*The Math of Homosocial Triangles*

Hazel Mackenzie

The second episode of the second season of *Crazy Ex-Girlfriend* (hereafter *CXG*) begins with our heroine Rebecca (Rachel Bloom) having conned a polyamorous "throuple" she found on Craig's List into meeting her under the guise of sociological research. In fact, her motivation in meeting them is an attempt to resolve her conflicted feelings for her ex-boyfriend/long-term crush Josh Chan (Vincent Rodriguez III) and friend-turned-lover Greg Serrano (Santino Fontana). Polyamory, Rebecca speculates, might be the answer. The throuple points out that what she is describing is not polyamory, but rather an old-fashioned love triangle. Here, as is the show's wont, we segue into a musical number, "The Math of Love Triangles." Love triangles proliferate in *CXG*: from Rebecca's triangle with Greg and Josh, to her triangle with Josh and Valencia (Gabrielle Ruiz), to her triangle with Josh and Nathaniel (Scott Michael Foster), to her triangle with Greg and Greg's dad (Robin Thomas)—the list goes on. As with many of the songs in the series, "The Math of Love Triangles" deconstructs specific cultural tropes while also providing a lens through which to reexamine the series' central characters and relationships.

"The Math of Love Triangles" both successfully undercuts the validity of the love triangle, portrayed by popular culture as a useful metaphor for human relationships, and simultaneously points to more productive meanings buried within the metaphor: the love triangle as a means of constructing and expressing homosocial relationships, as suggested by Eve

Kosofsky Sedgwick in *Between Men: English Literature and Male Homo-social Desire* (1985), and as an expression of the sense of individual lack and fragile subjecthood outlined in René Girard's classic structuralist text *Deceit, Desire, and the Novel: Self and Other in Literary Structure* (1965). In light of such works, it can be seen that lyrics such as "So I'm a triangle?" do more than point out the absurdity of such representations by taking them to their furthest extreme. They also point to deeper truths about the power dynamics that are both concealed and revealed in popular cultural tropes such as the love triangle and also in Rebecca's self-conception, for Rebecca both sees life in terms of stereotypical cultural tropes and defines herself by her relationships. It is only through a process of torturous self-discovery that she realizes that "Josh is Irrelevant" (3.06) and learns to strip herself bare of the cultural tropes behind which she has hidden.

### A Barbie with Two Perfect Kens:
### Deconstructing the Love Triangle

From its pilot episode, *CXG* invokes the love triangle as a plot device, setting up best friends Josh and Greg as rivals for Rebecca's affections. A staple of both romantic comedies and dramas in film and television, the love triangle has found a particular home on The CW network on which *CXG* aired. In fact, the two teen dramas on which its predecessor, the WB channel, made its name—*Dawson's Creek* (1998–2003) and *Felicity* (1998–2002)—were centered around similar love triangles in which a girl is torn between a long-term crush and a recently noticed friend. In both *Felicity* and *CXG*, the main characters move across the country to be closer to their crushes only to find themselves drawn to more obviously suitable male friends. Shows such as *One Tree Hill* (WB, 2003–6, CW, 2006–12) and *Gilmore Girls* (WB, 2000–2006, CW, 2006–7), which bridged the crossover period between the two networks, also frequently employed the love triangle as a plot device. Other key shows in The CW's 2015–18 lineup, such as *The Flash* (2014–), *Supergirl* (2015–), and *Arrow* (2012–20), all recurrently featured love triangles as a means of providing obstacles to clearly outlined central relationships. Season two of *CXG* was aired directly after *The Vampire Diaries* (2009–17), a show whose entire premise is the love triangle between two vampire brothers and their beloved. The CW's brand is strongly associated with the type of teen dramas in which the love triangle is a key plot device and marketing tool, helping to build the cultural reach of the shows beyond their weekly audiences.[1]

CXG knowingly plays upon this device, tapping into its audience's familiarity with and pleasure in the trope and using it to build tension and create conflict between its characters. At the same time the show's propensity for the deconstruction of cultural conventions, around which much of its humor is based, helps to create a different kind of tension as the audience comes to realize that a happy, stable heterosexual couple is unlikely to emerge from the triangle, leaving the audience increasingly caught between their pleasure in the familiar trope and their pleasure in its unraveling. "The Math of Love Triangles" is the peak of this latter pleasure. In true CXG style, the song dissects two quite distinct cultural tropes, the love triangle and the dumb blonde, with Bloom and her cowriters using the dissection of one trope to inform our response to the other. Formally, the number is a parody of Marilyn Monroe's performance of the song "Diamonds Are a Girl's Best Friend" (composed by Jule Styne and Leo Robin) in *Gentlemen Prefer Blondes* (1953, dir. Howard Hawks), with its costumes, choreography, and set design as well as Bloom's performance all mimicking the iconic film sequence. It takes the association of female sexuality with vulnerability, frivolity, and innocence embodied in the stereotype of the dumb blonde and pushes it ad absurdum, underlining its transgressive potential in aligning sexual attraction with vulnerable categories of people, such as children and the disabled with lyrics such as "sexy baby me" and "my learning difficulty." Monroe is an interesting figure in this respect, associated as she is with tragedy and mental instability. Numerous biographers have in fact speculated as to whether Monroe had borderline personality disorder.[2] A more substantiated claim is that she suffered from endometriosis, leading to a number of painful surgeries and an addiction to painkillers that she kept well hidden under her public persona. She was also, despite her roles, known to be intelligent and well-read. Furthermore, her character in the film *Gentlemen Prefer Blondes*, Lorelei Lee, was not the traditional dumb blonde, but rather the dumb blonde was an act she had perfected in her quest to hook a rich husband.

That Rebecca, a well-educated lawyer, is depicted as aping Monroe at this moment is suggestive of how we as the audience are to view her interpretation of her relationships with Josh and Greg. That this occurs while invoking an icon of female sexuality points to the role popular culture and its depiction of women and relationships have had in influencing Rebecca's thinking. Monroe's invocation in the song thus has multiple layers.

Lyrically, however, the main target of "The Math of Love Triangles" is the love triangle and its role in Rebecca's misconception of her relationships with men and herself. As a "Barbie" stuck between "two perfect Kens," Rebecca's fixation in the song is not her own feeling for either man but rather her belief that, as the focus of two men's rivalry, she is sexually desirable. This, after all, is the cultural logic of the love triangle. The song undercuts this through the bemused indifference of the dancing math professors that surround Rebecca, challenging her belief that "the center of the triangle is lil' ol' me!" by pointing out that mathematically "a triangle has multiple centers" and rebuffing her attempts at flirting, proclaiming, "Lady, we're all gay, we get nothing out of this!" As her therapist Dr. Akopian (Michael Hyatt) notes after the song closes, her "approach to this situation is fallacious." As well as pointing to the fallaciousness of Rebecca's understanding of the love triangle, however, the song also suggests that, properly understood, the metaphor of the triangle can reveal certain truths about her relationships with Josh and Greg as well as truths about her own self-conception.

Queer theorist Eve Kosofsky Sedgwick has argued that if we examine the love triangle as traditionally portrayed, the relationship between the two rivals is often as significant as that of the relationship between either of the rivals and the beloved. Sedgwick takes for her basis the work of French structuralist René Girard, who, according to Sedgwick, insisted that "in any erotic rivalry, the bond that links the two rivals is as intense and potent as the bond that links either of the rivals to the beloved: that the bonds of 'rivalry' and 'love,' differently as they are experienced, are equally powerful."[3] In other words, the rivalry with the other suitor is as important to the formation of the triangle and its maintenance as the desire for the beloved. The desire for the beloved may even be formed *because* she is already desired by the rival. In the case of Rebecca, Josh, and Greg, it could be argued that Josh is the center of the triangle, as he is the focus of both Rebecca's desire and Greg's envy. Greg's desire for Rebecca, after all, is formed after witnessing her desire for Josh. Later, Josh finds himself desiring Rebecca, in whom he has shown little romantic interest, when he realizes that she and Greg are in a romantic relationship. Initially confused by his emotional turmoil at this realization, when Father Brah (Rene Gube) asks him what provoked his turmoil, his response is "Greg made me so upset" (1.17). He then criticizes Greg in a manner that makes his envy clear, highlighting his differences from Josh, calling him a "know-it-all" (1.17) and "sarcastic and dark" (1.18), while Josh himself feels that he is always required to be lighthearted and laid-back: "What I can't be in a bad mood? It's like people think 'Oh, Josh is such a nice guy, Josh is so happy-go-lucky, Josh can't be in a bad mood!'" (1.17). Josh envies in Greg what he himself lacks, but it is not Rebecca that is the main focus of this envy. She is not the only possible center of the triangle: Josh and Greg are at least as invested in their rivalry with each other as they are in their desire for Rebecca. This results in head-to-head conflict in the final episode of the season, when Josh and Greg argue in the hospital over their respective positions in Rebecca's life, both clearly marking their territory. Josh's desire for Rebecca reaches its height here as does Greg's, although they both react differently to this, with Greg retreating into self-destructive patterns while Josh is inspired to take action to win Rebecca over. We see this again in the fourth season, when Josh and "new" Greg (Skylar Astin) come to physical blows, ostensibly regarding their rivalry over Rebecca (4.13), but in essence over their own deteriorating friendship.

Sedgwick's argument is not that the relationship between the two suitors is necessarily more significant than that of the suitors with the beloved, but rather that the heterosexual desire for the beloved can also be a conduit for the feelings between suitors. Rebecca's desire for Josh, for example, is clear, but her rivalry with Valencia reflects not just her desire for Josh but also her desire for Valencia, as does Valencia's rivalry with Rebecca. Both women desire in the other the qualities that they believe themselves to lack. As is demonstrated in both "I'm So Good at Yoga" and "Feelin' Kinda Naughty" (1.02), Rebecca envies Valencia's physical perfection, singing in the latter song that "I wanna kill you and wear your skin like a dress," but she also desires Valencia's approval: "But then also have you see me in the dress, and be like, 'O-M-G you look so cute in my skin!'" She wants to both be Valencia and be the object of her desire. Similarly, Valencia envies Rebecca's larger breasts, her academic credentials, and her agency, telling Josh, "Rebecca's a super-smart dynamo with a feminist bikini area that you should have treated with respect!" (2.05). This homosocial desire may or may not be erotically charged, although there are moments of slippage in Rebecca and Valencia's relationship, for example when Rebecca pictures herself and Valencia as Liberace and his lover Scott Thorson, or when Rebecca comments that Valencia is "so hot" in response to Valencia having read a feminist op-ed (2.05).

Sedgwick of course excludes female homosocial bonds from her argument, stating that the division between homosocial and homosexual desire among women in modern Western culture is less strict than between men: "The diacritical opposition between the 'homosocial' and the 'homosexual' seems to be much less thorough and dichotomous for women, in our society, than for men."[4] Sedgwick gives no evidence for this assertion. Sharon Marcus notes, "Yes, women's relations were less violently policed than men's, but are they therefore less interesting?"[5] Nor do they necessarily form a smooth continuum between homosociality and homosexuality simply because the demarcation is less outwardly violent, if that can be said to be definitively the case. Again, Sedgwick provides no evidence.

Certainly, we can see similar dynamics at work between the women of CXG as that which Sedgwick outlines between men in her study. We have already seen this in relation to Rebecca and Valencia, but a perhaps more significant example is the friendship between Rebecca and Paula. Here again it is the desire for Josh, albeit vicarious on Paula's part, that provides the medium through which the two women express their affection for each other. Paula is initially suspicious of Rebecca and sets out to expose her as a liar and a fraud. Their initial relationship is based upon enmity. It is upon her discovery of Rebecca's love for Josh that this changes, and Josh remains throughout the first season the conduit through which their relationship is enacted. Such is the significance of Josh to their relationship that Rebecca's renunciation of Josh in favor of Greg toward the end of the first season is seen by Paula primarily as a betrayal. "After everything I've done for you and your love story you betray me with sarcastic, alcoholic, unromantic Greg." In Paula's eyes Josh's role is fundamentally a means of consolidating female solidarity rooted in a shared ideology of romance.

## "Oh No, Professors, Am I Facing Suspension?"
## Patriarchal Power and Female Homosociality

On the most basic level then, we can see an equivalence between male-dominated and female-dominated triangles, in that in both a third figure of the opposite sex is often used as a conduit for the bond of the same-sex pair. Sedgwick's argument goes deeper than this however. Sedgwick argues that between men homosocial desire is often expressed through the channel of heterosexual desire for a female beloved in order that the structures of patriarchal power might be maintained. She also argues that embedded in male heterosexual desire is frequently "a desire to consolidate partnership with authoritative males in and through the bodies of females."[6] These are similar but different propositions. The first suggests that the cultural trope of the love triangle both reveals and conceals an inherent truth about the power dynamics of our social structures, but it leaves both forms of desire separate and intact. Heterosexual desire and rivalry effectively conceal homosocial desire and power but do not change our basic understanding of heterosexual desire. In contrast the second proposition suggests that heterosexual desire is predicated upon homosocial desire and the maintenance of homosocial power. Both propositions position the female beloved as an object to be competed over or exchanged, noting that while "an erotic triangle is likely to be experienced in terms of an explicit or implicit assertion of symmetry between genders," this symmetry will be "factitious or distorted both because of the raw differences in the amount and kinds of male and female power, and because in the discourse of most cultures . . . one gender is treated as a marginalized subset."[7] Despite this power advantage, Sedgwick argues that engagement in an erotic triangle has been depicted as posing a substantial risk to the male, that instead of the erotic triangle being a means of male omosocial bonding, it may allow one male to gain mastery over another, thus effectively feminizing one of the men. She notes, "Only the man who can proceed through that stage, while remaining in cognitive control of the symbolic system that presides over sexual exchange, will be successful in achieving a relation of mastery to other men."[8] Those who cannot will find themselves mastered.

Certainly we can see Paula's interest in Josh as at least partially a desire to consolidate her relationship with Rebecca. Similarly, while Rebecca's initial attempt to befriend Valencia is a strategy to win Josh's love, it also stems from a desire to both be like and be liked by Valencia. But can these relationships be seen to simultaneously reveal and conceal underlying power structures? Does the navigation of triangular desire pose a similar risk/gain scenario to women as it does to men? CXG rather explicitly, if flippantly, answers the former in 2.05 when Rebecca and Valencia confront Josh in the tent at Electric Mesa as both women realize the value of the other woman and the manner in which Josh has taken advantage of the competition between the two. This realization is couched in overtly feminist language and related by Rebecca to larger patriarchal structures: "This is the reason there is a pay gap, so what happens is women go into a job, not even—a raise doesn't even occur to them." That Rebecca is moments later, for the audience at least, jokingly rebuked for the pretentiousness of her use of this language does not negate the larger point: female competition promotes patriarchal power. It is the removal of the third point from their equation that allows for a true consolidation of female power. We can see a similar trajectory in the relationship between Rebecca and Paula: the third point in their relationship, ostensibly Josh, but truly the ideology of heterosexual romance, simultaneously conceals and points to Rebecca's lower social status as a single woman and the feeling of powerlessness Paula feels within her family (i.e., the ways in which traditional patriarchal structures isolate and weaken them). The strength of their relationship in the first season is built upon Josh, and the relationship is rendered vulnerable by the removal of this third point. Both women move toward other relationships, finding it difficult to communicate their feelings without the mediating desire for Josh and what he represents.

Here we come to the question of risk. Just as Sedgwick depicts triangular desire as allowing men a position of mastery over other men, we can see through Valencia that the successful culmination of triangular desire allows for a position of mastery over other women. In the first season Valencia has a similar although lesser form of authority over other women based upon her status as Josh's girlfriend. Her physical characteristics, showcased in "I'm So Good at Yoga," make her an apparently perfect sexual partner and the subject of Rebecca's envy. That these are subsidiary in value to her girlfriend status is shown clearly by her apparent loss of them following her breakup with Josh after falling foul of the love triangle with Rebecca.

We might also add to this risk of subjugation the risk of becoming or being deemed "crazy." Rebecca risks her own position as subject in every relationship: in attempting to bring romance into her life, Rebecca time and again risks life-threatening "craziness." This risk is hinted at in "The Math of Love Triangles," highlighting the dangers that beset Rebecca if she does not successfully navigate her triangular desire to establish a functioning relationship: "If not I'll be swinging from a hypote-noose." The pun on "noose" in this line is underlined by the hanging gesture made by Rebecca as she sings the line. In season three Rebecca refuses to take her relationship with Nathaniel to the next level because of the fear that she will once again come to the point where she wishes to take her own life (3.11). Love is madness for Rebecca, or so she thinks. The recontextualization of "Face Your Fears" from parody to sound advice when Rebecca goes to face Nathaniel, however, suggests that her more grounded and direct love for Nathaniel is different. It is not love itself that is madness but triangular love. A similar risk besets Paula: her desire to vicariously live Rebecca's dream leading her into behavior that is difficult to differentiate from Rebecca's "madness." Valencia falls into a milder version of the same behavior when she and Rebecca stalk Josh's new girlfriend in "Research Me Obsessively" (2.07).

They also risk their agency. Heather (Vella Lovell), who on first realization that Greg is in love with Rebecca immediately ends her relationship with Greg, bypasses triangular desire on the basis that she is "way too kick ass," showing that she is the female character most clearly in charge of her life and choices (1.13). That she does this without being fully aware of the extent to which Greg's desire for her was mediated by her proximity to Rebecca does not negate the importance of her choice. Neither Heather's sanity nor her agency is ever in question (the only other main character that this might also be true of is Darryl Whitefeather, who, as Kathleen Kollmann argues in the next chapter, is an exemplary figure in the comfort he exhibits in his relationship with both sexes and in his own sense of self), nor are the strengths of her friendships, which are not beset by the same difficulties as Rebecca's with Paula and Valencia. As with her friendship with Valencia, the solidity of Rebecca's bond with Paula is only firmly established once both Rebecca and Paula have said goodbye to the dynamics that previously structured their relationship and formed a direct and honest connection in which they both recognize their own agency—such as when Rebecca pleads guilty to Trent's (Paul Welsh) murder at the end of season three (3.13).

Sedgwick's paradigm therefore seems eminently applicable to female-based erotic triangles and female homosocial desire, even if the workings differ slightly. The end, however, is the same: the consolidation and maintenance of patriarchal power. The show demonstrates clearly that female empowerment and eroticism require the renunciation of triangular structures in both heterosexual and homosocial relationships. Sedgwick's paradigm, however, only goes so far in elucidating the workings of erotic triangles, at least within the context of *CXG*. It is interestingly the somewhat old-fashioned Girard, whose structuralist thesis Sedgwick reworks for her own purposes, who is perhaps most illuminating in unpacking the show's use of the triangle as a metaphor for human relationships but also for the show's central topic, Rebecca's self-conception.

### So I'm a Triangle? Triangular Desire and Self-Acceptance

Despite Sedgwick's characterization of Girard's primary interest in erotic triangles being in the rivalry between two suitors, Girard's real recurring area of interest is in the mediation of desire by whomever or whatever. In Girard's configuration the three points of the erotic or love triangle are the

subject, the object, and the mediator. The mediator can be but is not necessarily the subject's rival for the possession of the object. The mediator
may not even be human. Girard's first two examples of triangular desire
are Cervantes' *Don Quixote* (1615) and Flaubert's *Madame Bovary* (1856),
in which the third mediating point of the triangle is romantic literature.
Both Don Quixote's and Emma Bovary's desire for their beloved(s) are
mediated by their reading of romances. According to Girard, the value
that the object holds for the subject is a result of its association with the
mediator: "The mediator's prestige is imparted to the object of desire
and confers upon it an illusory value."[9] The subject's desire for the object
reflects the subject's desire for the mediator: "The object is only a means
of reaching the mediator. The desire is aimed at the mediator's being."[10]
Thus the value that Don Quixote and Emma Bovary bestow upon the
objects of their affection reflects the value they place upon the romantic
ideology they have imbibed through their obsessive reading of romances.

In many ways, we can see Rebecca as a modern-day Don Quixote
or Emma Bovary. In the final episode of the first season we flashback to
Rebecca as a child acting out stories of romance, frustrated at her male
friend who will not play his assigned role as her prince. Her life is a constant conflict between her romantic expectations and reality. She continues, however, to tilt at windmills. Even after her attempted suicide, this
desire does not abate. Removing Greg, Valencia, and Paula from the equation, we can still view Rebecca's desire for Josh as triangular. In the opening episode of the series, Rebecca's meet-cute with Josh on the streets of
New York signals that Rebecca's desire for Josh represents more than just
the reignition of a teenage crush, when a billboard advert for butter with
the tagline "When was the last time you were truly happy?" breaks and
points directly to Josh (1.01). He represents her desire for happiness, which
for Rebecca means the fulfillment of her romantic dreams. Rebecca's
statement that "she didn't move to West Covina for Josh" in the opening
musical number is thus simultaneously true and false. She desires West
Covina to the extent that it embodies Josh but simultaneously she desires
Josh to the extent he embodies West Covina, the anti–New York, a place
where for Rebecca dreams might come true. "West Covina" works by juxtaposition of the romantic idealism of the song's genre and the unromantic

reality of a small town beset by budget cuts and situated at least two hours from the beach (depending on traffic). This, presented alongside Rebecca's justification of her move there as being quite separate from her meeting with Josh, sends the clear message that she did move there for Josh, as why would anyone move to West Covina otherwise? However, it is noteworthy that Rebecca's and Josh's purest moment of identification is in 1.09 when Josh empathizes with Rebecca's desire to leave New York and move to West Covina—a moment marked by the two characters' reprisal of the "West Covina" refrain. The show repeatedly indicates that the root of Rebecca's desire for Josh has little to do with Josh himself.

Under Girard's thesis, furthermore, we are not required to oppose a same-sex pair with an object of affection of the opposite sex: all points of the triangle could be of the same sex. Earlier Josh was suggested as the third point in a triangle with Rebecca and Paula, but that third point could also be occupied by Rebecca's mother. The show frequently plays with this undercurrent in Rebecca and Paula's relationship, most notably in the song "After Everything I've Done for You" (1.18), in which Paula castigates Rebecca not only for her ingratitude but also in the infantilizing terms by which Paula refers to Rebecca, such as "cookie" and even straightforwardly as "baby" (1.17). Rebecca also refers to Paula as "Momma." Paula's desire for Rebecca can be seen as her desire for a daughter, while Rebecca's desire for Paula can be seen as a reflected desire for her mother or perhaps a cultural ideal of motherhood that she never experienced in her own mother.

As Kathleen Vandenberg notes, at the base of Girard's philosophy is a concern with imitation and identification, with "the category of human actions that are largely propelled by spontaneous, unconscious, internal, and self-directed processes."[11] For Girard, Don Quixote and Emma Bovary imitate those they wish to identify with (i.e., the mediator). If the mediator values an object, they too shall value the object. If an object appears to reflect the mediator, they will value the object. The object's own qualities are of little importance. As Girard notes, "The physical qualities of the object play only a subordinate role."[12] In fact, argues Girard, loss of or disappointment in the object in its attainment is not particularly important so long as the value of the mediator is not tarnished: "Mme Bovary could go on changing lovers endlessly without ever changing her dream."[13] It is only when the mediator draws too close to the object that the mediator is in danger of also being tarnished. Perhaps we might argue that as well as the cultural construction of romantic love, a prime mediator in Rebecca's relationship with Josh is her father. While he is distant, despite her many failures in love she can retain her belief in it, independent of how disappointing her relationships with Greg or Josh or her former professor Robert (Adam Kaufmann) prove to be. It is when her father is physically present at her latest disappointment when Josh stands her up at the altar that her disappointment stretches beyond Josh to the concept of romantic love. Being Rebecca, however, she simply latches onto another cultural construction to avoid her disappointment or what Girard would identify as her metaphysical angst.

For Girard, the basis of this desire for the mediator is a sense of lack in the subject. The subject suffers from a sense of inferiority while they see the mediator as whole and untarnished: "Each one believes that he alone is excluded from the divine inheritance and takes pains to hide this misfortune. Original sin is no longer the truth about all men as in a religious universe but rather each individual's secret, the unique possession of that subjectivity which broadcasts its omnipotence and its dazzling supremacy."[14] Lacking that secret, the subject seeks it in others: "It is the heroes themselves who see their own insufficiency and plunge into bovarysm in order to escape the condemnation which, deep in their consciousness, they are the first and possibly the only ones to make."[15] In winning the object, the subject hopes to obtain the mediator's secret and thus cure his or her insufficiency: "Every hero of a novel expects his being to be radically changed by the act of possession."[16] For Girard, therefore, triangular desire is ultimately about the subject's revulsion of its self. It is an existential crisis shaped by modern understandings of the individual's place in a godless universe.

Rebecca's revulsion for her own being is a recurring theme throughout the show, highlighted in numerous musical numbers such as "You Stupid Bitch" (1.11), "The Villain in My Own Story" (1.14), and "(Tell Me I'm Okay) Patrick" (2.12). Her attraction to Josh, who in his own words people think is "so happy-go-lucky," can convincingly be seen as a desire to experience the happiness he embodies. Similarly, Greg's attraction to Rebecca and his rivalry with Josh, as well as his alcoholism, result from his sense of his own insufficiency, which he overcomes through facing his alcoholism and going to Emory to study business. It is made clear on his return in season four that "new" Greg (Skylar Astin) still has issues that he is working through, but his interactions with other characters have much less destructive force than in the first two seasons, and he navigates the discovery of Rebecca's one-night-stand with his father far better than his discovery at the beginning of the second season of her new relationship with Josh.

Paula's vicarious desire for Josh is also predicated on a sense of a lack, on a life in which dreams do not work out ("Maybe This Dream" [2.02]), and in which she is not the Disney heroine at the heart of the story. Her desire to lose herself in Rebecca's romance diminishes not when she reconnects with her husband, but rather when she chooses to believe in her ability to be something more and enroll in law school. Valencia's triangular desire for Rebecca and Josh also disappears when she establishes herself as a party planner, her lack of desire for either represented by her willingness to act as their wedding planner. Nathaniel's love for Rebecca is rooted in his lack of emotional connection to those around him and deeply buried self-contempt. Again, while Nathaniel's love for Rebecca is the initial catalyst for his slow transformation, it is the loss of Rebecca and his acceptance of that loss that enables him to say "I'm nice now!" (4.10) and for the audience to believe that he has earned it. He must move past triangular desire to be fulfilled, a point reiterated in the finale, in which Rebecca, Nathaniel, and Greg are all single, and Josh has moved on to a new relationship.

Nathaniel's imaginary projection of himself into the "recognizable pop culture genre" of the romantic comedy in 4.11 places him at the "center" of three intersecting love triangles, but this in itself is the result of an attempt to connect and identify with Rebecca, who loves romantic comedies. In the fourth season, Nathaniel dabbles with the kind of rivalry that Sedgwick identifies, with Josh in 4.10 and Greg in 4.11, but in both cases, Nathaniel ultimately rejects the competitive hierarchical model of rivalry for the more egalitarian model of the sports team, quite literally. This jockeying over status is underscored in 4.11 when Nathaniel's journey into the world of romantic comedies is prefaced by his bemoaning his sense of "low status" to George (Danny Jolles), his complaint to Leonard (Marshall Givens) that he had been gym buddies with Greg "and then he jumped in there," and by his transformation from "suspiciously good-looking in ways that normal people are not" (2.09) to "a dumb ugly hopelessly-in-love nerd" while Greg is transformed into a frat-boy-esque boat-owning businessman. By the end of the episode, however, Nathaniel admits to Rebecca that "he's a good guy, he really is, he's a great guy, he's not some jerk who wears blazers and a sweater or sometimes two sweaters," and in 4.12 Nathaniel diffuses the tension between Greg and Josh by saying he sees "a lot of potential for a real-life friend trio" with his former rivals. In successfully navigating and moving beyond the tropes of the romantic comedy, Nathaniel finds the emotional connection to others that attracted him to Rebecca in the first place. He, to a large degree, becomes Rebecca in this episode, "trying on a persona to figure out something in his life," an identification underscored rather beautifully by Rebecca's wry "Yeah, I can relate" when he describes his "weird fantasy daydream" to her. It is in accepting this particular lack that he finds himself fulfilled.

Rebecca is unable to resolve her angst as easily as the other characters. For Girard, this is frequently the fate of the subject of triangular desire: "The hero goes through his existence, from desire to desire, as one crosses a stream, jumping from one slippery stone to another."[17] Ultimately, however, Don Quixote cannot escape disappointment, renounces romance, and in doing so ends his slavery to its ideals: "The hero triumphs in defeat; he triumphs because he is at the end of his resources; for the first time he has to look his despair and his nothingness in his face. But this look which he has dreaded, which is the death of pride, is his salvation."[18] From defeat, the subject emerges armed with self-acceptance and autonomy. Girard's heroes and heroines, however, are confined within the parameters of novels rather than serial television shows. Moreover, the lens through which he views their sense of insufficiency is metaphysical. In a television show with postmodern sensibilities, which frames its main character's issues as a mental health disorder, resolution is not so easy nor so tidy. As Caitlin Ray notes in the previous chapter, the experience of disability is often one of liminal temporality in which traditional ideas of progress are challenged. Facing death does not fully resolve Rebecca's issues nor does her diagnosis, despite her hopes. Living with her tendency to fantasize is clearly depicted as an ongoing struggle for Rebecca that she is unlikely to ever fully resolve, with the fourth season featuring numerous relapses.

In any given episode, CXG plays with half-a-dozen different cultural tropes and conventions, making explicit the absurdity of the underlying logic within. The throwaway manner of this, however, should not deceive us. Minor moments are frequently returned to within the larger arc of the show, recontextualized and shown to have vital significance to the story that is being told. That a Marilyn Monroe parody in which the leading lady cannot even understand the basic mathematical concept of a triangle should thus resonate with queer theorists and French structuralism is all par for the course, for even the silliest of jokes resonate with the show's underlying theme and its project: to reframe the stories we tell about who we are. Midway through "The Math of Love Triangles," Rebecca starts pointing at seemingly random objects and asking her dancing professors if they are triangles. "Is this a triangle?" she asks. "No, that's you," they reply. "So I'm a triangle?" she asks. "What? No," exclaim the teachers. This comical confusion on the part of Rebecca-as-Marilyn speaks to a larger misconception on the part of everyday-lawyer-Rebecca, as it is only through her relationships, which as we have seen are fundamentally triangular in structure, that she envisages herself as a fully rounded and autonomous subject. To an extent, Rebecca truly does see herself as a triangle. Without her triangular dreams of romance, she sees herself as nothing. What she has to learn, over and over again, is that it is only through proper recognition of the fallaciousness of her triangular desire with its deification of the mediator that she can truly realize her own subjecthood, not as a lack, but as something desirable in its own right. Oddly enough what Rebecca has to learn is that "the center of the triangle" really "is lil' old sexy little baby me!"

# 7

# "Gettin' Bi"

*Darryl Whitefeather as Bisexual Bellwether*

## Kathleen W. Taylor Kollman

Small-town attorney Darryl Whitefeather (Pete Gardner), a supporting character in The CW musical comedy series *Crazy Ex-Girlfriend* (hereafter *CXG*), goes through several relationship status changes in the first season.[1] He divorces his wife, battles her for their daughter's custody, and embarks on a new romance. Then, in a gleeful moment, Darryl comes out to his coworkers as bisexual. Darryl's revelation is groundbreaking for its dismantling of a stereotype. This contrasts with the treatment of bisexuality in other television series and films, not to mention a lack of or a problematic examination of bisexuality in queer theory scholarship and sex research. That Darryl is allowed—in a triumphant pop-rock musical performance, no less—not only to reconcile his sexual orientation but also to declare and name it—runs counter to common narratives that erase bisexual naming, keep characters' orientations ambiguous, or claim someone was always either gay or straight and that their bisexuality was a transitional phase. As Samantha Allen writes in a piece for *The Daily Beast*, research shows "that bisexual people are unlikely to be out," and acceptance of one's orientation by others is particularly weak for bisexual men. By tackling this subject in such a dramatically different way than other works, *CXG* reinforces its position as an example of television that stands out in the peak TV moment, exhibiting a high degree of self-reflexivity and use of parody to provide a response to developments in society and culture.

*Crazy Ex-Girlfriend* is a text that can be read through a queer lens in multiple ways. Caitlin Ray discusses the series as a cripped narrative in chapter 5 of this volume, and crip theory stems from both disability studies and queer theory. Similarly, Hazel Mackenzie argues in chapter 6 that the homosocial triangles of the show are not unlike the way Eve Sedgwick queers love triangles to explain how they are often more about power and homoeroticism between the same-sex participants in the triad than they are about heterosexual desire. To fully explain how CXG is revolutionary in its representation of queer themes, however, we must also look specifically at its LGBTQA+ characters.

The ambiguity of bisexual identity is uncomfortable for those with a binary understanding of sexual orientation. The hegemony of the gay/straight binary is not merely a homophobic one but a specifically biphobic stance with erasure coming from those who identify with a range of orientations. Though Michel Foucault and Sedgwick pioneered important work in queer theory, their statements about bisexuality have various and limited levels of usefulness for contemporary bisexuality scholars. By looking at the pre–queer theory era, turning to Alfred Kinsey's revolutionary views on bisexuality, we can achieve a new paradigm of bisexual theory, recapturing the possibilities of the scale spectrum, which has proved useful in looking at gender identity. For popular media creators, naming ambiguous identity destabilizes a heteronormative othering of the gay/straight understanding of sexual identity. That CXG (a series known for subverting expectations of gender, ethnicity, and mental illness) is willing to perform similar work in the name of bringing attention to an oft-maligned part of the LGBTQA+ community—and does so without angst—is remarkable.

This chapter will first provide a brief history of theoretical and representational bisexuality, followed by a look at comparative media, and finally apply that background to analyzing Darryl Whitefeather specifically. CXG manages to completely upend prevailing conceptions not just of bisexuality generally but also of male bisexuality specifically. To understand just how the series so profoundly shatters previous stereotypes, one must first look at those earlier representations and the psychoanalytical and cultural theories underpinning bisexuality.

## Bisexuality: A Theoretical and Representational Genealogy

Sigmund Freud's conception of bisexuality focused not on sexual orientation but on what we would now more appropriately understand as
either gender fluidity or transgender identities, depending on the degree
to which people identified with a gender not matching their biological
sex. This definition did not move much beyond Freud himself, with even
psychoanalytic theorists of his tradition disagreeing with his usage.[2] Starting with Havelock Ellis (1897), Wilhelm Stekel (1922), and Alfred Kinsey
(1948), a clearer picture of bisexuality as we understand the term today
emerges: a sexual orientation in which someone has the capacity to be
attracted to members of their own and other gender identities.

Despite these definitions, representation of bisexuality in popular culture has remained problematic, and film theorist Justin Vicari unpacks
many subconscious reasons for this. Vicari asserts that bisexuality threatens binaries, despite its binary-allegiant term. If culture at large prefers
dualism, even presenting the idea that heterosexuality and homosexuality "were not antipodes but rather complements, mirror images, merging
points along a continuum which is . . . more circular and cyclical than linear" is a radical notion.[3] Film theorist Nicole Richter further expounds on
this threat of cultural destabilization, noting that if we position "bisexuality
at the center of the discussion of sexual politics, a new understanding . . .
can emerge," which sees it "not as another sexual orientation between gay
and straight but rather a form of life" with the potential to unravel the
concept of sexual orientation itself.[4]

If, after all, the eternal "either/or" is instead changed to "and," and if
there is an inherent bisexual potential in all humans, does sexual orientation become meaningless? Due to this possibility, it may be tempting to
turn to other terms, such as "pansexual" or "queer," which could serve
not merely as a theoretical framework to discuss all matters of LGBTQA+
identity but the identities themselves (and, in the case of queer, adding the
Q to the initialism). For Steven Angelides, use of the term "queer"

> has provided a new discursive space through which to foster politi-
> cal alliance across class, gender, racial, and sexual borders. Here the

category of bisexuality in the present tense has for the first time found a welcoming space for the articulation of its identity.[5]

On the other hand, such a naming convention can instead act to obscure, as "the queer umbrella, while it may have sheltered a diverse group of practices, individuals, and organizations, also functioned as a 'cloaking device,' serving to render bisexuality invisible."[6] If we move past a "hetero/homo divide" and progress "into an unlabeled ambisexuality," does this signify acceptance and abandonment of prescriptive labels,[7] or does it make the problem of bisexual erasure—indeed, any erasure of someone able to claim queer identity—even worse than it already is? Embracing "bisexual" as an identity is not, as Richter insists, intended to play "'spot the bisexual' but to complicate the discourses of sexuality that otherwise limit our thinking and imagination about the sexual and the erotic to the gay/straight binary.'"[8] It is meant not to dismantle what could be a positive coalition under "queer," but to assert that "queer" is not just a synonym for "gay" or at least "non-straight."[9] One definition of "queer," as Siobhan B. Somerville writes,

> calls into question the stability of any such categories of identity based on sexual orientation . . . "queer" is a *critique* of the tendency to organize political or theoretical questions around sexual orientation per se. To "queer" becomes a way to denaturalize categories such as "lesbian" and "gay" (not to mention "straight" and "heterosexual"), revealing them as socially and historically constructed identities that have often worked to establish and police the line between the "normal" and the "abnormal."[10]

Identification assertion—often inspired by the comfort to be taken in positive representation—is an important step for many in the coming-out process. To be sure, some bisexuality theorists think the answer lies in the inherent multiplicity of and enthusiastic embrace of "queer," but it is specifically in the space of queer *theory* that we see bisexual marginalization, even if we don't see it in queer political and social movements.[11]

While this use is reasonable in the context of the academic field of queer theory, this tradition is based partly on the work of Foucault, who insisted "that sexuality 'must not be thought of as a kind of natural given,'" but that much of the work in the field—important work dismantling heteronormativity and Foucault's work, too—still caused bisexual erasure.[12]

In recent years, other terms have occasionally supplanted "bisexual" as the preferred label for someone asserting a plurisexual identity. One possible reason for this uses the logic that the label "bisexual" represents a lack of acceptance for or attraction to people who are transgender, agender, or nonbinary in gender identity. Several recent pieces have covered this issue, including work by April Scarlette Callis, Corey E. Flanders et al., and M. Paz Galupo et al.[13] Callis's work uses borderlands theory to differentiate among bisexual, pansexual, and queer identities via qualitative ethnographic research, while Flanders et al.'s and Galupo et al.'s work uses more quantitative surveying of plurisexual people. All three studies seek to note trends regarding when an individual tends to assert a bisexual identity versus a queer or pansexual identity, and the findings of each piece reveal that those asserting a bisexual identity do not necessarily subscribe to a binary idea of gender, nor are they more inclined to exhibit bias against people who are not cisgender. Furthermore, much of the data of each study reveals that many people label themselves in multiple ways, asserting queerness and/or bisexuality and/or pansexuality simultaneously. Thus, an asserted bisexual identity does not mean someone might not also identify with another term that carries with it a more multifaceted plurisexuality. Based on his age at coming to terms with his sexuality, it is not surprising that Darryl would prefer the term "bisexual," but given his eagerness to embrace his identity, it would not be out of character for him to adopt any number of other ways to describe a plurisexual orientation.

For Vicari, to pin down "a single monolithic bisexuality" or discover "a pre-written code of bisexual mores and behaviors" is impossible, particularly as identification is personal and does not necessarily involve behavior but may be limited to attraction. What is less important than acts, Vicari insists, is that assertive identity ensures that "the choice between gay and straight will not only cease to be controversial—it might cease to be at all."[14] To normalize is to reassure those who feel othered that, in fact, their preferences are as natural as anyone else's.[15]

One of the most helpful figures in bringing attention to the existence of male bisexuality is Kinsey, who "began to conduct interview-based research on human sexual behavior in the 1930s," ultimately producing *Sexual Behavior in the Human Male*, in which he derived from his data that "nearly half (46%) of the population engage in both heterosexual and homosexual activities, or react to persons of both sexes, in the course of their adult lives."[16] He established his famed Kinsey scale, which positioned bisexuality at the midpoint of a range of exclusively homosexual and heterosexual identity. Thinking of sexuality as a continuum rather than a binary, however, appears to have been lost in the intervening years, as the visibility of bisexuality is subsumed by both exclusively gay and exclusively straight identities. In terms of media representation, it's also ironic to note that Kinsey—who himself identified as bisexual and had an open marriage with his wife—had his own bisexuality somewhat erased in the biopic *Kinsey* (2004, dir. Bill Condon). In a close reading of *Kinsey*, Vicari describes how the dramatization of the sex researcher's life seems at first to position his bisexuality at the center of his life, not just within his work. However, as the threesome of Kinsey, his wife Mac, and his lover Clyde dissolves, it causes the film to end with Kinsey and Mac seeming to settle into a more traditional heterosexual marriage, which historical evidence does not bear out.[17] Thus, despite Kinsey's known bisexuality, the film about him remains heteronormative, emphasizing his relationship with a woman.

The frenzy over bisexual men's supposed culpability in bringing AIDS to the heterosexual sphere can best be illustrated by Eve Sedgwick's evisceration of a *New York Times* article from April 3, 1987. In Sedgwick's classic work of queer theory, *Epistemology of the Closet*, she discusses the piece, titled "AIDS Specter for Women: The Bisexual Man," and how *Times* writer Jon Nordheimer denigrated bisexual men. Nordheimer's argument is that bisexual men were the reason for AIDS spreading to the heterosexual population, and Sedgwick asserts this is a failure to consider the sexual practices of individual bisexual men as being potentially *more* diligent in concerns for safety for their partners.[18] She then criticizes

Nordheimer's infantilizing of "powerless" women against a phantom "small but 'dangerous' group of men who have very frequent sexual contact with both men and women," with the resulting article making bisexual men out to be "sociopathic-sounding."[19] This constitutes Sedgwick's limited acknowledgment of male bisexuality, an arguably blasé omission for which she, as well as Foucault in his own otherwise-exhaustive work, are frequently taken to task by later queer theorists.[20] However, Sedgwick's disapproval of the straw man/specter of the voracious and unsafe bisexual disease carrier proves a helpful step in dismantling hype from evidence and reprimanding those writing about AIDS for blaming victims or using harmful stereotypes to further unverified theories.

One arena in which positive change can be made is perhaps within media representation, which has the ability to depict bisexual characters more realistically and thereby help shape public and scholarly discourse. Until recently, though, depictions in narratives across many genres of media have remained fraught with problems that cause further erasure and stigmatization. The three primary ways that male bisexuality has been portrayed that raise concerns among bisexual film theorists are (1) overreliance on bisexuality as metaphor representing alien otherness and glamorous anarchy, (2) erasure of bisexuality through either plot devices suggesting the character had been in a transitional state toward gay or straight all along or critical erasure of bisexual characters, and (3) outright negative depictions of bisexual characters. Fortunately, *CXG* does not fall into any of these traps; Darryl is no glamorized metaphor, and his coming out is loud and unable to be erased.

Using male bisexuality as a metaphor can be seen as "potent and versatile,"[21] but this can also serve to exoticize and dehumanize real people. If the image and reality are overly conflated, this can lead to a variety of (usually negative and erroneous) assumptions, since the reality of the lived experience seldom resembles exoticized sexual freedom or predation. So while seeing someone coded as a member of a marginalized group as powerful, supernatural, otherworldly, or godlike can be thrilling, it does little to help uplift actual people and may in fact further cement the idea of them as the negative other in the minds of those looking for any excuse to cling to stereotypes.

On the other end of the spectrum from superhuman/allegorical bisexuality is the nonexistent or "resolved" bisexual. These stories involve a character's bisexuality being turned into hetero- or homosexuality through either the plot itself or the critical response to it. Even when a bisexual character was present, "critics often re-categorized it and explained it away as a more familiar and 'comfortable' scenario. Either a heterosexual male was dabbling, or a gay male was having trouble coming out."[22] Richter gives the example of the film *Brokeback Mountain* (2005, dir. Ang Lee) being called in the contemporary press the "gay cowboy movie," when, she asserts, the male lovers retain sexual relationships with women throughout the film.[23] Furthermore, the words "bi" or "bisexual" are often unsaid in pieces clearly depicting bisexual characters, relying instead on "a proliferation of verbal and visual codes."[24]

The "resolved" bisexual exists in a text that waves away the character's identity as not what it appears to be—in essence these texts see bisexuality as a problem requiring a resolution in which a character is decidedly located on one end of a sexual orientation binary. Vicari does a close reading of Todd Haynes's *Velvet Goldmine* (1998), in which the character of Brian Slade (Jonathan Rhys Meyers) behaves throughout the film in a wholly bisexual manner, yet the subtext of the narrative makes it clear we are meant to see him as a gay man who cannot admit the truth about his orientation.[25] By "resolving" the character's bisexuality as something other than the apparent, we erase the previous identity as legitimate and declare it an untruthful passage to either a gay or straight reality.

Erasure or "resolution" is arguably preferable to an outright negative portrayal. The bisexual male in 1990s films played out the AIDS locus onscreen, becoming a signifier of disease, reconfigured from the 1970s alien rock star into a figure of destruction and villainy. Allen cites a GLAAD report that says that when bisexual characters are televised at all they are "depicted as 'self-destructive,' 'untrustworthy,' and 'lacking a sense of morality.'"[26] Even though Darryl is in a relationship with a woman in the last few episodes of *CXG*, there is no indication that he has decided he is straight—ergo his bisexuality is not "resolved"—nor is he portrayed as lacking a moral compass.

## Comparative Media

The 1970s saw an uptick in media exploration of bisexuality. In 1974, *Time* and *Newsweek* covered the topic, and important books on the subject (including *The Bisexual Option* and *Bisexuality: A Study*) were released later in the decade.[27] At the same time, however, mental health professionals exhibited antagonistic attitudes toward legitimizing bisexuality. In entertainment media, the decade saw bisexual men in films and music depicted as aliens, rock stars, or sometimes both, thus turning the entire concept of bisexual men into more trope than human, "a bastion of vast sexual freedom, bordering on a thriving state of anarchy."[28] Indeed, queer theory scholar Gloria E. Anzaldúa advocated for this view to a certain extent, calling for an intersectional acceptance of queer people of all genders and races but simultaneously equating them with a sense of extraterrestriality and magic, but doing so in a way that emphasized queer identity as a position of opportunity and positive specialness.[29] In this way, as young researchers, journalists, and artists demonstrated the subversive potential and freedom available to bisexual people, the establishment of practicing psychoanalysts and the mindset of conservative politicians remained firm that the orientation was a disease, an impossibility, a rebellious perversion, or all three. But just as figures like Dr. Frank N. Furter (Tim Curry) in *The Rocky Horror Picture Show* (1975, dir. Jim Sharman), Mick Jagger's role in *Performance* (1970, dir. Donald Cammell and Nicolas Roeg), and David Bowie's Ziggy Stardust character gained followings and acceptance (at least among members of various subcultures), the perception of bisexual people—particularly bisexual men—would suffer a crushing blow brought on by the AIDS crisis, one damaging the potential for positive media portrayals for years to come.

In the twenty-first century, we have seen some measure of progress in post–AIDS crisis narratives, but the stigma surrounding bisexuality still results in uneven portrayals. In *This Is Us* (NBC, 2016–present),[30] there is a departure from this trend by actually depicting a male bisexual character, William Hill (played by both Ron Cephas Jones and Jermel Nakia at different ages), but the depiction is far more problematic than Darryl's.

William is Randall Pearson's (Sterling K. Brown) biological father and is shown throughout his time on the series as having had a troubled past, including drug abuse, the overdose death of his girlfriend, and abandonment of his infant son. When he reveals to his son that he has a male lover, William's identity as a bisexual man is elided and only infrequently referred to. When it is mentioned, it is with a sense of unease, as if this element of William's life is but one instance in a long line of examples of his messy, nontraditional choices that result in pain and suffering for himself and those around him. After William succumbs to cancer, Randall is hesitant to be open and upfront about it with William's boyfriend, Jessie (Denis O'Hare), who is not treated like a grieving partner but rather as just one of William's friends. While the choices to have William's sexual identity be more cloaked in euphemism and secrecy could have to do with the character's age and ethnicity, William himself is not embarrassed by his orientation; it is only those around him who find it uncomfortable.

*Jane the Virgin* (2014–19),[31] a series that aired on The CW alongside CXG, includes the storyline of Petra Solano (Yael Grobglas), who goes through a series of heterosexual relationships before falling in love with her attorney Jane Ramos (Rosario Dawson). Petra's coming out as bisexual is complicated by her position in the sprawling narrative of the telenovela-inspired series as essentially a villain. However, her same-sex relationship is portrayed as a humanizing element that brings out more positive elements of her personality. This portrayal could be seen as rebelling against prevailing images of bisexual women as being mentally unstable, evil, or both by using it to reform someone. Still, the character's overall arc does not always show her in a positive light.

A slightly better, more nuanced (but still imperfect) example of a recent bisexual-coming-out story is Detective Rosa Diaz (Stephanie Biatriz) on the police comedy *Brooklyn Nine-Nine* (Fox and NBC, 2013–present).[32] Rosa is depicted for four seasons as exclusively dating men, but in the first third of the fifth season, she reveals that the reason she has been cagey about discussing her new romance is that it is with a woman. She then comes out to her coworkers as bisexual, and every character is supportive and happy for her. Unfortunately, her coming out to her parents goes less well, and they admit to having difficulty with the news. This lack of acceptance on their part—while realistic—is disappointing.

### How Darryl Is Different

To counteract the negative narrative, erasure, and superhuman allegories, we have Darryl Whitefeather, the "awkward but good-hearted boss" of CXG's protagonist, Rebecca Bunch (Rachel Bloom). Critics have called Darryl "the single most authentic and positive portrayal of bisexuality ever seen on network television," and series cocreators Aline Brosh McKenna and Rachel Bloom went so far as to consult "a representative from [GLAAD] to provide input" on the character's coming out story, the showstopping moment of which is his "celebratory coming out tune" titled "Gettin' Bi," which occurs in episode 1.14.[33] The series' songwriters based the lyrics for "Gettin' Bi" on a list of negative stereotypes provided by Brosh McKenna. The song, in the style of a 1980s Huey Lewis and the News anthem, serves as a means of refuting preconceived notions and attempts at erasure and biphobia, even as it remains firmly humorous and cheerful:

> Now some may say
> "Oh, you're just gay
> Why don't you just go gay all the way?"
> But that's not it
> 'Cause bi's legit
> Whether you're a he or a she
> We might be a perfect fit
> And one more thing
> I tell you what
> Being bi does not imply that you're a player or a slut.[34]

The imagery accompanying the song intercuts between Darryl in the conference room of his law firm and him performing as the front man of a 1980s-style band consisting of men in popped-collar polo shirts and mullet hairstyles. During these scenes, Darryl wears a white suit and a purple polo shirt, signifying the use of purple as an LGBTQA+ symbol but most significantly the purple at the center of the "biangle" symbol for bisexuality. Behind the band is a flag mural of horizontal stripes of pink, lavender, and blue, which is the bisexual pride flag.[35] During the scenes in the conference room, these colors appear more subtly in gentle washes of light around the room. While Darryl's performance is clearly freeing and happy for him, his coworkers in the conference room scene seem alternately uncomfortable and bored by this coming out. These reactions could be interpreted variously as representing negative reactions to bisexuality or blasé acceptance, wherein Darryl's sexuality is so accepted as to be unworthy of much fanfare.

Darryl also represents a type of bisexual man that limited media portrayals of the past have failed to give us—a man realizing his sexual orientation later in life, coming to his epiphany after career establishment, marriage, fatherhood, and divorce. We are not, as viewers, given Darryl's exact age, but as the father of a preteen daughter and an attorney with his own (albeit small) firm who expresses anxiety over dating a younger man, we can place him most likely in his forties. Not only is the coming out story of a bisexual man unique in primetime network television, so is a later-in-life coming out. His romance with his personal trainer Josh Wilson (David Hull) becomes the turning point in his realization that sexuality does not need to be only gay or straight.[36] Darryl's awareness of the options offered to him if he is "bothsexual," as he initially puts it, could mirror that of viewers who may be lulled into the false narrative of its nonexistence. And though Darryl's realization of his own sexuality is somewhat slow to develop, as evidenced by moments such as exhibiting confusion about same-sex expressions of affection, by season four we see a relatively confident image of him, dating both men and women, without demonstrating internal confusion or angst.

The depiction of Darryl and Josh's romance does not shy away from displays of physical affection, nor does it present the education of a newly out man as idealized and seamless. The relationship, in fact, is as complicated as any other, though tellingly healthier than the romances of the titular, heterosexual character. During the show's second season, Darryl and Josh declare their love for each other, take trips together, and—while not officially living together—seem even more settled as a couple. Darryl introduces Josh to his daughter, who is supportive of their relationship. In episode 2.05, Darryl meets some of Josh's ex-boyfriends, all of whom are older men, and Darryl frets that he is merely Josh's "type," rather than Josh loving him on his own accord. However, this hurdle is quickly overcome, and the two become even closer. This storyline is notable due to its universality—one could easily imagine a couple of any gender pairing experiencing a similar quandary. That Darryl and Josh are able to resolve their misunderstanding and further solidify their relationship demonstrates the show's commitment to depicting the couple as having healthy communication skills.

Later in the second season, however, the two come to a crossroads: Josh reveals he is not interested in marriage, and Darryl comes to the realization that he not only wants marriage but also wants a second child. This becomes the breaking point for the couple, and they ultimately split up in season three. Again, the conflict is not surrounding their gender, their respective sexual orientations, or their shared identity as a same-sex couple. The conflict is instead a fundamental difference in life goals, something that could occur to any couple and be grounds for a breakup. Postbreakup, it is Josh—not Darryl—who is more devastated by the split. Josh is depicted in more normatively masculine ways than Darryl is: he is a fitness enthusiast, he is more interested in sports, and he is less talkative and demonstrative about his feelings. This is nuanced on another level, too, as Josh identifies as exclusively gay. Darryl is shown as more nurturing and is free with sharing his feelings; this, coupled with his desire for marriage and children, makes it more refreshing that he should be less visibly devastated by the breakup, and he demonstrates a marked practicality in moving on and pursuing voluntary single fatherhood.

Though Darryl and Josh do not wind up together, they do enter into a friendship. During the first half of season four, several characters appear to promote the idea of Darryl and Josh reuniting, particularly the office intern Maya (Esther Povitsky).[37] The musical number "The Group Mind Has Decided You're in Love" (4.05) depicts nearly the entire cast urging the two to reconcile. This number's genre and visual design are depicted as an homage to *Oklahoma!*, the 1943 Rodgers and Hammerstein collaboration generally seen as transitioning musical theater from operetta to the contemporary genre. This allusion could signify the stereotypical association of LGBTQA+ culture with musical theater, the Western imagery and trappings that Darryl is fond of using as decorative touches in his office, or a nod to the layers of gender presentation seen in the play—various characters in *Oklahoma!* perform traditional hypermasculinity, demure femininity, and sexually progressive femininity—all of which are arguably seen as traits in Darryl and Josh.

Once Darryl and Josh are solidly maintaining a friendship and not a romantic relationship, Darryl begins to date and express interest in other people. In episode 4.06, Darryl and Rebecca go on a road trip together, at the end of which they seem to share a quasiromantic moment that almost leads to a kiss. Both of them realize this is more about being able to move on from their recent long-term relationships rather than an actual attraction to one another, but Darryl does then subsequently go out on dates. In episode 4.10, Rebecca babysits for Darryl when he goes on a blind date, which he later reveals was with a woman. No one hearing of the date reveals any surprise that Darryl would leave a relationship with a man to then be open to dating women, further normalizing the idea that he remains attracted to multiple genders.[38] By the end of the series, Darryl has married April (Maribeth Monroe), a woman he met during episode 4.13. During the flashforward in episode 4.17, it is revealed they are expecting a child together.

Samantha Allen notes, "In 2016, it shouldn't be revolutionary to simply have a bi male character on television who's treated the same as any other character. But it is." In her discussion with bisexual advocate Alexandra Bolles, Allen learns those who identify as bisexual are "the majority" of LGBTQA+ people, despite being "less likely than their gay and lesbian peers to be out," due to misunderstandings surrounding bisexual identity, the very misunderstandings CXG seeks to dispel through Darryl.

It bears mentioning that, late in season three, the series depicts another character entering into a same-sex relationship. Valencia Perez (Gabrielle Ruiz) begins a party planning business and becomes romantically involved with a client-turned-business partner, Beth (Emma Willmann). Valencia never describes herself as bisexual, queer, pansexual, or with any other specific label, but for a show that is unafraid to use that term with Darryl, it would be logical and welcome for Valencia to more openly discuss her identity. Episode 4.08 reveals Valencia's teen romance with Joseph (Rene Gube), a former classmate who later became a priest. Despite her continued relationship with Beth, Valencia appears to be attracted to Joseph at their high school reunion. Still, later in season four, Valencia wants to marry Beth. This all seems to indicate that Valencia's sexual orientation cannot be described as a fixed attraction to only one gender, even if the series does not have her assign herself a label.

However, this coyness or lack of a label—while not unrealistic—is something that other characters have suffered from, including C. J. Lamb (Amanda Donohoe) on *L.A. Law* (NBC, 1986–94), various characters on *Xena: Warrior Princess* (syndicated, 1995–2001), Samantha Jones (Kim Cattrall) on *Sex and the City* (HBO, 1997–2003), Carol Rance (Kathleen Rose Perkins) on *Episodes* (Showtime/BBC, 2011–17), David Rose (Daniel Levy) on *Schitt's Creek* (CBC, 2015–present), and a host of other examples, mostly female characters whose sexuality is represented as fluid but unlabeled.[39]

It is unfortunate that the most groundbreaking example of an out, functional, and content bisexual man comes as a character who otherwise exhibits multiple markers of privilege,[40] considering that the African American character of William Hill and the Latina female character of Rosa Diaz have varying degrees of difficulty being accepted by those around them. Still, Darryl's presence is at least a step in the right direction and more palpable to a resistant audience and critical sphere who may still think, as he sings in his coming out song, that he is "just gay," which he is quick to counter, asserting "that's not it, 'cause bi's legit." After decades of media erasure, marginalization, and negative portrayals, being bluntly told bisexual people exist is the very message we need.

# Part Three

# Trauma, Vulnerability, and Mental Illness

# 8

# "I'm the Villain in My Own Story"

### Representations of Depression
### and the Spectatorial Experience

## Lauren Boumaroun

In New York City, people often express their feelings by defacing subway ads. The Rockettes receive Sharpie goatees, and supermodels are caught with snot coming out of their noses. Sometimes, this graffiti is pointed and controversial, like when a confused defacer made anti-Muslim remarks on an ad featuring Sikh jewelry designer and actor Waris Ahluwalia.[1] Similarly, several *Crazy Ex-Girlfriend* subway ads were defaced with aggressive comments, including "Fuck off for furthering a stereotype."[2] The ads feature protagonist Rebecca Bunch (Rachel Bloom) in a bright pink dress posed against a stark white background. In her hand she holds a broken pink string as a pink heart balloon floats away. The only other descriptive clues are the title and the tagline "NEVER. LET. GO." One defacer wrote "This oppresses women" on at least two separate posters, but fans came to the rescue, writing "No it doesn't, this is stupid" and "She's a lead actress! Good for her!" When asked on Twitter to weigh in, creator Rachel Bloom replied: "Can you write 'why don't you all settle this debate by watching the show on Mondays, 8/7c? This isn't Rachel Bloom btw.'"[3]

And with a characteristic touch of humor, Bloom said all she needed to say. Despite passersby reading the advertisements as furthering stereotypes of women, critics have overwhelmingly viewed the series as critical of stereotypes and even as feminist.[4] Rather than being a one-dimensional portrait of an overly attached girl uprooting her life for a man, Rebecca is

143

an intelligent and complicated woman whose actions are a result of her less-than-perfect mental health. The series is unique in its approach to mental illness, exploring the causes and effects of being "crazy." In this sense, *Crazy Ex-Girlfriend* (hereafter CXG) falls under Janet Walker's categorization of "trauma cinema," as it is a feminist text drawing on personal inspiration, giving "internal psychic phenomena . . . tangible expression" and representing personal trauma through nonrealist aesthetics, namely the series' musical numbers.[5] This chapter examines the spectatorial experience of season one of CXG. I analyze how paratextual information and formal characteristics encourage an interpretation of the series as subversive, yet ultimately true-to-life in its representation of childhood trauma and depression.[6] These analyses are supported by an interview I conducted with Bloom shortly after the first season aired. The complexity of her portrayal opens up the possibility for a therapeutic viewing experience by providing laughter, catharsis, and the potential for personal growth through identification with Rebecca.

### Paratexts/Creators

Paratextual materials can be viewed as "coherent clusters of meaning, expectation, and engagement," which often constitute people's first and only encounter with a text.[7] They exist outside and are separate from the text yet are inexorably tied to it. As potential viewers, we engage in what Jonathan Gray calls "speculative consumption," meaning we imagine what a text will be like based on the "hype" surrounding it.[8] Unfortunately, the paratext of CXG that most people encountered was the aforementioned ad that "both manages to communicate zero information to someone while simultaneously screaming, 'DO NOT, UNDER ANY CIRCUMSTANCES, WATCH THIS SHOW.'"[9] But advertising departments are separate from a show's creative departments, occasionally leading to dissonance between a series and its promotional materials.[10] As Bloom explained in our interview, she and cocreator Aline Brosh McKenna give ideas and feedback for promotional materials, but marketing and social media are independent departments. The pair are too busy with showrunner duties to create all of the advertising and marketing content.[11] Their previous work, especially Bloom's, is more representative of CXG and encourages the audience to see the show as deconstructing stereotypes rather than building them up.

Creative personnel, especially TV showrunners and film directors, are also paratexts that serve as "a mediating figure through which intertexts affect current interpretive strategies."[12] So, *Anchorman* (2004, dir. Adam McKay) and *The Newsroom* (HBO, 2012–14) may seem similar based on their titles, but knowing one is a film starring Will Ferrell and the other is an HBO series written by Aaron Sorkin will lead potential viewers to expect two very different products. Although *Morning Glory* (2010, dir. Roger Michell) is also about a cranky, drunk newscaster on a struggling news show, it is easily distinguished from the other two titles by the knowledge that it was penned by Brosh McKenna, screenwriter of *The Devil Wears Prada* (2006, dir. David Frankel) and *27 Dresses* (2008, dir. Anne Fletcher). Like Rebecca Bunch, *Morning Glory*'s protagonist Becky Fuller (Rachel McAdams) is a bit neurotic—twice during the film, she gets so worked up that other (male) characters ask if she is going to sing—but she is still portrayed as intelligent and competent. Becky is good at her job, and the film ends with her professional success. It also becomes clear that the love story was not between Becky and her romantic interest but rather about her and her father-figure, Mike Pomeroy (Harrison Ford).[13] Thus, Brosh McKenna's previous work encourages audiences to expect a well-crafted, yet slightly subversive, romantic comedy that plays with character types and tropes. She has even called CXG "an inside-out version" of her previous writing credits,[14] while Bloom more bawdily described it as a "fucked up version of the movies Aline had been writing."[15]

Though Brosh McKenna's authorial style is essential to the show, Rachel Bloom's previous work is even more influential. As the star of the show, Bloom's personality is not only felt in the writing and producing but also onscreen. She studied musical theater at New York University and sketch comedy at the Upright Citizens Brigade, and she has always had a macabre sense of humor, choosing *The Exorcist* for a book project in eighth grade.[16] Her training and penchant for irreverent humor are unmistakably present in the YouTube videos for which she first gained attention. In 2011, her music video "Fuck Me, Ray Bradbury" was nominated for a

Hugo Award for "Best Dramatic Presentation: Short."[17] As the title suggests, it is an explicitly sexual ode to science fiction writer Ray Bradbury. Bloom's schoolgirl costume and performance style are reminiscent of Britney Spears's "Baby One More Time" music video, though the lyrics waste no time with innuendo. With its irreverent pop culture references, it could easily be a number from CXG.

All of Bloom's music videos are similarly satirical, simultaneously criticizing and celebrating popular culture. "Historically Accurate Disney Princess Song" subverts the norms of fairy tales by presenting a kingdom more representative of historical realities—the princess coughs up blood, and it is explained that many townspeople died from a recent plague "spread by jealous witches," one of whom is being burned in the background. "We Don't Need a Man," a duet between Bloom and her friend Shaina Taub, enters the territory covered by CXG with its focus on romance and heartbreaks. While Shaina sings about looking and feeling good since her breakup, Bloom's reaction to her breakup involves eating lots of cheese and not showering for three days. The juxtaposition of the positivistic pop culture portrayal of newfound singleness as empowering and the more realistic representation of a sad woman in need of comfort takes aim at the contradictory messages that women receive from the mainstream media. Bloom's authorial style is one of deconstruction and camp, which, when combined with Brosh McKenna's neurotic rom-com style, forms the heart and soul of CXG.

## Form/Structure

The self-consciousness and performativity of camp keep the show from being stereotypical and uncritical of female representation. Like Bloom's previous music videos, CXG's campy style tackles mainstream culture with "irony, exaggeration, trivialization, theatricalization and an ambivalent making fun of and out of the serious and respectable."[18] But audiences do not need to know Bloom's work to understand the show. In addition to explaining the story's premise, the first season's opening credit sequence calls out the sexist nature of the term "crazy ex-girlfriend," showing a female protagonist who actively pushes back against the chorus of people labeling her as "crazy" and "broken inside" while maintaining a humorous bent. The animated opening credits also aesthetically reinforce the show's treatment of its protagonist as multidimensional, presenting Rebecca as the only three-dimensional object in a two-dimensional space. This "entryway paratext" effectively prepares the spectator for what they are about to see and encourages a certain interpretation of the show.[19]

Heather's (Vella Lovell) first interactions with Rebecca mirror the ideas put forth in the opening credit sequence. When she first meets Rebecca in 1.03, Heather is condescending and distancing, calling Rebecca "fascinating" and making her the subject of her abnormal psychology paper. When Rebecca thanks her with a weird voice and a little bow, Heather responds: "That right there would be an A." She exhibits no respect for Rebecca and immediately labels her as a "crazy person," which the viewer may be tempted to do. Heather is often the spectator's surrogate within the story world. She spends the entirety of Rebecca's housewarming party taking notes on Rebecca's behavior and, throughout the first season, often takes the position of a "reality TV" viewer, detachedly reveling in the drama that unfolds. The "most entertaining day" of her life was spent watching Rebecca try to steal a prescription pad from her doctor and catching Paula (Donna Lynne Champlin) being unfaithful to her husband (1.07).

Heather shifts from detached spectator to sympathetic friend in 1.04, which is bookended by two presentations in her abnormal psychology class. In the first presentation, Heather refers to her subject as "nuts" and is reprimanded by her instructor, but she insists that Rebecca is "bonkerballs." However, after spending more time with Rebecca and getting actual insight into her abnormal psychology, Heather gains a new perspective. In her second presentation, she refuses to use any labels and claims that Rebecca "doesn't fit into any of the categories of your little book" (referring to the *DSM-IV*). The teacher points out that Rebecca has a number of classifiable disorders, but Heather is no longer willing to see her as a subject. Spending time with Rebecca shows that one-dimensional labels are insufficient for describing the complexities of mental illness and that, as the opening credits state, "it's a lot more nuanced than that."

Structurally, the show's musical numbers serve as analogues for the series' construction overall. Like Bloom's earlier YouTube videos, they use preexisting generic forms in order to comment on those forms as well as critique larger themes and issues that the narrative is addressing. As Christine Prevas argues in chapter 11, the songs take "a truism about the world to an illogical extreme" thereby acting "as a microcosm in which notions of normality and conventionality are destabilized."[20] Darryl's (Pete Gardner) song "I Love My Daughter" (1.05) employs the country genre in order to mock the prevalence and content of songs about father-daughter love sung by country music stars. But as it calls out that songs like that can be creepy, the musical number expresses Darryl's genuine (noncreepy) love for his daughter. The song is an emotional moment and serves the narrative by helping Darryl convince Rebecca how important it is that he receives custody of his daughter. As Bloom has said in reference to the series overall, the approach is "doing the genre so hard that you're parodying the genre."[21] CXG consistently deconstructs televisual and cultural norms through campy musical satire while building up funny, realistic, and productive representations in their place.

## Trauma/Therapy

Through Rebecca's experience, the narrative probes the causes of depression and considers how childhood trauma can affect adult relationships and self-esteem, especially through the musical number "A Boy Band Made Up of Four Joshes" from episode 1.03.[22] We learned earlier in the episode that "the root of all [Rebecca's] party fears" is her father abandoning her while she was hosting a viewing party for her favorite boy band's pay-per-view concert. The song is obviously a reference to this memory and calls out the importance those bands had for adolescent girls in the late 1990s and early 2000s. I attended the Backstreet Boys' *Millennium* tour next to a girl who sobbed continuously throughout the entire concert—mascara streaking down her face, her hand occasionally reaching out toward the stage—not dissimilar to the way Rebecca and her younger self fawn over the boy band of Joshes. That emotional connection meant everything to my fellow concertgoer at the time, and Josh (Vincent Rodriguez III) is Rebecca's Nick Carter. He is cute, sensitive, and someone she is in harmony with (quite literally, as evidenced in 1.09's "West Covina Reprise II").

In keeping with Rebecca's subjectivity, "A Boy Band Made Up of Four Joshes" presents Josh as an unrealistic fantasy—a pop star, multiplied by four, who also happens to be a nationally recognized mental health professional. Josh has been equated with the "cure" for depression since the pilot, when an arrow below a butter advertisement posing the question "When was the last time you were truly happy?" pointed directly at him. The last time Rebecca was truly happy was at summer camp with Josh, and when she needed help livening up her housewarming party, he was there. But, in helping her solve that problem, he unwittingly reinforced her belief that he is the solution to all of her problems. In Rebecca's mind, the only way to be happy again is to be with Josh. As Bloom says, "the show is about the search for happiness" and not really about a guy: "Rebecca is in love with Josh because of all of the things Josh represents."[23]

"A Boy Band Made Up of Four Joshes" is only disguised as a love song. Its lyrics suggest instead that the proper treatment for Rebecca's childhood trauma is therapy, not romance. Although trauma is often discussed in terms of terrorist attacks, war, and abuse, other events not involving the threat of death, like familial disputes, divorce, and bullying, can also have long-term effects on our personalities. Kira et al. have argued for the insufficiency of the *DSM-IV* definition of trauma as being limited to "physical traumas," referring instead to Kira's two-way trauma taxonomy, which makes room for family traumas like abandonment by a parent. The APA Trauma Group sees trauma as "defined more by its negative outcomes" than its causes,[24] and it is obvious that Rebecca's abandonment by her father has had a lasting, negative effect on her. The boy band Joshes promise that she can "kiss all [her] childhood traumas goodbye," but only because they are "trained in cognitive behavioral therapy with specialties in personality and sleep disorders," which is what Rebecca really needs. Despite the song's comedic spin, it never belittles Rebecca's problems. Rather, it legitimizes her struggles by tying them to personal trauma and not some cultural construction of women as "hysterical" or irrationally emotional.

## Representations/Expectations

Unfortunately, many other media representations of depressed and mentally ill people are not as productive as *CXG*. Studies have found that media is a major contributor to the stigmatization of mental illness and, though representations of this sort are decreasing, mentally ill characters are often portrayed as violent, as Margaret Tally discusses in chapter 9.[25] This is especially problematic given that, for many people, their major source of information about mental health is television. People who watch a lot of television are more likely to hold values that resemble those seen on TV (cultivation theory) and may also gain knowledge about behaviors and social conventions through TV (social learning theory).[26] Although Rebecca's obsessive and problematic behavior could have easily fallen into the realm of stereotype, *CXG*'s formal characteristics and comedic style work together to destigmatize mental illness and humanize the characters. Rather than laughing at "crazy" Rebecca's quirks in a derisive or distancing way, the audience is encouraged to laugh "empathetically with Rebecca."[27] Comedy provides a "powerful emotional release"[28] and can soften the potentially triggering nature of her situation for viewers experiencing similar issues.[29] The series' uniqueness comes from its refusal to deride its protagonist, offering instead some insight into the emotional labor required to actively battle depression and appear "normal" to others.

  *CXG* tackles these issues head on in episode 1.07. While parked outside Josh's new apartment, Rebecca sees him ignore her phone call. Despite her attempts to "reject this feeling," the hurt of being ignored carries through the rest of the episode, and she falls into a deep depression. In a pop-up video on Rebecca's computer, Dr. Phil warns against avoiding feelings through ineffective and unhealthy means like alcohol and work, but Rebecca attempts to resist her depression by drinking vodka from the pen cup on her desk. It backfires when she bombs a meeting with an important client, and Darryl threatens to take her off the case. Dr. Phil, who requested to be on the show,[30] continues to pop up throughout the episode as Rebecca's conscience, calling out her destructive avoidance but seemingly having no effect. In actuality, Dr. Phil has been criticized for the ineffectual and exploitative methods used on his show as well as his generic, and occasionally problematic, advice.[31] In a sense, CXG represents the nuances of mental illness better than *Dr. Phil* (2002–, syndicated), as Dr. Phil's recurring appearances do nothing to stop Rebecca's spiraling.

The episode also exposes the emotional labor involved in hiding depression from friends. Darryl, who is sweet but naïve, tells Rebecca to come back on Monday as "the happy Rebecca that we all know and love." Rebecca, sarcastically though not maliciously, responds to his advice: "Such a good tip. So helpful. Be happy!" Cut to her laying miserably on her couch (1.07). The juxtaposition calls attention to the stigma of depression and the experience of interacting with someone who simplifies it into a switch that can be turned on and off. Paula calls, and Rebecca again puts on a happy performance but immediately drops the façade after hanging up. The quick shift is jarringly funny, yet reveals the effort depressed people put into appearing happy for those around them. Despite her ability to *act* like the "happy Rebecca" Darryl asked for, the reality is that her depression prevents her from *feeling* like that person.

The lyrics and visuals of the episode's first musical number, "Sexy French Depression," play with the contradiction between the sexy gloss of screen representations and the nasty reality of depression. Rebecca turns on the TV and sees Dr. Phil talking about the necessity of dealing with feelings head-on. Not yet ready to deal with her feelings, Rebecca flips through some channels, lands on a French film featuring a sad woman, and muses about how the French make depression look so sexy. This transitions into the black-and-white music video for "Sexy French Depression" in which Rebecca adopts the sexy/sad attitude of the French woman. The sequence mostly features Rebecca wandering through Paris, rolling around in her bed that "smells like a tampon," or sitting on her bathroom floor "black[ing] out on dessert wine." Rebecca sings of lips "red with pain" and how her "bosom heaves with sobs." This perfectly styled version of Rebecca with her winged eyeliner, little black dress, and dessert wine dribbling down her chin certainly appears to be much sexier than the disoriented Rebecca at the meeting with her teeth stained blue by drinking vodka from her pen cup.

The bridge is narrated by Rebecca, who is no longer wandering the streets of Paris in a little black dress but in pajamas—a sign she is finally leaning into the reality of her depression. With her blanket-like sweater hanging off her shoulder, Rebecca looks back at the camera. Her voiceover speaks in French while the English translation scrolls: "My anxiety is so out of control that all I can think about is thinking about thinking about thinking about fixing everything I've ever done wrong and all of the ways I've already messed up my life beyond repair. If I think about it hard enough eventually I'll get the answer but I've forgotten what the question was." The lyrics provide a straightforward, amusing, and heart-wrenching description of depressed thinking that defies an accepted view of musicals as "lightweight or ineffectual."[32] In fact, Bloom changed the original lyrics after deciding they were too "surface-y." Exhausted from speaking to the press to promote the show, she got "back in touch with [her] depression . . . and that's where the spoken bridge came from . . . this is how I feel when I'm truly miserable."[33] Actively rejecting the truism that musical comedy is more about "style and performance" than "plot and character conventions," CXG's musical numbers are more than space-filling spectacle.[34] They supplement the narrative and add depth to the characters.

### Shame/Self-Loathing

As implied in the bridge of "Sexy French Depression," depressed feelings are often accompanied by shame and self-loathing. This is tackled more explicitly in fan favorite "You Stupid Bitch," the final musical number from episode 1.11 and a song that is a "distillation of the entire show."[35] Having finally admitted that she is in love with Josh and moved to West Covina for him, Rebecca sends an emoji-filled text to Paula but is so Josh-focused that she accidentally sends it to him. Remembering that he left his phone at home, Rebecca breaks into his apartment to delete the text. She nearly ruins her relationship with Josh when he realizes that she is lying about why she is there and went to great lengths to cover up the truth. Unconcerned with the particulars, he walks out on her—just like her father did. Rebecca contemplates her mistakes, made tangible in the shattered glass on the floor in front of her, when a male announcer's voice welcomes her to the stage to sing a song about "self-indulgent self-loathing." Fade to

Rebecca in a glittery diva gown walking onto a dark stage lined with light bulbs and surrounded by a cheering crowd. Behind her hangs a beautiful chandelier of shattered glass, reminding us that what takes place in this fantasy space is tied to the reality of her situation.

Motivated by guilt, Rebecca sings of her shame. According to Sangmoon Kim, Randall S. Jorgensen, and Ryan Thibodeau, guilt is an outward-focused negative emotion toward a certain behavior or action, revealing awareness of someone else's pain. Shame is directed inward toward the self and focuses on personal emotional pain.[36] Rebecca's realization that her actions have hurt her friends sheds light on how others view her. Josh could barely look at her after realizing her story was untrue. Rebecca internalizes this external shame, finally beginning to see herself as others see her. This clarity manifests itself in "You Stupid Bitch." As Bloom explains, many depressive songs have a poetry to them, but "when you're actually angry at yourself, the things you say to yourself are not prolific, they're not song lyrics, they're very cruel," which is what makes the number so poignant.[37] The lyrics pull no punches with harsh, internally directed insults that simultaneously reveal Rebecca's newfound self-awareness: "You're just a poopy little slut who doesn't think and deceives the people she loves." The inward focus of shame gives Rebecca some perspective but also has the potential to "elicit ruminative processes" that are associated with depression.[38]

During the second chorus, Rebecca invites the audience members, diegetic and nondiegetic, to sing along with her saying, "Yes! I deserve this!" and asking for their help in inflicting emotional pain on her "bad self" as penance for her past actions.[39] Drawing on the form of a diva concert à la Barbra Streisand or Bernadette Peters, the musical number takes advantage of a form that enables the singer to look back on their career and, in Rebecca's case, all of the mistakes they have made. It is a recognition that Rebecca has been performing the same routine of self-denial and manipulation repeatedly, and maybe an acknowledgment that the act is getting old. She is telling the viewer that it is okay to be appalled by what happened, because she is too. Crazy does not mean unaware or uncaring. The things that make people "crazy" are often a result of being *deeply* caring and sensitive. With the self-reflective "You Stupid Bitch," CXG breaks new ground in providing a picture of how depressed people see themselves.

## Self-Awareness/Personal Growth

According to Bloom, one of the questions the show asks is: "What are the things that are getting in the way of you being the best version of yourself?" Discussing the "monsters" that plague us, Janina Scarlet explains that the "real enemy is avoidance, a trap set up by a villain to ensure that we fail before we even attempt to begin our hero's journey."[40] As exemplified in Rebecca's self-aware "I'm the Villain in My Own Story" (1.14), Rebecca has been villainous not only to others but also to herself by repressing feelings and avoiding her real issues. Throughout the season, Rebecca goes through a cycle of recognition and denial. She does something horrible, makes a promise to do better, but falls right back into her old habits, because she never addresses her real issues or seeks help. Her revelations in "You Stupid Bitch" all take place in the fantasy space of the concert hall, and she only becomes more manipulative after that. But the key lyrics in "I'm the Villain in My Own Story" are sung by Rebecca in the narratively real space of her bedroom. She realizes she is "the bad guy in [her] TV show" and that her "actions have gone way too far." For the first time, she looks at her story objectively and, in taking the position of observer, can fully acknowledge her manipulative behavior and work to change it. As Stephanie Salerno discusses in chapter 10, this is the type of "emotional growth in moments of personal turbulence [that] registers as candid, earnest, and relatable to viewers despite (or perhaps because of) being couched in dark humor."[41]

Due to the similarity of the cognitive and emotional processes that govern our experiences of reality and fiction, an active spectator can gain personal and social benefits from viewing and interpreting narratives. Viewers may watch a series because they can relate to the events being portrayed, which in turn helps them recognize situations and problems in their own lives.[42] They may also watch to relieve loneliness, learn about the self, relax, or heighten their mood.[43] Musicals may be uniquely adept at doing this, since music can affect "mood, attention, recall, and attitudes," and a musical number may have the power to "enhance the influence of its nonmusical counterpart."[44] Ben Sher has argued that aspects of trauma, such as compulsion and the tendency to blur fantasy and reality, complement aspects of cinephilia and suggests that viewing can be a way to process trauma.[45] Several members of the CXG Facebook fan group have found the show therapeutic, commenting that "Rachel Bloom is saving [the] lives of lots of people!!" and how the show "has been a godsend."

By identifying with Rebecca, we recognize our similarities and understand her choices, maybe even believe her self-delusions. But as objective viewers, we see the chaos that begins after she pours her medications down the sink in the pilot episode. Berys Gaut has argued that mirroring characters' emotional reactions can teach viewers how to respond emotionally to certain situations, learn from their mistakes, and grow with the character throughout the narrative.[46] Torben Grodal's bioculturalist approach similarly suggests that "mirror neurons in the premotor cortex" may provoke "action tendencies in viewers that mirror the actions and intentions of the characters."[47] This simulation of characters' actions not only helps us "to learn how and why they behave as they do, but also to learn how to behave ourselves."[48] This complements the positive psychological view that audiences can learn from films by empathizing with characters and reflecting on their emotions or by using exemplary fictional characters as role models in everyday life.[49] Although Rebecca is hardly an exemplary role model, much of the narrative is about her discovering and building her own character strengths. She does not want to be defined by negative labels like "crazy," nor will her friends let her be.

The therapeutic benefits are not restricted to the audience. Bloom's history of depression, which "runs rampant in [her] family," has made the production experience therapeutic as well. The audience's therapeutic identification with Rebecca, who shares many qualities with Bloom, becomes a two-way street: "The way that I have found that I deal with it is to talk about it and to write about it. . . . It's finding other people who have similarities, that's how I deal with it . . . this show is very much cathartic for me to write . . . people identify with it, and it means I'm not alone."[50] Bloom's songwriting partner and CXG producer Jack Dolgen echoed that sentiment at the finale concert taping and PaleyFest panel in Los Angeles, explaining how helpful it was to write about his own struggles with mental health and how validating it is to connect with fans through those issues.[51]

## Conclusion

Rather than reinforcing problematic ideas regarding gender and mental health as its title and initial advertising campaign implied, CXG complicates stereotypes, offering a complex and multidimensional protagonist whose psychological journey and personal growth can be mirrored by the viewer. By employing the satirical possibilities of comedy and the heightened emotionality of musical numbers, the show effectively debunks myths regarding mental illness and provides a uniquely complex portrayal of depression. It critiques the one-dimensional misrepresentations of mental illness in the media and goes deeper by exploring the causes of depression and its effects on self-perception. In addition to its entertainment value and relevant social critique, the series gives audiences a chance to learn from and through its main character, Rebecca Bunch.

Returning to the advertising campaign and further analyzing her facial expression, it becomes more difficult to pin down her emotions. Rebecca does not look crazy in love or psychotic like you might expect based on the surrounding text. Her facial expression is actually quite complex, with hints of annoyance and some underlying frustration. In that way, the billboard actually is fully representative of the show and its message. It looks just like a billboard for any other broadcast network television show and appears complicit in the standard practice of stereotyping women as hysterical. However, the star/showrunner utilizes these forms to actively fight back against these labels—annoyed by their use, frustrated by their pervasiveness, and ready to educate audiences about the complexities and nuances of femininity and mental health.

# 9

# "A Diagnosis!!"

Crazy Ex-Girlfriend *and the*
*Destigmatization of Mental Illness*
*in the Era of Postnetwork Television*

## Margaret Tally

In recent writings about the increasing importance of television in the lives of American citizens, much has been made of the ability of television to serve as a kind of public space in which trends related to social change can be explored. For example, scholars such as Horace Newcomb and Paul Hirsch have looked at the ways that television can present narratives that allow individuals to understand public issues and, in this way, can serve as a kind of public forum for the airing of competing views about these changes.[1] Similarly, Jason Mittell has underscored the mutual influence of American culture on television as well as television's influence on American culture over the past sixty years.[2] Speaking specifically to the representation of women on television, scholars such as Amanda Lotz have noted how recent shows about women have helped to redefine narrative conventions about gender and, in so doing, have influenced the female audiences who form a crucial demographic for these new shows.[3]

In the current era of television, where there has been a proliferation of outlets from which to view an increasing amount and variety of television content, more controversial or once-taboo topics such as mental illness have also been explored, although too often mental illness is portrayed in negative ways that can contribute to further misunderstandings and stigmatizing of those who have mental health issues. Media in general

157

are often a source of ideas about mental health and play an important role in how society understands issues around mental illness.[4] For example, while news reports highlight that most violent crimes are committed by people with mental illness, the evidence indicates that only 3 to 5 percent of people with mental illness commit violent acts.[5] Recent diatribes from President Donald Trump about "crazy" people as the ones who are committing mass shootings only adds fuel to the ways in which people who suffer from mental illness are portrayed as being criminal and violent and also serve as scapegoats for larger social problems and issues.

In prime time television especially, mentally ill characters are more likely to commit crimes than other characters. One common character type is the psychotic male character who is a serial killer of women and whose violence is directly attributable to his mental illness.[6] Another familiar character in "must see" television is the male antihero who is portrayed as a sociopath, including such characters as Tony Soprano of *The Sopranos* (HBO, 1999–2007), Don Draper on *Mad Men* (AMC, 2007–15), or Walter White on *Breaking Bad* (AMC, 2008–13). Other shows that also portray "difficult men," such as the show *House* (Fox, 2004–12), which aired in the early 2000s, portray the lead male antihero character not only as having sociopathic tendencies but also as being a kind of "mad genius" as a result of his mental conditions. These shows routinely offer a distorted picture of mental illness, such as a depiction that equates mental disorders with creative genius.[7] More recently, female characters who have mental health issues have become a common character type on contemporary television shows. Several dramatic shows, for example, featured characters who suffered from eating disorders or were suicidal, including such shows as *Pretty Little Liars* (Freeform, 2010–17) or *Lizzie McGuire* (Disney Channel, 2001–4). In 2017, Netflix's *13 Reasons Why* depicted teen suicide in a way that ended up romanticizing suicide as a form of revenge for the central character's mistreatment and ultimately made her death look inevitable.

In other recent television series, however, there is an attempt to offer a more nuanced portrait of women and mental health issues. For example, the actress, playwright, and writer Phoebe Waller-Bridge created and stars as a deeply flawed and angry comedic character in the Amazon Studios series *Fleabag* (BBC Three, 2016–19), about a woman who is coming to terms with the deaths of her best friend and her mother. In the series, she is portrayed as a sarcastic and sexually adventurous woman in London whose grief and guilt about the death of her friend lead her to contemplate suicide at one point. In addition, HBO's *Insecure* (2016–), about a young black woman named Issa (Issa Rae) and her friend Molly (played by Yvonne Orji), depicts Molly entering therapy on the advice of her friend and shows how she struggles with her own success as a corporate lawyer. Other recent shows have also had female characters struggle with anxiety and depression, such as Netflix's revival of *One Day at a Time* (2017). In this version, the mother is a military veteran (Justina Machado) whose anxiety and depression lead her to take antidepressants. In *You're the Worst* (FX, 2014–19), Gretchen (Aya Cash) is portrayed as struggling with clinical depression, resulting in episodes that cause her to stay in bed for days at a time. She pushes away the people who love her at times when she is depressed and is also shown working with a therapist (played by Samira Wiley). Another recent Marvel Netflix series, *Jessica Jones* (2015–19), also has a female character who suffers from PTSD as a result of seeing her family die in a car wreck as well as being the victim of sexual assault.

Like these other series, the award-winning *Crazy Ex-Girlfriend* (hereafter *CXG*) also takes as its subject matter the mental health of its lead character, Rebecca Bunch, played by Rachel Bloom. The series, which in its first two seasons was arguably more light-hearted, by the third season took on a more dramatic tone that was built around Rebecca obtaining a diagnosis for her erratic and self-destructive behavior. The diagnosis was Borderline Personality Disorder (BPD), which then formed the narrative arc for the rest of the season. For the creators, Aline Brosh McKenna and Rachel Bloom, there was a sense in which they felt that while they began telling this story many years ago, it was something they "owed" to their audience to explain why the character of Rebecca behaved in the ways she did.[8] At the same time, by taking the "crazy woman" character type and deconstructing it with humor, musical comedy, and genre-bending storylines, *CXG* plays an important role in destigmatizing mental illness.

In discussing the ways in which the show upends traditional notions of gender and mental illness, this chapter will focus specifically on the third season, where the character Rebecca attempts suicide and is then given a diagnosis of BPD. Whereas earlier the show focused more on the character's anxiety and depression, the new diagnosis creates an opportunity for the show to explore this disorder and, in so doing, arguably contributes to the larger cultural conversation around mental health issues and destigmatizes them. At the same time, the fact that women are overwhelmingly given the diagnosis of BPD when they engage in behaviors that would be considered within the range of normal behaviors if applied to men, such as anger, sexual impulsivity, or feelings of emptiness, raises the prospect that in trying to be progressive about mental health issues, CXG ends up reinforcing earlier cultural stereotypes about women. While these are potentially legitimate criticisms, CXG has nevertheless been able to create a narrative space to rewrite and open up the discussion about women and mental health in a way that is liberating for its television audience.

### Revelation of a Diagnosis: "Josh's Ex-Girlfriend Is Crazy"

*Crazy Ex-Girlfriend*'s background as a series originally developed for Showtime but ultimately airing on the broadcast channel The CW informs our understanding of its boundary-pushing content. The CW president Mark Pedowitz explained to *Variety* that it was a "perfect fit" for its channel. While the show was originally conceived of as a half-hour comedy, it was refashioned into an hour-long format and landed the 8 p.m. Monday slot, paired with *Jane the Virgin* (2014–19) to make a comedic block on that evening's lineup. While the show has had some restrictions because it is on a broadcast television channel, as opposed to a cable or streaming service such as Netflix or HBO, there is a broad range of material that has been allowed to be discussed on the show. The CW has allowed the writers to cover a range of topics that were once considered taboo, including, for example, the topics of bisexuality and abortions, which are dealt with as normal parts of people's lives. The show has demystified the biology behind women's orgasms and referred to a woman's clitoris. In addition, it has spoken directly about women's menstruation, tackled women's body images, shown men as emotionally vulnerable, and portrayed mental illness in a respectful way. In addition to Rachel Bloom, *The Devil Wears*

*Prada* screenwriter Brosh McKenna and director Marc Webb (*The Amazing Spider-Man*) were the creative minds behind the show. Bloom also became the star of the series, playing a woman who gives up her high-powered job as a law partner in New York City to follow her adolescent crush who was now living in the Los Angeles suburb of West Covina. In picking up this show, Pedowitz described Rachel Bloom as a "breakout," and compared her to Gina (Rodriguez), the star of *Jane the Virgin*.[9]

In its first two seasons, CXG focused on issues around romantic love and whether it is healthy or not by looking at it as a form of delusional behavior that overtakes otherwise sane people. As part of this narrative, Brosh McKenna and Bloom were clear that while the audience could view Rebecca's behavior as "crazy" in a humorous way, she was struggling with real, underlying issues. For example, while some of her behavior was viewed as depression, as when she sings about being in a "sexy French depression" in episode 1.07, it was clear from the pilot that Rebecca had also dealt with a suicide attempt. Brosh McKenna describes the first season as portraying Rebecca as Julie Andrews in *The Sound of Music*, singing at the top of the mountain. As the seasons progress, however, she starts to "tumble down the mountain" and ends up repeating some of her old patterns of behavior.[10] By the third season, then, the philosophical question of whether love creates a form of "mania" that afflicts otherwise sane people is replaced by focusing squarely on the underlying reasons for Rebecca's actions, and the question of her mental health issues comes to the fore.

Rebecca's mental health problems are revealed in the third season when her friends stage an intervention to try and get her help after they recognize her destructive behavior. They had been given a file from Josh (Vincent Rodriguez III), who had in turn received it from another man (Trent, played by Paul Welsh) who was stalking Rebecca and who had incriminating information about her. The file revealed that she had been briefly institutionalized after a scandal years earlier that involved her ex-lover and professor at Harvard Law School, whose home Rebecca had set fire to after he broke up with her. In response to the intervention, Rebecca flees West Covina, and in episode 3.05, she ends up back home in Scarsdale, New York, where she is depressed over how she destroyed her relationships in California. Her mother Naomi (Tovah Feldshuh) tries to reorganize her life and writes a letter of resignation to her law firm White-feather and Associates, moves her things back to the East Coast, and gets her New York law firm job back. Rather than be angry at her mother, as she was in previous episodes, in this episode Rebecca is so depressed that she is willing to reevaluate her mother, going so far as to sing, "Maybe She's Not Such a Heinous Bitch after All!"

While in her mother's house, though, she is despondent and unable to sleep, agonizing over the actions that led to her move back home. The small details of her collapse into despair at her mother's house are revealed by showing her in a catatonic state and unable to leave her bed; her hair is unwashed and unkempt and she is obsessing over her sabotaged relation-ships with friends and with Josh. In this semicomatose state, she cedes all control back to her mother for her day-to-day functions. At first thrilled that Rebecca has given her the power to run her life, her mother is soon horrified to discover that Rebecca has been researching the "least pain-ful" ways to commit suicide on her computer. Desperate to help Rebecca get over her depression, she goes so far as to drug Rebecca's drink in an attempt to commit her to an institution to prevent her from hurting her-self. When this doesn't work, Rebecca decides to fly back to California, only to find herself so depressed that she realizes she can't go back to West Covina and, at the same time, becomes aware that she can no longer return home to Scarsdale. The self-loathing and sense of paralysis is at such a fevered pitch that she finds that she can't "buy things or do things or get things or do things or say things or face things."

While on the plane, these revelations culminate in the ultimate decision to end her life. She swallows a bottle of antianxiety medication chased down with a glass of wine given to her by a kindly flight attendant. The suicide attempt is not Rebecca's first, as in season two she nearly flung herself off a cliff when Josh left her at the altar on their wedding day. In this episode, however, the difference is that she realizes she has made a mistake and calls the airline attendant to get help.

In the next episode, "Josh Is Irrelevant" (3.06), the title itself becomes a way of revealing that he was never, in the end, the whole point of the series but rather a symptom of Rebecca's struggles around her mental health. She is hospitalized after the suicide attempt and has a new doctor, the hospital psychiatrist Dr. Dan Shin (Jay Hayden), who explains to her that, often after a suicide attempt, the individual can have a new period of intense energy. The most important dramatic and comedic arc in the episode becomes Rebecca's discovery that she finally has a new psychological diagnosis. The diagnosis that she is given is BPD. Dr. Shin then tells her that, unlike some other diagnoses, this one can't be treated with medication. Explaining this diagnosis, Dr. Shin says, "Well, a person with BPD is essentially someone who has difficulty regulating their emotions, someone that lacks the protective emotional skin to feel comfortable in the world."

In their discussion of why they chose this particular disorder to be the revelatory mental health diagnosis that Rebecca receives, Brosh McKenna and Bloom reveal that they brought in a panel of doctors to watch earlier episodes of the show and to make their own evaluations as to what issues Rebecca may be exhibiting, and they independently arrived at the diagnosis of BPD. The creators then attempted to offer the most accurate representation of what this diagnosis looks like, and in this way were able to humanize it for the audience by having a main character who has already generated sympathy and empathy from them find herself with this diagnosis. Her illness, then, unlike earlier representations of mental disorders on television, is not simply a plot device but a way to bring the experience of mental health issues to the foreground, and her character is not just a "spectacle" but a woman whom we have come to care about who feels as if she is "broken" when she learns she has this disorder.

One of the ways that the writers also try to show compassion for Rebecca is through showing the audience that even though Rebecca "has a diagnosis," this doesn't mean that recovery will happen overnight. On other television shows, when a character is revealed to have a mental illness, they might go into therapy, but they usually don't show what it is actually like to be in therapy and they also usually show that the character can be "cured." Having given Rebecca a diagnosis of BPD, the creators of *Crazy Ex-Girlfriend* instead show the audience that recovery is a process and that individuals are not cured overnight, or as Brosh McKenna offered, "It's a very long struggle, and a lot of people pass through it, but it can take a very long time—and Rebecca's issues are very deep-seated."[11]

The musical number in the episode, called "My Diagnosis," reveals how excited Rebecca is that she finally has an explanation for her behavior, instead of never really knowing which diagnosis might be the right one, or "What could be right? / Schizophrenic / Or bipolar light? I could really rock a tinfoil hat." Once she is told that she has BPD, furthermore, she is elated to learn that she is not alone, or as she sings, "Doc, prescribe me my tribe, give me my throng. Tell me this whole time I've belonged / with those other people who share my diagnosis."

Unfortunately, however, she ignores her doctor's advice not to look up this diagnosis on the internet and finds out that there is no "cure" for BPD. There is also no medication that could be taken to treat it. Rebecca then goes into denial over the diagnosis, because it has a stigma associated with it, and so she searches desperately for a new diagnosis. So, while she is first thrilled and relieved that she has a diagnosis, and that there are other people who have the same illness and that she can begin to "fix" herself, the reality that the show portrays is that a diagnosis will not solve everything in her life.

## Discussion

*Crazy Ex-Girlfriend* joins such other recent shows centered on women, including *Girls* (HBO, 2012–17), *Fleabag*, and *Insecure*, that can be considered "dramedies," a genre that combines comedy with melodramatic elements. These shows, which are considered "prestige dramedies," follow a line of earlier shows that starred female protagonists on cable, such as *Weeds* (Showtime, 2005–12) and *Nurse Jackie* (Showtime, 2009–15). These were then followed by other shows featuring strong women characters on streaming television, such as *Transparent* (Amazon, 2014–19), *I Love Dick* (Amazon, 2017), and *Orange Is the New Black* (Netflix, 2013–19). These shows all draw on the dramedy narratives that had been earlier associated with male-centered quality television, such as *The Sopranos*, *Breaking Bad*, or *Mad Men*. Julia Havas and Maria Sulimma have referred to these new female-centered dramedies as being informed by a "cringe" aesthetic that informs how the characters "negotiate the tensions between drama and comedy."[12] They also make the point that in a cultural climate in which female comedians have been continually subject to the persistent question "Can women be funny?" and in which humor has still been equated with men rather than women, these female characters have opened up a space to explore oftentimes serious subject matter with humor. They also, almost without exception, portray women who are going through heightened emotional states and struggling with mental health issues as a result of life-altering situations. Whether they are in prison, dealing with a parent who is transitioning from male to female, or wrestling with an obsession with a male artist, these shows are distinguished by their unwavering gaze on the ways that their female protagonists struggle to maintain a grip on their sanity.

From an industry standpoint, cable and online content providers such as Netflix and Amazon Prime, as well as the cable channels HBO and FX, have realized the potential of producing these kinds of female-centered dramedies with women who are often "on the edge of a nervous breakdown" as a way to increase their own prestige in the era of "Peak TV."[13] Borrowing from Jason Mittell's work (2015) on male antihero television characters in "complex TV,"[14] Havas and Sulimma have found that many of these female-centered dramedies are also able to adopt prestige drama's focus on the complexity of their main characters to allow for more depth in their portrayal of female characters who are facing profound emotional traumas.

This invocation of female subjectivity and complex characterizations through cringe aesthetics can be seen in any number of television shows that center on female millennial characters, including Issa Rae on *Insecure*, Lena Dunham on *Girls*, and Rachel Bloom on *Crazy Ex-Girlfriend*. Jorie Lagerwey, Julia Leyda, and Diane Negra have similarly described the rise of programs that feature female leads, including such examples as *Homeland* (Showtime, 2011–), *Orange Is the New Black*, *Girls*, *Veep* (HBO, 2012–19), *Scandal* (ABC, 2012–18), and *The Good Wife* (CBS, 2009–16).[15] In their view, these shows share storylines in which women's work and their personal lives are so interconnected as to be "conflated."[16] Moreover, they all live in a postrecession period where female resilience is identified with surviving within this new economically precarious world and where, unlike in earlier eras of television, long-term romance is no longer viewed as the most important feature of women's happiness.

At the same time that CXG challenges the heteroromantic focus of earlier shows featuring female protagonists, there is also a sense in which it is obviously part of another tradition, which Michael Newman has referred to as the "rom-comification" of the sitcom.[17] This refers to the ways in which many of the comedies in recent years on television have focused on romance and heterosexual courtship as their primary storyline. Such shows as *The Office* (NBC, 2005–13), *Friends* (NBC, 1994–2004), or *Cheers* (NBC, 1982–93) all contain a long-simmering romantic interest taking place over several years, and these storylines variously take the forms of unrequited love turning to love triangles, missed opportunities, or being with the wrong mate initially. Unlike these other shows, which make it seem normal to have a long-simmering romance, CXG challenges this trope by questioning the sanity and impact on the character's mental health of holding onto a romantic attachment indefinitely as these other shows do.

Despite the initial focus on the romantic aspects of Rebecca's behavior, then, the cocreators Brosh McKenna and Bloom knew they were trying to portray "the most unromantic romantic comedy possible." They were always trying to push back against the fantasy of romantic love and, in the third season, they did something that was "rare for network television: discussing a very specific mental health diagnosis, and suicide attempts, and sleeping with your ex-boyfriend's Dad."[18] They did this by showing that Rebecca's behavior was evidence of a kind of mental disorder that is set off by feelings of love for someone. This is a radically different reading of how romance is usually portrayed in our culture. In fact, romance and love are often viewed as leading to acts of heroism. By contrast, in the third season infatuation itself is understood as a kind of "trigger"—Bloom describes it as being addicted to the chase itself, and the term she draws on is "limerence," in which you are in a heightened state and feel like being with the desired individual is what will keep you alive.

More generally, this new attempt to humanize mental health problems and treat them with compassion is part of a small but growing trend in some recent television series, including such shows as *You're the Worst* and *Lady Dynamite* (Netflix, 2016–17), to take seriously television's power to influence audiences about a variety of socially relevant issues. The narrative transition in the series—from viewing Rebecca's behavior as due simply to being "just a girl in love" who "can't be held responsible for her actions," as the theme song from season two implies, to one where her issues are confronted head-on—represents, as Kelly Lawler has pointed out, a sea change in how mental illness has been portrayed in recent television shows.[19] Shows like FX's *You're the Worst* or NBC's *This Is Us*, where the characters exhibit chronic depression and anxiety, are part of this new wave of series that try to deal with these characters with compassion, even as the main characters themselves often invite mixed feelings from their viewers because of their status as antiheroes.

### Progressive Diagnosis or Antifeminist Backlash?

The responses to the revelation that Rebecca has a diagnosis of BPD have been mixed. Not everyone has been positive about the show's portrayal of suicide and the subsequent diagnosis of BPD. While acknowledging the show's progressive aspects, there is the potential for a backlash against individuals, especially women, who are given this diagnosis.[20] Borderline Personality Disorder has traits that are often stigmatized in real life, including having very unstable relationships, extremely emotional reactions to life events, and intensive anxiety about being abandoned. These traits, furthermore, are often associated with stereotypes about women and, in fact, about 75 percent of those who are diagnosed with this disorder are women. Earlier representations of this illness in popular culture included Glenn Close's character Alex Forrest in *Fatal Attraction* (1987, dir. Adrian Lyne), where the scorned woman was driven to destroy her lover's family with violent actions because she was so distraught at not being able to be with him. In reality, this disorder is often misunderstood, and it is even stigmatized by mental health professionals themselves compared to other diagnoses, with some mental health providers even refusing treatment.

The diagnosis itself, then, may reveal a kind of gender bias in mental health treatment, and the line between behaviors such as female anger and a diagnosis of BPD may be blurred due to cultural norms against women expressing anger or being excessively emotional. In thinking about recent mental health diagnoses in the general population, some analysts in the mental health profession have found that there is a trend toward diagnosing women with BPD while diagnosing men with narcissistic personality disorder, which is associated with gendered male traits such as selfishness or self-centeredness and lacking in empathy.[21]

More generally, while it is true that some of these symptoms are a reflection of gendered norms, it is important to note that there are also implications for Rebecca in terms of her feeling that her problems stem not so much from her actions as who she is. At first she is despondent that she can't just change her behaviors and, in this way, the bar is much higher for her than for a man, who might be counseled instead to go into a substance abuse program. This, too, is potentially stigmatizing, because it means that Rebecca, in finally having a diagnosis to hold on to, at the same time is traumatized by the fact that it is viewed as a fundamental aspect of her identity and thus not amenable to other forms of treatment that, say, anxiety or depression might be.

Other writers are much more encouraged by the portrayal of a female television character as having a diagnosis of BPD. Maggy Vaneijk has expressed her gratitude for finally seeing this disorder being portrayed in such an "understanding" way.[22] As someone who herself suffers from this disorder, she found that other shows such as *Homeland*, *EastEnders* (BBC One, 1985–), or *You're the Worst* have portrayed female characters with bipolar disorder, postpartum psychosis, or post-traumatic stress disorder, respectively, as dangerous or "scary ladies you can't trust." For writers like Vaneijk, however, the ultimate acceptance by Rebecca that she has BPD is revelatory because it allows her to have insight into her "inner self," which had been shadowed by the symptoms of dissociation, obsessive romantic love, or impulsive behavior. When Rebecca finally realizes that after two years of obsessively chasing Josh, whom she gave up her life in New York to pursue, "It's not about Josh. . . . Maybe it never was," this is a defining moment for viewers who also have dealt with obsessive romantic attachments.

For other writers, such as Angelica Jade Bastien,[23] the fact that the disorder isn't linked to other stereotypes about mental illness, particularly as it relates to women, is a real victory in terms of finally offering honest portrayals of mental disorders on television. She notes that men have long been portrayed in stereotypical and damaging ways in relation to mental health issues. More recently, female characters such as Rachel on *UnREAL* (Lifetime, Hulu, 2015–18) are now also portrayed as having autism-like features, and these characters often resist taking medication or going into therapy. That CXG offers a diagnosis is progress for Bastien, as are the ways in which it endorses seeking treatment for a mental health disorder, as opposed to earlier portrayals on television of viewing medication and treatment as somehow robbing an individual of their essential nature or personality.

While it is not a foregone conclusion how successful the creators will be in moving the needle on attitudes about mental illness, Brosh McKenna and Bloom have already arguably done a public health service by creating a television show with characters who are struggling with mental health issues and allowing them to be fully dimensional characters. As cultural critic Sadie Doyle observes about the service that the writers of CXG have done for their audience:

> It's a worthwhile pursuit, not just for people with mental illness. Every day, women's very real pain and anger is dismissed as "crazy," which gives us permission to put those women in the box labeled People We Can Ignore. If we can empathize with someone who really is "crazy," then we will have done something to broaden our definitions of women who deserve to be seen and heard.[24]

And, in an era when women are struggling to have their voices heard, the question of how to support women who struggle with mental health disorders is arguably more relevant than ever. Television has a role to play in educating the public about a number of social issues and mental health issues, which are experienced by a large portion of the population and are long overdue for a more public conversation to destigmatize those who suffer oftentimes in silence.

# 10

## "Let Us Ugly Cry"

### Spoofing Emotional Vulnerability
### in Season Three of Crazy Ex-Girlfriend

### Stephanie Salerno

## Introduction

A gay strip club where pulsing lights and dance rhythms do little to cure two fitness buffs' post-breakup depression. A psychiatric clinic where a woman scans a community bulletin board, eagerly reaching for a glittery envelope labeled "Rebecca's Diagnosis." A stark holding cell where a pair of egotistical lawyers give in to their feelings, letting their emotional defenses plummet. In season three of CW's *Crazy Ex-Girlfriend* (hereafter *CXG*), these settings become flexible spaces where reality melts away and musical parody blooms, allowing these four characters to encounter the consequences of emotional trauma. Rebecca Bunch (the "crazy bitch," played by Rachel Bloom) is plagued by persistent mental illness and misdiagnosis amid continuous family dysfunction; Nathaniel Plimpton III (the "metrosexual playboy," played by Scott Michael Foster) is distant due to childhood emotional abuse; Josh Wilson (aka White Josh or WhiJo, the "superficial gay guy," played by David Hull), negotiates the effects of childhood bullying through a fitness obsession; and Josh Chan (the "adolescent man-boy," played by Vincent Rodriguez III), a Filipino American, lacks a clear identity or direction in adulthood.

Parody, with its tendencies toward imitation and repetition at a critical distance, establishes the circumstances for the characters to address their damaged lives and self-inflicted troubles through a gauze of humor.[1] Stereotypes reduce these characters to mere tropes suspended within the liminality of queer time. Though they pass as healthy and functional, they travel along a nonlinear life path as the result of traumatic experiences and "failing" to adhere to socially constructed expectations.[2] In this chapter, "queer" describes how characters navigate their lives, deviating from prescribed paths and establishing alternative and nonnormative outcomes that empower rather than suppress them.[3] The "out of time" aspect of musical parody exemplifies the disruptive quality of queer temporality through glib lyrics, fantastical settings and costumes, and capricious musical styles. With underlying themes of failure, family trauma, and chronic depression,[4] CXG elucidates how nonnormative (traumatized, ill, and/or Othered) bodies express vulnerability along a flexible temporal spectrum that shifts between fantasy and reality.

An interconnected group who wrestle with the pitfalls of romance, friendship, and self-discovery, Rebecca, Nathaniel, White Josh, and Josh crash into emotional walls in season three. Though only WhiJo identifies as gay/experiences queer sexuality, all four of these characters live queer trajectories that complicate their ability to fit into heteronormative society. Rebecca swings wildly from vengeful to suicidal as all of her life expectations crumble after Josh bails on their wedding. Suffering from a major identity crisis, Josh regresses from an almost married man to unemployed and living with his parents. Nathaniel, the romantic foil to Rebecca's idyllic happiness, struggles with the repressed emotional trauma her mental illness stirs in him. White Josh, Chan's best friend, leaves his loving relationship with Darryl (Pete Gardner), Rebecca and Nathaniel's law firm colleague, when they reach an impasse about raising children together. For the CXG gang, singing and dancing erupt at points in their lives when their feelings eclipse stereotypical tendencies; typically rigid or oblivious characters express themselves freely, allowing emotional vulnerability to peek through previously erected walls. In the distorted space between fantasy and reality and along the spectrum of queer time, these characters acknowledge their traumas and embrace vulnerability, thus encouraging productive emotional journeys. In this chapter, visual and narrative analysis of three musical parodies, "Fit Hot Guys Have Problems Too" (3.09),

"A Diagnosis" (3.06), and "Nothing Is Ever Anyone's Fault" (3.13), illuminate how emotional growth in moments of personal turbulence registers as candid, earnest, and relatable to viewers despite (or perhaps because of) being couched in dark humor. Nathaniel, WhiJo, Josh, and Rebecca become vulnerable within the gay club, hospital, and holding cell as their inhibitions are stripped away via music/dance/alcohol, amid a medical crisis, or while under arrest. In these spaces, temporality is queered, or disrupted, allowing unexpected or "offline" emotions to be expressed.[5]

## Musical Parody and Trauma

Lauded as a "subversive show with a terrible name"[6] and one of the lowest-rated shows on broadcast television,[7] CXG is a musical dramedy that expertly explores serious life challenges, using irony, satire, and even slapstick comedy. CXG's musical numbers function as narrative devices, creating space for emotion to bubble to the surface and burst out of characters' mouths.[8] High stylization (both visual and musical),[9] visual markers that define characters, time, and place,[10] and the freedom to shift between "narrative and spectacle" firmly root the show in the musical genre.[11] CXG's parodies emerge organically from the "diegesis, the fictional world created" within the show as opposed to background music that stems from nowhere.[12]

Musical numbers break up the teleplay to signal loudly and melodramatically that intimidating feelings are about to be expressed. Functioning within a hybrid genre (dramedy), parody offers a levity that makes the darker aspects of CXG's narrative palatable to a wide audience.[13] Parody's tendencies toward satire and ironic "trans-contextualization," or situating one art form next to another (e.g., musical and teleplay), lightens the show's mood.[14] Acerbic humor and the presentation of canonical cultural material enable "a shared understanding between the encoder and the decoder."[15] For CXG's viewers, popular music parodies create touchstones for understanding across class, gender, ethnicity, and cultural experiences; the characters' emotional journeys are exaggerated on television but are ultimately relatable.

Childhood traumas, abandonment issues, and fear shaped Rebecca, Nathaniel, Josh, and WhiJo's emotional health and reactions to hiccups in life. Their bodies are vulnerable, carrying marks of emotional abuse as children (Rebecca and Nathaniel), low self-esteem (WhiJo), and a lack of a clear ethnic and spiritual identity leading to a stagnant adulthood (Josh). Because traumatic events are experienced out of time, the resulting "damage" and "destabilization" can be neither interpreted nor controlled.[16] The lack of closure that accompanies trauma ensures that these characters' responses to traumatic experiences in adulthood are self-destructive and rooted in fantastic ideations of appropriate/healthy responses. Building upon the idea that CXG's narrative exists within "crip time," or along a nonlinear and atemporal spectrum,[17] I argue that parody's disruption in linear time is a self-reflexive, queer temporal act that hits the pause button on reality and provides a private, emotional outlet for these characters. For example, the parody "I Go to the Zoo" (3.03) portrays Nathaniel retreating inward, imagining himself visiting zoos to fill his emptiness without ever leaving his apartment. In the parody he performs as an unflappable playboy who abandons the vices of the club to find comfort around exotic animals.[18] Similarly, while sitting on the toilet with earbuds in and puzzling over her new diagnosis, Rebecca imagines "You Do/You Don't Want to Be Crazy," the recurring season three theme song that parodies a singing talent show (3.06). With lyrics that include "Crazy is when I go off the rails / This is what you've done to me" and "Don't mess with a bitch who's crazy in the head," the parody functions both in and out of narrative time, establishing the tone for the season while signposting Rebecca's continuing struggle with her mental health.[19] Both types of interruptions intensify the parodic device that creates space for emotional vulnerability while also pausing reality.

## Analyzing Distorted Realities along the Queer Spectrum

A key strength of CXG is its resistance to stereotypical representations through satirizing the characters' range of emotions expressed and/ or repressed. The following examples represent a smattering of CXG's genre-fluid songs that reject stereotypes while permitting emotional expression within highly policed spaces (literally and figuratively). While Nathaniel, WhiJo, and Josh confront toxic masculinity at the gay club, Rebecca finds herself considering the meaning of personal responsibility at the hospital and later in a jail cell. Within these precarious spaces, Rebecca, Nathaniel, WhiJo, and Josh queer their one-dimensional stereotypical tendencies and convey emotionally accessible, human narratives.

"Fit Hot Guys Have Problems Too"

Bursting biceps, sculpted abs, and the pulse of electronic dance music set up episode 3.09's high-energy anthem "Fit Hot Guys Have Problems Too," a parody that explores male bonding across social and class distinctions. "Fit Hot Guys" proffers the gay club as a space for Nathaniel and White Josh, stereotypically attractive men, to lay bare their feelings as well as their bodies. While bonding in their misery after "mutual" breakups, a bachelorette partygoer tells them that their sour moods are "killing the vibe" and attractive guys "don't have real problems." Commiserating that no one understands them, Nathaniel and WhiJo slip into a daydream in which they become dancers on stage. Educating clubgoers that their sexiness does not negate their feelings, the pair declaim while go-go dancing: "Cause fit hot guys have problems too / don't look at us / we're not dancing for you / this is our quiet personal time to reflect / we both have almost no body fat / but we're too bummed out to talk about that."[20] As sexy guys, they are gazed upon by the judging eyes of society and unable to escape notice: "Everyone is at our sexual mercy / be them a mister or miss / but when we're down on our knees / no one has sympathy / because they only see this."[21] After ripping off their button-down shirts, a nod to strip-tease escalation and the baring of their emotions, they explain: "It's just hard to process emotions with our clothes on / our pecs are perfect but we have bad days / so don't objectify us with your male and female gaze / we have childhood traumas just like you."[22] Despite their outward perfection, these men are emotionally battered, and the male and female gazes that pierce them challenge their masculinity and freedom to express vulnerability. It's clear the audience in the club, viewing the men as sex symbols, misses the nuance in their strip tease: that exposing their bodies signifies an excavation of layers of emotional body armor.

Examining Nathaniel and White Josh's individual traumas minimizes their vast sociocultural differences. Nathaniel's fragility is rooted in waspy passive-aggression, repression, and toxic masculinity stemming from a web of lies surrounding his mother's mental health. The realities of his upbringing, coupled with Rebecca's recent suicide attempt, have shaken Nathaniel to his core; he is wrecked when Rebecca privileges her recovery over their blossoming relationship. Comparatively, WhiJo, taunted as a "tubby tubster" in childhood, embraced a life of physical fitness to combat the psychological scars of bullying.[23] In order to keep their emotions locked down, Nathaniel and WhiJo pushed their bodies past physical exhaustion, deprived themselves of nonsexual pleasure (i.e., junk food), and largely sought uncomplicated relationships. Nathaniel's outer shell begins to crack when he realizes he is attracted to Rebecca, who is far from the stereotypical trophy he typically dates, thoroughly disrupting the brand of masculinity he believed he needed to uphold.[24] WhiJo strives to live his truth, whether that means devoting his life to nutrition regimens or admitting he is not ready to be a parent. For this pair, queer temporality offers a respite from normative expectations as they realize they cannot escape their evolving emotions and must articulate their feelings within a culture that champions toxic masculinity and the silencing of male pain.

As Nathaniel and WhiJo wrestle with their exposed bodies and feelings (pleading during a musical interlude for the audience to give them back their shirts), Josh Chan appears on stage dressed as a sexy fireman. Recognizing an intrusion to their fantasy, WhiJo asks, "Hold on, are you actually here? Like, in reality?" Josh explains that he's a go-go dancer at the club, and not a "volunteer fireman" as he described earlier in the episode.[25] A perpetual adolescent, Josh frequently refers to himself as a "big boy," clinging to dead-end jobs, fearing commitment, and living with maternal figures. His entanglement with Rebecca reinforced his identity struggles, and his refusal to fully engage with reality after their breakup rooted him to the queer spectrum. It is only at the club, nearly naked, that Josh is able to reveal that he's unhappy.

In this liminal and pivotal moment, the trio recognize one another's similarities and muster a sense of community that encourages empathy. Despite inequality on economic, educational, and social levels, the trio's empathy is built upon the setbacks and deviations from prescribed paths in their lives and the rejection of toxic masculinity. The unpredictability of queer temporality connects them as they focus for the first time on *their unhappiness*, not someone else's (usually Rebecca's). "Fit Hot Guys" parodies the gay club scene's penchant for dancing and spectacle and the stereotypical suppression of male tears. Whereas traditional gender roles and negative responses to male vulnerability yield judgment and presumptions of weakness, within their common fantasy the gay club stage becomes a space of sincerity amid a culture of superficiality. Earnestly, the three men sing: "Leave us alone / we have to twerk out our sad. / We're expressing our pain through the art of dance / but we'll express so much better without these pants / there's so much pressure when you're a fit hot guy / so just let us ugly cry."[26] Nathaniel, WhiJo, and Josh are able to express themselves within the fictional space because their "fit, hot" bodies conform to the expectations of clubgoers. Passing as three hunks with only sex on their minds, the trio uses stereotyping as a shield, bonding with one another, safely succumbing to vulnerability, and unloading their pain in a cathartic, constructive manner in a space that embraces candor and zeal.

When the parody shifts back to normative time, the men are seated at the bar ugly crying, a queer act that resists normative expressions of male grief. For all three, the act of stripping was a method of divesting themselves of their emotions in the present, rejecting the toxic masculinity that permeates the club. From tango to ballet to tap to pole dancing, all styles of dance featured in the series, turning to the "art of dance" transforms emotions into movement that communicate feelings too complex to articulate through speech. Theorized as an "extended closet," gay clubs are at once communal, public, and private, upholding the tensions of LGBTQ* identity and assumptions about safety.[27] By using their bodies to express pain, the men queer the reductive expectations the bachelorette party thrust upon them at the beginning of the parody—that the gay club is exclusively a place for fun and joy when it is actually a complex, multifaceted space. As such, "Fit Hot Guys" comments on the limited and/or traditionally queer public spaces that men are given to fully express their pain.

*"A Diagnosis" and "Nothing Is Ever Anyone's Fault"*

While "Fit Hot Guys" challenges toxic masculinity, "A Diagnosis" and "Nothing Is Ever Anyone's Fault" challenge the notion of responsibility. Distorted reality connects the parodies, acting as thematic bookends to Rebecca's and Nathaniel's journeys: one that begins by unearthing repressed trauma and ends with the pair baring their souls to one another without pretense at last. If "A Diagnosis" asks the question "who am I?," then "Nothing" answers with a frank presentation of Rebecca's and Nathaniel's warped understanding of responsibility and consequences. "A Diagnosis" is Rebecca's identity anthem as she, post–suicide attempt, looks to a new diagnosis to define herself. Though Nathaniel is not part of the parody, his persistent attempts to excavate repressed memories and emotions about his mother's suicide attempt complement Rebecca's journey to know "what" she is. In "Nothing," Rebecca finally reaches a point where the urge to be responsible wins (though the function of the parody is to remove blame from themselves), just as Nathaniel pronounces his love for her, urging her to plead insanity to save herself. The excavation of traumatic wounds in these parodies acts as a narrative leitmotif across the second half of season three. Highlighting their past and future on the queer temporal spectrum elucidates the fractured process of healing and the emotional growth that has occurred between fantasy and reality.

The question/answer relationship between "A Diagnosis" and "Nothing" is connected through similar musical styles; both are classic musical showtunes of the "I Want" and "Love Song" varieties respectively.[28] Considering the variety of musical styles in the CXG series, this similarity provides thematic continuity among several major plot points, shifts in parodic musical style, and a narrative time jump. The parodies themselves are fairly minimalist in terms of sets, costumes, lighting, and makeup; it is abundantly clear that the narrative progress and emotional journeys of these characters are vastly more important than making fun of pop music, pop culture, or the frivolousness and camp of Broadway.[29] The parodies are designed to point out the ways that queer temporality affects vulnerable bodies, producing relatable experiences for viewers who also travel along the queer spectrum and reject normative tropes and social demands.

Following the show's most serious narrative to this point, "A Diagnosis" is a parodic performance intensely rooted in reality but tied to unrealistic expectations of wellness and recovery. In the aftermath of a suicide attempt at the end of episode 3.05, Rebecca sings this delightfully buoyant song proclaiming that a new name for the illness that has plagued her for almost thirty years will change her life. She begins the song in drab pajamas with flat hair and a pale face in her hospital room. As the scene transitions to her house, Rebecca reflects upon her struggle to solve her psychological problems: "And when I tried to find the reason for my sadness and terror, all the solutions were trial and error / take this pill, say this chant, move here for this guy."[30] A television moment later, she enters Mount Christine Outpatient Clinic, eager for her appointment in full makeup, wavy hair, and a sunny yellow floral-print dress, singing: "Doc, prescribe me my tribe, bring me my throng, tell me that this whole time I belonged with those other people who share / my diagnosis."[31] Rebecca's enthusiasm about a new diagnosis is momentous in part because she embraces the outpatient clinic, a stigmatized space, as that which holds the answers to her problems.

"A Diagnosis" reframes the clinic/hospital thus as a space that will free rather than trap her. Having been institutionalized prior to beginning law school, Rebecca and her mother, Naomi (Tovah Feldshuh), see the hospital as a symbol of shame and derailment from heteronormative goals. From Rebecca's standpoint, Naomi's house/New York hold negative associations (depression, anxiety, and loneliness), while West Covina represents new possibilities (happiness, friendship, and love). However, when West Covina fails Rebecca, her hospitalization marks a moment of regeneration as her California friends rally around her, upholding her original associations with the place. Rebecca's nonlinear navigation and reappropriation of traumatized spaces represent how queer bodies redefine happiness and success, becoming queerer over time because heteronormative restrictions and exclusions must perpetually be evaluated and negotiated. "A Diagnosis" is a moment of renewal and deliberate choice:

Rebecca gives herself over to vulnerability in order to regain a sense of identity within a space that has otherwise erased her individuality in the name of treatment.

Considering the lasting impact of emotional wounds, "A Diagnosis" emphasizes the deeply personal aspect and individuality of childhood trauma that follows one into adulthood. While Rebecca's suicide attempt was an expression of her total isolation and emptiness, a new diagnosis marks a moment of rebirth: a step toward understanding how her actions affect others and an optimistic desire to embrace community. In the parody, her former doctors appear, piling bottles of pills in her arms as Rebecca recounts the various afflictions she had been diagnosed with, including anxiety, insomnia, and sex addiction.[32] Her extreme reactions to situations over the years speciously label her as a "crazy bitch." For example, her revenge plan after Josh bails on their wedding includes mailing him poop, shooting a sex tape with a British lookalike, and suing him; her response to her former Harvard law professor/lover breaking off their affair was setting fire to his home.[33] However, Rebecca's reactions are not rooted in evil, but in the inability to cope with abandonment and isolation. She thus sees a new label as a ticket to fresh opportunities, a definitive identity, and a means to amend previous mistakes. Rebecca's readiness to understand herself, empathize with others, and work toward wellness is a queer act of reclamation within the type of space that previously ostracized and branded her as mentally ill, unlovable, and "crazy." When Rebecca's new label is revealed to be one of the most misunderstood diagnoses, Borderline Personality Disorder (BPD), her initial response is deflation and despair, the gusto and commitment to change of "A Diagnosis" forgotten.

Imperfect as her journey is, the conceivability of trying to get well is crucial to Rebecca recognizing that she is part of something larger than herself. Her nonnormative lived experience echoes that of vulnerable and traumatized bodies in the queer community who lack supportive families/mentors and do not see themselves represented in the world. Her tendency to internalize pain as a means of self-preservation is a relatable response to the traumatic events vulnerable bodies endure. In this sense, Rebecca's journey fits into a larger queer archive of nonnormative lived experiences. More than a "repository," the queer archive is "a theory of cultural relevance, a construction of collective memory, and a complex record of queer activity."[34] By showing the messy and exhausting process of mental illness, diagnosis, and treatment, "A Diagnosis" asserts a cultural statement about community and emotional support that transcends the show's limited audience. Significantly, this lesson ensures that Rebecca is able to make a meaningful change in her life, owning her mistakes and accepting the consequences with a clear mind and heart.

While "A Diagnosis" carries the promise of identity and belonging, "Nothing" presents Rebecca and Nathaniel with two options: blame everyone else or take responsibility for their lives. The final episode of season three finds Rebecca in deep trouble after an elaborate blackmail scheme orchestrated by Trent (Paul Welsh), former fake boyfriend/current stalker. Thinking Trent is about to murder Nathaniel and his girlfriend Mona (Lyndon Smith), Rebecca pushes him off a rooftop in her attempt to protect Nathaniel. Despite their complicated history, Nathaniel wants to represent her in court, admitting that he is doing so because he loves her. The resulting love ballad presents the idea that queer, or traumatized, bodies are trapped in adolescence because emotional distress derailed normative timelines and societal expectations: "Before I knew you / I did bad things and didn't know why / But now I know you / And I learned to look inside / I understand what makes me frightened and sad / so yes I do bad things, but are they actually bad?"[35] Rebecca's and Nathaniel's emotional immaturity stems from childhood traumas rooted in their parents' frigidness and adamant adherence to traditional gender roles. The stability that Rebecca and Nathaniel lack becomes a reason for their families to habitually reject their perceived failures, drawing parallels to the habits of nonqueer entities who perceive queer lives as off-track or directionless.[36] More than physical attraction or shared life goals, Rebecca and Nathaniel bond because they both play "adult" badly; their dysfunctional similarities and mutual understanding of their issues intensify their romance.

Despite the ridiculous stance that trauma excuses all bad behavior, "Nothing" marks the moment when Rebecca and Nathaniel bond emotionally, as opposed to connecting intimately through sex. The holding cell is a queer space because, despite its suppressing tendencies, it authenticates the emotional vulnerability and growth the couple are experiencing.

As a manifestation of emotional freedom and understanding rather than fear and hopelessness, the holding cell is a space for connection without pretense and where time is insignificant. Halfway through the song, the stark table and chairs in the scene disappear. Though the duet parodies the tenderness and melodrama of love ballads by becoming egotistical and self-righteous, the emotional vulnerability erupting out of these characters inches them beyond their comfort zones as their emotional paralysis melts. Rebecca and Nathaniel eschew the normative script of courtship, confessing their feelings out of time and in a surveilled space. While they blame everything from their parents to the Big Bang for their problems, they creep toward the reality that taking responsibility for their actions is an act of logic and an expression of agency.

Rebecca's and Nathaniel's positions of privilege and social/cultural capital ensure that they have been able to get away with treating other people badly and making mistakes that would jeopardize other people's careers (Rebecca blows off work for almost two weeks straight in her haste to plan her and Josh's wedding; Nathaniel carries on an affair with Rebecca, his subordinate, in the supply closet of their firm for months). However, even their agency and comfort cannot spare them emotional pain that eventually disrupts their lives. Rebecca and Nathaniel explore how their adulthoods are troubled because of their parents' behavior in "Nothing" ("we're all just products of childhood trauma / nothing is ever anyone's fault / pain causes anger and fear causes drama").[37] Whereas Rebecca's family life was chaotic with her mother constantly harping on Rebecca's weight and clingy personality as a driving factor of her father's abandonment ("I was brought up by a fat-shaming mom / Who made me take laxatives a week before prom. . . . Yup! / Now I overeat ever since that abuse"),[38] Nathaniel's relationship with his "dick" father "filled [him] with hate."[39] His family's refusal to talk about his mother's secret hospitalization after a suicide attempt when Nathaniel was young sent a clear message that emotions were never to be discussed, nurturing Nathaniel's tendencies toward shallow relationships, emotional detachment, and replacing meaningful relationships with sex, wealth, and status symbols. As both Nathaniel and Rebecca grew into adulthood, they veered farther from the normative expectations placed on them by family and society, becoming queerer like WhiJo and Josh. For Rebecca and Nathaniel, queer temporality functions as a brittle bridge between versions of their lives. They resist affirming their stereotypes ("crazy bitch" and "playboy"), instead connecting to one another via traumatic childhood experiences. After months of trickery, deception, and selfishness, the isolation of the holding cell fosters Rebecca's and Nathaniel's emoting, acting like a cocoon keeping accountability out. In the last scene of season three, Rebecca pleads "Responsible," or guilty, a bold act of maturity that promises to interrupt their love story yet again.[40] This ultimate expression of vulnerability and agency signifies the lasting effects of trauma that continuously interrupt plans and reshape dreams, yet another point of relatability between CXG and the queer lived experience of viewers.

## Conclusion

As a television musical, CXG shows how queer temporality can be expressed through both musical form and narrative content via musical parodies. Rather than continue to pigeonhole queer lives and experiences, CXG encourages an alternative dialogue (through song) about what it means to be a happy, healthy, whole, and mature adult. Rebecca, Nathaniel, WhiJo, and Josh are, at times, unable to appropriately and healthily process their grief, anger, resentment, and self-loathing. In these moments they eschew responsibility, commitment, and even self-actualization in order to present a version of themselves that appears powerful, content, and fulfilled in reality.

In their efforts to pass as "normal," Rebecca, Nathaniel, WhiJo, and Josh progress along the queer time/space continuum, following a parallel heteronormative track that society recognizes as appropriate or well-adjusted for adults with privilege, agency, and ability. But within their fantasies, their true selves emerge. "Fit Hot Guys" represents how men deal with low self-esteem and insecurity through the rejection of toxic masculinity. "A Diagnosis" signifies old scar tissue, emotional wounds, and the possibility of a clean slate through wellness and recovery. And "Nothing" tackles taking responsibility for one's actions, regardless of the scars that previous traumas left behind. As points along the queer spectrum, these three musical parodies connect experiences, explain behaviors, and bond these individuals together. Haunted by trauma, their futures are thus interconnected, dependent upon one another's honesty, emotional vulnerability, and patience as they each pursue a way forward along their unique life paths.

# 11

## Failure and the Family
## in *Crazy Ex-Girlfriend*

### Christine Prevas

REBECCA: Whatever this turns out to be, I think it could make me
    happy. Truly happy.
VALENCIA: But what if it doesn't? And I am telling you from expe-
    rience, sometimes the thing or person you think will make you
    happy, doesn't.
    —"I'm Finding My Bliss," *Crazy Ex-Girlfriend*

At the end of season three of *Crazy Ex-Girlfriend*, when Rebecca (Rachel
Bloom) has been arrested for pushing her stalker off of a building, she joins
her boss/attorney/ex-boyfriend Nathaniel (Scott Michael Foster) in song,
explaining all the reasons they are not responsible for their actions. After
all, they explain, they had abusive, absent, or emotionally unavailable parents, and the harm done by those parents is responsible for all the bad
things they've done. The song takes this premise to its illogical extreme—
John Wayne Gacy was hit by his dad, Hitler's brother died, and "nothing is
ever anyone's fault" because "we're all just products of childhood trauma"
(3.13). And yet, when the song comes to its conclusion, the overwrought
absurdity of its thesis—"Adam and Eve were messed up by God / Who
was messed up originally by the Big Bang— / Everything is the Big Bang's
fault!"—encapsulates one of the show's core themes. Among other things,
CXG is a show about people from unhappy families and the ways they
are maladjusted because of those families and the pressures exerted by
them. Through its examination of families and familial pressures, CXG

184

condemns nostalgia for monogamy, domesticity, and traditional success as an impossible way of life.

"Nothing Is Ever Anyone's Fault" utilizes a common rhetorical strategy for CXG's writers: in taking a truism about the world to an illogical extreme, the songs within the show act as a microcosm in which notions of normality and conventionality are destabilized. The viewer is asked to question their own assumptions about whatever facet of the world the song broaches. When the show turns its sights on the family, it illustrates a world in which children are destined to repeat their parents' mistakes, make mistakes in rebellion against them, or else aggressively break free of the cycle of the conventional family. Through its characters' twisted relationships to happiness, the self, and success, it illustrates the harm that familial pressure does to its subjects and twines together notions of success and the family. Often, TV families are swathed in an idealistic nostalgia, a sentimentalism rooted in an outdated model of the conventional "happy family." And even when they are not, they usually find their way to a reaffirmation of the importance of the family space. CXG has no such agenda: every family in the show is troubled. From Rebecca's strained relationship with her overbearing mother and the father who abandoned her, to Greg's (Santino Fontana; Skylar Astin) lingering resentment at the divorced mother he believes abandoned him, to Nathaniel's distant and unaffected parents or Paula's (Donna Lynne Champlin) insecurity based on her father's dismissal of her, every family in the show is unhappy. The show does not strive to redeem these families—to tell its members that they need only compromise, forgive, or do better in order to achieve the happiness they were promised. Instead, families in CXG fail, and an examination of those failures allows its characters the ability to pursue other ways of being in the world, free from the pressure to reproduce the conventional and painful families in which they grew up and the high standards of success they have inherited from them.

### Just Out of Reach

Failure is at the crux of CXG. Rebecca's plans never quite come to fruition, and her antics never quite go the way she wanted. The series is structured around the never-ending comedy of Rebecca's increasingly elaborate plots and their failure to have the desired effect. Ultimately, though, it is Rebecca's various failures that open up possibilities for her—whether it is the failure of her career, the failure of her many romantic relationships, or the failure of her numerous plots and plans, Rebecca's failures drive the show's plot and the direction of her life along with it. These failures are not the end of Rebecca's story, nor are they stops along the way to her eventual success; instead, they generate meaning in her life. They represent a failure that is not subordinate to success, but an alternate way of life. Failure is not an endpoint, but a possibility: as Jack Halberstam writes in *The Queer Art of Failure*, "Under certain circumstances failing, losing, forgetting, unmaking, undoing, unbecoming, not knowing may in fact offer more creative, more cooperative, more surprising ways of being in the world."[1]

Failing, as Halberstam writes, "can stand in contrast to the grim scenarios of success that depend upon 'trying and trying again.' In fact if success requires so much effort, then maybe failure is easier in the long run and offers different rewards."[2] Success, the ultimate measure of life and worth in an American society obsessed with winning and with winners, is an endless task: once obtained, a life must be spent in maintaining and retaining it—a life without error, without mistake, without any risk that might turn *winner* into *loser*. To embrace failure is to embrace a life of possibility outside the never-ending self-surveillance and self-policing necessary to retain success. For Halberstam, "success" in a heteronormative, capitalist society means two things: "specific forms of reproductive maturity" and "wealth accumulation."[3] A successful person is (re)productive, through both procreation and the production of capital, so that their success benefits their society. Thus, success can be measured against a standard of (re)productivity: How much money do they make? What kind of family do they create? What are they worth, with "worth" measured as their tangible benefit to their society? What materials do they produce and what values do they reproduce? Success is a generalized set of standards, a universal set of achievements or landmarks—metrics that cannot be adapted to fit the reality of individual lives.

Rebecca is not successful by either of the standards Halberstam posits. Though she starts out as a big-shot lawyer in a big-shot New York City firm where she's being promoted to junior partner, she runs away from the promise of her own success, abandoning everything to move to West Covina. Rebecca's lost success is literalized in the recurring form of her frenemy and rival Audra Levine (Rachel Grate). Their "lifelines have been parallel like corduroys," with similar upbringings, similar expectations, and ostensibly similar goals (1.13). Audra has everything that Rebecca once believed she should have. In season one, this is her Jewish fiancé and the promotion Rebecca turned down, and by season four, it is the perfect family-to-be: as Audra's mother brags, "She's having triplets. All boys. She and David had to move into an even bigger Tribeca apartment" (4.07). In comparison, Rebecca is a parody of failure: she has been left at the altar, quit her job as an attorney, moved into a murder house, and has virtually no contact with the baby for whom she was an egg donor. Audra is the specter of success, the ghost of who Rebecca might once have been. When, at the end of the fourth season, Audra "pull[s] a Rebecca Bunch" by fleeing to Las Vegas—"I'm just doing exactly what you did," she tells Rebecca; "I've actually secretly admired you for it for a really long time"— the show deliberately calls into question the validity of their competition and the validity of the success Audra has represented, and it posits Rebecca's failure to obtain conventional success as a viable alternative (4.15).

Despite Rebecca's desperation for success in work, in love, or in her life more broadly, her failures *do* something: they help her to understand the impossible standards she has always been held to, and they help her to begin to escape them. In *The Queer Art of Failure*, Halberstam discusses failure with regard to the 2006 film *Little Miss Sunshine* (dir. Jonathan Dayton and Valerie Faris); yet his conclusion on the topic could have just as well been written about Rebecca Bunch as about *Sunshine's* aspiring preteen beauty queen Olive Hoover. Halberstam writes, "While her failure could be the source of misery and humiliation, and while it does indeed deliver precisely this, it also leads to a kind of ecstatic exposure of the contradictions of a society obsessed with meaningless competition. By implication it also reveals the precarious models of success by which American families live and die."[4] Failure reveals the standards against which success is measured. When those standards are unfair or imbalanced, it also reveals the absurdity with which those standards have been set. Failure "allows us to escape the punishing norms that discipline behavior and manage human development with the goal of delivering us from unruly childhoods to orderly and predictable adulthoods."[5] This unruly disorder, this childlike playfulness, is the method by which CXG works. The show's wacky hijinks, parodied songs, and absurd situations are an "ecstatic exposure" of those places in society where expectations of success break down. From female sexuality ("The Sexy Getting Ready Song" [1.01]) to motherhood ("The Miracle of Birth" [3.13]) to career success ("Don't Be a Lawyer" [4.03]), CXG playfully takes those standards to their extreme.[6] However, it does more than just point out the societal flaws that obstruct success or happiness; it provides a radical alternative in the form of West Covina.

West Covina is not so much a destination as it is an idealized fantasy of escape—escape from the suffocating pressure to succeed that Rebecca feels in her high-pressure career. West Covina is a place steeped in failure, or at least in a kind of second-best-ness, always "just two hours from the beach!" (1.01). West Covina is presented in sharp visual contrast to the glamour of Rebecca's former New York life; our initial introduction is of graffiti, adult superstores, and street-side advertisements for buying gold. The promise of West Covina is that "true happiness is so near"—but it's also "where all of your dreams can stay just out of reach" (1.06). Happiness and success are always near but, much like the beach, a certain fixed distance away, relieving Rebecca of the pressure to pretend she has already achieved them. The ability to keep these dreams at arm's-length allows her to look at them critically and see them as what they really are: her family's dreams for her, rather than her own.

## The Unhappy Bunch

Television has long been a site for portraying and examining the "happy family." As Erin Lee Mock notes, families have been a central part of television since some of the earliest sitcoms of the 1950s—*I Love Lucy* (CBS, 1951–57), for instance, or *Leave It to Beaver* (CBS, ABC, 1957–63)—which "provided an ideal form through which to visit and revisit concerns about marriage and family in the postwar era."[7] These sitcoms portrayed the proverbial "happy family," the idealized suburban family of the mid-twentieth century. These serialized families remain happy because, despite their trials and tribulations, they always circle back around to happiness and stability by the end of their weekly timeslot. In these sitcoms, Mock writes, "women, children, and men all understand family happiness as both hard work and masquerade" in which "happy families [are] not easy or 'natural'" but achieved through a denial of that which threatens to make them unhappy, the shadows and tensions of abuse and fear carefully disguised to mimic normality.[8] Even in television that satirizes the nuclear family, there is a certain unavoidable nostalgia for the "happy family" that cannot be escaped. A show such as *The Simpsons* (Fox, 1989–), for instance—one of the series most famous for its satirical take on both the nuclear family and conventional metrics of success—still finds "its own odd way to defend the nuclear family."[9] Where *The Simpsons* may allow characters to fail, and may paint a less than perfect, more honest picture of the family, "no matter how much . . . the Simpsons satirizes or critiques the institution of the American family, the program continually comes back to reaffirm" the foundation of the family.[10] In CXG, the family is a deliberate site of failure, unhappiness, and possibility. The show works to dismantle the masquerade of the family, to express how hard the "happy family" is to maintain and what happens to its members when they *do* maintain it. The show is post–happy family—these unhappy families lie in the past, and rather than trying to reconcile or reaffirm them, the characters simply try to exist in spite of them.

This post–happy family critique is timely, as the happy family in contemporary America feels more like a myth than ever. The happy family has become just another impossible form of success. If success is bolstered because it is productive, then the happy family is bolstered because it is *re*productive: it reproduces itself and, along with it, those values in which it is based. Family, we are taught to believe, is the *good* "F-word." As inspirational speaker Troy Dunn writes, a "functioning, happy family is the greatest gift you can give yourself, your husband, wife, partner, and children, and really, the world. . . . When family members are devoted to each other, they are also good neighbors and good citizens."[11] Not only is having a happy, stable, functional family considered the best thing one can do for one's own health, well-being, and personal happiness, but it is also framed as a civic duty, a responsibility each person has to their community. Happy families are figured not just as the ultimate human goal but also as something we owe to the world.

The valorization of the traditional family, and the idea that families must be happy, successful, and productive, is a coercive ideal, rewarding those who conform and penalizing those who don't—"single parents, gay families, and other 'deviant' family forms."[12] However, marriage in contemporary America is a setup for failure:

> We have one of the highest marriage rates among Western countries: 90 percent of us marry in the course of our lives, only 5 percent down from the all-time high of the 1950s. Further, more than three-quarters of us think that marriage should be permanent and ended only in "extreme circumstances," and we have become more disapproving of extramarital sex than in the past. Yet, we also divorce more than people in other countries. We have more live-in partners, and we break up with them more often. . . . Marriage today is an optional part of life rather than a required one, but it is so prestigious that people try and try again.[13]

Marriage seems almost destined to fail thanks to the high pedestal on which we have set it, an impossibly romanticized goal in a world rapidly evolving out of the economic and social system in which it is frozen. Or, at least, the highly coercive ideal of family and marriage, the nostalgic model in which "it is not so much discussed as assumed that a family is supposed to be a variation on a productive marriage that features a husband, a wife, and children."[14] If marriage is destined for failure, then so is the traditional family and all misplaced nostalgia for it.

Happy families are, according to Sara Ahmed, "a myth of happiness, of where and how happiness takes place, and a powerful legislative device, a way of distributing time, energy, and resources."[15] Traditional families act as a "pressure point," bestowing upon their members an unwanted inheritance: the expected upkeep of the family's happiness and harmony. Those who refuse that inheritance, who refuse to go along with the masquerade, or who don't want that which the happy family offers, become what Ahmed calls "affect aliens," alienated not only from the family itself but from the society that bolsters it.[16] CXG's characters are affect aliens, isolated by families that are disturbed by divorce, distance, or abuse; traditional families and standard notions of success and happiness have failed them, and they are left trying to navigate the world in search of an alternative option. For many of them, their strained relationships against the flow of their families cause a disconnect with the world around them.

This alienation is most apparent with Rebecca, as her issues with her family are often presented as the root of her many problems. Her father Silas's (John Allen Nelson) absence and neglect are examined as the cause of her fear of abandonment. As her therapist Dr. Akopian (Michael Hyatt) realizes, "Your father's behavior in the past has set a pattern for you—seeking the love of men who don't fully love you back, men you have to pursue, men who are taken or emotionally unavailable" (2.13). At the same time, her mother Naomi's (Tovah Feldshuh) nagging is held responsible for Rebecca's perfectionism, her history of bulimia, and her overly critical perception of herself. Because Naomi doesn't hold back her criticisms, she becomes a potent reminder of all the ways in which Rebecca fails. She is there not only to criticize but to push Rebecca back onto the path of success. By season four, when Rebecca has failed by every possible standard her mother could measure her against, the absurdity of these standards is abundantly clear. She is the ultimate realization of the system that demands we meet every point in a long line of increasingly impossible tasks in order to be considered successful.

Naomi first arrives explosively onto the scene with the Gilbert and Sullivan–esque patter song "Where's the Bathroom" (1.08). Bursting into Rebecca's apartment, she criticizes everything from Rebecca's weight and eczema to the lack of vases in her apartment. The song is rife with contradiction: "Where's my purse?" Naomi demands, snatching her bag from Rebecca moments after shoving it unceremoniously into her hands; "Don't interrupt me! You're always with the talking," she berates Rebecca, after Rebecca has gotten out only a handful of words amid the barrage of her mother's constant questions; "You haven't told me where your stupid bathroom is!" she exclaims, though Rebecca has already answered the repeated question. Naomi, it's clear, is impossible to appease. Even if Rebecca were to succeed by every one of Naomi's standards, she would still be found lacking, and so we must question the validity of every one of Naomi's demands. Discontented with her daughter's career, her love life, her figure, her lax Judaic practice, and her home decor, Naomi leaves us wondering *what* Rebecca would need to do to fully be a success in her mother's eyes, and the answer appears to be: more than is humanly possible.

When Rebecca fails, Naomi turns that failure back on her as a measure of her *own* success. She frames Rebecca's failures as a direct reflection of herself, focusing on the way Rebecca's choice affects *her* reputation, bringing her pain and shame:

> So you want I should be known as the mother of a loser?
> Meet my daughter, former lawyer, now a failure, please excuse her.
> And you want I should see the look upon the rabbi's face
> When she learns that Miss Ivy League Attorney's a disgrace?
> [ ... ]
> In your search for happiness, you never thought of me.
> You haven't caused me so much pain since my episiotomy. (4.07)

Though Naomi is a caricature of the overbearing Jewish mother, she is also representative of the voice of society at large, both the pressure of success and the "pressure point" of the happy family. When she sings about her disappointment in Rebecca, she doesn't sing alone. A chorus of mothers come together to inform Rebecca that "Moms don't suffer tsuris and pain / to have their daughters bring them shame" (4.07). Naomi, perhaps, cannot be entirely blamed for her behavior: families are irreconcilably intertwined with the idea of success, and motherhood is defined by how well one raises their child. Naomi is just as desperate to succeed herself as she is to see Rebecca succeed. She is not blameless; she is complicit in the toxic environment in which Rebecca was forged. But the show allows us empathy for her by showing the passive-aggressive, competitive culture that surrounds her and the impossible standards to which *she* is also held.

*Crazy Ex-Girlfriend* is revolutionary in that it allows Rebecca to put herself before her family, even if it means losing them. Rebecca distances herself from Silas entirely after he comes to her wedding only to ask her to pay for his son's orthodontia, and she presents Naomi with an ultimatum regarding their relationship. Uninterrupted for once, Rebecca makes her demands:

> REBECCA: It's over. The old Rebecca let you manipulate her, but not anymore. I don't want your opinion anymore. I don't want your opinion on my career, on my hair, on my clothes, on my love life. Nothing. They are my choices, and as of right now they are off-limits to you. . . . Now you respect me and my boundaries, or we will have no relationship at all. Do I make myself clear? (4.07)

Rebecca is able to realize that, like success, this model of the family is hurting her. She is able to both imagine and demand a better alternative, one in which she can find support and companionship without the pressure exerted by the conventional family.

## The Un(re)productive Family

Rebecca is freed not only from the family she was born into but also from the expectation to reproduce the family as a social form through marriage and motherhood. With Rebecca's engagement to Josh (Vincent Rodriguez III) and their wedding at the end of the second season, Rebecca believes she has a second chance at the happy family she is supposed to have. She sees marriage as a way to repair her previous failures, as if starting a new family is a solution to the problem of the happy family she lacked. Her love with Josh is portrayed as a cure-all, the two of them singing, "Do you remember back when we had problems? . . . now our love has magically solved them / And there won't be any more in our future at all" (2.10) While the song lampshades (i.e., deliberately draws attention to) the unlikeliness of this sentiment, particularly for Rebecca, as a child of divorce—"Some say we're all repeating patterns taught by our parents / But that's just— No, that's not. . . . No, it's not" (2.10)—the two are steadfast in their determinedly optimistic outlook on the decision to marry.

Rebecca fully deludes herself into believing that her wedding will not only repair her life but also repair her nonexistent relationship with her father. She reprises a medley of some of her most self-loathing songs, including "You Stupid Bitch" ("You ruined everything / You stupid, stupid bitch / You're just a lying little bitch who ruins things") and "I'm the Villain in My Own Story" ("We're told love conquers all / But that only applies to the hero. / Is the enemy what I'm meant to be? / Is being the villain my destiny?"). Her self-deprecating observations transform into positive affirmations of how her life will change for the better: "You've gotten everything you said you wanted / So take a moment and take a breath / After today, you'll start fresh / And I'll finally be the hero of my story" (2.13). By reprising the moments in which she feels the most like an irredeemable failure, and by turning them into something hopeful, the song illustrates that she truly believes that getting married will solve all of her problems:

> But now that I'm a bride
> He'll look at me with pride,
> 'Cause my daddy will love me
> And then, in a wonderful way
> Everything in the past will just fall away.
> My daddy will love me
> And my mommy will love me
> And Josh will love me and then
> I'll never have problems again. (2.13)

Reproducing the social form of the family through her marriage to Josh, she believes, will not only promise her a new happy family but also fix the family that she has lost. Yet by the end of the episode, Rebecca has not only been left at the altar but also lost the father whose love she hoped to win back. What should have been the fulfillment of her childhood dream has been utterly destroyed. She has, in her own eyes, failed entirely, destroying her last chance at happiness.

### Putting the "Hap" Back in "Happy"

Accepting that happiness, like success, may be better just out of reach is central to Rebecca's journey. Throughout the show, people constantly tell Rebecca *I just want you to be happy*, particularly in the midst of her biggest failures. But if moving to West Covina is Rebecca's moment of allowing herself to give up on the idea of traditional success, the show encapsulates her journey of questioning, complicating, and personalizing the meaning of happiness. To wish for happiness is not as simple as it seems. Like success, happiness is also a manufactured goal constructed by a set of standards one must achieve: "living a certain kind of life, one that reaches certain points, and which, in reaching these points, creates happiness for others."[17] Rebecca's failure may allow her a better life, but before it can, she must also give up on this particular kind of happiness, one that aligns itself with the standards of success. She must, as Halberstam advocates, accept and express "a basic desire to live life otherwise."[18] She must escape a happiness that defines itself as the controlled and predictable reaching of a line of predetermined points.

Through the course of the show, Rebecca comes to understand the world in more nuanced terms, ones in which happiness and love and family and success are not the sole reason for her life. Failure does not make Rebecca happy, nor is it a painless experience: "While failure certainly comes accompanied by a host of negative affects, such as disappointment, disillusionment, and despair, it also provides the opportunity to use these negative affects to poke holes in the toxic positivity of contemporary life."[19] Rebecca's failures allow her to see the scaffolding that makes it so difficult for her to live in the world. One of these failures—during a theatrical revue—reveals to her the literal scaffolding of both the show and her life: the conventions of musical theater. "What if these classic musical theater songs that I've loved for so long and kind of based my life around are . . . bad?" she asks, faced with a sexist, degrading song about the worth of women, suddenly realizing that the model against which her life is matched is upholding the same standards that have been destroying her (4.14). Though the episode title declares her firm belief that musical theater will allow her to "find her bliss," what it truly does is show her that she has to write her own script in life, instead of following the one laid out for her.

Rebecca's new happiness is a different kind of happiness, one rooted in *hap* and *happenstance*, one that does not resist the unpredictable flow of life but embraces it. "Happiness cannot eliminate the hap of what happens," Ahmed writes; "Happiness means living with the contingency of this world."[20] Rebecca's story complicates not only traditional notions of a happy ending, as hers is thwarted at every turn, but also the primacy of happiness as a goal. When Rebecca feels as if she's reached happiness, something inevitably happens. *Hap* disrupts *happiness* as we would see it, and posits the question: What goals can there be, aside from happiness and success? For Rebecca, happiness and success are counterproductive or even harmful goals. Maybe the ultimate goal is taking life for all of its speed bumps, all of its setbacks, all of its twists and wrong turns, and finding the joy in the hap of things, without the pressure of what everyone else thinks happiness should be.

Rebecca's failures are crucial to her ability to accept a counterintuitive understanding of happiness. Failure gives Rebecca a new kind of life; it allows her to form a life in which each blow need not be devastating, each disappointment need not be the end of the world, each setback need not be irredeemable. It allows her to trade the fairy-tale image of the world she begins the show with—one in which she is destined to move somewhere new, have Josh Chan fall madly in love with her, and finally find happiness—into something else, something like Halberstam's "new kind of optimism," which does not "insist upon the bright side at all costs" but "produces shade and light in equal measure and knows that the meaning of one always depends upon the meaning of the other."[21] After all, even for the most successful people, the world is not black and white, and nothing is ever guaranteed.

To its very end, *CXG* remains committed to this questioning of what success means in a society driven by obsessive competition and impossible standards, and what happiness means in a post–happy family world. Though the finale is set up to provide answers and closure—after three last first dates with Josh, Nathaniel, and Greg, Rebecca is finally slated to make the choice that will give her the happy, successful future she's always dreamed of—it subverts its own premise, instead giving the audience a glimpse into the unexpected *hap*pinesses each of its characters finds. Each character's future carries its own surprises, far from what they would have once dreamed of: Nathaniel stands up to his father, quits his job, and moves to Mexico to work at an animal sanctuary; Greg, previously desperate to leave West Covina, comes to accept all the possibility of its decisive mediocrity. Each one is unexpected, drastically different, and, most importantly, not a perfect image of success and happiness. But each character takes a chance and lets the hap of life push them on toward their undefined futures. And for Rebecca, the finale refuses the neat and tidy endings of not only the romantic comedies it parodies but also the soul-searching dramas—there is no happy ending, only a gesture of possibility toward other ways of being. Rebecca's romantic fate is left explicitly open-ended, and so too is her personal fate: she has spent a year writing a song to perform, a song to help her understand herself, and the song is left unplayed as the final credits roll. If the piano and voice lessons of her flashbacks are any indication, it's likely that her song *isn't good*. After all, outside of her fantasies, Rebecca has never been a good singer. But whether or not her song is good doesn't matter. Whether or not she has succeeded is irrelevant. The show has never cared about her success: it has only ever cared about the real-life messes that happen along the way, and the new and surprising possibilities they provide.

By illustrating the absurdity of society's standards for success and happiness, CXG is able to break free of them, allowing Rebecca to move beyond and create her own alternate way of life. And in relating Rebecca's struggle to those of the other characters, the show universalizes this message. Even when Rebecca thinks that she is alone in her experience, when "no one else is singing [her] song," CXG puts her in "eleven-part harmony" with "the entire company" of the show to show how these standards are unlivable for everyone, not just for her (4.01). Each of the show's characters are allowed to fail and to find new ways of living—even if they are all just "products of childhood trauma," they "hold out [their] lonely hands" ("No One Else Is Singing My Song," 4.01) and come together in a unison of their desire to "live life otherwise."[22] Rather than reproducing the "happy family," Rebecca's friends and West Covina companions become a community of different rewards, which questions the pressures of success and embraces the *hap* of happiness, the absurdity of the world, and the craziness that comes with it all.

# Part Four

# New Feminisms

# 12

# Crazy Ex-Girlfriend's Female Networks

*From Hacking and Selfies to Taking Responsibility*

Marija Laugalyte

Although *Crazy Ex-Girlfriend* (The CW, 2015–19, hereafter CXG) is not fundamentally about technology, technology is part of the CXG world in a way that shapes the themes, storylines, and issues that are grappled with in the show. In CXG, the trope of the woman on the phone, or the technologized woman, features throughout, meaning that it is a show that is part of a lineage of cultural artifacts concerned with women and technology.[1] The trope of the woman using communication technology is one that pervades our cultural imagination, especially since the telephone was transformed from its initial designation as a tool for business and adopted by women to alleviate domestic isolation in the home.[2] In this chapter, I focus on the representations of CXG's female characters using technology, and I read these representations "as if in a female network."[3] Ned Schantz's conception of "female networks" describes connections between female characters in narratives that are "at once fragmented and technologically extended, operating around and against powerful men with all of their advantages, redirecting the flows of knowledge, money, and affect that maintain gender among so many other devastating social asymmetries."[4] To read "as if in a female network," then, is to direct sympathy toward these connections and to "return insistently to the forgotten interests of female characters."[5] Though the female characters of CXG do not suffer from oppressive male characters or neglected

201

interests, I look at how technology facilitates female networks in CXG to provide the female characters with a respite from the demands and pressures of heteronormativity. Whereas Christine Prevas has argued in the previous chapter how CXG reformulates "failure" to subscribe to heteronormativity into legitimate alternative ways of being, in this chapter I focus on how CXG binds negotiations of heteronormativity to female networks.

In particular, the female network that is constituted by Rebecca Bunch (Rachel Bloom) and Paula Proctor (Donna Lynne Champlin) holds this subversive aspect of operating as an alternative to heteronormativity. The network is initiated by Paula, who does operate within the domestic sphere as a mother and wife but is not limited to the home through her work as a paralegal and, in later seasons, her role as a law student. Paula is highly skilled with computers and uses her talents to help Rebecca seduce Josh Chan (Vincent Rodriguez III), the happy-go-lucky West Covina native and Rebecca's summer camp boyfriend from her teenage years. Even though this scheme of seduction is another focus on and creation of a romantic plot, on other levels, this scheme facilitates the two female characters to act on their desires and escape heteronormativity.[6]

This chapter highlights the productive aspect of female networks in CXG as they appear outside dominant circuits of value through reading "as if in a female network."[7] This type of reading recognizes a sensibility of "fabrication" inherent in female networks as they invent new narratives and worlds, rather than accepting the narratives that are dealt to the female characters at the outset of the show. We see this sensibility enacted through the scheming of Paula and Rebecca, who, in their pursuits, implement technology and technological skill—themselves symbolizing world-building. At the same time, the world of CXG is one in which social media maintains desire for the normative relations of heterosexual couplehood and certain forms of sociality.[8] Ultimately, the show turns toward a more conservative ending in which both Rebecca and Paula take responsibility for their own well-being, and their use of technology comes to symbolize this.

### Schemes of Romance, Female Affiliation, and Cyberstalking

The female network of Paula and Rebecca operates subversively in season one where together they hatch a scheme that serves purposes beyond heteronormativity. Initially, it is Paula who instigates the female network of the show by encouraging Rebecca to pursue Josh with her help. As the show begins, Paula's motivation to see Rebecca and Josh together is introduced as Paula's infatuation with love stories, but as the season progresses, it is revealed that the underlying purpose of the scheme is to become friends with Rebecca. Paula believes that their aim of getting Josh to fall in love with Rebecca sustains Paula and Rebecca's friendship. In episode 1.16, Paula confesses this worry: "If we are not chasing Josh, then you're not going to want to hang out with me anymore, I know it." Here, the "romance" interest in the show is used for maintaining female friendship by providing a common interest through which the friendship can flourish, especially from Paula's point of view. This "happily ever after" for Rebecca and Josh is strived for through Paula's implementation of technology; the scheme requires breaking into Rebecca's computer, Valencia's (Gabrielle Ruiz) photo stream, and West Covina's cell tower system, among other cybersecurity-cracking instances.

Though I focus primarily on Paula and Rebecca as forming a technologically enhanced female network, other instances of female affiliation through technological practices appear in the show, for instance, in the activity of cyberstalking Josh's girlfriends. In these moments Rebecca is portrayed as desiring other women that Josh dates without this desire being clearly delineated. Rebecca uses social media to establish an initial encounter with Josh's girlfriends: first Valencia in season one after their initial encounter in a supermarket, and then Anna (Brittany Snow), where it is through social media that Rebecca and Valencia find out about Josh having a new girlfriend. In the first instance, when Rebecca is acquainted with Valencia (1.02), she is initially infatuated and resolves to become Valencia's friend. Paula argues that the reason Rebecca desires to be friends with Valencia is because she, in fact, hates her as the competition for Josh's attention. Rebecca denies this, and indeed, the episode never turns into a story about women in competition for a man (though the episode does end with the two women on bad terms after Valencia discovers that Rebecca used to date Josh). Though Rebecca does not "cyberstalk" Valencia in this episode per se—her only online contact with Valencia is a short scene in which she "friends" Valencia on social media—the episode is dedicated to Rebecca's ambiguous desiring of Valencia, which continues in later episodes when Rebecca surveilles couple photos of Valencia and Josh online (such as in 1.07). As Bibi Burger and Carel van Rooyen point out in the next chapter, and Hazel Mackenzie discusses in chapter 6, much of this infatuation has to do with aspiration for the self or, in other words, "being like" Valencia. At the same time, however, the line between wanting to "be like" and wanting to "be with" is blurred in Rebecca and Valencia's relationship in this episode, even sexually with the "Feeling Kind of Naughty" musical number and Rebecca kissing Valencia in the club at the end of the episode. In episode 2.07, Valencia and Rebecca (at this point friends and housemates) cyberstalk Josh's new partner Anna. This common activity is parodied in the musical number "Research Me, Obsessively," a song about spending thirteen hours compulsively cyberstalking Anna through her various social media accounts.

In the instances of both Paula and Rebecca's scheming female network as well as in the cyberstalking instances described above, women use technology to gain access to other women from whom they are separated by heterosexual norms and narratives. In the former case, a romantic interest mediates Paula and Rebecca's relationship; in the latter case, Rebecca's curiosity about Valencia and, subsequently, Anna is mediated through a narrative of obsession about a past partner's love life. This raises questions about the norms and narratives that mediate female affiliation, but also highlights the practice of cyberstalking as a structure or genre that enables a form of female affiliation. Cyberstalking produces a situation in which a female network can operate, though only ambiguously, as it navigates dominant circuits of heteronormative values and logics, producing incoherent responses from Rebecca toward the women she cyberstalks.

## Hacking, Fabrication, and Irreverence

The technological practice that gives the female network of Paula and Rebecca its subversive character is that of hacking. The hacking Paula performs on computers—breaking into Rebecca's computer, Valencia's photo stream, and West Covina's cell tower system—is concerned with overcoming security barriers and resembles the practices of 1980s and 1990s hackers, preoccupied with overcoming security, passwords, and PINs.[9] However, Paula can also be seen as a hacker of earlier decades—the 1950s and 1960s—who were programmers and pranksters focused on reconfiguring systems (computers or other networks) in creative ways. Paula does this too when she hacks and reprograms the romantic relationships of the CXG world through her schemes with Rebecca. Through hacking computers and phones, and through her manipulation of the information that she obtains through this hacking, Paula gains control of the events of the plot in the first season, which she channels towards Valencia and Josh's breakup as well as Josh and Rebecca's romantic relationship. This agency of Paula's is exemplified humorously in the musical number "After Everything I've Done for You (That You Didn't Ask For)" where she enumerates all the ways that she has been manipulating other characters and their lives without Rebecca's or the audience's knowledge. In it she sings,

> Want to know all the things I've done for you?
> I broke into Josh's old high school
> and made copies of all his grades!
> I bumped into Lourdes at Starbucks
> and insisted you be a bridesmaid!
> I blackmailed Valencia's boss
> so now I control when she teaches!
> That's right!
> I make all the yoga class schedules!
> There's no limit to where my reach is! (1.18)

Paula can be seen to embody the character of the first generation of hackers—both Paula and 1950s/1960s hackers are focused on understanding a system, taking it apart, and putting it back together in creative ways. The practice of hacking offers a structure for the female network in which an impulse to take apart and recreate offers the ground on which a shared project can be used for fulfillment. In this way, the female network plays with and reconfigures the system of heteronormativity in CXG.

Thus, Paula's manipulation and scheming to obtain control over the CXG world and to change its order of things in the narrative works in tandem with her computer and phone hacking. The latter facilitates the former, but the parallel also works symbolically. Technology, in its broadest sense, can be defined as "attempts to shape the physical world."[10] Fabrication and creation through technology (as well as other means), thus, represents Paula's creativity and rejection of her world as it is, which is characterized by the limitations of domesticity and the effects of growing up with a discouraging father (3.07).

This sensibility of "fabrication" does not only characterize Rebecca and Paula's initial relationship but can be said to characterize female networks more generally as they represent that which exists outside of patriarchal arrangements of living and affiliating, that is, the traditional, normative ways of living. When Paula initiates her plan to unite Rebecca and Josh romantically, she fabricates a new plot, a new interest, a new trajectory that provides her with a friend and also de-centers the importance of Paula's family in her life. In reconfiguring the relationships around her through manipulation, Paula intervenes in her own responsibility-filled domestic life in which she is a mother and wife, roles she has no interest in (something noted throughout the first two seasons). Paula's representation as technologically savvy matters to Paula as someone who embraces this sensibility of fabrication and who is able to reconfigure and reprogram story lines.

Though the pursuit of Josh and the attendant schemes of Paula and Rebecca may be read as destructive, manipulative, and escapist, the productive aspect of Rebecca's and Paula's scheming must also be considered, especially as it is a creative force outside the acceptable and the normative—as noted by Schantz: "to resist a sadistic reading may be to license a little ruthlessness in others, particularly in female characters, the regular victims of masculine sadism."[11] In the same way that Prevas reads failure to fit into heteronorms as productive in CXG (chapter 11, this volume), I also frame the failure of female networks to fit into moral standards as productive of alternatives to heteronormative values.

The choice of Rebecca and Josh's love story as the endpoint of the female network's scheme must also be considered as the embrace of interests that are generally derided as feminine and, thus, often deemed as not worthy of serious attention. In fact, when Paula uses technology to facilitate the fabrication of the romance plot, to make friends, and to escape domesticity, she shows irreverence toward the masculinization of high-skilled technologies and exalts this often-derided interest in romance narratives and female friendships. Paula's taking up of this technology for the purposes of the subject matter of romance, categorized as feminine, challenges the patriarchal value system that demeans femininity, a value system in which "sport [is] 'important'; the worship of fashion, the buying of clothes 'trivial,'" as famously noted by Virginia Woolf.[12]

This irreverence toward value hierarchies is about satiating the interests and appetites of the women joined in female networks, rather than aligning their desires with heteronorms (for a further discussion of women's desires and their irreconcilability with desirable femininity in CXG, see Christi Cook's discussion of the *vagina dentata* in the last chapter of this volume). Importantly, because Paula and Rebecca are irreverent about their appetites and interests fitting into desirable femininity, their relationship should not be equated with what Alison Winch calls "girl-friendships." Winch argues that, in contemporary culture, many representations of female friendships are often bound to women's policing of other women's bodies. This creates representations of female affiliation that serve the surveillance and disciplining of women to fit into heteronormativity under the guise of friendship and "empowerment."[13] However, the female network constituted by Paula and Rebecca in season one provides a model of female affiliation that is focused on the women's desires, not their disciplining, providing a model of friendship operating outside the norms of Winch's policing girlfriendships.

## Fabrication versus Deconstruction and Revealing

The sensibility of fabrication, however, does not dominate the vision of CXG. It exists alongside a discourse of "revealing" and "uncovering" what is already present, though not evidently visible. This revealing or deconstructing tendency is evident when Paula's interest in Rebecca and Josh as a couple is revealed as a desire for female friendship, which is then revealed to be a desire for escape from her own limited domestic life. This idea that much of what we see hides some more profound desires is reflected in Rachel Bloom's description of the show: "The show has always been about the pursuit of happiness and how do you figure out what you really, really want in your life and not what other people expect you to want."[14] The show itself has much to do with deconstructing in a manner that promises to reveal a truth behind a façade or a stereotype. As a television show, CXG is highly self-referential, and its very basis hinges on the promise to deconstruct stereotypes and to play on the audiences' expectations and their points of reference (see Salerno's discussion of stereotypes in chapter 10). Likewise, as it deconstructs stereotypical plots, it also plays a part in the deconstruction of character desires and motivations, peeling away false desires to reveal more "truthful" ones. For instance, the show presents us with the narrative of a female protagonist who moves cities for love—narratives figuring in previous female-centered television series such as Ally McBeal (Fox, 1997–2002) and Felicity (The WB, 1998–2002). This logic is then undone when love is shown to be a focus that has been covering up Rebecca's search for fulfillment and reconciliation with her past and present. The premise of the show is that female-centered television series often stereotype women and their motivations and do not reflect women's actual experiences or desires. The initial move to another city for love by a female protagonist as well as other stereotypes of women that center on romance, marriage, and motherhood are, in many ways, challenged in the show, where TV's female characters' "traditional" motivations are replaced by those centering on female friendships and one's own psyche. The clearest example is Rebecca's diagnosis of Borderline Personality Disorder (BPD) in season three, which leads to Rebecca's realization that her fixation on Josh was a symptom of her mental state, a turn of events foreshadowed by the title of the show. Desire for a romantic relationship is "figured out" as being only a mask for Rebecca's desire for better mental health.

Fabrication is about creating newness, whereas deconstruction is about revealing "truth" that is not evident or covered up by falsehood. Fabrication is artistic and appeals to fantasy, new worlds, and imagination, whereas deconstruction appeals to claims of hidden truths, to origins, to reality and reason pertaining to taking things apart and explaining how they operate. In CXG, both discourses exist, with fabrication holding a predominant place as Paula and Rebecca scheme in season one, and with the discourse of deconstruction taking over in subsequent seasons as the characters of CXG develop and take responsibility for their lives. Though the discourse of deconstruction still produces an alternative to what is first presented to us, it has a quality of determining what *is* and the way things must be. Thus, it lacks the creative life-building quality of fabrication of Paula and Rebecca's female network, meaning the show moves toward a more deterministic attitude than it begins with.

### Norms and Social Media

But technology in CXG does not only benefit female networks through facilitating connection and this sensibility of fabrication. Social media also creates an environment in which a more individualist practice of self-promotion perpetuates the very norms that female networks attempt to overtake in the show. Several episodes take up this theme of self-promotional culture around social media: in 1.10 Josh takes selfies throughout the episode hoping to increase his "LPP's" ("likes per post"); and in 2.07 Rebecca and Valencia spend thirteen hours cyberstalking Anna's social media profiles. Besides moments where characters call attention to social media through their dialogue, goals, and musical numbers, social media appears as part of the fabric of the CXG world, and these media reveal the normative desires and aspirations such as heterosexual coupledom and popularity.

Throughout the show, characters check other characters' social media accounts, and, in so doing, both the consumption of the social media images and the performance that is captured in the images delineates what is desirable.[15] For instance, when Rebecca sees a selfie of Josh and Valencia in Hawaii, smiling with their arms around each other, Rebecca is negatively affected and falls into a spell of depression for the rest of the episode, and she tries to alleviate the symptoms with casual sex, pills, and marijuana (1.07). In a similar moment in 1.02, Paula is shown staying after hours at work and scrolling through pictures on social media after Rebecca cancels their plans to go to the *Spider's* nightclub with Josh and Valencia. She looks at selfies of Rebecca and Valencia while snacking and avoiding phone calls from her family. And in episode 2.06, Rebecca's boss Darryl (Pete Gardner) and her colleague Maya (Esther Povitsky) feel left out after seeing social media images of Rebecca's new "girl group"—consisting of her roommate Heather (Vella Lovell) and Valencia.

In these instances, pictures of socializing, specifically the couple or group selfie, induce unhappiness in characters who are excluded from that which is documented and posted on social media. In this episode, Darryl observes this exclusion when he tells Rebecca that her girl group's social media photos might make her other close friends, meaning himself, feel left out. As Mary McGill observes, "Social media commodifies and exacerbates our need to belong, filling our gaze with idealized images that gain a large part of their power through exclusion,"[16] indicating the centrality of "exclusion" to social media's flows of desire.

This exclusion that invokes desire and unhappiness in its spectators is constructed through characters' performance in the production of these social media images. In these productions, a compulsory "happiness filter" dictates that the performance captured in a social media image express the good life, success, and happiness. This "filter" is not the digital coloring of social media images through editing. Rather, it refers to all the factors that render the social media image into one that expresses heteronormative success, like the bodily performance of happiness by the subject of the image, the absence of which is used to show conflict in the show. As Sara Ahmed notes, "Happiness is used to justify social norms as social goods," meaning that social media is a component of the world of CXG that reproduces the normative both by the limited array of subject matter deemed worth social media documentation as well as by the "happiness" filter that accompanies these images.[17] For example, in "I'm Back at Camp with Josh" (1.10), Rebecca's absent smile in the selfie that Josh takes of them at Blowie Point signifies her heartbreak after Josh laughs at her love letter. And in 2.06, Paula is reluctant to join the selfie that Rebecca tries to take of the "gurl group," which conveys their troubled friendship in this episode. Otherwise, "happy" is the norm for social media image production and conveys the absence of conflict.

Moreover, social media's images are usually limited to documenting heterosexual coupledom and desirable sociality in CXG. These contents are then bound to the happiness filter. For instance, being in a heterosexual couple is never framed in online images in relation to negative feelings, only positive ones. The show, however, presents this vision of the online world critically. When Josh and Rebecca finally consummate their relationship in season two, they perform their relationship through taking selfies. As they document their smiling faces pressed up against each other, Heather enters the room and, upon seeing Rebecca and Josh posing for a selfie, comments that their behavior may be hiding their insecurity about the relationship (2.10), offering an alternative reality behind the happy couple selfie.[18]

The happiness frame around social media documentation shows how heterosexual coupledom and popularity/having many friends is a norm in CXG that is a point of both desire and unhappiness for the characters in the show. Social media is bound with specific norms that then dictate happiness. We see this in the shifts in Rebecca's mood depending on what she sees on social media in relation to Josh and in her insistence on documenting online her relationship with Josh and her friends framed in a positive light throughout the first two seasons. We also see characters who long to partake in social situations that, as they learn through social media, they have been left out of. This amounts to a connection between how social media mediate couplehood, friendship, and popularity; other signifiers of success and happiness; and Rebecca's and other characters' mental states.

## Responsibilization of Technology

As the show progresses, both women take on (or realize that they must take on) responsibility for themselves in their everyday life, and technology's employment, too, begins to mirror this goal of becoming responsible for the self. Rebecca's use of Skype to contact Valencia and Heather (4.06) after they move away from West Covina signifies Rebecca's learning to handle changing circumstances in her life. Similarly, her decision to go on "the dating apps" (also in 4.06) signifies Rebecca's growing security in herself. Importantly, Paula abandons her hacking and the sensibility of fabrication to study for her bar exams in the pursuit of becoming a lawyer. Technology is not being used here to create alternative projects that do not fit into heteronorms as in Paula and Rebecca's scheme in season one; instead technology is employed to strive toward aspirational and normative achievements and ways of coping. It becomes associated with Rebecca's adaptation to life and to change as well as with her learning to live with BPD, and for Paula, technology becomes a part of her focus on her own life and career.

Contrasting the first season with later seasons, desires focused on initially (friendship, fantasy, and reprieve from everyday familial and work life) are revealed to be superficial compensations for "actual" desires, especially through (the technology of) therapy in Dr. Akopian's (Michael Hyatt) and Dr. Shin's (Jay Hayden) offices. The desires and schemes that have been pursued by the female characters throughout the first season are seen as fabrications of Rebecca's as well as Paula's psyches. A search for a root cause, for the "real" cause of unhappiness, becomes the focus of the show, rather than a playful scheming of achieving and creating a romantic plot. The show ultimately presents characters who desire, who desire wrongly, and who must be fixed. In this way, the sensibility/ethics of fabrication and artifice is denounced. Instead, as the show comes to a close with the fourth season, the female network, or at least its creative fabricating aspect, can be said to dissipate as the women take responsibility for their own lives. The discourses of mental health and therapy play a part in this education of norms and what it means to act responsibly as Rebecca sees her therapist Dr. Akopian and undergoes treatment for BPD with Dr.

Shin. Winch notes that "because health is a cultural ideal, the inability to be healthy . . . is the failure to be normative."[19] Hence, Rebecca's negotiation with her BPD diagnosis must be read as a negotiation of norms. However, Rebecca's learning of healthy, but also normative, behaviors and ways to cope with her unhappiness and her disorder lead her away from the creative energy of female networks and toward more conventional and normative ways of living and coping with her life.

## Conclusion

Using the concept of reading "as if in the female network" to analyze CXG highlights how a sensibility of fabrication, through technology, scheming, and creation of alternative storylines by the female characters, facilitates an alternative trajectory to that of heteronormativity. However, because the female network is bound to negative valuations and failings of personhood (obsession and stalking), it must be forsaken. Instead, to reach life satisfaction, Paula and Rebecca take "responsibility" for the self. Thus, the female network that holds alternative values to a self-responsible individuality ceases in the show when the women embrace normative paths to satisfaction. At the same time, the technological world of CXG is constituted by a social media–normativity complex in which social media images and norms are wedded and influence characters to desire the norms that social media perpetuates, envisioning social media as synonymous with heteronormativity.

This reflection on how technology and gender intersect in the world of CXG leads to a mapping of desire where different technological practices in the show highlight the different routes to fulfilment that exist in the CXG world. Perhaps most significantly, it poses key questions: To what extent does technology construct our discourses and narratives of desire, happiness, and fulfillment? And how much does technology have to do with, as Rachel Bloom says, "what [we] really really want"?

# 13

# "Put Yourself First in a Sexy Way"

## *Metamodernist Feminism in* Crazy Ex-Girlfriend

### Bibi Burger and Carel van Rooyen

## Introduction

Contemporary notions of feminism seem to be informed by either second wave feminism (which can be likened to a modernist paradigm) or post-feminist ideas of empowerment through self-stylization (associated with postmodernist sensibilities). We argue that these contradicting modes of thinking within feminism are explored in *Crazy Ex-Girlfriend* (hereafter CXG), which we analyze in terms of the oscillation described by Timotheus Vermeulen and Robin van den Akker in "Notes on Metamodernism."[1] They describe a pendulum-like movement between modernist and postmodernist ideas as characteristic of contemporary art and culture, and they term this phenomenon "metamodernism." Vermeulen and Van den Akker's (European) metamodernism can be used to understand the ways in which CXG not only acknowledges and portrays the sway of the postfeminist aesthetic but also criticizes it by pointing to the patriarchal structures influencing it. We first provide a background on theories surrounding metamodernism and bring it into dialogue with feminist debates in contemporary popular culture before launching into a discussion of "The Sexy Getting Ready Song" (from episode 1.01) and "Put Yourself First" (1.10).

Whereas postmodern philosophy, art, and popular culture are generally associated with cynicism, irony, and nihilism, Vermeulen and Van den Akker claim that the contemporary zeitgeist is characterized by "a (often guarded) hopefulness and (at times feigned) sincerity."[2] They analyze the works of Jacques Herzog and Pierre de Meuron, Bas Jan Ader, David Thorpe, Kaye Donachie, and Michel Gondry to assert that a metamodernist ideology underlies these artists' works:

> Ontologically, metamodernism oscillates between the modern and the postmodern. It oscillates between a modern enthusiasm and a postmodern irony, between hope and melancholy, between naïveté and knowingness, empathy and apathy, unity and plurality, totality and fragmentation, purity and ambiguity.[3]

Seth Abramson claims that European metamodernism focuses on the in-between, the oscillation between qualities associated with modernism and those associated with postmodernism.[4] In contrast, North American metamodernism is underpinned by an assumption that the opposition between these qualities can be transcended. Abramson relates this assumption to "the self-mythologizing drive that typifies the American ethos and much of American history."[5] While CXG is a North American television show, we are of the view that the ways in which issues of gender are explored in the show relates more to the metamodernism of Vermeulen and Van den Akker than the American metamodernism described by Abramson. A song such as "Put Yourself First," which we discuss in detail later in this chapter, does not represent a transcendence of oppositions within contemporary pop culture and its relationship to gender but rather describes those oppositions as an impasse.

The concept of metamodernism has been influential, but thus far very little has been written on the implications and potentialities of metamodernism for understanding gender. We address this by arguing that aspects of CXG, and especially the song "Put Yourself First" are manifestations of oscillations within contemporary feminism, and that the concept of metamodernism can help us understand contradictions and debates within feminism.

## Metamodernism and Feminism

Only a few studies bring Vermeulen and Van den Akker's work into dialogue with gender studies. Griffin Hansbury and Hilary Offman use Vermeulen and Van den Akker's focus on the oscillations between "postmodern detachment" and "modern commitment" to understand their transgender patients' desire to both transcend gender binaries (in a postmodern way) but also to conform to certain modernist essentialist gender identities.[6] James B. Cronin et al. refer to Vermeulen and Van den Akker to explain the paradoxical aspects of "women's food-related behaviours."[7] They argue that women "in their production of 'homey hyper-reality' can be seen as performatists attempting to negotiate the two opposite poles of past and present through the use of food."[8]

Gry Rustad comes perhaps the closest to using metamodernism in the way we have in mind.[9] Rustad contrasts Zooey Deschanel's character, Jess, on the sitcom *New Girl* (Fox, 2011–18) with the characters in the film *Me and You and Everyone We Know* (2005) and the character of Leslie Knope (Amy Poehler) in the sitcom *Parks and Recreation* (NBC, 2009–15). Rustad concludes that the representation of Jess on *New Girl* cannot be considered metamodernist because it ultimately corresponds to a postfeminist celebration of consumerism and self-stylization (albeit in a different form than in "girl power" narratives).[10] She contends that Leslie is portrayed as a character with what is traditionally considered "second wave" ideals *as well as* a postfeminist enthusiasm for self-stylization. Leslie can therefore be considered a metamodern feminist because of how her character is "constantly oscillating between different poles of femininity."[11]

Rustad thus uses Vermeulen and Van der Akker's analysis of oscillations between modern and postmodern ideals to analyze a similar oscillation between aspects associated with second wave feminism and those associated with postfeminism. Second wave feminism cannot be equated with modernism—and in fact sometimes involves a critique of modernism's ideals and practices (see Rita Felski's "Feminism, Postmodernism, and the Critique of Modernity").[12] It does, however, share the "hopefulness" (and implicit belief in progress and truth) that Vermeulen and Van den Akker associate with modernism.[13] Correspondingly, postfeminism cannot be equated with postmodernism, but does share with it a fascination with consumerist self-fashioning as well as an attitude of individualistic cynicism.[14]

These theoretical claims can be more concretely explained using Rustad's example of Leslie Knope as a metamodernist feminist—and specifically Leslie's coinage of "Galentine's Day," a day celebrating female friendship (*Parks and Recreation*, 2.16, 2010).[15] On the one hand (and as Rustad claims), Galentine's Day is a (second wave–like) feminist subversion of the heteronormativity associated with Valentine's Day.[16] On the other hand, some of the aspects Leslie delights in sharing with her female friends on this day are traditionally feminine, for example "a bouquet of hand-crocheted flower pens." Her enjoyment of items that are stereotypically feminine is in line with postfeminism's emphasis on individual choice.

Rosalind Gill, for example, argues that the discourse of postfeminism is characterized by, among other "elements,"

> the notion that femininity is a bodily property; the shift from objectification to subjectification; . . . a focus on individualism, choice and empowerment [and] the dominance of a makeover paradigm.[17]

Postfeminist critics contend that "patriarchal suppression is something that belongs in the history books" and that women can harness their agency by employing their sexuality and by exercising their individualistic ability to "buy, wear, want and do whatever (or whomever) they want."[18]

We read postfeminism as a reaction to second wave feminism's focus on the ways that structures impact on the individual. Laura Mulvey's analysis of the representation of women as passive objects existing for consumption by the "male gaze" is a seminal example of second wave feminism's critique of the subjugation of women within patriarchal structures.[19] More recently, there seems to have been a turn in popular discourse away from postfeminism, toward a (more second wave–like) critique of the representation of women in the media. This includes the exploration of feminism in television shows such as *Parks and Recreation* and, as we shall argue later in the chapter, CXG, but also the media discourse on female celebrities. An example is the outcry over Rich Cohen's profile of the actor

Margot Robbie in *Vanity Fair*.[20] Cohen was criticized for the way in which he objectified Robbie and fetishized her body (see, for example, the commentary of Maddison Connaughton and Steph Harmon).[21] The critical reception of Miley Cyrus's Terry Richardson–directed music video for "Wrecking Ball" is a slightly older example.[22]

At the same time, the critique of a female public figure's sexualized image is often perceived and criticized as an attempt to curtail her (postfeminist) right to self-expression. The discourse around any number of prominent female celebrities, including Miley Cyrus, can be referenced to illustrate this point. Hermione Hoby writes the following about the reaction to Cyrus's sexualized image:

> Fairy-tale logic dictates that any woman performing in scanty clothing is compromised. The possibility that a woman might *want* to be naked, might choose that, happily, while feeling more than comfortable in her skin, seems too difficult or frightening to countenance.[23]

In the South African context in which we write, feminist writer Pumla Dineo Gqola explores this conflict in contemporary feminism (between a critique of the ways in which patriarchal social structures influence women and an acknowledgment of individual women's agency).[24] Gqola admits to being conflicted by the phenomenon of girl power and its "overt celebrations of patriarchally sanctioned performances of womanliness."[25] Gqola sees girl power as confounding, a dilemma:

> Popular discourse at UFS [University of the Free State, South Africa] labelled these young women as empowered, in control and exhibiting "girl power." These adolescents listen to the Destiny's Child liberal feminist anthem, "Independent women," at the same time that they dance to lyrics that ask "don't you wish your girlfriend was hot like me?" where women compete for the ultimate prize: the heterosexual man.[26]

The heterosexual man's purpose is to give them money, "in exact contradiction to their anthem that asserts the importance of a woman buying things . . . for herself and not needing a man to take care of her."[27]

The contrast between second wave feminism and postfeminism should not be overstated, and in fact our contention is that our current era is one in which these supposedly oppositional ideologies are intersecting in interesting and seemingly contradictory ways. Sarah Banet-Weiser, for example, contends that there are currently many forms of feminism circulating but that a hegemonic neoliberal form of feminism that she calls "popular feminism" has infiltrated mainstream culture.[28] According to her, popular feminism, despite its acknowledgment that women are "injured" by patriarchy, bolsters postfeminism in its celebration of individual empowerment rather than structural change. Although she does not call it "popular feminism," it is this same hegemonic neoliberal feminism that Jia Tolentino sees as entailing a "vision of 'women's empowerment' that often feels brutally disempowering in the end."[29] At the same time, Tolentino's structural critique of popular feminism is itself circulating within mainstream feminist discourse—her book *Trick Mirror* having made it onto the New York Times Best Seller list. In the next section, we will discuss how the competing narratives within contemporary feminist discourse manifest in CXG, with a specific focus on how the songs "The Sexy Getting Ready Song" and "Put Yourself First" are explorations of the conflict between second wave critique of social structures and the postfeminist celebration of self-fashioning and women's agency.

## The Oscillation between Second Wave Feminism and Postfeminism in *Crazy Ex-Girlfriend*

Twenty-six minutes into the first episode of CXG, the show launches into the musical number "The Sexy Getting Ready Song" (1.01). This song is the first indication of the show's engagement with the complicated relationship between feminism and pop culture. This R&B/hip hop–style song and its accompanying visuals reveal the "horrifying" (in the words of Nipsey Hussle, the rapper featured in the song) reality of the discomfort that goes into appearing sexy. Rebecca Bunch (Rachel Bloom), the titular "crazy ex-girlfriend," is shown burning herself while straightening her hair, drawing blood while waxing her pubic hair, and forcing herself into shapewear to get an "hourglass silhouette."[30] At the end of the episode, Nipsey Hussle phones various so-called video vixens to apologize for the ways in which he had demeaned them after reading *The Second Sex* by Simone de Beauvoir. The viewer, as the result of "The Sexy Getting Ready Song" earlier in the episode, has a newfound appreciation of the (physical and emotional) labor video vixens put into appearing sexy on screen. Humor is, however, also mined from the fact that the video vixens that Nipsey Hussle crosses off his to-call list (entitled "Bitches to Apologize To") include such humorous names as Tittany, Tundra, and Trinity. Such sincere feminist statements that are relativized, simultaneously, by irony and humor are characteristic of CXG in general. This characteristic is typical of metamodernist art. "The Sexy Getting Ready Song" also serves to characterize Rebecca. Rebecca sings the song in the first person, and the viewer learns that she goes to great lengths to appeal to societal beauty standards, even as she is aware of the double standards involved—at one stage, Rebecca says "let's see how the guys get ready," and the video cuts to her date, Greg (Santino Fontana), asleep on a couch. This song in the first episode therefore already shows Rebecca oscillating between the postfeminist narrative of empowering herself through her sexuality and an awareness of the second wave critique of this narrative.

Both Rebecca and her best friend Paula (Donna Lynne Champlin) rely on pop culture to make sense of their realities. Rebecca occupies especially two dominant pop-culture female identities, that of the idealized fairy-tale princess and the villain/scorned woman. In the third season, Rebecca says that she has only ever known how to be "really good or really bad. But being a human is living within that kinda in-between space" (3.07). This statement points to the way in which the show explores a more nuanced approach to femininity. Talking about the conception of the show, Bloom said that they were writing from a female perspective from the beginning, and that even the title of the show is critical commentary: "The title is a commentary . . . we're deconstructing that label from a female point of view."[31] She also elaborated on Rebecca's reliance on pop culture: "I think Rebecca is someone who doesn't have an inner sense of self, so she is trying on all of these personas and all of these pop-culture stereotypes."[32]

One of the characteristics associated with postmodernist art and theory is a fascination and engagement with pop culture, which can be exemplified through the intertextuality of parody.[33] "The Sexy Getting Ready Song" and "Put Yourself First" both contain intertextual references and parodic elements. Both also explore postfeminist conceptions of the empowering potential of female beauty. "The Sexy Getting Ready Song" illuminates the usually unacknowledged labor and "horrifying" bodily manipulation that goes into being a video vixen, while "Put Yourself First" comments on the paradox of empowering yourself by making yourself appealing to men. CXG, however, does not nihilistically mock pop-culture narratives with the cynicism that has been associated with postmodernism,[34] but rather explores and portrays its allure, explaining why it has become dominant in the collective imagination in the first place.

When Rebecca learns that Josh volunteers at a summer camp, she decides to present a "female empowerment seminar" there in order to be close to him (1.10). The irony is that she is presenting this feminist seminar for the sake of a man's attention. She aims to harness the camp setting to rekindle Josh's feelings for her. This is not successful, and Josh interprets her sincere declaration of love as a joke. As a result Rebecca admits to the young women attending her seminar that "I'm not one to speak about feminism or empowerment. I am desperately in love with a man who will never love me back. I'm the one who needs to be empowered" (1.10). The young women's reaction is one of the show's most distinct comments on feminism, and the main focus of this chapter, the musical number "Put Yourself First."

This girl power anthem, a parody of the Fifth Harmony songs "BO$$"[35] and "Worth It,"[36] involves the teenagers advising Rebecca on how to "Put yourself first for him." "The Sexy Getting Ready Song" is echoed in their advice to

Push them boobs up
Just for yourself
Wear six-inch heels
Just for yourself.

Rebecca responds by asking, "If it's just for myself, shouldn't I be comfortable?" She again interjects in the song's second verse, asking, "If I put myself first for him, then by definition, aren't I putting myself . . . second?" The young women respond:

> Don't think about it too hard
> Too, too hard
> Don't think about it too hard
> Too, too hard
> It's a wormhole, it's a Mobius strip
> It's snake eats tail, it's the infinity sign.

This "wormhole" or "Mobius strip" refers to the dilemma of the conflict between notions of individual empowerment and an acknowledgment of the ways women are subjugated by cultural scripts and social structures. The Mobius strip, ouroboros, and infinity signs are here all symbols of never-ending and entangled thought. The women enjoining Rebecca not to think about it "too hard" are implying that she will not be able to arrive at an answer, that the question of whether a woman's use of her own beauty can ever be considered empowering is too convoluted to solve. This convoluted problem is the same impasse faced by contemporary feminist discourse discussed earlier in the chapter: it is the girl power narrative that confounds Gqola.

When the young women at the camp speak about putting oneself first, Rebecca understands this in terms of (a caricatured) second wave feminism: "You're right, I should read Gloria Steinem, take ceramics class, and grow my pit hair out, stuff like that" (1.10). Incredulous, the women reply: "No. What you need is a makeover." In spite of her interjections, the fantasy of confidence and self-reliance enchants Rebecca and she thanks them for their advice.

The young women sing "when a dude sees you put yourself first / he'll be like, 'damn, you're hot, let's buy a house in Portland'" (1.10), alluding to the irony that in a patriarchal paradigm this "self-reliance" is only available to "hot" women. This verse also conveys an underlying need for (material and, perhaps, relational) security, despite the song's overt rhetoric of self-reliance and independence.

In CXG, Rebecca is not dependent on Josh for money, but her happiness and sense of fulfillment depend on him. Even though she is empowered by her relative wealth and education, her status as a liberated woman is belied by her emotional dependency. The irony mined from this situation, and Rebecca's self-aware grappling with this contradiction, set her apart from other postfeminist characters.

In the second season, after feeling humiliated and disempowered by her breakups with Greg (Santino Fontana) and Josh, Rebecca again tries to change her own and others' perceptions of her by giving herself a makeover in the song, "Makey-Makeover" (2.4). In postfeminist culture, the makeover signals that anyone can attain the mode of femininity it proposes.[37] In spite of its prominence in popular culture, the outside-in approach epitomized by the complete makeover proves to be ultimately unsuccessful for Rebecca, who finds that the confidence it brings is short-lived. After "Makey-Makeover," Rebecca runs into Josh, who initially thinks her new appearance is a funny costume. A few moments later, he interprets it as evidence that Rebecca is going through some crisis and in need of assurance. Josh was more impressed with her first makeover attempt at the camp, but her need for his affection immediately overshadows her recently acquired convictions about the attitude of independence and the ethos of self-focus.

Carl Wilson considers the songs on the show "deconstructions of the implicit content of their chosen genre—the fantasy narratives and social values that it's selling under the surface."[38] The "fantasy narrative" that by being financially successful, women can prove themselves just as powerful as men, if not more so, is one of those deconstructed on CXG. The two Fifth Harmony videos ("BO$$" and "Worth It") referenced in "Put Yourself First" present not only a narrow view of success and power but also the model for achieving it. Success is defined as money (note the dollar signs in "BO$$"'s title), fame (represented by the spotlights and catwalk), and confidence through beauty (in both videos, a glossy, manicured picture of femininity is on display). In this way, women are encouraged to use their bodies to achieve what they want.

It is noteworthy that both Fifth Harmony songs are explicitly posited as anthems of female independence, empowerment, and success, similar to Destiny's Child's "Independent Woman."[39] This is not only conveyed lyrically, but also through the visual cues in the videos. In the video for "BO$$," men and women are physically pitted against each other in arm wrestling, the women winning every time.[40] In the video for "Worth It," female sexuality and empowerment are conflated in a confounding way: Phrases including "Many women in power," "To break through / the glass ceiling," "Feminism is sexy," as well as figures that seem to represent the bankability of Fifth Harmony and/or women in general scroll on a stock market billboard behind the group.[41] The ideals of postfeminist empowerment are reflected in the fact that the men in the video are working for the women who are in executive positions. Even so (and in keeping with the ironies of so-called girl power that Gqola points out),[42] the appearances of the women seem integral to the power and status they represent. This version of empowerment and this depiction of the female body share an ability to sell: "It's uniquely marketable, like the female body, which is where women's empowerment is forced to live."[43]

In the video for "BO$$," men photograph the Fifth Harmony members on the catwalk. In "Put Yourself First," a Terry Richardson lookalike with the words "male gaze" printed on his sweater photographs the women. One of the Fifth Harmony members takes a photo of the men taking photos of her, highlighting an awareness that she is being scrutinized and framed in a particular way. By labeling the Terry Richardson lookalike in "Put Yourself First" the "male gaze," he (and, implicitly, the male photographers in the "BO$$" music video) is positioned as the "determining male gaze" who "projects its fantasy on the female figure which is styled accordingly[,] . . . coded for strong visual and erotic impact so that they can be said to connote *to-be-looked-at-ness*."[44] The "male gaze" sweater could also be a reference to the way that Richardson was initially positioned as a photographer who uses postmodern irony to document the "sexualization of female empowerment."[45] More recently, allegations of sexual harassment have marked Richardson's career.[46] By critiquing Richardson's supposedly ironic appropriation of the "male gaze" label, "Put Yourself First" possibly also comments on the Fifth Harmony members' implicit suggestion that they are manipulating the male gaze by also photographing the photographers who are photographing them. Richardson's persona as supposedly ironic chauvinist turns out to be underpinned by an actual objectification of women, and similarly Fifth Harmony's manipulation of the male gaze can be critiqued as actually supporting the patriarchy and its objectification of women.

Wilson notes that, with the formation and rise of girl groups, women were given a voice that they never had before but that men in the music industry often dictated that voice.[47] The Fifth Harmony lyrics for "BO$$" veer into the explicitly suggestive. The fact that only one of the six writers of "BO$$" is female brings into question the authenticity of this image of femininity and female sexuality and dominance.[48]

The featured rapper in the video for "Worth It," Kid Ink, brings the rapper of "The Sexy Getting Ready Song" to mind, but here, there is no feminist metanoia; he admonishes the woman he is singing to to "stop playing," asking her why she's "acting shy." Originally, the song was written for Kid Ink, and the lyrics were then changed to fit "[Fifth Harmony's] perspective."[49] Kid Ink's verse on the original version of the song, "Wit It," includes the lyrics "Bitch, please, you don't wanna be no tease,"[50] dismissing and denying female agency and autonomy. A song that was actively disempowering to women was thus turned into a song championing female empowerment, but as "Put Yourself First" points out, such girl power anthems are often prescriptive of women's behavior—in a way that can be seen (from a second wave perspective) as ultimately disempowering. "Put Yourself First" explores the allure of the fantasy narrative of enacting agency through self-fashioning and the patriarchal structures informing this fantasy.

Apart from the "fantasy narratives" deconstructed in its songs, CXG's approach is also metamodern in its critique of gender and romance through the show's various plots. An example is the oscillation between Rebecca and Paula's pop culture–inspired conceptions of romantic love and an often-disillusioning reality. An example is when Valencia (Gabrielle Ruiz) unexpectedly invites Rebecca on a beach trip with the "crew" (1.09). Rebecca sees this as a time to bond with Josh and rents a party bus to take them to the beach. Rebecca's unrealistic expectations that she will share a romantic time with Josh on the bus are left unfulfilled when she witnesses Josh and Valencia's togetherness.

Earlier on in the series, the sway of the postfeminist aesthetic is explored through Rebecca's infatuation with Valencia (see, for example, 1.02). Although Rebecca's fascination with Valencia is inextricably linked to the fact that she has what Rebecca wants (a seemingly stable relationship with Josh), Rebecca is also spellbound by Valencia's beauty, her body-consciousness, and her aura of personal wellbeing. Insofar as Valencia initially represents these postfeminist qualities to Rebecca, Rebecca is willing—and eager—to sacrifice her own identity to embody these postfeminist qualities and espouse their accompanying cultural capital. After showing up to West Covina's club "Spider's" in identical metallic mini-dresses, Rebecca and Valencia dance.

Rebecca's infatuation is then explored in the song "Feeling Kinda Naughty" (1.2). Rebecca's desire to be beautiful, as beautiful as Valencia, is stated in drastic, body-altering terms, which brings the painful effort of "The Sexy Getting Ready Song" and "Put Yourself First" to mind: "Cause I'm feelin' kinda naughty, take measurements of your body, then go up to a surgeon, make my body like your body." Rebecca subsequently reveals by accident that she and Josh used to date. Valencia is simultaneously betrayed by both Josh, who lied to her, and Rebecca, whom she thought wanted to be her friend. Valencia is later further humanized as someone with her own insecurities (an example is when she admits to Rebecca that she considered getting breast implants because "guys love big boobs") (1.16), in opposition with the "skinny bitch" or "witch" initially set up for Rebecca to conquer.[51] Instead of pitting these modes of femininity against each other, CXG does not invalidate the postfeminism that Valencia arguably represents, but shows that it is informed by men's perceptions and often underpinned by feelings of insecurity.

## Conclusion

Rebecca's denial of that which motivates her actions can conceivably alienate viewers, but they invest in the character again after instances characterized by sincerity and honesty (notably occurring in the musical numbers "You Stupid Bitch" [1.11] and "I'm the Villain in My Own Story" [1.14]). Rebecca Bunch is not only the lovesick ingénue, but a complex and occasionally self-aware character whose flaws and mental health problems are contextualized. She is a Harvard-educated lawyer whose skills are not only referenced but also demonstrated, and she is also a loyal friend. While Rebecca is often depicted humorously and irony is used to critique her actions, the viewer is also encouraged to identify and sympathize with her. The show asks for involvement with the characters and their situations and not a distancing from them. Speaking about the (incorrect) notion that the show operates at the expense of the titular "crazy ex-girlfriend," Bloom said "that's so not what the show is," and that one of the goals of the show is to "enlighten" people by fostering an understanding of the character.[52] This renewed engagement with the concepts of identification, involvement, and connection (after the distancing, irony, and cynicism associated with postmodernism) is described as a metamodern endeavor by Vermeulen and Van den Akker,[53] and is instrumental to Brosh McKenna and Bloom's feminist vision for the show.

*Crazy Ex-Girlfriend* ultimately represents a nuanced exploration of the opposing forces that shape Rebecca's sense of self as well as her actions. As we argued, these opposing forces are related to inter alia different discourses around feminism and female empowerment. Mainstream feminist discourse currently faces a quandary. Second wave critiques of patriarchal power structures are still circulating, but they are simultaneously opposed by postfeminist ideals of individual empowerment through the manipulation of capitalist and patriarchal structures. Our contention is that CXG engages with these contradictory discourses in a way that Vermeulen and Van den Akker term "metamodern"—oscillating between a celebration of ideals that could be considered modernist and/or second wave feminist and ideals that are associated with postmodernism and postfeminism.

# 14

## "I'm Ravenous"

### *Hunger for Food, Sex, and Power in* Crazy Ex-Girlfriend

### Christi Cook

Young women's bodies are commodities in today's cultural landscape. This is evident when turning on the television and viewing programming such as *16 and Pregnant* (MTV, 2009–14) and *American Idol* (Fox, 2002–16; ABC, 2018–), among many others, in addition to the commercials that run in between the programs. Young women flounce about, generally scantily clad, and we consume them. Society hungers for the bodies of young women, but the girls themselves are not supposed to have their own appetites. Where society's hunger for young women and simultaneous insistence that they not have their own hunger intersects with ambivalent expressions about appetite from the young women themselves is where those young women are able to find resistance and agency. Examination of pop culture through books, TV programs, music, and movies illustrates the cultural script that young women should not be hungry for either food or sex. This is especially significant since TV shows and young adult literature hold great sway over their audiences. As Roberta Trites and Beth Younger[1] discuss, young adult novels, and TV shows and movies by extension, often portray young women's sexuality as a menacing and overwhelmingly negative component of their lives. For young women, "sexual desire is often viewed as a primitive, taboo drive that must be regulated," and the pregnancy problem genre is widespread.[2] Additionally, girls are not typically portrayed as having notable appetites for food. Quite to the contrary, a girl on the screen or on the pages is more likely to have an eating disorder than to take pleasure in food. I have chosen to examine the types of hunger found in *Crazy Ex-Girlfriend* (hereafter *CXG*) and to explore the significance of hunger to the characters' sense of agency and reclamation of their bodies. In this chapter, I will utilize the folkloric image of the *vagina dentata*, a symbol to connect hunger for food and for sex and an overarching metaphor for the resistance of Rebecca Bunch (Rachel Bloom) and other female characters in *CXG*, as I examine the significance of the male fear of the devouring vagina, which I argue is present in both the series and in society writ large. In my interpretation, a hungry, toothed vagina represents a woman with her own sexual drives and appetites. Since women are conditioned not to discuss their appetites forthrightly, reframing the symbol of the *vagina dentata*, just as Rebecca Bunch reframes so much that is emblematic of femininity and the body, is one way to understand and to embrace the connections between different types of female hunger and avenues of resistance for young women.

Rebecca and other characters, like Paula (Donna Lynne Champlin) and Valencia (Gabrielle Ruiz), find power during frequent or intermittent moments of rebellion against the dominant culture's expectations of them. These moments of rebellion exist at the intersection of society's appetite for young women and the appetites of the women themselves. An apt symbol for this interstitial tension is the *vagina dentata*, a widespread, obscure, and fearsome motif primarily from American Indian folklore in which a man is unable to have intercourse with a woman due to her toothed vagina.[3] This symbol shows men's common "fear that in intercourse with women they may be castrated, that they may be laughed at, that they may die. The woman's power must therefore be neutralized by 'pulling the teeth' from her vagina or by killing her first and then remaking her as a nonthreatening, procreative partner."[4] Society tends to fear women and women's sexuality, and yet is also obsessed with what it fears. Man is drawn to a woman's sexual organs, but he has longstanding trepidation about those very organs. A contemporary example is the 2007 horror film *Teeth* (dir. Mitchell Lichtenstein), in which the young female protagonist has a *vagina dentata* that bites off the penises of several male characters who attempt to assault her. In my interpretation, a hungry, toothed vagina represents a woman with her own sexual drives and appetites, but women are conditioned not to discuss their appetites forthrightly. As younger women are on the outskirts of human sexuality since they are recently developed, they are even more desirable and even less able to take ownership of their appetites. Reframing the symbol of the *vagina dentata* is one way to understand and to embrace the connections between different types of female hunger and avenues of resistance for women of all ages.

In this chapter, I will utilize the *vagina dentata* as an overarching metaphor for the resistance of the female protagonists of CXG. I will begin by examining the relationship between power and generic conventions in the show, and then I will briefly discuss the function of class and race/ethnicity. Following that, I will inquire into the relationship between food, bodies, and sexuality. I will then delve into the types of hunger apparent in CXG. Drawing on work by Susan Bordo, Maggie Helwig, and Susie Orbach, I explore how women use their bodies to speak to others.

## The Show, Hunger, and Food

Recent novels, TV programs, and movies show hungry young women utilizing their bodies in various ways to achieve their goals.[5] *Crazy Ex-Girlfriend* has been anomalous in its treatment of these same themes with transgressive humor in the form of a musical. This show "rides the line between drop-dead serious and just joking," often in the same sentence.[6] It boasts a diverse cast, which the casting director and show creators take pride in as they are aware of the relative dearth of roles for diverse television actors. The show features a rare Asian male romantic lead along with a supporting cast of varying ages, sizes, ethnicities, and sexualities. Aline Brosh McKenna, the show's cocreator, "emphasizes that telling new stories—something that often comes from highlighting underrepresented populations or hyper-specific characters or both—is simply something that she finds interesting and makes an effort to do."[7] The focus on diversity affects the bawdy, female-centric sense of humor as well; a Jewish studies professor notes that "one of the hallmarks of Jewish humor created by millennials is a refusal to accept that some things can't be joked about, and we see that with CXG working mental illness, suicide, medications, etc.

into a comedy show."[8] Nothing is off-limits, particularly themes of female sexuality, hunger, and mental wellness/illness.

This show itself is framed by food; many of the episodes begin and/or end with a discussion of food and the reality of the women's hunger. The opening episode features Rebecca noting the unusually large size of West Covina's pretzels before being hoisted into a gigantic pretzel to soar, singing, above the rest of the town at the end of the number. Pretzels are a recurring leitmotif: in season four, Rebecca hits her stride on her journey of self-discovery and healing, and one of her notable accomplishments is quitting her practice of law and opening "Rebetzel's Pretzels," her own pretzel shop. Referring to the hunger she experiences, we learn in episode 1.06 about Rebecca's very beginnings: she ate her twin in the womb. While complaining about her life and her family of origin and emphasizing how she doesn't belong, Rebecca tells Paula about her natal twin and then clarifies, "Medically speaking I didn't eat it; I just metabolized its body parts for my own use." I find this harkening back to a primal hunger for survival to be telling. Rebecca's pivotal decision to move to California is also rooted in food: she encounters an advertisement for butter three times throughout the first episode of the series. The ad features text asking, "When was the last time you were truly happy?" Rebecca takes this question as an opportunity for reflection and as a sign that she needs to make a drastic lifestyle change. The beginnings of Rebecca's story are situated in food, hunger, and domination.

The communal and cultural aspects of food are highlighted later in the series. Food is often equated with love: in episode 2.05, Rebecca thoughtfully packs Paula's lunch for the first day of law school, but she steals an extra juice box for herself. Seeking to impress Josh's family in episode 1.06, Rebecca secures an invitation to their Thanksgiving celebration and then brings the Filipino dish, *dinuguan*, which is pork cooked in pigs' blood. Interestingly, the food causes intestinal distress for Rebecca, which leads to her running to the bathroom where she inadvertently becomes trapped while, to her chagrin, Josh and Valencia have sex in the bedroom next to her. In season four, Josh returns the favor of preparing an ethnic dish from the recipient's heritage by serving Rebecca matzo. During episode 2.08, Rebecca sends Josh chicken soup, another dish associated with being Jewish, but he thinks it's from his girlfriend and Rebecca is upset—when the misunderstanding is revealed, Josh realizes that Rebecca is the one for him.

The cultural connotations of food and its association with gender roles can be more complicated for women than for men. In addition to facing cultural opposition to self-expression along the axis of gender, Rebecca also faces opposition to creativity along the axis of ethnicity. Heller and Moran note:

> The kinds of ideological tensions that we have identified in women's literature—where daughters are caught up in changing beliefs about gender roles—are exacerbated when cultural dislocation is part of the brew. For instance, in ethnic and postcolonial narratives, while women can feel nostalgia for an originary culture threatened by assimilation or colonization, they can also feel alienated from a traditional role for women within the originary culture; such dissatisfaction with traditional gender roles, however, does not mean that they can easily find an alternative substitute in the colonizing or assimilating culture which is obliterating or diluting their cultural heritage.

Rebecca's attempts to formulate her identity are evident in the interactions she has with her mother and with her mother's food, particularly in episode 3.05: she rejects and retreats, but then she feels remorse and she approaches again only to retreat once more. The cycle repeats itself, illustrative of the dynamic Rebecca and her mother share. Perhaps this tension mirrors the "tension between a native and a colonizing culture abound[ing] with nostalgic evocations of traditional food, an association strengthened by the role of women (mothers, grandmothers, aunts) in food preparation."[9] Rebecca's mother is not usually linked with traditional food preparation, but in the episode where she focuses on feeding her needy daughter, Rebecca consistently loathes and appreciates her simultaneously. Plying her daughter with popcorn, full-fat strawberry milkshakes, and promises about fun quality time they'll spend together, Naomi (Tovah Feldshuh) begins slipping antidepressants into her daughter's milkshakes once she discovers Rebecca's intent to commit suicide. Rebecca eventually gives in to her appetites; she is in one of her lowest moments, and she very simply needs her mother. The viewer sees a stark portrayal of "Rebecca's relationship with her mother, distilled to its essence with one horrible and manipulative choice motivated by terrified, bone-deep love."[10] Although she is always already attempting to manipulate her daughter, in this instance, Naomi's food has life-saving properties. Rebecca, of course, does not view the situation through that lens, and she sees this betrayal as a consequence of her own appetites. She flees her mother once again in order to attempt suicide. She temporarily loses her fearsome spirit of resistance symbolized with the *vagina dentata* as she faces her lowest low in the series.

## Women's Bodies

Focus on food in this show serves as a gateway to examining the bodies that crave that food. Female characters exist on opposite ends of the continuum of bodies: Paula and, to some extent, Rebecca exhibit self-pride in their larger bodies, while Valencia and Heather (Vella Lovell) have thinner bodies. Rebecca and Paula eat and Valencia doesn't. Valencia's desire for a socially acceptable, thin body outweighs her desire to eat. The character's possible anorexia doesn't appear to be deeply shocking either to the other women in the show or to the viewer. During the Thanksgiving with the Chan family (1.06), Rebecca jokes ebulliently while clearing dishes about her desire to lick all the plates clean shortly before arguing with her (at that point) romantic rival, Valencia. Rebecca resists societal norms by unabashedly devouring food while Valencia goes along with the dominant narrative. Rebecca adopts a mock caring attitude and asks Valencia whether she's hungry. Valencia replies, "Of course I'm starving. I've been starving since 1998." A woman starving herself to achieve a perfect body is status quo since, according to Maggie Helwig, "we have normalized anorexia and bulimia, even turned them into an industry."[11] However, this is not, Helwig continues, "just a problem of proportion. This is the nightmare of consumerism acted out in women's bodies."[12] Women want to consume food to nourish their bodies, but they are discouraged from doing so; instead, they are encouraged to spend copious amounts of money on perfect clothing and beauty products for their idealized shrinking bodies. In the same scene, Rebecca makes the feminist but at that moment insincere observation: "That is the media telling you what your body should be and it just gets my goat." This is what CXG does: it makes feminist arguments, sometimes seriously and sometimes in jest, and it moves on; feminism is merely part of the show's oeuvre.[13] As Bibi Burger and Carel van Rooyen argue in the previous chapter in this collection, this simultaneous relativization of a sincere feminist statement by irony and humor is characteristic of this series. Rebecca and Valencia continue sniping at each other when chicken soup makes another appearance: Rebecca, cloyingly as a pretense of caring, asks if she can get Valencia a hot cup of *arroz caldo*. Valencia responds, "I don't need chicken soup! It's just hot melted fat water" before wishing Rebecca luck "digesting all that gross food," referring to the traditional Filipino fare. Rebecca points out the cultural insensitivity of that remark before, in fact, getting sick digesting the meal. At this point, her devouring is punished and her appetites, along with her resistance, are kept in check.

Along the same lines, in *Unbearable Weight*, Susan Bordo asserts that eating disorders aren't anomalous but are continuous with the experience of being female in this culture; she sees women using eating disorders as an attempt to create a body that will speak for the self in a meaningful and powerful way. Helwig furthers this line of thinking: "To be skeletally, horribly thin makes one strong statement. It says, I am hungry. What I have been given is not sufficient, not real, not true, not acceptable. I am starving. To reject food, whether by refusing it or by vomiting it back, says simply, I will not consume. I will not participate. This is not real."[14] Valencia can be seen as rejecting her surroundings to some extent; she wants to be upwardly mobile and she is restless in relationships as she wrestles with her sexuality. Perhaps she starves herself away from the Latina body ideal, which is more accepting of larger hips and thighs, in order to meld with a more upwardly mobile Anglo "American Dream."[15]

Even though she no longer has an eating disorder,[16] Rebecca also sends powerful messages through her body. Susie Orbach discusses the phenomenon of women speaking through their bodies, noting that food and body-image issues are "the language of women's inner experience," and arguing that "food is a metaphor through which women speak of their inner experiences. Until we have a real voice in the body politic, individual women are likely to use their bodies as their mouthpieces to express the forbidden and secluded feelings we carry inside."[17] Hélène Cixous theorizes about women's writing through their bodies, *écriture feminine*, in her essay "The Laugh of the Medusa" (1975), where she asserts "woman must write her self: must write about women and bring women to writing, from which they have been driven away as violently as from their bodies" because their sexual pleasure has been repressed and denied expression. Scenes illustrating Rebecca's use of her body as a mouthpiece find their roots in actor and series cocreator Rachel Bloom's life experiences. Bloom and the series have been nominated for numerous awards, which necessitate a wardrobe full of ball gowns. Bloom notes, "A lot of fashion houses are reluctant to lend clothes that aren't in the sample sizes of 0 and 2, so it's getting harder and harder for me to find clothes without buying them. That's the whole problem with the fashion industry: My body size is literally normal and healthy, but when you put me next to a model, I look obese."[18] Bloom and Rebecca write and speak through their bodies: imperfections are highlighted rather than shied away from, and there is no shame in not being a size 0 or 2. As one critic observes, "'Crazy Ex-Girlfriend' showed us something we almost never see on television," referring to the pre-Spanx squishy tummy closeup in "Sexy Getting Ready Song."[19] The audience might experience some shock viewing a fleshy body on screen, since "a non-flat female tummy is practically a body part non grata on television, with the notable exception of Lena Dunham's performance as Hannah Horvath on Girls."[20] As Christine Prevas points out in chapter 11 of this collection, this song represents an "ecstatic exposure" of the societal place where female sexuality breaks down. For Rebecca, her body speaks. Her weight speaks. She extols both the virtues and the challenges of large breasts in "Heavy Boobs" (1.16), but she illustrates that she, like the majority of women living in our media-driven society, also falls victim to self-deprecation in "You Stupid Bitch" (1.11), which includes lines like "you're just a lying little bitch who ruins things and wants the world to burn, bitch, you're a stupid bitch, and lose some weight." Although she is a conscious feminist who embraces and speaks through her body with agency, she is also a woman who wants to be pretty and to be attractive to men. As much as Bordo and others reject Cartesian dualism and the equation of women with body and men with mind, these associations are engrained in Western society. Therefore, it is women with eating disorders who embody the "monster" by acting out "the equation of food and sin, who deny hunger and yet embody endless, unfulfilled appetite."[21] Also monstrous, by extension, are the women's *vagina dentatas*, which advocate for the hidden and so often shameful presence of physical appetites. Good girls aren't supposed to be hungry, but sometimes they eat.

### Hunger for Sex

Similarly, good girls are supposed to maintain an acceptable level of sexual desirability without ever actually desiring or having sex themselves. Throughout the series, there are numerous instances of the conflation of two types of hunger: for food and for sex. Food and sexuality are linked, which calls to mind our guiding motif of the ravenous, toothed vagina image. For example, alongside the previously explored series fixation on pretzels, another significant occurrence from the show's beginning is that we are introduced to awkward teenaged Rebecca hungering for Josh and being rejected by him: at drama camp, she excitedly tells him, "You've awakened my sexual being for the first time" (1.01). In the same line, Rebecca mentions using suicidal thoughts to manipulate her parents into letting her go to drama camp, which conflates her mental state with her sexual longing. This is an instance of Rebecca being a "bad feminist"; in episode 2.05, Rebecca alludes to Roxane Gay, who has written extensively about being a "bad feminist," the kind who wants independence but also a partner who's financially stable and so on. Interestingly enough, Roxane Gay authored a memoir titled *Hunger*. Another conflation of these two types of hunger is seen in grocery stores, which are the settings for several important scenes where sex and food are juxtaposed: Josh and Valencia have a steamy make-out session in an aisle of the grocery store just before Valencia meets Rebecca (1.02), and Paula does her "First Penis I Saw" routine in the grocery store, focusing her sexual attention on several phallic vegetables (3.07). Appetites for food and sexuality are juxtaposed to high-light their similarities.

As explored previously, Rebecca attempts to enter the signifying econ-omy by inscribing meaning on her body, and this meaning contains her various appetites. Reminiscent of Luce Irigaray in *This Sex Which Is Not One*, Rebecca has two sets of lips, horizontal and vertical, and two cor-responding appetites; both her hunger and her sexuality are prominent features in the series. Her sexual partners are numerous, and songs like "Period Sex" (2.03) and "Oh My God I Think I Like You" (1.17) show viewers how comfortable she is with her bodily functions, her raunchy desires, and her feelings of affection coexisting alongside one another. In addition to normalizing women's sexual appetites, the show delves into a level of sexual knowledge that is atypical of most comedies. In this sense, the show gives vaginas a mouth and a voice. In season three's "To Josh, With Love" (3.02), we see the first time a network show has explained the purpose of the clitoris.[22] Bloom herself was inspired to write this episode after reading an article about "the orgasm gap" between men and women; she was distraught at how long the article took to mention the clitoris. This episode frames Rebecca's coworker who fails to bring his wife to orgasm as a pitiable man, and his female colleagues all take the time to educate him about what women want and need in order to experience orgasm. Vaginas continue to have a voice in episode 3.13 in Paula's song "The Miracle of Birth." Paula, dressed as a goddess sitting on a vaginal throne, sings, "Tear, tear, tear goes your vagina. Never will it be its cute little self again." Paula illuminates the process of childbirth to the audience of people who have (and have not) experienced it, and she doesn't hold back on the visceral and painful parts like explosive diarrhea, the ring of fire, and placental expulsion. Thus, the vertical and horizontal lips speak as one through the dissemination of radical sex and body knowledge.

Rebecca's hunger to express herself is also interesting to view through the lens of Julia Kristeva's work on the role of the abject within the mother-daughter relationship. In *Powers of Horror*, Kristeva identifies the mother's body as the first "thing" to be abjected or cast off in the infant's process to gain a concept of self as the infant enters inevitably into the patriarchal order, where women's voices are devalued. However, the mother's body in the form of the feminine *chora*[23] and the nonpatriarchal realm of semiotics continually returns by rupturing through the borders of selfhood and phallogocentric language. Per Kristeva, the creation of the subject occurs through the processes of exclusion and violence, which oppose the feminine, the *chora*, and the abject. The importance of the mother-daughter dyad in CXG highlights the importance of the mother-daughter dynamic in the creative process: Rebecca struggles to find meaning within the phallic economy while at the same time struggling against the maternal force that she finds smothering and inhibitive of growth. The daughter attempts to spit her mother, the abject, out, and to establish her selfhood, but she finds herself spitting herself out as well since the abject is not an object. The audience watches Rebecca grapple with finding her place within her family and her new community of West Covina without the understanding of where she will end up at the end. Rebecca flees to her mother and New York when she has her mental breakdown, but it is her California friends and West Covina location that help her rebuild.

Food, hunger, and bodies are the concrete representations of the complex intertwining of body image, language, gender, ethnicity, and socioeconomically motivated oppression, tradition, and culture in CXG. Hunger for food, for sex, and for knowledge/self-expression motivate the women throughout the series, but most notably compel Rebecca along her journey to make peace with her own feelings, mental health, and future. Rebecca is able to take charge of her body and her life; she helps the women around her to accept their bodies as they are and to envision a world where their bodies are welcome. As Maria Figueroa puts it: "To become beautiful one must conform to the systematic formation of beauty, which historically in Western culture has been a 'normative' white beauty."[24] Though thickness has historically been valued by Latinxs and African Americans, "normative" white beauty standards are inescapable. Bloom creates Rebecca's body image as an almost unachievable paragon: she loves herself as she is, which is an ideal most women within Western culture are unable to attain. She hungers for more knowledge and for self-expression, and she gains the courage not only to eschew her initial invitation to be partner in a New York law firm but also eventually to leave the legal profession altogether. As Rebecca manages her appetites, she serves as a success story if one measures success in equal measures of self-love and achievement of the American dream.

One critic, when writing about *The Hunger Games*, observes that "girls are continuously resisting both patriarchy's constraints as well as the constraints of feminist portrayals of them as victims,"[25] but I argue that ignoring the pervasive component of victimization and commodification of girls is dangerous. Resistance is present and possible for young women, but their resistance is multivalent and complex as it is found in the interstices of their individual appetites and society's appetite for them. In CXG, there is a covert commodification of Rebecca's body, which is marked as larger than desirable and as ethnic. Designers do not literally attempt to inscribe Rebecca's body as the designers do in *The Hunger Games*, but she feels the inscription of designers who make clothes for size 2 women, along with the inscription of her mother's projected self-hatred.

Although Rebecca and the other female characters on CXG are protagonists with intelligence and grit, they each must grapple with authentic representation in a society that is fixated on their outward appearance. As Marija Laugalyte asserts in chapter 12 of this collection, the female characters often move beyond gender stereotypes like marriage and motherhood and focus instead on the empowerment of female friendships and self-examination. They have to marshal their appetites in order to find moments of agency in an unjust world. The *vagina dentata* serves as a symbol for uniting the women's sexual hunger and hunger for food along with their hunger for self-expression and for justice. The show creators model the possibilities of female hunger and female resistance for viewers. For the majority of episodes, the authors convey the idea that overt and covert resistance are possible in the interstices of society's demands for young women and the women's own will and desire. The creators do not fall short of their ideals by removing the *dentata* from their protagonists in a finale that provides the protagonists with traditional "happy endings." Instead, they actively subvert that: instead of choosing among her three suitors for one final time, Rebecca tells a room full of all the show's characters that "Romantic love is not an ending, not for me or for anyone else here. It's just a part of your story, a part of who you are." She continues, "When I'm telling my own story, for the first time in my life I am truly happy. It's like I met myself." She then sits down to play a song of her own to express her true self. As Prevas discusses in chapter 11, Rebecca spent a year writing this song to help her understand herself, and yet the song is actually left unplayed as the episode ends. Prevas speculates that Rebecca's song is likely not good but reminds us that "whether or not her song is good doesn't matter. Whether or not she has succeeded is irrelevant. The show has never cared about her success: it has only ever cared about the real-life messes that happen along the way, and the new and surprising possibilities they provide." Rebecca finds her resistance in opting out of romance and focusing instead on loving and listening to herself. Nonetheless, hunger is an important motif in the series since it helps crystallize the intersection of society's hunger for the bodies of women and the women's individual appetites.

*Appendix*

*Notes*

*Bibliography*

*Contributors*

*Index*

# Appendix

# Complete Episode List, *Crazy Ex-Girlfriend*

*2015–19. Created by Rachel Bloom and Aline Brosh McKenna*

### Season One

1.01. "Josh Just Happens to Live Here!" Directed by Marc Webb. Written by Rachel Bloom and Aline Brosh McKenna. The CW. October 12, 2015.

1.02. "Josh's Girlfriend Is Really Cool!" Directed by Don Scardino. Written by Rachel Bloom and Aline Brosh McKenna. The CW. October 19, 2015.

1.03. "I Hope Josh Comes to My Party!" Directed by Tamra Davis. Written by Rachel Bloom and Aline Brosh McKenna. The CW. October 26, 2015.

1.04. "I'm Going on a Date with Josh's Friend!" Directed by Stuart McDonald. Written by Erin Ehrlich. The CW. November 2, 2015.

1.05. "Josh and I Are Good People!" Directed by Alex Hardcastle. Written by Michael Hitchcock. The CW. November 9, 2015.

1.06. "My First Thanksgiving with Josh!" Directed by Joanna Kerns. Written by Rene Gube. The CW. November 16, 2015.

1.07. "I'm So Happy That Josh Is So Happy!" Directed by Lawrence Trilling. Written by Sono Patel. The CW. November 23, 2015.

1.08. "My Mom, Greg's Mom and Josh's Sweet Dance Moves!" Directed by Steven Tsuchida. Written by Rachel Specter and Audrey Wauchope. The CW. November 30, 2015.

1.09. "I'm Going to the Beach with Josh and His Friends!" Directed by Kenny Ortega. Written by Dan Gregor and Doug Mand. The CW. January 25, 2016.

1.10. "I'm Back at Camp with Josh!" Directed by Michael Schultz. Written by Jack Dolgen. The CW. February 1, 2016.

1.11. "That Text Was Not Meant for Josh!" Directed by Daisy Von Scherler Mayer. Written by Elisabeth Kiernan Averick. The CW. February 8, 2016.

1.12. "Josh and I Work on a Case!" Directed by Steven Tsuchida. Written by Rachel Bloom and Aline Brosh McKenna. The CW. February 22, 2016.

1.13. "Josh and I Go to Los Angeles!" Directed by Michael Patrick Jann. Written by Aline Brosh McKenna. The CW. February 29, 2016.

1.14. "Josh Is Going to Hawaii!" Directed by Erin Ehrlich. Written by Sono Patel. The CW. March 7, 2016.

1.15. "Josh Has No Idea Where I Am!" Directed by Steven Tsuchida. Written by Rachel Bloom and Aline Brosh McKenna. The CW. March 21, 2016.

1.16. "Josh's Sister Is Getting Married!" Directed by Alex Hardcastle. Written by Rachel Specter and Audrey Wauchope. The CW. March 28, 2016.

1.17. "Why Is Josh in a Bad Mood?" Directed by Joanna Kerns. Written by Jack Dolgen. The CW. April 11, 2016.

1.18. "Paula Needs to Get Over Josh!" Directed by Aline Brosh McKenna. Written by Rene Gube. The CW. April 18, 2016.

### Season Two

2.01. "Where Is Josh's Friend?" Directed by Marc Webb. Written by Rachel Bloom, Aline Brosh McKenna, and Marc Webb. The CW. October 21, 2016.

2.02. "When Will Josh See How Cool I Am?" Directed by Jay Chadrasekhar. Written by Rene Gube. The CW. October 28, 2016.

2.03. "All Signs Point to Josh . . . Or Is It Josh's Friend?" Directed by Stuart McDonald. Written by Rachel Specter and Audrey Wauchope. The CW. November 4, 2016.

2.04. "When Will Josh and His Friend Leave Me Alone?" Directed by Paul Briganti. Written by Erin Ehrlich. The CW. November 11, 2016.

2.05. "Why Is Josh's Ex-Girlfriend Eating Carbs?" Directed by Erin Ehrlich. Written by Sono Patel. The CW. November 18. 2016.

2.06. "Who Needs Josh When You Have a Girl Group?" Directed by Stuart McDonald. Written by Jack Dolgen. The CW. December 2, 2016.

2.07. "Who's the Cool Girl Josh Is Dating?" Directed by Jude Weng. Written by Michael Hitchcock. The CW. December 9, 2016.

2.08. "Who Is Josh's Soup Fairy?" Directed by Linda Mendoza. Written by Rachel Specter and Audrey Wauchope. The CW. January 6, 2017.

2.09. "When Do I Get to Spend Time with Josh?" Directed by Kabir Akhtar. Written by Rachel Bloom and Aline Brosh Mckenna. The CW. January 6, 2017.

2.10. "Will Scarsdale Like Josh's Shayna Punim?" Directed by Alex Hardcastle. Written by Dan Gregor and Doug Mand. The CW. January 13, 2017.

2.11. "Josh Is the Man of My Dreams, Right?" Directed by Michael Patrick Jann. Written by Elisabeth Kiernan Averick. The CW. January 20, 2017.

2.12. "Is Josh Free in Two Weeks?" Directed by Alex Hardcastle. Written by Katie Schwartz. The CW. January 27, 2017.

2.13. "Can Josh Take a Leap of Faith?" Directed by Aline Brosh McKenna. Written by Aline Brosh McKenna. The CW. February 3, 2017.

### Season Three

3.01. "Josh's Ex-Girlfriend Wants Revenge." Directed by Erin Ehrlich. Written by Rachel Bloom and Aline Brosh McKenna. The CW. October 13, 2017.

3.02. "To Josh, with Love." Directed by Kabir Akhtar. Written by Rachel Specter and Audrey Wauchope. The CW. October 20, 2017.

3.03. "Josh Is a Liar." Directed by Stuart McDonald. Written by Michael Hitchcock. The CW. October 27, 2017.

3.04. "Josh's Ex-Girlfriend Is Crazy." Directed by Joseph Kahn. Written by Rachel Bloom and Aline Brosh McKenna. The CW. November 3, 2017.

3.05. "I Never Want to See Josh Again." Directed by Stuart McDonald. Written by Jack Dolgen. The CW. November 10, 2017.

3.06. "Josh Is Irrelevant." Directed by Max Winkler. Written by Rachel Bloom, Aline Brosh McKenna, and Ilana Pena. The CW. November 17, 2017.

3.07. "Getting Over Jeff." Directed by Stuart McDonald. Written by Erin Ehrlich. The CW. December 8, 2017.

3.08. "Nathaniel Needs My Help!" Directed by Jude Weng. Written by Rachel Specter and Audrey Wauchope. The CW. January 5, 2018.

3.09. "Nathaniel Gets the Message!" Directed by Kabir Akhtar. Written by Elisabeth Kiernan Averick. The CW. January 12, 2018.

3.10. "Oh, Nathaniel, It's On!" Directed by Jude Weng. Written by Sono Patel. The CW. January 26, 2018.

3.11. "Nathaniel and I Are Just Friends!" Directed by Erin Ehrlich. Written by Rene Gube. The CW. February 2, 2018.

3.12. "Trent?!" Directed by Stuart McDonald. Written by Dan Gregor and Doug Mand. The CW. February 9, 2018.

3.13. "Nathaniel Is Irrelevant." Directed by Aline Brosh McKenna. Written by Aline Brosh McKenna and Michael Hitchcock. The CW. February 16, 2018.

## Season Four

4.01. "I Want to Be Here." Directed by Stuart McDonald. Written by Rachel Bloom. The CW. October 12, 2018.

4.02. "I Am Ashamed." Directed by Rachel Specter and Audrey Wauchope. Written by Erin Ehrlich. The CW. October 19, 2018.

4.03. "I'm on My Own Path." Directed by Jude Weng. Written by Alden Derck. The CW. October 26, 2018.

4.04. "I'm Making Up for Lost Time." Directed by Stuart McDonald. Written by Elisabeth Kiernan Averick. The CW. November 2, 2019.

4.05. "I'm So Happy for You." Directed by Erin Ehrlich. Written by Ilana Pena. The CW. November 9, 2018.

4.06. "I See You." Directed by Dan Gregor. Written by Jack Dolgen. The CW. November 16, 2018.

4.07. "I Will Help You." Directed by Kabir Akhtar. Written by Aline Brosh McKenna. The CW. November 30, 2018.

4.08. "I'm Not the Person I Used to Be." Directed by Stuart McDonald. Written by Rene Gube. The CW. December 7, 2018.

4.09. "I Need Some Balance." Directed by Kimmy Gatewood. Written by Elisabeth Kiernan Averick. The CW. January 11, 2019.

4.10. "I Can Work with You." Directed by Kabir Akhtar. Written by Rachel Specter and Audrey Wauchope. The CW. January 18, 2019.

4.11. "I'm Almost Over You." Directed by Erin Ehrlich. Written by Michael Hitchcock. The CW. January 25, 2019.

4.12. "I Need a Break." Directed by Jack Dolgen. Written by Ilana Pena. The CW. February 1, 2019.

4.13. "I Have to Get Out." Directed by Stuart McDonald. Written by Rene Gube. The CW. February 8, 2019.

4.14. "I'm Finding My Bliss." Directed by Kabir Akhtar. Written by Elisabeth Kiernan Averick and Michael Hitchcock. The CW. March 15, 2019.

4.15. "I Need to Find My Frenemy." Directed by Stuart McDonald. Written by Alden Derck and Aline Brosh McKenna. The CW. March 22, 2019.

4.16. "I Have a Date Tonight." Directed by Dan Gregor. Written by Erin Ehrlich. The CW. March 29, 2019.

4.17. "I'm in Love." Directed by Aline Brosh McKenna. Written by Aline Brosh McKenna and Rachel Bloom. The CW. April 5, 2019.

4.18. "Yes, It's Really Us Singing: The Crazy Ex-Girlfriend Concert Special!" Directed by Marty Pasetta Jr. Written by Rachel Bloom, Adam Schlesinger, and Jack Dolgen. The CW. April 5, 2019.

# Notes

## Introduction

1. Joshua Alston, "Crazy Ex-Girlfriend Is the Sharpest Pop Satire You're Not Watching (or Hearing)," *AV/TV Club*, February 22, 2016, https://tv.avclub.com/crazy-ex-girlfriend-is-the-sharpest-pop-satire-you-re-n-1798244533.

2. Samantha Allen, "'Crazy Ex-Girlfriend' Is Smart, Sexy, Unapologetically Feminist TV," *The Daily Beast*, November 2, 2015, https://www.thedailybeast.com/crazy-ex-girlfriend-is-smart-sexy-unapologetically-feminist-tv (accessed February 14, 2018).

3. Matt Zoller Seitz, "The Best Show on TV Is *Crazy Ex-Girlfriend*," *Vulture*, 2016, http://www.vulture.com/2016/06/best-show-crazy-ex-girlfriend-c-v-r.html.

4. Kevin Fallon, "'Crazy Ex-Girlfriend' Is Still the Most Charming Show on TV," *The Daily Beast*, October 13, 2017, https://www.thedailybeast.com/crazy-ex-girlfriend-is-still-the-most-charming-show-on-tv.

5. See Emily Nussbaum, "Definitely Not a Top Ten List: The Best TV Shows of 2017," *The New Yorker*, December 18, 2017, https://www.newyorker.com/culture/2017-in-review/definitely-not-a-top-ten-list-the-best-tv-shows-of-2017; and "Glee Club," *The New Yorker*, January 25, 2016, https://www.newyorker.com/magazine/2016/01/25/glee-club.

6. Alison Herman, "How Aline Brosh McKenna Reinvented the Romantic Comedy—for TV," *The Ringer*, November 9, 2017, https://www.theringer.com/tv/2017/11/9/16625682/aline-brosh-mckenna-profile (accessed December 28, 2019). See also Lauren Boumaroun in this volume.

7. Susan Dominus, "Rachel Bloom's Twisted Comedy," *New York Times Magazine*, January 19, 2016, https://www.nytimes.com/2016/01/24/magazine/make-em-laugh.html?auth=login-email&login=email (accessed December 28, 2019).

8. Dominus, "Rachel Bloom's Twisted Comedy."

9. Dominus, "Rachel Bloom's Twisted Comedy."

10. Dominus, "Rachel Bloom's Twisted Comedy."

11. Scott Meslow, "Rachel Bloom Has a Lot to Say," *GQ*, June 13, 2018, https://www.gq.com/story/rachel-bloom-has-a-lot-to-say.

12. Jon Lafayette, "Bet on The CW Paying Off for the Network's Parents," *Broadcasting & Cable,* October 27, 2014, 16.

13. Maureen Ryan, "For Women, The CW Is Still the Gold Standard," *Variety,* October 21, 2016, 28.

14. Amanda D. Lotz, *We Now Disrupt This Broadcast: How Cable Transformed Television and the Internet Revolutionized It All* (Cambridge, MA: MIT Press, 2018), 69.

15. Michael Z. Newman and Elana Levine, *Legitimating Television: Media Convergence and Cultural Status* (New York: Routledge, 2012), 5.

16. Jennifer Gillan, *Television and New Media: Must-Click TV* (New York: Routledge, 2011), 74. Gillan cites Mike Shields, "New Net, New Business," *MediaWeek,* January 30, 2006, 5.

17. Paige Abiniak, "CW-Netflix Deal Puts Broadcasters on Edge," *Broadcasting & Cable,* October 24, 2011, 26.

18. See Caryn Murphy, "The CW: Media Conglomerates in Partnership," in *From Networks to Netflix: A Guide to Changing Channels,* ed. Derek Johnson, 35–44 (New York: Routledge, 2018), 36.

19. Sarandos quoted in Liz Calvario, "Netflix and The CW Reach New Multi-Year Licensing Deal for Scripted Series," *IndieWire,* July 5, 2016, http://www.indiewire.com/2016/07/netflix-the-cw-network-announce-new-agreement-streaming-1201702652/.

20. Calvario, "Netflix and The CW."

21. Daniel Holloway, "The CW's Male-Pattern Boldness," *Broadcasting & Cable,* October 27, 2014, 13.

22. Michael Depp, "CW Steers Viewers from Streaming to Broadcast," *TVNewsCheck,* March 9, 2020, https://tvnewscheck.com/article/245601/cw-steers-viewers-from-streaming-to-broadcast/.

23. Amanda D. Lotz, *We Now Disrupt This Broadcast: How Cable Transformed Television and the Internet Revolutionized It All* (Cambridge, MA: MIT Press, 2018), 148.

24. Lotz, *We Now Disrupt,* 146.

25. Murphy, "The CW," 37.

26. Kaitlin Thomas, "The CW Boss Defends Renewing Crazy Ex-Girlfriend," *TV Guide,* January 8, 2017.

27. There were 700,000–800,000 viewers in the live +7 window. The first season averaged about a million viewers per episode; the last season averaged about 400,000 viewers per episode.

28. Meslow, "Rachel Bloom Has a Lot to Say."

29. Jason Mittell, *Complex TV: The Poetics of Contemporary Television Storytelling,* (New York: New York Univ. Press, 2015), 34.

30. Mittell, *Complex TV,* 16.

31. Mittell, *Complex TV,* 16.

32. Willa Paskin, "What Does 'Peak TV' Really Mean?" *Slate*, December 23, 2015, https://slate.com/culture/2015/12/what-does-peak-tv-really-mean.html.

33. Paskin, "What Does 'Peak TV' Really Mean?"

34. Percentages of scripted originals in 2018, according to FX's Networks Research, were 32 percent online, 30 percent broadcast, 29 percent basic cable, and 9 percent pay cable; see Lesley Goldberg, "Peak TV Update: Scripted Originals Hit Yet Another High in 2018," *Hollywood Reporter*, December 13, 2018, https://www.hollywoodreporter.com/live-feed/peak-tv-update-scripted-originals-hit-high-2018-1169047 (accessed December 28, 2019).

35. Elaine Low, "John Landgraf: Nearly 60% of FX's Writing Staff Are Now Not White Men," *Variety*, October 26, 2019, https://variety.com/2019/tv/news/john-landgraf-usc-gould-entertainment-law-1203384643/ (accessed December 28, 2019).

36. James Poniewozik, "Review: Crazy Ex-Girlfriend, a Musical with Twisted Songs," *New York Times*, October 11, 2015, https://www.nytimes.com/2015/10/12/arts/television/review-crazy-ex-girlfriend-a-musical-with-twisted-songs.html.

37. Constance Grady, "Crazy Ex-Girlfriend Succeeds Where Most TV Musicals Fail Thanks to This One Trick," *Vox*, October 21, 2016, https://www.vox.com/2016/4/20/11463132/crazy-ex-girlfriend-tv-musicals

38. Ron Rodman, "'Coperettas,' 'Detecterns,' and Space Operas: Music and Genre Hybridization in American Television," in *Music in Television: Channels of Listening*, ed. James Deaville, 35–56 (New York: Routledge, 2011), 41–42.

39. Rodman, "'Coperettas,'" 53.

40. I am leaving out of this discussion those television musicals aimed at an audience of children or tweens, such as the Disney Channel hits *Hannah Montana* (2006–11), *Phineas and Ferb* (2007–15), and the *High School Musical* trilogy (2006–8) as well as the *Descendants* trilogy (2015–19).

41. Mary Jo Lodge, "Beyond 'Jumping the Shark': The New Television Musical," *Studies in Musical Theatre* 1, no. 3 (2007): 294.

42. Lodge, "Beyond 'Jumping the Shark,'" 300.

43. Richard Dyer, "Entertainment and Utopia," in *Movies and Methods*, vol. 2, ed. Bill Nichols, 220–32 (Berkeley: Univ. of California Press, 1977), 220–32.

44. Janet K. Halfyard, *Sounds of Fear and Wonder: Music in Cult TV* (London: I. B. Tauris, 2016), 142.

45. Meslow, "Rachel Bloom Has a Lot to Say."

46. Lodge, "Beyond 'Jumping the Shark,'" 301.

47. Raymond Knapp, *The American Musical and the Performance of Personal Identity* (Princeton: Princeton Univ. Press, 2006), 205.

48. Meslow, "Rachel Bloom Has a Lot to Say."

49. Eliza Berman, "Rachel Bloom on Crazy Ex-Girlfriend and Flipping the Bechdel Test on Its Head," *Time.com*, October 14, 2015, https://time.com/4068058/rachel-bloom-crazy-ex-girlfriend/ (accessed December 28, 2019).

50. Sara Ahmed, *Living a Feminist Life* (Durham, NC: Duke Univ. Press, 2017).

51. Whitney Friedlander, "Ten Ways Crazy Ex-Girlfriend Changed TV," *Paste*, April 4, 2019, https://www.pastemagazine.com/articles/2019/04/10-ways-crazy-ex-girlfriend -changed-tv.html (accessed December 3, 2019). For more on the show's depiction of various aspects of Jewishness, see *Journal of Modern Jewish Studies* 19 (2020), edited by Jennifer Caplan, https://www.tandfonline.com/toc/cmjs20/19/1?nav=tocList.

52. Jonathan Gray, Jeffrey P. Jones, and Ethan Thompson, "The State of Satire, the Satire of State," in *Satire TV: Politics and Comedy in the Post-Network Era*, ed. Jonathan Gray, Jeffrey P. Jones, and Ethan Thompson, 3–46 (New York: New York Univ. Press, 2009), 9.

53. Linda Mizejewski, *Pretty/Funny: Women Comedians and Body Politics* (Austin: Univ. of Texas Press, 2014), 6.

54. Linda Mizejewski and Victoria Sturtevant, "Introduction," in *Hysterical! Women in American Comedy*, ed. Linda Mizejewski and Victoria Sturtevant, 1–34 (Austin: Univ. of Texas Press, 2017), 6.

55. Dominus, "Rachel Bloom's Twisted Comedy."

56. Shweta Khilnani, "Of Nasty, Unlikeable Women: Veep and the Comedic Female Anti-Hero," *Flow*, April 24, 2017, https://www.flowjournal.org/2017/04/of-nasty-unlikeable -women/. See also Margaret Tally, *The Rise of the Anti-Heroine in TV's Third Golden Age* (Cambridge: Scholars Publishing, 2016), 8.

57. Julia Havas and Maria Sulimma, "Through the Gaps of My Fingers: Genre, Femininity, and Cringe Aesthetics in Dramedy Television," *Television and New Media* 21, no. 1 (2018): 80.

58. Havas and Sulimma, "Through the Gaps," 84.

59. See Melissa Dahl, *Cringeworthy: A Theory of Awkwardness* (New York: Portfolio/ Penguin, 2018), 11.

60. Jorie Lagerwey and Taylor Nygaard, "Liberal Women, Mental Illness, and Precarious Whiteness in Trump's America," *Flow*, November 27, 2017, https://www.flow journal.org/2017/11/whiteness-in-trumps-america/ (accessed December 3, 2019).

61. Lagerwey and Nygaard, "Liberal Women."

## 1. "Crazy for *Crazy Ex-Girlfriend*"

1. Robert Bianco, "Review: Ex-Girlfriend Is Crazy Musical Fun," *USA Today* (October 9, 2015); Josh Bell, "Musical Comedy Crazy Ex-Girlfriend Brings an Appealing Mix," *Las Vegas Weekly* (October 7, 2015).

2. Daniel Fienberg, "Crazy Ex-Girlfriend: TV Review," *Hollywood Reporter* (October 8, 2015); Scott D. Pierce, "Crazy Ex-Girlfriend Is Daft. You'll Love It!," *Salt Lake Tribune* (October 9, 2015); Sarah Rodman, "CW's Crazy Ex-Girlfriend Could Be a Winner," *Boston Globe* (October 12, 2015).

3. Molly Eichel, "Crazy Ex-Girlfriend Is a Smart, Dark Delight," *AV Club* (October 12, 2015); Jeff Jensen, "Crazy Ex-Girlfriend: TV Review," *Entertainment Weekly* (October 12, 2015).

4. Emily Nussbaum, "Glee Club: Fresh Starts on Crazy Ex-Girlfriend and Younger," *New Yorker* (January 18, 2016).

5. Henry Jenkins, Jane Shattuc, and Tara McPherson, "The Culture That Sticks to Your Skin: A Manifesto for a New Cultural Studies," in *Hop on Pop: The Politics and Pleasures of Popular Culture*, ed. Henry Jenkins, Jane Shattuc, and Tara McPherson, 3–25 (Durham, NC: Duke Univ. Press, 2002), 13.

6. Jenkins, Shattuc, and McPherson, "The Culture That Sticks to Your Skin."

7. Jenkins, Shattuc, and McPherson, "The Culture That Sticks to Your Skin." The person who epitomizes that liminal position today is Henry Jenkins, the Provost Professor of Communication, Journalism, Cinematic Arts and Education at the University of Southern California who had earlier spent a decade at MIT as Director of the Comparative Media Studies Program. As he acknowledges in many of his published pieces, including university textbooks, articles for Salon.com and the Huffington Post, and more than 2,000 blog posts that are archived at his "Confessions of an Aca-Fan" website, Jenkins's passion for participatory culture—his personal connection to fan communities—is what drives his scholarly productivity; but so does the idea of speaking to a broad base of non-academics: individuals whose knowledge of media has developed organically outside of institutions of higher learning.

8. Karen Hellekson and Kristina Busse, "Introduction: Work in Progress," in *Fan Fiction and Fan Communities in the Age of the Internet: New Essays*, ed. Karen Hellekson and Kristina Busse, 5–32 (Jefferson, NC: McFarland, 2006), 25.

9. Camille Bacon-Smith, *Enterprising Women: Television Fandom and the Creation of Popular Myth* (Philadelphia: Univ. of Pennsylvania Press, 1992); John Fiske, "The Cultural Economy of Fandom," in *The Adoring Audience: Fan Culture and Popular Media*, ed. Lisa A. Lewis (New York: Routledge, 1992), 30–49; Henry Jenkins, *Textual Poachers: Television Fans and Participatory Culture* (New York: Routledge, 1992).

10. Matt Hills, *Fan Cultures* (New York: Routledge, 2002); Mark Jancovich and Nathan Hunt, "The Mainstream, Distinction, and Cult TV," in *Cult Television*, ed. Sara Gwenllian-Jones and Roberta E. Pearson, 27–44 (Minneapolis: Univ. of Minnesota Press, 2004); Cornell Sandvoss, *Fans: The Mirror of Consumption* (Cambridge: Polity Press, 2005); Rebecca Williams, *Post-Object Fandom: Television, Identity and Self-Narrative* (New York: Bloomsbury Academic, 2015); and Melissa Click and Suzanne Scott, eds., *The Routledge Companion to Media Fandom* (New York: Routledge, 2018).

11. John Sullivan, *Media Audiences: Effects, Users, Institutions, and Power* (Thousand Oaks, CA: SAGE, 2012), 194.

12. Sullivan, *Media Audiences*, 209.

13. Sullivan, *Media Audiences*, 206.

14. George Dohrmann, *Superfans: Into the Heart of Obsessive Sports Fandom* (New York: Random House, 2018); Adam Geczy, Paul Mountfort, and Anne Peirson-Smith, eds., *Planet Cosplay: Costume Play, Identity and Global Fandom* (Bristol: Intellect, 2019); Alan McKee, "The Fans of Cultural Theory," in *Fandom: Identities and Communities in a Mediated World*, ed. Jonathan Gray, C. Lee Harrington, and Cornel Sandvoss, 88–97 (New York: New York Univ. Press, 2007).

15. Daisy Asquith, "Crazy About One Direction: Whose Shame Is It Anyway?," in *Seeing Fans: Representations of Fandom in Media and Popular Culture*, ed. Lucy Bennett and Paul Booth (New York: Bloomsbury, 2018), 82.

16. Mark Duffett, *Understanding Fandom: An Introduction to the Study of Media Fan Culture* (New York: Bloomsbury, 2013), 103.

17. Duffett, *Understanding Fandom*, 85–122.

18. Duffett, *Understanding Fandom*, 103.

19. Brian Lowry, "TV Review: Crazy Ex-Girlfriend," *Variety* (October 8, 2015).

20. Hanh Nguyen, "Crazy Ex-Girlfriend Finally Went to Its Darkest Place Yet on Friday's Pivotal Episode," *IndieWire* (November 10, 2017), https://www.indiewire.com/2017/11/crazy-ex-girlfriend-i-never-want-to-see-josh-again-suicide-cw-1201896470/.

21. In addition to being uttered by characters within *CXG*, the word "stalker" has been frequently used by the show's many supporters when describing Rebecca. An example of this rhetorical move occurs in the opening paragraph of Emily Nussbaum's *New Yorker* article, "Glee Club: Fresh Starts on Crazy Ex-Girlfriend and Younger" (January 18, 2016), which begins with her calling the protagonist a "delusional stalker."

22. Jensen, "Crazy Ex-Girlfriend: TV Review."

23. Mark Dawidziak, "Crazy Ex-Girlfriend Tops Network Newcomers with Its Music-Comedy Mix," *Cleveland.Com TV Blog* (October 17, 2015).

24. Lowry, "TV Review"; Willa Paskin, "Crazy Ex-Girlfriend Is Peak #PeakTV," *Slate* (October 8, 2015).

25. Jensen, "Crazy Ex-Girlfriend: TV Review"; Fienberg, "Crazy Ex-Girlfriend: TV Review."

26. Bianco, "Review: Ex-Girlfriend Is Crazy Musical Fun."

27. Eichel, "Crazy Ex-Girlfriend."

28. Dawidziak, "Crazy Ex-Girlfriend Tops Network."

29. Mary McNamara, "And They All Live Sardonically Ever After on the Intoxicating, Daffy Crazy Ex-Girlfriend," *Los Angeles Times* (October 12, 2015).

30. Rob Owen, "Tuned In: Crazy for Crazy Ex-Girlfriend," *Pittsburgh Post-Gazette* (October 8, 2015); Jensen, "Crazy Ex-Girlfriend: TV Review."

31. Fienberg, "Crazy Ex-Girlfriend: TV Review."

32. Eichel, "Crazy Ex-Girlfriend."

33. Eichel, "Crazy Ex-Girlfriend."

34. Fienberg, "Crazy Ex-Girlfriend: TV Review."

35. Paskin, "Crazy Ex-Girlfriend Is Peak #PeakTV."

36. Paskin, "Crazy Ex-Girlfriend Is Peak #PeakTV."

37. Casey Mink, "Crazy Ex-Girlfriend Recap: Meet Rebecca, Who Is Totally Not at All Crazy," *Hollywood Life* (October 12, 2015); Eichel, "Crazy Ex-Girlfriend."

38. Paskin, "Crazy Ex-Girlfriend Is Peak #PeakTV"; Bell, "Musical Comedy."

39. James Poniewozik, "Review: Crazy Ex-Girlfriend, a Musical with Twisted Songs," *New York Times* (October 11, 2015).

40. Poniewozik, "Review"; Eichel, "Crazy Ex-Girlfriend."

41. McNamara, "And They All Live."

42. Jensen, "Crazy Ex-Girlfriend: TV Review."

43. Jensen, "Crazy Ex-Girlfriend: TV Review."

44. Jensen, "Crazy Ex-Girlfriend: TV Review."

45. Jensen, "Crazy Ex-Girlfriend: TV Review."

46. Matt Zoller Seitz, "The Best Show on TV Is Crazy Ex-Girlfriend," *Vulture* (June 29, 2016), https://www.vulture.com/2016/06/best-show-crazy-ex-girlfriend-c-v-r.html.

47. Matt Zoller Seitz, *Mad Men Carousel: The Complete Critical Companion* (New York: Harry N. Abrams, 2015); Matt Zoller Seitz and Alan Sepinwall, *The Sopranos Sessions* (New York: Harry N. Abrams, 2019).

48. Seitz, "The Best Show on TV."

49. Seitz, "The Best Show on TV."

50. Seitz, "The Best Show on TV."

51. Seitz, "The Best Show on TV."

52. Jensen, "Crazy Ex-Girlfriend: TV Review."

53. Jensen, "Crazy Ex-Girlfriend: TV Review"; Eichel, "Crazy Ex-Girlfriend."

54. Pierce, "Crazy Ex-Girlfriend Is Daft."

55. Jenkins, Shattuc, and McPherson, "The Culture That Sticks to Your Skin," 6.

56. Matt Hills, "'Twilight' Fans Represented in Commercial Paratexts and Inter-Fandoms: Resisting and Repurposing Negative Fan Stereotypes," in *Genre, Reception, and Adaptation in the "Twilight" Series*, ed. Anne Morey, 113–29 (Burlington, VT: Ashgate, 2012), 116.

57. Rebecca Williams, "'Anyone Who Calls Muse a *Twilight* Band Will be Shot on Sight': Music, Distinction, and the 'Interloping Fan' in the Twilight Franchise," *Popular Music and Society* 36, no. 3 (2013): 337–38.

58. Dean Barnes Leetal, "Those Crazy Fangirls on the Internet: Activism of Care, Disability and Fan Fiction," *Canadian Journal of Disability Studies* (University of Waterloo: Canadian Disability Studies Association, 2019), https://cjds.uwaterloo.ca/index.php/cjds/article/view/491/736.

59. "Gender and Women's Mental Health," *World Health Organization*: https://www.who.int/mental_health/prevention/genderwomen/en/.

60. Arielle Bernstein, "How Crazy Ex-Girlfriend Became TV's Most Surprising Feminist Comedy," *The Guardian* (November 13, 2018), https://www.theguardian.com/tv-and-radio/2018/nov/13/crazy-ex-girlfriend-rachel-bloom-feminist-comedy.

61. Bernstein, "How Crazy Ex-Girlfriend."

62. Lori Morimoto, "Ontological Security and the Politics of Transcultural Fandom," in *A Companion to Media Fandom and Fan Studies*, ed. Paul Booth, 257–75 (Hoboken, NJ: Wiley-Blackwell, 2018), 266.

### 2. Musicals Have a Place

1. Kelsea Stahler, "'Crazy Ex-Girlfriend' Star Rachel Bloom Is Living Proof That Fangirling Is a Radical Act," *Bustle* (July 24, 2018), https://www.bustle.com/p/crazy-ex-girlfriend-star-rachel-bloom-is-living-proof-that-fangirling-is-a-radical-act-9844149.

2. She has remarked that it was one of her central career goals (Stahler, "'Crazy Ex-Girlfriend' Star Rachel Bloom Is Living Proof").

3. Lesley Goldberg, "Network TV's Live Musical Boom Hits Sour Note," *Hollywood Reporter* (February 13, 2019), https://www.hollywoodreporter.com/live-feed/network-tvs-live-musical-boom-hits-sour-note-1186035.

4. For example, Kevin Fallon writes, "The TV musical experiment has failed," in response to the downturn in *Glee* and *Smash*, and they conclude that "it's time to put this genre to rest" ("The TV Musical Is Dead," *The Atlantic* [April 10, 2012], https://www.theatlantic.com/entertainment/archive/2012/04/the-tv-musical-is-dead/255643/).

5. Kyra Hunting and Amanda McQueen, "A Musical Marriage: The Mash-Up Aesthetic as Governing Logic in *Glee*," *Quarterly Review of Film and Video* 31, no. 4 (2014): 297.

6. CW Press Release (July 31, 2015), https://cwtvpr.com/the-cw/releases/view?id=43222.

7. Isobel Lewis, "How *Crazy Ex-Girlfriend* revived the TV Musical Genre—And Liberated Its Heroine," *The Atlantic* (April 5, 2019), https://www.theatlantic.com/entertainment/archive/2019/04/crazy-ex-girlfriend-revived-tv-musical-the-cw/586555/.

8. Devon Ivie, "*Crazy Ex-Girlfriend*'s Producers Tell the Stories Behind 9 Songs from Season Two," *Vulture* (February 3, 2017), https://www.vulture.com/2017/02/crazy-ex-girlfriend-songs-rachel-bloom-aline-brosh-mckenna.html.

9. Jason Mittell, *Genre and Television* (New York: Routledge, 2004), 187.

10. Mittell, *Genre and Television*, 153.

11. Hunting and McQueen, "A Musical Marriage," 292.

12. Hunting and McQueen, "A Musical Marriage," 292, 294.

13. For example, the success of *Parks and Rec* (NBC, 2009–15) and *This Is Us* (NBC, 2016–present) prompted people to speculate as to whether cynical television had given way to more heartwarming and tearjerking fare. See Morgan Glennon, "Is the Age of the Cynical Sitcom Over?" *Huffpost* (February 22, 2013), https://www.huffpost.com

/entry/is-the-age-of-the-cynical_b_2744154; and Rick Bentley, "In Cynical TV Landscape, This Is Us Defies the Odds," *Times Colonist* (January 22, 2017), https://www.times colonist.com/entertainment/television/small-screen-in-cynical-tv-landscape-this-is-us -defies-the-odds-1.8242488).

14. Pierre-Emmanuel Jacques, "The Associational Attractions of the Musical," in *The Cinema of Attractions Reloaded*, ed. Wanda Strauven, 281–88 (Amsterdam: Amsterdam Univ. Press, 2006), 284.

15. Katherine Spring, *Saying It with Songs* (Oxford: Oxford Univ. Press, 2013), 97.

16. Spring, *Saying It with Songs*, 101.

17. Maureen Ryan, "'Crazy Ex-Girlfriend' Plans 'Our Version of a Happy Ending,'" *New York Times* (October 10, 2018), https://www.nytimes.com/2018/10/10/arts/television /crazy-ex-girlfriend-rachel-bloom-aline-brosh-mckenna-interview.html.

18. Bloom quoted in Ryan, "'Crazy Ex-Girlfriend' Plans 'Our Version of a Happy Ending.'"

19. For example: "JAP Battle (Reprise)" (4.14); "The Math of Love Quadrangles" (4.14); "There's No Bathroom" (4.16); and "Eleven O'Clock" (4.17), which consists of a medley of nine previous songs.

20. Chris Harnick, "From Anxiety to Revenge: Rachel Bloom on *Crazy Ex-Girlfriend* Season 3 and Diagnosing Rebecca Bunch," *ENews* (October 12, 2017), https://www .eonline.com/news/885137/from-anxiety-to-revenge-rachel-bloom-on-crazy-ex-girlfriend -season-3-diagnosing-rebecca-bunch.

21. Viewing numbers found on: https://tvseriesfinale.com/tv-show/crazy-ex-girlfriend -season-one-ratings-38641/, https://tvseriesfinale.com/tv-show/crazy-ex-girlfriend-season -two-ratings/, https://tvseriesfinale.com/tv-show/crazy-ex-girlfriend-season-three-ratings/, https://tvseriesfinale.com/tv-show/crazy-ex-girlfriend-season-four-ratings/.

22. Lisa de Moraes, "Final 2016–17 TV Rankings," *Deadline* (May 25, 2017), https:// deadline.com/2017/05/2016-2017-tv-season-ratings-series-rankings-list-1202102340/.

23. Viewership remained low in season four, ranging from .3 to .5 million viewers an episode (https://tvseriesfinale.com/tv-show/crazy-ex-girlfriend-season-four-ratings/).

24. Stahler, "'Crazy Ex-Girlfriend' Star Rachel Bloom Is Living Proof," http://www .bustle.com/p/crazy-ex-girlfriend-star-rachel-bloom-is-living-proof-that-fangirling-is-a -radical-act-9844149.

25. Kaitlin Thomas, "The CW Boss Defends Renewing *Crazy Ex-Girlfriend*," *TV Guide* (January 8, 2017), https://www.tvguide.com/news/crazy-exgirlfriend-renewed-season -3-mark-pedowitz-cw/.

26. Laura Bradley, "Crazy Ex-Girlfriend Will End after Its Fourth Season—As It Should," *Vanity Fair* (April 2, 2018), https://www.vanityfair.com/hollywood/2018/04/crazy -ex-girlfriend-renewed-season-4-final-season.

27. Press Release (January 24, 2006), https://cwtvpr.com/the-cw/releases/view?id =12625.

28. Paul Gough and James Hibberd, "'90210' Upfront and Center for CW," *Hollywood Reporter* (May 13, 2008), https://www.hollywoodreporter.com/news/90210-upfront-center-cw-111620.

29. Cynthia Littleton, "Birth of the CW: UPN-WB Network Merger Deal Rocked TV Biz 10 Years Ago," *Variety* (January 24, 2016), https://variety.com/2016/tv/news/cw-wb-network-upn-merger-announcement-10-years-ago-1201687040/.

30. Andrew Wallenstein, "CW Courts Digital Auds with Original Content" (May 17, 2012), https://variety.com/2012/tv/news/cw-courts-digital-auds-with-original-content-1118054214/.

31. CW Press Release (January 19, 2016), https://cwtvpr.com/the-cw/releases/view?id=44450.

32. Littleton, "Birth of the CW."

33. Cynthia Littleton, "Netflix, CW Near Deal That Accelerates Streaming Window as Hulu Ends In-Season Pact," *Variety* (June 20, 2016), https://variety.com/2016/tv/news/netflix-cw-output-deal-the-flash-hulu-1201799176/.

34. Wallenstein, "CW Courts Digital Auds."

35. Michael Schneider, "The CW Looks to the Future as Its Parent Companies Evolve," *Variety* (August 7, 2019), https://variety.com/2019/tv/news/cw-cbs-warnermedia-1203294203/.

36. Hunting and McQueen, "A Musical Marriage," 290.

37. Hunting and McQueen, "A Musical Marriage," 291.

38. Hunting and McQueen, "A Musical Marriage," 291.

39. Ryan, "'Crazy Ex-Girlfriend' Plans 'Our Version of a Happy Ending.'"

40. Viewing numbers as of December 2019. "Heavy Boobs" and "Settle for Me" are not explicit versions.

41. Emily Yahr, "'Crazy Ex-Girlfriend's' Raunchy, Hilarious Concert Tour Proves Low TV Ratings May Not Matter," *Washington Post* (April 9, 2018), https://www.washingtonpost.com/news/soloish/wp/2018/04/09/crazy-ex-girlfriends-tv-ratings-are-low-but-its-fans-are-loyal/?noredirect=on&utm_term=.44e2b418b2d8.

42. Stahler, "'Crazy Ex-Girlfriend' Star Rachel Bloom."

### 3. Deconstructing Crazy

1. Jeffrey Sconce, "Irony, Nihilism and the New American 'Smart' Film," *Screen* 43, no. 4 (2002): 349.

2. David Bordwell, *Narration in the Fiction Film* (Madison: Univ. of Wisconsin Press, 1985), 157.

3. Laura Mulvey, "Visual Pleasure and Narrative Cinema," *Screen* 16, no. 3 (1975): 11.

4. Frank Krutnik, "Conforming Passions? Contemporary Romantic Comedy," in *Genre and Contemporary Hollywood*, ed. Steve Neale, 130–47 (London: BFI, 2003), 140.

5. Krutnik, "Conforming Passions," 142.

6. Krutnik, "Conforming Passions," 140.

7. For a detailed discussion of the stereotype and its prevalence in popular media, see Ruth R. Wisse, *No Joke: Making Jewish Humor* (Princeton, NJ: Princeton Univ. Press, 2013), 1–28.

8. Thomas Elsaesser, "Media Archeology as Symptom," *New Review of Film and Television Studies* 14, no. 2 (2016): 207–8.

9. Laura Mulvey, *Citizen Kane* (London: Bloomsbury Publishing, 2017), 80.

10. Steven Shaviro, "The Life, After Death, of Postmodern Emotions," *Criticism* 46, no. 1 (2004): 140.

11. Slavoj Žižek, *The Sublime Object of Ideology* (London: Verso, 1989), 82.

## 4. Television after Complexity

1. Amanda Lotz, *The Television Will Be Revolutionized* (New York: New York Univ. Press, 2007), 12–14.

2. Jason Mittell, *Complex TV: The Poetics of Contemporary Television Storytelling* (New York: New York Univ. Press, 2015), 40.

3. Mittell, *Complex TV*, 40.

4. Mittell, *Complex TV*, 40.

5. Mittell, *Complex TV*, 41.

6. Mittell, *Complex TV*, 42–43.

7. Steven Shaviro, "Post-continuity," *The Pinocchio Theory*, March 26, 2012, http://www.shaviro.com/Blog/?p=1034 (accessed October 25, 2019).

8. Joy Press, *Stealing the Show: How Women Are Revolutionizing Television* (New York: Atria Books, 2018), 2.

9. Lili Loofbourow, "TV's New Girls' Club," *New York Times Magazine*, January 16, 2015, https://www.nytimes.com/2015/01/18/magazine/tvs-new-girls-club.html (accessed October 25, 2019).

10. Loofbourow, "TV's New Girls' Club."

11. Loofbourow, "TV's New Girls' Club."

12. Naja Later, "Quality Television (TV) Eats Itself: The TV-Auteur and the Promoted Fanboy," *Quarterly Review of Film and Video* 35, no. 6 (2018): 531.

13. Caetlin Benson-Allott, "Made for Quality Television?: Behind the Candelabra (Steven Soderbergh, 2013) Anna Nicole (Mary Herron, 2013)," *Film Quarterly* 66, no. 4 (2013): 5.

14. Press, *Stealing the Show*, 9–10.

15. Press, *Stealing the Show*, 11.

16. Loofbourow, "TV's New Girls' Club."

17. Loofbourow, "TV's New Girls' Club."

18. Loofbourow, "TV's New Girls' Club."

19. "Nathaniel and I Are Just Friends!," *Crazy Ex-Girlfriend*, Season 3, Episode 11. Original air date February 2, 2018. Written by Rene Gube, directed by Erin Ehrlich.

20. Loofbourow, "TV's New Girls' Club."

21. Loofbourow, "TV's New Girls' Club."

22. Loofbourow, "TV's New Girls' Club."

23. Brenda R. Weber and Joselyn K. Leimbach, "Ellen Degeneres's Incorporate Body: The Politics of Authenticity," in *Hysterical! Women in American Comedy*, ed. Linda Mizejewski and Victoria Sturtevant, 303–23 (Austin: Univ. of Texas Press, 2017), 304.

### 5. "This is What Happy Feels Like"

1. Stacy Wolf, *A Problem Like Maria: Gender and Sexuality in the American Musical* (Ann Arbor: Univ. of Michigan Press, 2002); both Mackenzie (chapter 6) and Kollman (chapter 7) highlight how queer theory can be read through musical numbers such as "Gettin' Bi" and "The Math of Love Triangles."

2. Margaret Price, "The Bodymind Problem and the Possibilities of Pain," *Hypatia* 30, no. 1 (2015): 268–84. "Bodymind" is a term that combines the body and mind from two distinct entities into one. Price writes, "I said bodymind every time I wanted to mark the fact that I believe mental disability matters, that it is an important category of analysis."

3. John Moe, "Rachel Bloom Finds Her Voice, Then Uses It to Sing about Stealing Pets and Moving to West Covina, California," January 22, 2018, in *The Hilarious World of Depression*, produced by American Public Media, podcast, MP3 audio, 53:44, https://www.hilariousworld.org/episode/2018/01/22/rachel-bloom-finds-her-voice-then-uses-it-to-sing-about-stealing-pets-and-moving-to-west.

4. Arthur Kleinman, *The Illness Narratives: Suffering, Healing, and the Human Condition* (New York: Basic Books, 1989), 49.

5. Judy Segal, "Breast Cancer Narrative as Public Rhetoric: Genre Itself and the Maintenance of Ignorance," *Linguistics and the Human Sciences* 3, no. 1 (2007): 3–23.

6. Arthur Frank, *The Wounded Storyteller: Body, Illness, and Ethics* (Chicago: Univ. of Chicago Press, 2013).

7. Frank, *Wounded Storyteller*, 2–3.

8. David T. Mitchell and Sharon L. Snyder, *Narrative Prosthesis: Disability and the Dependences of Discourse* (Ann Arbor: Univ. of Michigan Press, 2000), 9.

9. Tim Dean, "Queer," in *Keywords for Disability Studies*, ed. Rachel Adams, Benjamin Reiss, and David Serlin (New York: New York Univ. Press, 2015), 143–44. For example, Mackenzie's essay (chapter 6) uses Sedgwick's theories on love triangles and homosocial desire to examine how Rebecca understands herself through others. This

work challenges normative heterosexual romantic pairings as the typical goal of "love triangles" and instead highlights female homosocial bonds.

10. Nancy Mairs, "On Being a Cripple," in *Plaintext: Essays* (Tucson: Univ. of Arizona Press, 1986), 9–20.

11. When I refer to "abled" or "abledness," I am referring to people and experiences typically coded as "nondisabled" and do not identify as having a physical, psychological, or developmental disability.

12. Victoria Ann Lewis, "Crip," in *Keywords for Disability Studies*, ed. Rachel Adams, Benjamin Reiss, and David Serlin (New York: New York Univ. Press, 2015), 46–47.

13. Robert Menzies, Brenda A. LeFrançois, and Geoffrey Reaume, "Introducing Mad Studies," in *Mad Matters: A Critical Reader in Canadian Mad Studies*, ed. Brenda A. LeFrançois, Robert Menzies, and Geoffrey Reaume (Toronto: Canadian Scholars' Press, 2013), 1–22.

14. Lennard J. Davis, "Constructing Normalcy," in *The Disability Studies Reader*, ed. Lennard J. Davis, 2nd ed. (New York: Routledge, 2006), 3–16.

15. United States Census Bureau, "Nearly 1 in 5 People Have a Disability in the U.S., Census Bureau Reports," July 25, 2012.

16. Lennard J. Davis, "Introduction," in *The Disability Studies Reader*, ed. Lennard J. Davis, 2nd ed. (New York: Routledge, 2006), xv–xviii.

17. Davis, "Introduction," xv.

18. Alison Kafer, *Feminist, Queer, Crip* (Bloomington: Indiana Univ. Press, 2013), 36.

19. Kafer, *Feminist, Queer, Crip*, 36.

20. Critics have disagreed about the role of perspective in songs performed by characters who are not Rebecca. The songs "Settle for Me" (1.4) and "After Everything I've Done for You" (1.17) are not performed by Rebecca, but they are performed in Rebecca's presence and thus from her perspective. As for other songs performed by characters not in Rebecca's presence, there is debate as to how those songs fit into the premise of the show. I argue that since this entire show is in Rebecca's perspective (connected by the show's metaconversation about writing songs in the finale of the series), the songs sung outside of her presence are still influenced by her cripped bodymind.

21. Devon Ivie, "Crazy Ex-Girlfriend Creators Tell the Stories Behind 6 Songs from Season 3," *Vulture*. February 28, 2018, https://www.vulture.com/2018/02/crazy-ex -girlfriend-making-of-season-3-songs.html.

22. The lyrics to "I'm Just a Girl in Love" are also recalled in 4.15, when Rebecca tries to bring Audra Levine (Rachel Grate) back from Las Vegas. Audra uses the lyrics to justify why she should stay in Las Vegas with a guy she just met at a bachelorette party. Recalling the lyrics help to contrast Rebecca with Audra and highlight the growth Rebecca has had since season two.

23. Maria Elana Fernandez. "Rebecca Bunch Is 'Just a Girl in Love' in *Crazy Ex-Girlfriend*'s Season Two Theme Song," October 17, 2016, https://www.vulture.com /2016/10/crazy-ex-girlfriend-season-two-theme-im-just-a-girl-in-love.html.

24. Scott Meslow, "Rachel Bloom Has a Lot to Say," *GQ*, June 13, 2018, https://www .gq.com/story/rachel-bloom-has-a-lot-to-say.

25. Like "You Stupid Bitch" (1.11), "The End of the Movie" (3.04) is also recalled later when she faces a crossroads in her life. In season three, the decision in result of this song is to leave West Covina and try to rejoin her life in New York (which leads to her suicide attempt). However, in season four, the song instead leads her to decide to audition for a musical—a much healthier decision that foregrounds her decision to pursue writing songs in the season finale.

26. Michele Lent Hirsch, *Invisible: How Young Women with Serious Health Issues Navigate Work, Relationships, and the Pressure to Seem Just Fine* (Boston: Beacon Press, 2018).

27. Hirsch, *Invisible*, 93.

28. Moe, "Rachel Bloom Finds Her Voice."

29. Kollman (chapter 7), discussing representation of bisexuality through an analysis of Darryl, also notes that "[it is] unfortunate that the most groundbreaking example of an out, functional, and content bisexual man comes as a character who otherwise exhibits multiple markers of privilege."

30. Christine Vines. "The Damage of "Crazy Ex-Girlfriend," March 22, 2017, https://electricliterature.com/the-damage-of-crazy-ex-girlfriend-be86d9d2b10.

### 6. "Lady, We're All Gay!"

1. See Will Brooker, "Living on Dawson's Creek: Teen Viewers, Cultural Convergence, and Television Overflow," *International Journal of Cultural Studies* 4, no. 4 (2001): 456–72.

2. See, for example, Anthony Summers, who appears to be the first biographer to make this claim, in *Goddess: The Secret Lives of Marilyn Monroe* (London: Hachette, 2013), 18–89. A number of guides to the disorder also cite Marilyn as a famous example: Constance M. Dolecki, *The Everything Guide to Borderline Personality Disorder: Professional, Reassuring Advice for Coping with the Disorder and Breaking the Destructive Cycle* (New York: Simon & Schuster, 2012), 80; Richard A. Moskovitz, *Lost in the Mirror: An Inside Look at Borderline Personality Disorder* (Lanham: Rowman & Littlefield, 2001), 7; John G. Gunderson and Paul Links, *Borderline Personality Disorder: A Clinical Guide* (Arlington: American Psychiatric Publishing, 2008), 323.

3. Eve Kosofsky Sedgwick, *Between Men: English Literature and Male Homosocial Desire* (New York: Columbia Univ. Press, 1985), 21.

4. Sedgwick, *Between Men*, 2–3.

5. Sharon Marcus, *Between Women: Friendship, Desire, and Marriage in Victorian England* (Princeton: Princeton Univ. Press, 2007), 10.

6. Sedgwick, *Between Men*, 38.

7. Sedgwick, *Between Men*, 47.

8. Sedgwick, *Between Men*, 51.

9. René Girard, *Deceit, Desire, and the Novel: Self and Other in Literary Structure* (Baltimore: Johns Hopkins Univ. Press, 1965), 17.

10. Girard, *Deceit*, 53.

11. Kathleen M. Vandenberg, "René Girard and the Rhetoric of Consumption," *Contagion: Journal of Violence, Mimesis & Culture* 12/13, no. 1 (2006): 261.

12. Girard, *Deceit*, 88.

13. Girard, *Deceit*, 89.

14. Girard, *Deceit*, 57.

15. Girard, *Deceit*, 63.

16. Girard, *Deceit*, 53.

17. Girard, *Deceit*, 90.

18. Girard, *Deceit*, 294.

## 7. "Gettin' Bi"

1. Rachel Bloom and Aline Brosh McKenna, creators, *Crazy Ex-Girlfriend*, Warner Bros. Television and CBS Television Distribution, 2015–present.

2. Merl Storr, *Bisexuality: A Critical Reader* (London: Routledge, 1999), 3–4.

3. Justin Vicari, *Male Bisexuality in Current Cinema: Images of Growth, Rebellion and Survival* (Jefferson, NC: McFarland, 2011), 1–2.

4. Nicole Richter, "Bisexual Erasure in 'Lesbian Vampire' Film Theory," *Journal of Bisexuality* 13 (2013): 274–75.

5. Storr, *Bisexuality*, 29.

6. Kristin G. Esterberg, "The Bisexual Menace Revisited: Or, Shaking Up Social Categories Is Hard to Do," in *Introducing the New Sexuality Studies*, ed. Steven Seidman, Nancy Fischer, and Chet Meets, 278–84 (London: Routledge, 2011), 283.

7. Esterberg, "The Bisexual Menace Revisited," 283.

8. Esterberg, "The Bisexual Menace Revisited," 275.

9. Siobhan B. Somerville, "Queer," in *Keywords for American Culture Studies*, ed. Bruce Burgett and Glenn Hendler, 203–7 (New York: New York Univ. Press, 2014), 203.

10. Somerville, "Queer," 203.

11. Steven Angelides, "The Queer Intervention," in *The Routledge Queer Studies Reader*, ed. Donald E. Hall, Annamarie Jagose, Andrea Bebell, and Susan Potter, 60–73 (London: Routledge, 2013).

12. Somerville, "Queer," 205–7.

13. April Scarlette Callis, "Bisexual, Pansexual, Queer: Non-Binary Identities and the Sexual Borderlands," *Sexualities* 17 (2014): 63–80; Corey E. Flanders, Marianne E. LeBreton, Margaret Robinson, Jing Bian, and Jaime Alonso Caravaca-Morera, "Defining Bisexuality: Young Bisexual and Pansexual People's Voices," *Journal of Bisexuality* 17 (2017): 39–57; M. Paz Galupo, Johanna L. Ramirez, and Lex Pulice-Farrow, "'Regardless of Their Gender': Descriptions of Sexual Identity among Bisexual, Pansexual, and Queer Identified Individuals," *Journal of Bisexuality* 17 (2017): 108–24.

14. Storr, *Bisexuality*, 3.

15. On the point of the sexually voracious bisexual male, we should employ the same arguments against "slut-shaming" the woman who enjoys sex; the man who enjoys sex—even if that includes sex with other men as well as women—should similarly not be maligned. A bisexual man should not be viewed as "fickle or indecisive," and his partner should not "be wary of his propensity to 'cheat' with either gender," as if they are somehow more driven by this urge than an exclusively homosexual or heterosexual man. This anxiety speaks to a patriarchal insistence that men must perform their gender in a specific, sexually voracious way.

16. Storr, *Bisexuality*, 31; Alfred C. Kinsey, Wardell B. Pomeroy, and Clyde E. Martin, "Extracts from Sexual Behavior in the Human Male (1948)," in Storr, *Bisexuality*, 36.

17. Storr, *Bisexuality*, 99–103.

18. Eve Kosofsky Sedgwick, *Epistemology of the Closet* (Berkeley: Univ. of California Press, 1990).

19. Corey E. Flanders, Marianne E. LeBreton, Margaret Robinson, Jing Bian, and Jaime Alonso Caravaca-Morera, "Defining Bisexuality: Young Bisexual and Pansexual People's Voices," *Journal of Bisexuality* 17 (2017): 249–51.

20. Steven Angelides, author of *A History of Bisexuality* (Chicago: Univ. of Chicago Press, 2001), is particularly wary of Foucault's usefulness in studying bisexuality. While acknowledging that Foucault's "methodological innovations have been groundbreaking in reorienting the discipline of history" and even inform Angelides' own work, particularly Foucault's "notions of problematization and genealogy" (11), he ultimately finds Foucault's theory to be "limited for undertaking [the] task" of "deconstructing sexuality in general and the hetero/homosexual opposition in particular," as Foucault's "intervention and reception has been yet another foreclosure (albeit in different ways for different reasons than those occurring in psychomedical discourses) of any consideration of the category of bisexuality" (18). If Foucault and Sedgwick are the parents, after a fashion, of queer theory, yet do not spend much real estate in their work acknowledging it, it's no wonder, then, that Richter writes of bisexuality's "strained relationship with queer theory" (273). Instead of Sedgwick's epistemology of the closet, bisexual theory employs the metaphor of the "epistemology of the fence," which "collapses dichotomies between gender, sexuality, and identity categories, thus opening up multiplicitous and fluid desire" (Richter, "Bisexual Erasure," 275).

21. Vicari, *Male Bisexuality in Current Cinema*, 8.

22. Storr, *Bisexuality*, 99–103.

23. Richter, "Bisexual Erasure," 274.

24. Richter, "Bisexual Erasure," 276.

25. Storr, *Bisexuality*, 38.

26. GLAAD also revealed that in 2015, "there were only two male bisexual characters on broadcast TV." Samantha Allen, "Crazy Ex-Girlfriend Is Smashing Stereotypes of Male Bisexuality, One '80s Jam at a Time," *The Daily Beast*, March 8, 2016, accessed October 5, 2016, http://www.thedailybeast.com/articles/2016/03/07/crazy-ex-girlfriend-is -smashing-stereotypes-of-male-bisexuality-one-80s-jam-at-a-time.html.

27. Storr, *Bisexuality*, 38.

28. Vicari, *Male Bisexuality in Current Cinema*, 8.

29. Gloria E. Anzaldúa, *Borderlands/La Frontera: The New Mestiza* (San Francisco: Aunt Lute Books, 1987).

30. Dan Fogelman, creator, *This Is Us*, 20th Television, 2016–present.

31. Jennie Snyder Urman et al., executive producers, *Jane the Virgin*, Poppy Productions, 2014–19.

32. Dan Goor and Michael Schur, creators, *Brooklyn Nine-Nine*, NBC Universal Television Distribution, 2013–present.

33. Allen, "Crazy Ex-Girlfriend."

34. Pete Gardner, "Gettin' Bi," 2016, *Crazy Ex-Girlfriend: Original Television Soundtrack* (Season 1—Vol. 2), Digital Album, WaterTower Music.

35. Matt Petronzio, "A Storied Glossary of Iconic LGBT Flags and Symbols," *Mashable*, June 13, 2014, https://mashable.com/2014/06/13/lgbt-pride-symbols/#dIkoP7vwmgqJ.

36. Also called "White Josh," to distinguish him from his friend Josh Chan, who is of Filipino descent. In this way, by racializing the white character rather than the person of color, CXG further destabilizes hegemonic expectations; too, by not making his differential nickname "Gay Josh," it further normalizes nonheterosexual identities, essentially proclaiming it to not be Josh's most distinctive characteristic.

37. Maya is also openly bisexual and even came out in the same episode as Darryl. In season four, she is shown having recently broken up with a woman, while Nathaniel (Scott Michael Foster) imagines dating her to make Rebecca jealous.

38. Later, in "I Have to Get Out" and "I'm Finding My Bliss," Darryl expresses romantic interest in the mother of one of his daughter's classmates.

39. David Rose is a notable male exception herein, and he generally identifies as pansexual and has relationships with both men and women; a particularly poignant conversation around this issue occurs in episode 1.10, in which David and his friend Stevie liken plurisexuality to choosing wine. David states that he drinks red wine "but I also drink white wine. And I've been known to sample the occasional rosé . . . I like the wine and not the label."

40. Though Darryl himself states he is "one eighth Chippewa" in the series pilot episode, Darryl still enjoys white privilege, is highly educated, and by all appearances enjoys financial solvency. He also experiences de facto masculine privilege, despite there being very little support for his purposeful capitalization on it; there is evidence to suggest he may have feminist leanings, even if the label is not used, as he counts several avowedly feminist female characters among his close friends.

## 8. "I'm the Villain in My Own Story"

1. Christine Hauser, "A Defaced Gap Ad Goes from the Subway to the Web to Its Demise," *The New York Times: The Lede*, November 27, 2013, http://thelede.blogs.nytimes .com/2013/11/27/a-defaced-gap-ad-goes-from-the-subway-to-the-web-to-its-demise/?_r=0.

2. Giselle, Twitter post, January 10, 2016, 8:26 p.m., https://twitter.com/giselle_m7 /status/686358460590600193; Franny Anderson, Instagram post, November 2015, https:// www.instagram.com/p/9MXu1cKsCX/.

3. Scenes of Big Apple, Twitter post, October 27, 2015, 2:16 a.m., https://twitter .com/bigapplescenes/status/658890057558990848; Eddie Brawley, Twitter post, October 28, 2015, 9:03 p.m., https://twitter.com/ebrawley/status/659535891711598592/photo/1.

4. Some examples: Samantha Allen, "'Crazy Ex-Girlfriend' Is Smart, Sexy, Unapologetically Feminist TV," *The Daily Beast*, November 2, 2015, https://www.thedailybeast .com/crazy-ex-girlfriend-is-smart-sexy-unapologetically-feminist-tv; Eliza Berman, "Rachel Bloom on Crazy Ex-Girlfriend and Flipping the Bechdel Test on Its Head," *Time*, October 12, 2015, https://time.com/4068058/rachel-bloom-crazy-ex-girlfriend/.

5. Janet Walker, *Trauma Cinema: Documenting Incest and the Holocaust* (Berkeley: Univ. of California Press, 2005), 19, 58.

6. Rebecca is not diagnosed with Borderline Personality Disorder until season three, and it was not part of the creators' original plan for the character. See Laura Bradley, "How Crazy Ex-Girlfriend Found an Even Stronger Voice in Season 3," *Vanity Fair*, November 17, 2017, https://www.vanityfair.com/hollywood/2017/11/crazy-ex-girlfriend-borderline -personality-disorder-rachel-bloom-aline-brosh-mckenna-interview.

7. Jonathan Gray, *Show Sold Separately: Promos, Spoilers, and Other Media Paratexts* (New York: New York Univ. Press, 2010), 47.

8. Gray, *Show Sold Separately*, 24.

9. Drew Millard, "'Crazy Ex-Girlfriend' Is the Funniest Show on TV You're Not Watching," *Vice*, October 27, 2015, http://www.vice.com/read/crazy-ex-girlfriend-is-like -if-broad-city-and-seinfeld-combined-to-create-a-musical-1027.

10. Gray uses ABC's *Six Degrees* as a case study to reveal the potential for a gap between the way a series is presented and its actual meaning in Gray, *Show Sold Separately*, 47–79.

11. Rachel Bloom, Interview with Lauren Boumaroun, April 28, 2016.

12. Gray, *Show Sold Separately*, 136.

13. Brosh McKenna said the real love story in *CXG* is between Rebecca and her pseudo-mom/best friend Paula. Samantha Allen, "'Crazy Ex-Girlfriend': How Paula and Rebecca's Unlikely Friendship Became TV's Best Love Story," *The Daily Beast*, April 18, 2016, https://www.thedailybeast.com/crazy-ex-girlfriend-how-paula-and-rebeccas-unlikely -friendship-became-tvs-best-love-story.

14. Jessica Goldstein, "The 'Crazy Ex-Girlfriend' Showrunner Takes Us Inside the Show Subverting the Stereotype," *ThinkProgress*, January 27, 2016, http://thinkprogress .org/culture/2016/01/27/3742920/the-crazy-ex-girlfriend-showrunner-takes-us-inside-the -show-subverting-the-stereotype/.

15. Rachel Bloom, Interview with Lauren Boumaroun, April 28, 2016.

16. Susan Dominus, "Rachel Bloom's Twisted Comedy," *The New York Times Magazine*, January 19, 2016, https://www.nytimes.com/2016/01/24/magazine/make-em-laugh .html.

17. Rachel Bloom, "Fuck Me, Ray Bradbury," YouTube.com, August 15, 2010, https:// www.youtube.com/watch?v=eIIxOS4VzKM.

18. Richard Dyer, "Judy Garland and Camp," in *Hollywood Musicals: The Film Reader*, ed. Steven Cohan, 107–14 (New York: Routledge, 2002), 107.

19. Gray, *Show Sold Separately*, 35.

20. Christine Prevas, "Failure and the Family in Crazy Ex-Girlfriend," chapter 11, this volume.

21. Berman, "Rachel Bloom on Crazy Ex-Girlfriend."

22. Berman, "Rachel Bloom on Crazy Ex-Girlfriend."

23. Rachel Bloom, Interview with Lauren Boumaroun, April 28, 2016.

24. Kira Ibrahim, Linda Lewandowski, Thomas Templin, Vidya Ramaswamy, Bulent Ozkan, and Jamal Mohanesh, "Measuring Cumulative Trauma Dose, Types, and Profiles Using a Development-Based Taxonomy of Traumas," *Traumatology* 14, no. 2 (2008): 62–87.

25. Patricia A. Stout, Jorge Villegas, and Nancy A. Jennings, "Images of Mental Illness in the Media: Identifying Gaps in the Research," *Schizophrenia Bulletin* 30, no. 3 (2004): 543, 552.

26. Stout, Villegas, and Jennings, "Images of Mental Illness," 544.

27. Rachel Bloom, Interview with Lauren Boumaroun, April 28, 2016.

28. Dirk Eitzen, "The Emotional Basis of Film Comedy," in *Passionate Views: Film, Cognition, and Emotion*, ed. Carl Plantinga and Greg M. Smith, 84–101 (Baltimore: Johns Hopkins Univ. Press, 1999), 85.

29. Therapists in the *CXG* Facebook fan group discussed how and when they might suggest the show to some of their clients, though they would have to be careful since some of the moments may be a trigger: https://www.facebook.com/groups/1143784535651988/.

30. Rachel Bloom, Interview with Lauren Boumaroun, April 28, 2016.

31. Corinne Heller, "'Appallingly Cruel': Dr. Phil Slammed for 'Exploitative' Interview with Mentally Ill Shelley Duval," *NBC New York*, November 18, 2016, https://www.nbcnewyork.com/entertainment/entertainment-news/Dr-Phil-Slammed-for-Shelley-Duvall-Interview-401700775.html; Laurie Essig, "Dr. Phil's Very Bad Advice," *Psychology Today*, February 10, 2011, https://www.psychologytoday.com/us/blog/love-inc/201102/dr-phils-very-bad-advice; Sam Barsanti, "Former Guests Accuse *Dr. Phil* Staff of Helping Them Get Drugs and Alcohol," *AV Club*, December 30, 2017, https://www.avclub.com/former-guests-accuse-dr-phil-staff-of-helping-them-get-1821668922.

32. Frederick J. Heide, Natalie Porter, and Paul K. Saito, "Do You Hear the People Sing? Musical Theatre and Attitude Change," *Psychology of Aesthetics, Creativity, and the Arts* 6, no. 3 (2012): 228.

33. Rachel Bloom, Interview with Lauren Boumaroun, April 28, 2016.

34. Harriet and Irving Deer, "Musical Comedy: From Performer to Performance," *Journal of Popular Culture* 12, no. 3 (1978): 406.

35. Glen Weldon, "The Top 27 Songs of 'Crazy Ex-Girlfriend,' Ranked, Ruthlessly and Dispassionately," *NPR*, April 8, 2019, https://www.npr.org/2019/04/08/709062466/the-top-27-songs-of-crazy-ex-girlfriend-ranked-ruthlessly-and-dispassionately. The idea of the song embodying the essence of the series becomes clear when considering the line "Yes, Josh completes me, but how can that be when there's no me left to complete?" in light of Rebecca's decision in the series finale (4.18) to choose herself over her three love interests. The last reference to "You Stupid Bitch" is in the finale's "Eleven O'Clock" number. She looks back on the different versions of herself represented throughout the series, referring to them in the past tense until she gets to the reprise of "You Stupid Bitch" when she switches to the present tense and admits she still "doesn't know how to love." The number ends with Rebecca surrounded by costumes representing these past versions of herself, but she is still wearing the gown from "You Stupid Bitch." It is the one version of herself that she has not worked through, which encourages her to finally prioritize self-love over a romantic relationship. For the first time, she truly chooses herself, thus beginning a new chapter in her life and resolving the series' main conflict.

36. Sangmoon Kim, Randall S. Jorgensen, and Ryan Thibodeau, "Shame, Guilt, and Depressive Symptoms: A Meta-Analytic Review," *Psychological Bulletin* 137, no. 1 (2011): 70–71.

37. Rachel Bloom, Interview with Lauren Boumaroun, April 28, 2016.

38. Kim, Jorgensen, and Thibodeau, "Shame, Guilt, and Depressive Symptoms," 73.

39. Kim, Jorgensen, and Thibodeau, "Shame, Guilt, and Depressive Symptoms," 73.

40. Janina Scarlet, *Superhero Therapy: Mindfulness Guide to Help Teens and Young Adults Deal with Anxiety, Depression and Trauma* (Oakland: New Harbinger Publications, 2017), 23.

41. Stephanie Salerno, "'Let Us Ugly Cry': Spoofing Emotional Vulnerability in Season Three of Crazy Ex-Girlfriend," chapter 10, this volume.

42. Sonia Livingstone, *Making Sense of Television: The Psychology of Audience Interpretation* (London: Routledge, 1998), 56.

43. Ed S. Tan, *Emotion and the Structure of Narrative Film: Film as an Emotion Machine* (Mahwah: Erlbaum, 1996), 17, 28.

44. Heide, Porter, and Saito, "Do You Hear the People Sing?," 228.

45. Ben Sher, "Fraught Pleasures: Domestic Trauma and Cinephilia in American Culture," PhD diss., Univ. of California, Los Angeles, 2015, 7, 150.

46. Berys Gaut, "Identification and Emotion in Narrative Film," in *Passionate Views: Film, Cognition, and Emotion*, ed. Carl Plantinga and Greg M. Smith, 200–215 (Baltimore: Johns Hopkins Univ. Press, 1999), 213.

47. Torben Grodal, *Embodied Visions: Evolution, Emotion, Culture, and Film* (New York: Oxford Univ. Press, 2009), 150.

48. Grodal, *Embodied Visions*, 190.

49. Ryan M. Niemiec and Danny Wedding, *Positive Psychology at the Movies: Using Films to Build Virtues and Character Strengths* (Ashland: Hogrefe, 2013).

50. Rachel Bloom, Interview with Lauren Boumaroun, April 28, 2016.

51. Jack Dolgen, "Yes It's Really Us Singing: The Crazy Ex-Girlfriend Concert Special," taping, March 16, 2019; panel, PaleyFest LA, March 20, 2019.

## 9. "A Diagnosis!!"

1. Horace M. Newcomb and Paul M. Hirsch, "Television as a Cultural Forum: Implications for Research," *Quarterly Review of Film Studies* 8, no. 3 (1983): 45–55.

2. Jason Mittell, *Television and American Culture* (New York: Oxford Univ. Press, 2010).

3. Amanda D. Lotz, *Redesigning Women: Television after the Network Era* (Champaign: Univ. of Illinois Press, 2006), http://www.jstor.org/stable/10.5406/j.ctt1xcqg7.

4. Natalie Slopen, Amy Watson, Gabriela Gracia, and Patrick Corrigan, "Age Analysis of Newspaper Coverage of Mental Illness," *Journal of Health Communication* 1, no. 12 (2007): 3–15.

5. Heather Stuart, "Violence and Mental Illness: An Overview," *World Psychiatry* 2, no. 2 (2003): 121–24, https://www.ncbi.nlm.nih.gov/pmc/articles/PMC1525086/.

6. Angelica Jade Bastien, "What Television Gets Wrong about Mental Illness," *The Week*, September 17, 2016, http://theweek.com/articles/648229/what-tv-gets-wrong-about-mental-illness.

7. In the recent era of television, the portrayal of individuals with mental health issues evolved from characters who were psychopaths to those who were sociopaths, particularly in male characters. In one common trope, these men had certain special powers that allowed them to solve crimes, but their conditions made it difficult for them in their relationships with others. For example, in 2002, the title character of the show *Monk*

(USA Network, 2002–9), played by Tony Shalhoub, was a police consultant who had the ability to solve crimes in part because he suffered from obsessive-compulsive disorder (OCD). Another character who had similar qualities was *Sherlock Holmes* (BBC One, 2010–17), played by Benedict Cumberbatch, whose OCD qualities also allowed him to solve crimes.

8. Yvonne Villareal, "'Crazy Ex-Girlfriend' Creators Weigh in on the Exploration of Rebecca's Mental Health," *LA Times.com*, December 8, 2017, http://www.latimes.com /entertainment/tv/la-et-st-rachel-bloom-crazy-ex-girlfriend-20171208-htmlstory.html#.

9. Cited in Debra Birnbaum, "How 'Crazy Ex-Girlfriend' Moved from Showtime to The CW," *Variety.com*, May 14, 2015, https://variety.com/2015/tv/news/crazy-ex -girlfriend-cw-showtime-comedy-rachel-bloom-1201495301/.

10. Villareal, "'Crazy Ex-Girlfriend' Creators."

11. Laura Bradley, "How Crazy Ex-Girlfriend Found an Even Stronger Voice in Season 3," *Vanity Fair.com*, November 18, 2017, https://www.vanityfair.com/hollywood/2017 /11/crazy-ex-girlfriend-borderline-personality-disorder-rachel-bloom-aline-brosh-mckenna -interview.

12. Julia Havas and Maria Sulimma, "Through the Gaps of My Fingers: Genre, Femininity, and Cringe Aesthetics in Dramedy Television," *Television & New Media*. First Published May 30, 2018, https://doi.org/10.1177/1527476418777838.

13. Megan Garber, David Sims, Lenika Cruz, and Sophie Gilbert, "Have We Reached 'Peak TV'?," *The Atlantic*, August 12, 2015, http://www.theatlantic.com/entertainment /archive/2015/08/have-we-reached-peak-tv/401009/ (accessed March 15, 2016).

14. Jason Mittell, *Complex TV: The Poetics of Contemporary Television Storytelling* (New York: New York Univ. Press, 2015).

15. Jorie Lagerwey, Julie Leyda, and Diane Negra, "Female Centered TV in an Age of Precarity," *Genders* 1, no. 2 (Fall 2016), https://www.colorado.edu/genders/2016/05/19 /female-centered-tv-age-precarity.

16. Lagerwey, Leyda, and Negra, "Female Centered TV."

17. Michael Z. Newman, "The Rom-com/Sitcom/YouTube Musical: Crazy Ex-Girlfriend," *Film Criticism* 40, no. 3 (2016), https://quod.lib.umich.edu/f/fc/13761232.00 40.311?view=text;rgn=main.

18. Villareal, "'Crazy Ex-Girlfriend' Creators."

19. Kelly Lawler, "The Quietly Revolutionary Way 'Crazy Ex-Girlfriend' Addresses Mental Health," *USA Today*, November 9, 2017, https://www.usatoday.com/story/life/tv /2017/11/09/crazy-ex-girlfriend-mental-health/840665001/.

20. Sadie Doyle, "With a Groundbreaking Diagnosis, 'Crazy Ex-Girlfriend' Insists That Even 'Psycho' Women Deserve to be Heard," *Elle.com*, November 27, 2017, https:// www.elle.com/culture/movies-tv/a13938654/crazy-ex-girlfriend-borderline-personality -disorder-diagnosis/.

21. Jay Watts, "I'm a Psychologist, and This Is the Truth about Whether You Can Tell If Someone Is a 'Psychopath' or Not," *The Independent*, July 5, 2017, https://www.independent.co.uk/Voices/personality-disorder-mental-health-girl-interrupted-fatal-attraction-misdiagnosis-a7825066.html.

22. Maggy Vaneijk, "How Crazy Ex-Girlfriend Is Having the Smartest, Most Empathetic Conversations about Mental Health," *Pool.com*, November 22, 2017, https://www.the-pool.com/health/mind/2017/47/Maggy-Vaneijk-on-Crazy-Ex-Girlfriend-and-mental-health.

23. Angelica Jade Bastien, "What Television Gets Wrong about Mental Illness," *The Week*, September 17, 2016, http://theweek.com/articles/648229/what-tv-gets-wrong-about-mental-illness.

24. Doyle, "With a Groundbreaking Diagnosis."

### 10. "Let Us Ugly Cry"

1. Linda Hutcheon, *A Theory of Parody* (Urbana and Chicago: Univ. of Illinois Press, 2000 [1985]).

2. Judith Halberstam, *In a Queer Time and Place: Transgender Bodies, Subcultural Lives* (New York: New York Univ. Press, 2005). See also Caitlin E. Ray's chapter in this volume.

3. Halberstam, *In a Queer Time and Place.*

4. See essays by Christine Prevas and Lauren Boumaroun in this volume.

5. Sara Ahmed, *Queer Phenomenology: Orientations, Objects, Others* (Durham: Duke Univ. Press, 2006), 161.

6. Maureen Lenker, "The Subversive Show with the Terrible Name 'Crazy Ex-Girlfriend' Satirizes Sexist Tropes with Song and Dance," *Bitch Media*, October 12, 2016, https://www.bitchmedia.org/article/subversive-show-terrible-name/crazy-ex-girlfriend-satirizes-sexist-tropes-song-and-dance.

7. Todd VanDerWerff, "Crazy Ex-Girlfriend's Unexpected Season 3 Renewal Shows How TV's Rules Are Changing," *Vox*, January 10, 2017, https://www.vox.com/culture/2017/1/10/14206016/crazy-ex-girlfriend-season-3-renewal.

8. Richard Dyer, *In the Space of a Song* (New York: Routledge, 2012).

9. Jean-Loup Bourget, "Social Implications in the Hollywood Genres," in *Film Genre Reader III*, ed. Barry Keith Grant, 51–59 (Austin: Univ. of Texas Press, 2003), 55.

10. Edward Buscombe, "The Idea of Genre in the American Cinema," in *Film Genre Reader III*, ed. Barry Keith Grant, 12–26 (Austin: Univ. of Texas Press, 2003), 19.

11. Barbara Klinger, "'Cinema/Ideology/Criticism' Revisited: The Progressive Genre," *Film Genre Reader III*, ed. Barry Keith Grant, 75–91 (Austin: Univ. of Texas Press, 2003), 89.

12. Rick Altman, *The American Film Musical* (Bloomington: Indiana Univ. Press, 1987), 12.

13. See Margaret Tally, this volume, for an examination of how CXG rewrites the narrative of mental illness.

14. Hutcheon, *Theory of Parody*, 10–12.

15. Miguel Mera, "Is Funny Music Funny?: Contexts and Case Studies of Film Music Humor," *Journal of Popular Music Studies* 14 (2002): 95.

16. Maurice E. Stevens, "Trauma Is as Trauma Does," in *Critical Trauma Studies: Understanding Violence, Conflict and Memory in Everyday Life*, ed. Monica J. Casper and Eric Wertheimer, 19–36 (New York: New York Univ. Press, 2016), 25–26.

17. Ray, this volume.

18. The CW Network, "I Go to the Zoo," YouTube video, 0:25–0:32, https://www.youtube.com/watch?v=UEhTmETAt9A.

19. See 3.06, 0:00–0:49 and 34:55–36:55. "Josh Is Irrelevant," *Crazy Ex-Girlfriend*, season 3, episode 6, The CW, November 17, 2017, Netflix, https://www.netflix.com/watch/80215252.

20. The CW Television Network, "Fit Hot Guys Have Problems Too," YouTube video, 0:53–1:14, https://www.youtube.com/watch?v=rLESEq2dRVY.

21. The CW Television Network, "Fit Hot Guys," 1:31–1:51.

22. The CW Television Network, "Fit Hot Guys," 1:59–2:17.

23. See 1.09 and 3.09 for specific examples of White Josh's weight-related backstory.

24. See the song "Let's Have Intercourse" (2.11).

25. The CW Television Network, "Fit Hot Guys," 2:22–2:58.

26. The CW Television Network, "Fit Hot Guys," 3:07–3:30.

27. Tatiana Matejskova, "Straights in a Gay Bar: Negotiating Boundaries Through Time-Spaces," in *Geographies of Sexualities*, ed. Kath Browne, Jason Lim, and Gavin Brown, 137–50 (Burlington: Ashgate, 2007), 138–39.

28. John Kenrick, *Musical Theatre: A History* (New York: Continuum, 2008).

29. "A Diagnosis" was meant to be a huge Broadway showstopper, but the production team ran out of money. From the creators' perspective, the song was "more about doing the genre than making fun of the genre." See Devon Ivie, "Crazy Ex-Girlfriend Creators Tell the Stories Behind 6 Songs from Season 3," *Vulture*, February 28, 2018, http://www.vulture.com/2018/02/crazy-ex-girlfriend-making-of-season-3-songs.html.

30. The CW Television Network, "A Diagnosis," YouTube video, 0:30–0:43, https://www.youtube.com/watch?v=nK2DlLmVc20&t=50s.

31. The CW Television Network, "A Diagnosis," 1:03–1:16.

32. The CW Television Network, "A Diagnosis," 2:18–2:38.

33. As a result of Rebecca's actions, she is dismissed from Harvard and attends Yale Law instead, a secret she kept from everyone in West Covina.

34. Halberstam, *In a Queer Time and Place*, 169–70.

35. The CW Television Network, "Nothing Is Ever Anyone's Fault," YouTube video, 0:17–0:41, https://www.youtube.com/watch?v=sqJ6YWbBGVk.

36. Halberstam, *In a Queer Time and Place*, 4–5.

37. The CW Television Network, "Nothing Is Ever Anyone's Fault," 0:49–1:00.

38. The CW Television Network, "Nothing Is Ever Anyone's Fault," 1:39–1:49.

39. The CW Television Network, "Nothing Is Ever Anyone's Fault," 1:32–1:35.

40. "I Want to Be Here," the first episode of the fourth season, aired on October 12, 2018. It picked up moments after Rebecca apologized and declared that she was ready to be held responsible, resulting in Nathaniel's abrupt departure from the courtroom. This episode explores Rebecca's elective, brief stint in jail, in which she realizes how deep her privilege runs. Nathaniel attempts to self-punish, using deprivation and adrenaline highs to avoid emotional pain. Josh Chan is convinced he has a disorder or mental illness, echoing Rebecca's desire to find a label that explains/defines her.

## 11. Failure and the Family in *Crazy Ex-Girlfriend*

1. J. Halberstam, *The Queer Art of Failure* (Durham: Duke Univ. Press, 2011), 2–3.

2. Halberstam, *Queer Art*, 3.

3. Halberstam, *Queer Art*, 2.

4. Halberstam, *Queer Art*, 5.

5. Halberstam, *Queer Art*, 4.

6. For more on the nature of parody's queer function within the show, see Stephanie Salerno's analysis of "Fit Hot Guys Have Problems Too," "A Diagnosis," and "Nothing Is Ever Anyone's Fault" in chapter 10.

7. Erin Lee Mock, "The Horror of 'Honey, I'm Home!': The Perils of Postwar Family Love in the Domestic Sitcom," *Film & History: An Interdisciplinary Journal of Film and Television Studies* 41, no. 2 (2001): 30.

8. Mock, "The Horror of 'Honey, I'm Home!,'" 30–32.

9. Paul A. Cantor, "The Simpsons: Atomistic Politics and the Nuclear Family," in *The Simpsons and Philosophy: The D'oh! of Homer*, ed. William Irwin et al., 160–78 (Chicago: Open Court, 2001), 166.

10. Robert Sloane, "Who Wants Candy? Disenchantment in The Simpsons," in *Leaving Springfield: The Simpsons and the Possibility of Oppositional Culture*, ed. John Alberti, 137–71 (Detroit: Wayne State Univ. Press, 2004), 140.

11. Troy Dunn, *Family: The Good F-Word* (Los Angeles: Bird St. Books, 2014), xviii.

12. Arlene Skolnick, "Beyond the 'M' Word: The Tangled Web of Politics and Marriage," *Dissent* 53, no. 4 (2006): 82.

13. Arlene Skolnick, "Talking about Family Values after 'Family Values,'" *Dissent* 57, no. 4 (2010): 101.

14. Leonardo Cassuto, "The Real-Life Myth of the American Family," *American Literary History* 20, no. 3 (2008): 487.

15. Sara Ahmed, *The Promise of Happiness* (Durham: Duke Univ. Press, 2010), 45.

16. Ahmed, *Promise of Happiness*, 49.

17. Ahmed, *Promise of Happiness*, 48.

18. Halberstam, *Queer Art*, 2.

19. Halberstam, *Queer Art*, 3.

20. Ahmed, *Promise of Happiness*, 31.

21. Halberstam, *Queer Art*, 5.

22. Halberstam, *Queer Art*, 2.

## 12. *Crazy Ex-Girlfriend*'s Female Networks

1. See Mary Celeste Kearney's "Birds on the Wire: Troping Teenage Girlhood through Telephony in Mid-Twentieth-Century U.S. Media Culture," *Cultural Studies* 19, no. 5 (2005): 580, for a discussion of the "girl on the phone" trope in 1950s and 1960s US advertisements and screen texts.

2. Kearney, "Birds on the Wire," 580.

3. Ned Schantz, *Gossip, Letters, Phones: The Scandal of Female Networks in Film and Literature* (Oxford: Oxford Univ. Press, 2008), 4.

4. Schantz, *Gossip, Letters, Phones*, 3.

5. Schantz, *Gossip, Letters, Phones*, 4.

6. See Hazel Mackenzie's chapter on "The Math of Homosocial Triangles" in this volume for a discussion of the ways Paula's and Rebecca's relationship is triangulated through Josh as well as through Rebecca's mother.

7. Schantz, *Gossip, Letters, Phones*, 4.

8. In this chapter I conceive of "norms" and "normativity" as the socially defined aspirations that signify that which is worth attainment and which is a cause of a happy, successful "good life" including, among many other things, certain types of relations and health.

9. Douglas Thomas, *Hacker Culture* (Minneapolis: Univ. of Minnesota Press, 2002), ix–xi.

10. Stephen Wilson, *Information Arts: Intersections of Art, Science, and Technology* (Cambridge, MA: MIT Press, 2002), 13.

11. Schantz, *Gossip, Letters, Phones*, 33.

12. Virginia Woolf, *A Room of One's Own* (1928; reprint ed., London: Penguin, 2000), 74.

13. Alison Winch, *Girlfriends and Postfeminist Sisterhood* (Hampshire: Palgrave Macmillan, 2013), 5.

14. Rachel Bloom in Danielle Turchiano, "Rachel Bloom Reflects on Emotional 'Crazy Ex-Girlfriend' Season and Plans for Final Year," *Variety*, May 17, 2018, https://variety.com/2018/tv/features/rachel-bloom-crazy-ex-girlfriend-final-season-interview-1202793228/.

15. Episode 1.10 illustrates humorously the prescriptive aspect of social media when Rebecca tells Josh about an article showing that sunset photos get most likes after "fitness girls with big butts and slow-motion dogs."

16. Mary McGill, "#Obsessed: Ingrid Goes West and Instagram's Toxic Gaze," *Another Gaze* 1, no. 2 (2018): 71.

17. Sara Ahmed, *Living a Feminist Life* (Durham: Duke Univ. Press, 2017), 254.

18. Heather's comment also needs to be considered as a disciplining voice in this scene as she is generally the voice of reason in the show, obtaining this status through her reliance on psychology discourse to explain the behavior of the characters around her—a discourse that consolidates the normative through its dependence on delineating normal and deviant behavior.

19. Winch, *Girlfriends and Postfeminist Sisterhood*, 42.

## 13. "Put Yourself First in a Sexy Way"

1. Timotheus Vermeulen and Robin van den Akker, "Notes on Metamodernism," *Journal of Aesthetics and Culture* 2, no. 1 (2010): 1.

2. Vermeulen and Van den Akker, "Notes on Metamodernism," 2.

3. Vermeulen and Van den Akker, "Notes on Metamodernism," 5–6.

4. Seth Abramson, "On American Metamodernism," *Huffington Post*, December 6, 2017, https://www.huffingtonpost.com/seth-abramson/on-american-metamodernism_b_4743903.html.

5. Abramson, "On American Metamodernism."

6. Griffin Hansbury, "King Kong & Goldilocks: Imagining Transmasculinities through the Trans-Trans Dyad," *Psychoanalytic Dialogues* 21, no. 2 (2011): 219, http://dx.doi.org/10.1080/10481885.2011/562846; Hillary Offman, "The Princess and the Penis: A Post Postmodern Queer-y Tale," *Psychoanalytic Dialogues* 24, no. 1 (2014): 85.

7. James B. Cronin et al., "Paradox, Performance and Food: Managing Difference in the Construction of Femininity," *Consumption Markets & Culture* 17, no. 4 (2014): 367.

8. Cronin et al., "Paradox, Performance and Food," 386.

9. Gry Rustad, "Metamodernism, Quirky and Feminism," *Notes on Metamodernism*, February 29, 2012, http://www.metamodernism.com/2012/02/29/metamodernism-quirky-and-feminism/.

10. Rustad, "Metamodernism."

11. Rustad, "Metamodernism."

12. Rita Felski, "Feminism, Postmodernism, and the Critique of Modernity," *Cultural Critique* 14 (1989): 33–56.

13. Vermeulen and Van den Akker, "Notes," 2.

14. Rustad, "Metamodernism."

15. Rustad, "Metamodernism."

16. Rustad, "Metamodernism."

17. Rosalind Gill, "Postfeminist Media Culture: Elements of a Sensibility," *European Journal of Cultural Studies* 10, no. 2 (2007): 147.

18. Rustad, "Metamodernism."

19. Laura Mulvey, "Pleasure and Narrative Cinema," in *Film Theory and Criticism*, ed. Leo Braudy and Marshall Cohen, 58–69 (Oxford: Oxford Univ. Press, 2004), 841.

20. Rich Cohen, "Welcome to the Summer of Margot Robbie," *Vanity Fair*, July, 2016, https://www.vanityfair.com/hollywood/2016/07/margot-robbie-cover-story.

21. Maddison Connaughton, "Vanity Fair's Article on Margot Robbie is Fascinatingly Awful," *Vice*, July 7, 2016, https://www.vice.com/en_au/article/av9jp4/vanity-fair-tears-australia-a-new-one; Steph Harmon, "Margot Robbie Calls Her Vanity Fair Profile 'Really Weird,'" *The Guardian*, July 26, 2016, https://www.theguardian.com/film/2016/jul/26/margot-robbie-calls-her-vanity-fair-profile-really-weird.

22. See Zoe Williams, "Lady Gaga, Miley Cyrus and the Rape Generation," *The Guardian*, June 24, 2014, https://www.theguardian.com/music/womens-blog/2014/jun/24/lady-gaga-do-what-u-want-rape-generation.

23. Hermione Hoby, "Miley Cyrus Isn't a Child: She's 21 and She Can Twerk If She Wants To," *The Guardian*, November 24 2013, https://www.theguardian.com/culture/2013/nov/24/miley-cyrus-21-twerk-if-she-wants.

24. Pumla Dineo Gqola, *Reflecting Rogue: Inside the Mind of a Feminist* (Johannesburg: Jacana, 2017).

25. Gqola, *Reflecting Rogue*, 134.

26. Gqola, *Reflecting Rogue*, 136.

27. Gqola, *Reflecting Rogue*, 136.

28. Sarah Banet-Weiser, *Empowered: Popular Feminism and Popular Misogyny* (Durham: Duke Univ. Press, Kindle e-book, 2018), loc. 581.

29. Jia Tolentino, *Trick Mirror: Reflections on Self-Delusion* (New York: Random House, Kindle e-book, 2019), loc. 1268.

30. See also Cook in this volume.

31. Eliza Berman, "Rachel Bloom on *Crazy Ex-Girlfriend* and Flipping the Bechdel Test on Its Head," *Time*, October 12, 2015, http://time.com/4068058/rachel-bloom-crazy-ex-girlfriend/.

32. Berman, "Rachel Bloom."

33. Ingeborg Hoesterey, *Pastiche: Cultural Memory in Art, Film, Literature* (Bloomington: Indiana Univ. Press, 2001), 105.

34. Vermeulen and Van den Akker, "Notes," 1.

35. Fifth Harmony, "BO$$," YouTube, last modified July 8, 2014, https://www.you tube.com/watch?v=Y4JfPlry-iQ.

36. Fifth Harmony, "Worth It ft. Kid Ink," YouTube, last modified March 28, 2015, https://www.youtube.com/watch?v=YBHQbu5rbdQ.

37. Gill, "Postfeminist Media," 156–57.

38. Carl Wilson, "Crazy Exegesis," *Slate*, January 4, 2018, https://slate.com/arts/2018 /01/crazy-ex-girlfrienddeconstructs-pop-music-and-destigmatizes-mental-illness.html.

39. Gqola, *Reflecting Rogue*, 136.

40. Fifth Harmony, "BO$$."

41. Fifth Harmony, "Worth It."

42. Gqola, *Reflecting Rogue*, 136.

43. Jia Tolentino, "How 'Empowerment' Became Something for Women to Buy," *New York Times*, April 17, 2016, https://www.nytimes.com/2016/04/17/magazine/how -empowerment-became-something-for-women-tobuy.html.

44. Mulvey, "Visual Pleasure," 841.

45. Benjamin Halligan, "Modeling Affective Labor: Terry Richardson's Photography," *Cultural Politics* 13, no. 1 (2017): 58–80.

46. Hannah Ellis-Petersen, "Fashion Brands Drop Terry Richardson over Allegations of Abuse on Shoots," *The Guardian*, October 24, 2017, https://www.theguardian .com/artanddesign/2017/oct/24/terry-richardsonphotographer-dropped-fashion-brands -allegations.

47. Wilson, "Crazy Exegesis."

48. Fifth Harmony, "Worth It."

49. Carl Lamarre, "Interview: Fifth Harmony Talk Their Platinum Hit 'Worth It' and Their Love for Drake, Fetty Wap, and Kendrick Lamar," *Complex*, June 22, 2015, http:// www.complex.com/music/2015/06/fifth-harmonyinterview-worth-it-reflections-tour.

50. Kid Ink, "Wit It Feat the Rangers," YouTube, last modified May 29, 2013, https:// www.youtube.com/watch?v=Rm8arOH4Dws.

51. As Laugalyte says in chapter 12 of this volume, "the episode never turns into a story about women in competition for a man."

52. Berman, "Rachel Bloom."

53. Vermeulen and Van den Akker, "Notes," 2 and 6.

### 14. "I'm Ravenous"

1. In Roberta Trites, *Disturbing the Universe: Power and Repression in Adolescent Literature* (Iowa City: Univ. of Iowa Press, 2000); and Beth Younger, *Learning Curves: Body Image and Female Sexuality in YA Literature* (Lanham, MD: Scarecrow Press, 2009), respectively.

2. Younger, *Learning Curves*, 2. The pregnancy problem novel depicts young women becoming pregnant the first time they have intercourse; pregnancy is a punishment for sex in these typically sex-negative, didactic novels.

3. Maria Leach, ed., *Funk & Wagnalls Standard Dictionary of Folklore, Mythology, and Legend* (San Francisco: Harper & Row, 1972), 1152.

4. Jill Raitt, "The Vagina Dentata and the Immaculatus Uterus Divini Fontis," *Journal of the American Academy of Religion* 48, no. 3 (September 1980): 415–31.

5. *Hunger Games* (Lionsgate, 2012–15); *Real Women Have Curves* (HBO Films, 2002); *Survivor* (CBS 2000–).

6. Matt Zoller Seitz, "*Crazy Ex-Girlfriend* Season 4 Beats the Odds," *Vulture*, October 10, 2018, vulture.com/2018/10/crazy-ex-girlfriend-season-4-review.html (accessed February 4, 2019).

7. Samantha Rollins, "'Crazy Ex-Girlfriend' Proves That On-Screen Diversity Is Actually Really Easy to Achieve," *Bustle*. March 5, 2018.

8. Caplan, quoted in Jamie Kravitz, "The Particularly Jewish Humor of Crazy Ex-Girlfriend," *Alma*, October 15, 2018, heyalma.com (accessed January 4, 2019).

9. Tamar Heller and Patricia Moran, *Scenes of the Apple: Food and the Female Body in Nineteenth- and Twentieth-Century Women's Writing* (Albany: State Univ. of New York Press, 2003), 7.

10. Allison Shoemaker, "A Hard-to-Watch *Crazy Ex-Girlfriend* Is Imperfect, Honest, and Remarkable," *The AV Club*, November 11, 2017, avclub.com (accessed March 8, 2018).

11. Maggie Helwig, "Hunger," in *The Norton Reader*, ed. Linda H. Peterson and John C. Brereton (New York: W. W. Norton, 2004), 199.

12. Helwig, "Hunger," 199.

13. This oeuvre illustrates what Rosalind Gill identifies as a postfeminist sensibility and what Diane Negra, in her article in *Cinema Journal*, identifies as central to postfeminism. Yvonne Tasker and Diane Negra, "In Focus: Postfeminism and Contemporary Media Studies," *Cinema Journal* 44, no. 2 (Winter 2005): 107–10 (accessed July 7, 2019).

14. Helwig, "Hunger," 201.

15. Compare Deborah Schooler's 2008 article, "Real Women Have Curves: A Longitudinal Investigation of TV and the Body Image Development of Latina Adolescents," *Journal of Adolescent Research* 23, no. 2 (2008): 132–53, *Sage Journals Online* (accessed October 2, 2011).

16. Rebecca mentions having gone through a bulimic phase while she was in college.

17. Quoted in Heller and Moran, *Scenes of the Apple*, 26.

18. "'Crazy Ex-Girlfriend's' Rachel Bloom Spends $500 to $3,000 on Event Dresses Because She's Not Sample Size," *Hollywood Reporter*, August 16, 2017, hollywood reporter.com (accessed March 8, 2018).

19. Molly Fitzpatrick, "'Crazy Ex-Girlfriend' Showed Us Something We Almost Never See on TV," October 13, 2015, *Splinter*, splinternews.com (accessed April 4, 2018).

20. Fitzpatrick, "'Crazy Ex-Girlfriend' Showed Us."

21. Helwig, "Hunger," 202.

22. Sarah Midkiff, "Crazy Ex-Girlfriend Broke a Major Taboo on TV," *Yahoo! Life*, October 21, 2017, yahoo.com/lifestyle (accessed June 6, 2018).

23. The first stage of infant development: liquid, changing, and feminine since there is no noticed separation between baby and mother.

24. Maria Figueroa, "Resisting 'Beauty' and Real Women Have Curves," in *Velvet Barrios: Popular Culture and Chicano/a Sexualities*, ed. Alicia Gaspar de Alba, 265–82 (New York: Palgrave Macmillan, 2003), 266.

25. Renee Curry, "I Ain't No FRIGGIN' LITTLE WIMP," in *The Girl: Construction of the Girl in Contemporary Fiction by Women*, ed. Ruth Saxton, 95–106 (New York: St. Martin's Press, 1998).

# Bibliography

Abramson, Seth. "On American Metamodernism." *Huffington Post*, December 6, 2017. https://www.huffingtonpost.com/seth-abramson/on-american-meta modernism_b_4743903.html.

Ahmed, Sara. *Living a Feminist Life*. Durham: Duke Univ. Press, 2017.

———. *The Promise of Happiness*. Durham: Duke Univ. Press, 2010.

———. *Queer Phenomenology: Orientations, Objects, Others*. Durham: Duke Univ. Press, 2006.

Allen, Samantha. "'Crazy Ex-Girlfriend': How Paula and Rebecca's Unlikely Friendship Became TV's Best Love Story." *The Daily Beast*, April 18, 2016. https://www.thedailybeast.com/crazy-ex-girlfriend-how-paula-and-rebeccas -unlikely-friendship-became-tvs-best-love-story.

———. "'Crazy Ex-Girlfriend' Is Smart, Sexy, Unapologetically Feminist TV." *The Daily Beast*, November 2, 2015, https://www.thedailybeast.com/crazy -ex-girlfriend-is-smart-sexy-unapologetically-feminist-tv.

———. "*Crazy Ex-Girlfriend* Is Smashing Stereotypes of Male Bisexuality, One '80s Jam at a Time." *The Daily Beast*, March 8, 2016. http://www.thedaily beast.com/articles/2016/03/07/crazy-ex-girlfriend-is-smashing-stereotypes-of -male-bisexuality-one-80s-jam-at-a-time.html.

Alston, Joshua. "*Crazy Ex-Girlfriend* Is the Sharpest Pop Satire You're Not Watch-ing (or Hearing)." *AV/TV Club*, February 22, 2016. https://tv.avclub.com /crazy-ex-girlfriend-is-the-sharpest-pop-satire-you-re-n-1798244533.

Altman, Rick. *The American Film Musical*. Bloomington: Indiana Univ. Press, 1987.

Angelides, Steven. *A History of Bisexuality*. Chicago: Univ. of Chicago Press, 2001.

———. "The Queer Intervention." In *The Routledge Queer Studies Reader*, ed-ited by Donald E. Hall, Annamarie Jagose, Andrea Bebell, and Susan Potter, 60–73. London: Routledge, 2013, 61.

Anzaldúa, Gloria E. *Borderlands/La Frontera: The New Mestiza.* San Francisco: Aunt Lute Books, 1987.

Asquith, Daisy. "*Crazy about One Direction*: Whose Shame Is It Anyway?" In *Seeing Fans: Representations of Fandom in Media and Popular Culture*, edited by Lucy Bennett and Paul Booth, 79–88. New York: Bloomsbury, 2018.

Bacon-Smith, Camille. *Enterprising Women: Television Fandom and the Creation of Popular Myth.* Philadelphia: Univ. of Pennsylvania Press, 1992.

Banet-Weiser, Sarah. *Empowered: Popular Feminism and Popular Misogyny.* Durham: Duke Univ. Press, 2018.

Barber, Stephen. *Abandoned Images: Film and Film's End.* London: Reaktion, 2010.

Barsanti, Sam. "Former Guests Accuse *Dr. Phil* Staff of Helping Them Get Drugs and Alcohol." *AV Club*, December 30, 2017. https://www.avclub.com /former-guests-accuse-dr-phil-staff-of-helping-them-get-1821668922.

Bastien, Angelica Jade. "What Television Gets Wrong about Mental Illness." *The Week*, September 17, 2016. http://theweek.com/articles/648229/what-tv -gets-wrong-about-mental-illness.

Bazin, Andre. "Some Films Are Better on the Small Screen Than the Large." In *Andre Bazin's New Media*, edited by Dudley Andrew, 160–62. Berkeley: Univ. of California Press, 2004.

Bell, Josh. "Musical Comedy *Crazy Ex-Girlfriend* Brings an Appealing Mix." *Las Vegas Weekly*, October 7, 2015. https://lasvegasweekly.com/ae/film/2015 /oct/07/crazy-ex-girlfriend-tv-review-musical-comedy/.

Benson-Allott, Caetlin. "Made for Quality Television?: Behind the Candelabra (Steven Soderbergh, 2013) Anna Nicole (Mary Herron, 2013)." *Film Quarterly* 66, no. 4 (2013): 5–9.

Bentley, Rick. "In Cynical TV Landscape, This Is Us Defies the Odds." *Times Colonist*, January 22, 2017. https://www.timescolonist.com/entertainment/television /small-screen-in-cynical-tv-landscape-this-is-us-defies-the-odds-1.8242488.

Berlant, Lauren, and Michael Warner. "Sex in Public." *Critical Inquiry* 24, no. 2 (1998): 547–66.

Berman, Eliza. "Rachel Bloom on *Crazy Ex-Girlfriend* and Flipping the Bechdel Test on Its Head." *Time*, October 12, 2015, https://time.com/4068058/rachel -bloom-crazy-ex-girlfriend/.

Bernstein, Arielle. "How *Crazy Ex-Girlfriend* Became TV's Most Surprising Feminist Comedy." *The Guardian*, November 13, 2018. https://www.theguardian .com/tv-and-radio/2018/nov/13/crazy-ex-girlfriend-rachel-bloom-feminist -comedy.

Bianco, Robert. "Review: *Ex-Girlfriend* Is Crazy Musical Fun." *USA Today*, October 9, 2015. https://www.greenbaypressgazette.com/story/life/tv/columnist/2015/10/09/review-ex-girlfriend-crazy-musical-fun/73597696/.

Birnbaum, Debra. "How 'Crazy Ex-Girlfriend' Moved from Showtime to The CW." *Variety.com*, May 14, 2015. https://variety.com/2015/tv/news/crazy-ex-girlfriend-cw-showtime-comedy-rachel-bloom-1201495301/.

Bloom, Rachel. "Fuck Me, Ray Bradbury." *YouTube.com*, August 15, 2010. https://www.youtube.com/watch?v=e1IxOS4VzKM.

———. Interview with Lauren Boumaroun, April 28, 2016.

Bordwell, David. *Narration in the Fiction Film*. Madison: Univ. of Wisconsin Press, 1985.

Bourget, Jean-Loup. "Social Implications in the Hollywood Genres." In *Film Genre Reader III*, edited by Barry Keith Grant, 51–59. Austin: Univ. of Texas Press, 2003.

Bradley, Laura. "*Crazy Ex-Girlfriend* Will End after Its Fourth Season—As It Should." *Vanity Fair*, April 2, 2018. https://www.vanityfair.com/hollywood/2018/04/crazy-ex-girlfriend-renewed-season-4-final-season.

———. "How *Crazy Ex-Girlfriend* Found an Even Stronger Voice in Season 3." *Vanity Fair*, November 17, 2017. https://www.vanityfair.com/hollywood/2017/11/crazy-ex-girlfriend-borderline-personality-disorder-rachel-bloom-aline-brosh-mckenna-interview.

Brooker, Will. "Living on Dawson's Creek: Teen Viewers, Cultural Convergence, and Television Overflow." *International Journal of Cultural Studies* 4, no. 4 (2001): 456–72.

Buscombe, Edward. "The Idea of Genre in the American Cinema." In *Film Genre Reader III*, edited by Barry Keith Grant, 12–26. Austin: Univ. of Texas Press, 2003.

Callis, April Scarlette. "Bisexual, Pansexual, Queer: Non-Binary Identities and the Sexual Borderlands." *Sexualities* 17 (2014): 63–80.

Calvario, Liz. "Netflix and The CW Reach New Multi-Year Licensing Deal for Scripted Series." *IndieWire*, July 5, 2016. http://www.indiewire.com/2016/07/netflix-the-cw-network-announce-new-agreement-streaming-1201702652/.

Cantor, Paul A. "The Simpsons: Atomistic Politics and the Nuclear Family." In *The Simpsons and Philosophy: The D'oh! Of Homer*, edited by William Irwin et al., 160–78. Chicago: Open Court, 2001.

Caruth, Cathy. *Trauma: Explorations in Memory*. Baltimore: Johns Hopkins Univ. Press, 1995.

Cassuto, Leonardo. "The Real-Life Myth of the American Family." *American Literary History* 20, no. 3 (Fall 2008): 487–96. Project MUSE.

Chan, Stephanie. "Crazy Ex-Girlfriend's Rachel Bloom Spends $500–$3000 on Event Dresses Because She's Not Sample Size." *Hollywood Reporter*, August 16, 2017. https://www.hollywoodreporter.com/news/crazy-girlfriend-star-rachel -bloom-paying-500-3000-sample-size-dresses-1030129.

Chocano, Carina. "Rachel Bloom's Mission Is to Unravel the Stories Women Tell Themselves." *Elle*. Hearst Digital Media, October 8, 2018. https://www .elle.com/culture/movies-tv/a23639652/rachel-bloom-crazy-ex-girlfriend/.

Chun, Wendy Hui Kyong. *Updating to Remain the Same: Habitual New Media*. Cambridge, MA: MIT Press, 2017.

Click, Melissa, and Suzanne Scott, eds. *The Routledge Companion to Media Fandom*. New York: Routledge, 2018.

Cohen, Rich. "Welcome to the Summer of Margot Robbie." *Vanity Fair*, August 2016. https://www.vanityfair.com/hollywood/2016/07/margot-robbie -cover-story.

Connaughton, Maddison. "Vanity Fair's Article on Margot Robbie Is Fascinatingly Awful." *Vice*, July 7, 2016. https://www.vice.com/en_au/article/av9jp4 /vanity-fair-tears-australia-a-new-one.

Couser, G. Thomas. *Signifying Bodies: Disability in Contemporary Life Writing*. Ann Arbor: Univ. of Michigan Press, 2009.

Cronin, James B., Mary B. McCarthy, Mark A. Newcombe, and Sinéad N. McCarthy. "Paradox, Performance and Food: Managing Difference in the Construction of Femininity." *Consumption Markets & Culture* 17, no. 4 (2014): 367–91.

Curry, Renee. "I Ain't No FRIGGIN' LITTLE WIMP." In *The Girl: Construction of the Girl in Contemporary Fiction by Women*, edited by Ruth Saxton, 95–106. New York: St. Martin's Press, 1998.

CW Press Release. July 31, 2015. https://cwtvpr.com/the-cw/releases/view?id=43222.

CW Press Release. January 19, 2016. https://cwtvpr.com/the-cw/releases/view?id =44450.

Dahl, Melissa. *Cringeworthy: A Theory of Awkwardness*. New York: Portfolio/ Penguin, 2018.

Davis, Lennard J. "Constructing Normalcy: The Bell Curve, The Novel, and the Invention of the Disabled Body in the Nineteenth Century." In *The Disability Studies Reader*, edited by Lennard J. Davis, 3–15. 2nd ed. New York: Routledge, 2006.

————. "Introduction." In *The Disability Studies Reader*, edited by Lennard J. Davis, xv–xviii. 2nd ed. New York: Routledge, 2006.

Dawidziak, Mark. "*Crazy Ex-Girlfriend* Tops Network Newcomers with Its Music-Comedy Mix." *Cleveland.Com TV Blog*, October 17, 2015. https://www.cleveland.com/tv-blog/2015/10/crazy_ex-girlfriend_hitting_high_notes_with_music-comedy_mix.html.

Dean, Tim. "Queer." In *Keywords for Disability Studies*, edited by Rachel Adams, Benjamin Reiss, and David Serlin, 46–47. New York: New York Univ. Press, 2015.

Deer, Harriet, and Irving Deer. "Musical Comedy: From Performer to Performance." *Journal of Popular Culture* 12, no. 3 (1978): 406–21.

de Moraes, Lisa. "Final 2016–17 TV Rankings." *Deadline*, May 25, 2017. https://deadline.com/2017/05/2016-2017-tv-season-ratings-series-rankings-list-1202102340/.

Denson, Shane. *Postnaturalism: Frankenstein, Film, and the Anthropotechnical Interface*. New York: Transcript Verlag, 2014.

Depp, Michael. "CW Steers Viewers from Streaming to Broadcast." *TVNewsCheck*, March 9, 2020. https://tvnewscheck.com/article/245601/cw-steers-viewers-from-streaming-to-broadcast/.

Dohrmann, George. *Superfans: Into the Heart of Obsessive Sports Fandom*. New York: Random House, 2018.

Dolecki, Constance M. *The Everything Guide to Borderline Personality Disorder: Professional, Reassuring Advice for Coping with the Disorder and Breaking the Destructive Cycle*. New York: Simon & Schuster, 2012.

Dolgen, Jack. "Yes It's Really Us Singing: The Crazy Ex-Girlfriend Concert Special" taping, March 16, 2019; PaleyFest LA, March 20, 2019.

Dolmage, Jay Timothy. *Disability Rhetoric*. Syracuse: Syracuse Univ. Press, 2014.

Dominus, Susan. "Rachel Bloom's Twisted Comedy." *New York Times Magazine*, January 19, 2016. https://www.nytimes.com/2016/01/24/magazine/make-em-laugh.html?auth=login-email&login=email.

Doyle, Sadie. "With a Groundbreaking Diagnosis, "Crazy Ex-Girlfriend" Insists That Even "Psycho" Women Deserve to be Heard." *Elle.com*. November 27, 2017. https://www.elle.com/culture/movies-tv/a13938654/crazy-ex-girlfriend-borderline-personality-disorder-diagnosis/.

Duffett, Mark. *Understanding Fandom: An Introduction to the Study of Media Fan Culture*. New York: Bloomsbury, 2013.

Dunn, Troy. *Family: The Good F-Word*. Los Angeles: Bird St. Books, 2014.

Dunne, Peter. "Inside American Television Drama: Quality Is Not What Is Produced, But What It Produces." In *Quality TV: Contemporary American Television and Beyond*, edited by Janet McCabe and Kim Akass, 98–109. New York: I. B. Tauris, 2007.

Dyer, Richard. *In the Space of a Song*. New York: Routledge, 2012.

———. "Judy Garland and Camp." In *Hollywood Musicals: The Film Reader*, edited by Steven Cohan, 107–13. New York: Routledge, 2002.

Eichel, Molly. "*Crazy Ex-Girlfriend* Is a Smart, Dark Delight." *AV Club*, October 12, 2015. https://tv.avclub.com/crazy-ex-girlfriend-is-a-smart-dark-delight-1798185200.

Eitzen, Dirk. "The Emotional Basis of Film Comedy." In *Passionate Views: Film, Cognition, and Emotion*, edited by Carl Plantinga and Greg M. Smith, 82–101. Baltimore: Johns Hopkins Univ. Press, 1999.

Ellis, Sarah Taylor. "Doing the Time Warp: Queer Temporalities and Musical Theater." PhD diss., University of California, Los Angeles, 2013.

Ellis-Petersen, Hannah. "Fashion Brands Drop Terry Richardson over Allegations of Abuse on Shoots." *The Guardian*, October 24, 2017. https://www.theguardian.com/artanddesign/2017/oct/24/terry-richardson-photographer-dropped-fashion-brands-allegations.

Elsaesser, Thomas. "Contingency, Causality, Complexity: Distributed Agency in the Mind-Game Film." *New Review of Film and Television Studies* 16, no. 1 (2018): 1–39.

———. "Media Archeology as Symptom." *New Review of Film and Television Studies* 14, no. 2 (2016): 181–215.

Essig, Laurie. "Dr. Phil's Very Bad Advice." *Psychology Today*, February 10, 2011. https://www.psychologytoday.com/us/blog/love-inc/201102/dr-phils-very-bad-advice.

Esterberg, Kristin G. "The Bisexual Menace Revisited: Or, Shaking Up Social Categories Is Hard to Do." In *Introducing the New Sexuality Studies*, edited by Steven Seidman, Nancy Fischer, and Chet Meets, 278–84. London: Routledge, 2011.

Fallon, Claire. "*Crazy Ex-Girlfriend* Is a Bad Feminist, Just Like Us." *Huffington Post*, November 17, 2015. https://www.huffingtonpost.com.au/entry/crazy-ex-girlfriend-bad-feminist_us_56464b02e4b060377349016b.

Fallon, Kevin. "'Crazy Ex-Girlfriend' Is Still the Most Charming Show on TV." *The Daily Beast*, October 13, 2017. https://www.thedailybeast.com/crazy-ex-girlfriend-is-still-the-most-charming-show-on-tv.

———. "The TV Musical Is Dead." *The Atlantic*, April 10, 2012. https://www
.theatlantic.com/entertainment/archive/2012/04/the-tv-musical-is-dead/255
643/.

Fawcett, Kirsten. "How Mental Illness Is Misrepresented in the Media." *U.S. News and World Report*, April 16, 2015. https://health.usnews.com/health-news /health-wellness/articles/2015/04/16/how-mental-illness-is-misrepresented -in-the-media.

Felski, Rita. "Feminism, Postmodernism, and the Critique of Modernity." *Cultural Critique* 14 (1989): 33–56.

Fernandez, Maria Elana. "Rebecca Bunch Is 'Just a Girl in Love' in *Crazy Ex-Girlfriend's* Season Two Theme Song." *Vulture*, October 17, 2016. https:// www.vulture.com/2016/10/crazy-ex-girlfriend-season-two-theme-im-just-a -girl-in-love.html.

Fienberg, Daniel. "*Crazy Ex-Girlfriend*: TV Review." *Hollywood Reporter*, October 8, 2015. https://www.hollywoodreporter.com/review/crazy-girlfriend-tv -review-830806.

Fifth Harmony. "BO$$." YouTube. Last modified July 8, 2014. https://www.you tube.com/watch?v=Y4JfPlry-iQ.

———. "Worth It ft. Kid Ink." YouTube. Last modified March 28, 2015. https:// www.youtube.com/watch?v=YBHQbu5rbdQ.

Figueroa, Maria. "Resisting 'Beauty' and *Real Women Have Curves*." In *Velvet Barrios: Popular Culture and Chicano/a Sexualities*, edited by Alicia Gaspar de Alba, 265–82. New York: Palgrave Macmillan, 2003.

Fiske, John. "The Cultural Economy of Fandom." In *The Adoring Audience: Fan Culture and Popular Media*, edited by Lisa A. Lewis, 30–49. New York: Routledge, 1992.

Fitzpatrick, Molly. 'Crazy Ex-Girlfriend' Showed Us Something We Almost Never See on Television." *Splinter*, October 13, 2017. https://splinternews .com/crazy-ex-girlfriend-showed-us-something-we-almost-never-1793851836.

Flanders, Corey E., Marianne E. LeBreton, Margaret Robinson, Jing Bian, and Jaime Alonso Caravaca-Morera. "Defining Bisexuality: Young Bisexual and Pansexual People's Voices." *Journal of Bisexuality* 17 (2017): 249–51.

Frank, Arthur. *The Wounded Storyteller: Body, Illness, and Ethics*. Chicago: Univ. of Chicago Press, 2013.

Friedlander, Whitney. "Ten Ways *Crazy Ex-Girlfriend* Changed TV." *Paste*, April 4, 2019. https://www.pastemagazine.com/articles/2019/04/10-ways-crazy-ex -girlfriend-changed-tv.html.

Galupo, M. Paz, Johanna L. Ramirez, and Lex Pulice-Farrow. "'Regardless of their Gender': Descriptions of Sexual Identity among Bisexual, Pansexual, and Queer Identified Individuals." *Journal of Bisexuality* 17 (2017): 108–24.

Garber, Megan, David Sims, Lenika Cruz and Sophie Gilbert. "Have We Reached 'Peak TV'?" *The Atlantic*, August 12, 2015. http://www.theatlantic .com/entertainment/archive/2015/08/have-we-reached-peak-tv/401009/.

Gaut, Berys. "Identification and Emotion in Narrative Film." In *Passionate Views: Film, Cognition, and Emotion*, edited by Carl Plantinga and Greg M. Smith, 200–215. Baltimore: Johns Hopkins Univ. Press, 1999.

Geczy, Adam, Paul Mountfort, and Anne Peirson-Smith, eds. *Planet Cosplay: Costume Play, Identity and Global Fandom*. Bristol, UK: Intellect, 2019.

"Gender and Women's Mental Health." World Health Organization: https:// www.who.int/mental_health/prevention/genderwomen/en/.

Gill, Rosalind. "Postfeminist Media Culture: Elements of a Sensibility." *European Journal of Cultural Studies* 10, no. 2 (2007): 147–66.

Gillan, Jennifer. *Television and New Media: Must-Click TV*. New York: Routledge, 2011.

Gillespie, Claire. "Crazy Ex-Girlfriend Succeeds in Portraying Mental Illness Where So Many Other TV Shows Have Failed." *Self.com*, February 15, 2018. https://www.self.com/story/crazy-ex-girlfriend-portraying-mental-illness.

Girard, René. *Deceit, Desire, and the Novel: Self and Other in Literary Structure*. Baltimore: Johns Hopkins Univ. Press, 1965.

Glennon, Morgan. "Is the Age of the Cynical Sitcom Over?" *Huffpost*, February 22, 2013. https://www.huffpost.com/entry/is-the-age-of-the-cynical_b_274 4154.

Goldberg, Lesley. "Network TV's Live Musical Boom Hits Sour Note." *Hollywood Reporter*, February 13, 2019. https://www.hollywoodreporter.com/live -feed/network-tvs-live-musical-boom-hits-sour-note-1186035.

Goldstein, Jessica. "The 'Crazy Ex-Girlfriend' Showrunner Takes Us Inside the Show Subverting the Stereotype." *ThinkProgress*, January 27, 2016, http:// thinkprogress.org/culture/2016/01/27/3742920/the-crazy-ex-girlfriend-show runner-takes-us-inside-the-show-subverting-the-stereotype/.

Gough, Paul, and James Hibberd. "'90210' Upfront and Center for CW." *Hollywood Reporter*, May 13, 2008). https://www.hollywoodreporter.com/news /90210-upfront-center-cw-111620.

Gqola, Pumla Dineo. *Reflecting Rogue: Inside the Mind of a Feminist*. Johannesburg: Jacana, 2017.

Grady, Constance. "*Crazy Ex-Girlfriend* Succeeds Where Most TV Musicals Fail Thanks to This One Trick." *Vox*, October 21, 2016. https://www.vox .com/2016/4/20/11463132/crazy-ex-girlfriend-tv-musicals.

Gray, Jonathan. *Show Sold Separately: Promos, Spoilers, and Other Media Paratexts*. New York: New York Univ. Press, 2010.

Gray, Jonathan, Jeffrey P. Jones, and Ethan Thompson, "The State of Satire, the Satire of State." In *Satire TV: Politics and Comedy in the Post-Network Era*, edited by Jonathan Gray, Jeffrey P. Jones, and Ethan Thompson, 3–36. New York: New York Univ. Press, 2009.

Grodal, Torben. *Embodied Visions: Evolution, Emotion, Culture, and Film*. New York: Oxford Univ. Press, 2009.

Gunderson, John G., and Paul Links. *Borderline Personality Disorder: A Clinical Guide*. Arlington: American Psychiatric Publishing, 2008.

Halberstam, Jack. *The Queer Art of Failure*. Durham: Duke Univ. Press, 2011.

Halberstam, Judith. *In a Queer Time and Place: Transgender Bodies, Subcultural Lives*. New York: New York Univ. Press, 2005.

Halfyard, Janet K. *Sounds of Fear and Wonder: Music in Cult TV*. London: I. B. Tauris, 2016.

Halligan, Benjamin. "Modeling Affective Labor: Terry Richardson's Photography." *Cultural Politics* 13, no. 1 (2017): 58–80.

Hansbury, Griffin. "King Kong & Goldilocks: Imagining Transmasculinities Through the Trans-Trans Dyad." *Psychoanalytic Dialogues* 21, no. 2 (2011): 210–20.

Harmon, Steph. "Margot Robbie Calls Her Vanity Fair Profile 'Really Weird.'" *The Guardian*, July 26, 2016. https://www.theguardian.com/film/2016/jul /26/margot-robbie-calls-her-vanity-fair-profile-really-weird.

Harnick, Chris. "From Anxiety to Revenge: Rachel Bloom on *Crazy Ex-Girlfriend* Season 3 and Diagnosing Rebecca Bunch." *ENews*, October 12, 2017. https:// www.eonline.com/news/885137/from-anxiety-to-revenge-rachel-bloom-on -crazy-ex-girlfriend-season-3-diagnosing-rebecca-bunch.

Hauser, Christine. "A Defaced Gap Ad Goes from the Subway to the Web to Its Demise." *New York Times: The Lede*, November 27, 2013, http://thelede.blogs .nytimes.com/2013/11/27/a-defaced-gap-ad-goes-from-the-subway-to-the -web-to-its-demise/?_r=0.

Havas, Julia, and Maria Sulimma. "Through the Gaps of My Fingers: Genre, Femininity, and Cringe Aesthetics in Dramedy Television." *Television & New Media* 21, no. 1 (2018): 75–94.

Heide, Frederick J., Natalie Porter, and Paul K. Saito. "Do You Hear the People Sing? Musical Theatre and Attitude Change." *Psychology of Aesthetics, Creativity, and the Arts* 6, no. 3 (2012): 224–30.

Hellekson, Karen, and Kristina Busse, "Introduction: Work in Progress." In *Fan Fiction and Fan Communities in the Age of the Internet: New Essays*, edited by Karen Hellekson and Kristina Busse, 5–32. Jefferson, NC: McFarland, 2006.

Heller, Corinne. "'Appallingly Cruel': Dr. Phil Slammed for 'Exploitative' Interview with Mentally Ill Shelley Duval." NBC New York, November 18, 2016. https://www.nbcnewyork.com/entertainment/entertainment-news/Dr-Phil-Slammed-for-Shelley-Duvall-Interview-401700775.html.

Heller, Tamar, and Patricia Moran. *Scenes of the Apple: Food and the Female Body in Nineteenth- and Twentieth-Century Women's Writing*. Albany: State Univ. of New York Press, 2003.

Helwig, Maggie. "Hunger." In *The Norton Reader*, edited by Linda H. Peterson and John C. Brereton. New York: W. W. Norton, 2004.

Herman, Alison. "How Aline Brosh McKenna Reinvented the Romantic Comedy—for TV." *The Ringer*, November 9, 2017. https://www.theringer.com/tv/2017/11/9/16625682/aline-brosh-mckenna-profile.

Hills, Matt. *Fan Cultures*. New York: Routledge, 2002.

———. "'Twilight' Fans Represented in Commercial Paratexts and Inter-Fandoms: Resisting and Repurposing Negative Fan Stereotypes." In *Genre, Reception, and Adaptation in the "Twilight" Series*, edited by Anne Morey, 113–29. Burlington, VT: Ashgate, 2012.

Hoby, Hermione. "Miley Cyrus Isn't a Child: She's 21 and She Can Twerk If She Wants To." *The Guardian*, November 24, 2013. https://www.theguardian.com/culture/2013/nov/24/miley-cyrus-21-twerk-if-she-wants.

Hoesterey, Ingeborg. *Pastiche: Cultural Memory in Art, Film, Literature*. Bloomington: Indiana Univ. Press, 2001.

Holloway, Daniel. "CW Chief Looks to Lure Women Viewers Back with 'Dynasty,' 'Riverdale.'" *Variety*, August 2, 2017. https://variety.com/2017/tv/news/dynasty-riverdale-tca-1202513508/.

———. "The CW's Male-Pattern Boldness." *Broadcasting & Cable*, October 27, 2014, 13.

Holmes, Lindsay. "Media Is Perpetuating a Dangerous Myth about Mental Illness." *Huffington Post*, June 6, 2016. https://www.huffpost.com/entry/media-mental-illness-violence-study_n_57556f96e4b0eb20fa0e5443.

Horn, Katrin. *Women, Camp and Popular Culture: Serious Excess*. London: Palgrave Macmillan, 2017.

Hu, Tung-Hui, *A Prehistory of the Cloud*. Cambridge, MA: MIT Press, 2016.

Hunting, Kyra, and Amanda McQueen. "A Musical Marriage: The Mash-Up Aesthetic as Governing Logic in Glee." *Quarterly Review of Film and Video* 31, no. 4 (2014): 289–308.

Hutcheon, Linda. *A Theory of Parody*. 1985; reprint ed., Urbana and Chicago: Univ. of Illinois Press, 2000.

Iggy and the Stooges. "Search and Destroy." YouTube video, 3:28. December 26, 2016. https://www.youtube.com/watch?v=KjXgxbVXrrU.

Ivie, Devon. "*Crazy Ex-Girlfriend* Creators Tell the Stories Behind 6 Songs from Season 3." *Vulture*, February 28, 2018. https://www.vulture.com/2018/02/crazy-ex-girlfriend-making-of-season-3-songs.html.

———. "*Crazy Ex-Girlfriend*'s Producers Tell the Stories Behind 9 Songs from Season Two." *Vulture*, February 3, 2017. https://www.vulture.com/2017/02/crazy-ex-girlfriend-songs-rachel-bloom-aline-brosh-mckenna.html.

Jacques, Pierre-Emmanuel. "The Associational Attractions of the Musical." In *The Cinema of Attractions Reloaded*, edited by Wanda Strauven. Amsterdam: Amsterdam Univ. Press, 2006.

Jancovich, Mark, and Nathan Hunt. "The Mainstream, Distinction, and Cult TV." In *Cult Television*, edited by Sara Gwenllian-Jones and Roberta E. Pearson, 27–44. Minneapolis: Univ. of Minnesota Press, 2004.

Jenkins, Henry. *Textual Poachers: Television Fans and Participatory Culture*. New York: Routledge, 1992.

Jenkins, Henry, Jane Shattuc, and Tara McPherson. "The Culture That Sticks to Your Skin: A Manifesto for a New Cultural Studies." In *Hop on Pop: The Politics and Pleasures of Popular Culture*, edited by Henry Jenkins, Jane Shattuc, and Tara McPherson, 3–25. Durham, NC: Duke Univ. Press, 2002.

Jensen, Jeff. "*Crazy Ex-Girlfriend*: TV Review." *Entertainment Weekly*, October 12, 2015.

Johnson, Merri Lisa. "Bad Romance: A Crip Feminist Critique of Queer Failure." *Hypatia* 30, no. 1 (2015): 251–67.

Kafer, Allison. *Feminist, Queer, Crip*. Bloomington: Indiana Univ. Press, 2013.

Kearney, Mary Celeste. "Birds on the Wire: Troping Teenage Girlhood through Telephony in Mid-Twentieth-Century U.S. Media Culture." *Cultural Studies* 19, no. 5 (2005): 568–601.

Kelly, J. P. "'A Stretch of Time': Extended Distribution and Narrative Accumulation in *Prison Break*." In *Time in Television Narrative: Exploring Temporality in Twenty-First-Century Programming*, edited by Melissa Ames. Jackson: Univ. Press of Mississippi, 2014.

Kenrick, John. *Musical Theatre: A History*. New York: Continuum, 2008.

Khilnani, Shweta. "Of Nasty, Unlikeable Women: *Veep* and the Comedic Female Anti-Hero." *Flow*, April 24, 2017. https://www.flowjournal.org/2017/04/of-nasty-unlikeable-women/.

Kid Ink. "Wit It Feat the Rangers." YouTube. Last modified May 29, 2013. https://www.youtube.com/watch?v=Rm8arOH4Dws.

Kim, Sangmoon, Randall S. Jorgensen, and Ryan Thibodeau, "Shame, Guilt, and Depressive Symptoms: A Meta-Analytic Review." *Psychological Bulletin* 137, no. 1 (2011): 70–71.

Kinsey, Alfred C., Wardell B. Pomeroy, and Clyde E. Martin. "Extracts from *Sexual Behavior in the Human Male* (1948)." In Merl Storr, ed., *Bisexuality: A Critical Reader*, 31–37. London: Routledge, 1999.

Kira, Ibrahim, Linda Lewandowski, Thomas Templin, Vidya Ramaswamy, Bulent Ozkan, and Jamal Mohanesh, "Measuring Cumulative Trauma Dose, Types, and Profiles Using a Development-Based Taxonomy of Traumas," *Traumatology* 14, no. 2 (2008): 62–87.

Klinger, Barbara. "Cinema/Ideology/Criticism Revisited: The Progressive Genre." In *Film Genre Reader III*, edited by Barry Keith Grant. Austin: Univ. of Texas Press, 2003.

Knapp, Raymond. *The American Musical and the Performance of Personal Identity*. Princeton: Princeton Univ. Press, 2006.

Kort, Alicia. "Women to Watch: An Interview with Rachel Bloom." *Newsweek Special Edition: She Persisted*, January 25, 2018. https://www.newsweek.com/women-watch-interview-rachel-bloom-789698.

Kravitz, Jamie. "The Particularly Jewish Humor of 'Crazy Ex-Girlfriend.' *Alma*. https://www.heyalma.com/the-particularly-jewish-humor-of-crazy-ex-girlfriend/. Accessed December 4, 2018.

Krutnik, Frank. "Conforming Passions? Contemporary Romantic Comedy." In *Genre and Contemporary Hollywood*, edited by Steve Neale, 130–47. London: BFI, 2003.

Lafayette, Jon. "Bet on The CW Paying Off for the Network's Parents." *Broadcasting & Cable*, October 27, 2014, 16.

Lagerwey, Jorie, and Taylor Nygaard. "Liberal Women, Mental Illness, and Precarious Whiteness in Trump's America." *Flow*, November 27, 2017. https://www.flowjournal.org/2017/11/whiteness-in-trumps-america/.

Lagerwey, Jorie, Julie Leyda, and Diane Negra, "Female Centered TV in an Age of Precarity." *Genders* 1, no. 2 (Fall 2016). https://www.colorado.edu/genders/2016/05/19/female-centered-tv-age-precarity.

Lamarre, Carl. "Interview: Fifth Harmony Talk Their Platinum Hit 'Worth It' and Their Love for Drake, Fetty Wap, and Kendrick Lamar." *Complex*, June 22, 2015. http://www.complex.com/music/2015/06/fifth-harmony-interview-worth-it-reflections-tour.

Later, Naja. "Quality Television (TV) Eats Itself: The TV-Auteur and the Promoted Fanboy." *Quarterly Review of Film and Video* 35, no. 6 (2018): 531–51.

Lawler, Kelly. "The Quietly Revolutionary Way 'Crazy Ex-Girlfriend' Addresses Mental Health." *USA Today*, November 9, 2017. https://www.usatoday.com/story/life/tv/2017/11/09/crazy-ex-girlfriend-mental-health/840665001/.

Leach, Maria, ed. *Funk & Wagnalls Standard Dictionary of Folklore, Mythology, and Legend*. San Francisco: Harper & Row, 1972.

Leetal, Dean Barnes. "Those Crazy Fangirls on the Internet: Activism of Care, Disability and Fan Fiction." *Canadian Journal of Disability Studies* (University of Waterloo: Canadian Disability Studies Association, 2019). https://cjds.uwaterloo.ca/index.php/cjds/article/view/491/736.

Lenker, Maureen. "The Subversive Show with the Terrible Name 'Crazy Ex-Girlfriend' Satirizes Sexist Tropes with Song and Dance." *Bitch Media*, October 12, 2016. https://www.bitchmedia.org/article/subversive-show-terrible-name/crazy-ex-girlfriend-satirizes-sexist-tropes-song-and-dance.

Lewis, Isobel. "How Crazy Ex-Girlfriend Revived the TV Musical Genre—And Liberated Its Heroine." *The Atlantic*, April 5, 2019. https://www.theatlantic.com/entertainment/archive/2019/04/crazy-ex-girlfriend-revived-tv-musical-the-cw/586555/.

Lewis, Victoria Ann. "Crip." In *Keywords for Disability Studies*, edited by Rachel Adams, Benjamin Reiss, and David Serlin, 46–48. New York: New York Univ. Press, 2015.

Littleton, Cynthia. "Birth of the CW: UPN-WB Network Merger Deal Rocked TV Biz 10 Years Ago." *Variety*, January 24, 2016. https://variety.com/2016/tv/news/cw-wb-network-upn-merger-announcement-10-years-ago-1201687040/.

————. "Netflix, CW Near Deal That Accelerates Streaming Window as Hulu Ends In-Season Pact." *Variety*, June 20, 2016. https://variety.com/2016/tv/news/netflix-cw-output-deal-the-flash-hulu-1201799176/.

Livingstone, Sonia. *Making Sense of Television: The Psychology of Audience Interpretation*. London: Routledge, 1998.

Lodge, Mary Jo. "Beyond 'Jumping the Shark': The New Television Musical." *Studies in Musical Theatre* 1, no. 3 (2007): 293–305.

Loofbourow, Lili. "TV's New Girls' Club." *New York Times Magazine*, January 16, 2015. https://www.nytimes.com/2015/01/18/magazine/tvs-new-girls-club.html.

Lotz, Amanda D. *Redesigning Women: Television after the Network Era*. Urbana: Univ. of Illinois Press, 2006.

————. *The Television Will Be Revolutionized*. 2nd ed. New York: New York Univ. Press, 2014.

————. *We Now Disrupt This Broadcast: How Cable Transformed Television and the Internet Revolutionized It All*. Cambridge, MA: MIT Press, 2018.

Low, Elaine. "John Landgraf: Nearly 60% of FX's Writing Staff Are Now Not White Men." *Variety*, October 26, 2019. https://variety.com/2019/tv/news/john-landgraf-usc-gould-entertainment-law-1203384643/.

Lowry, Brian. "TV Review: *Crazy Ex-Girlfriend*." *Variety*, October 8, 2015. https://variety.com/2015/tv/reviews/crazy-ex-girlfriend-review-rachel-bloom-musical-cw-1201607885/.

Mahaney, Emily. "How *Crazy Ex-Girlfriend's* Rachel Bloom Survived the Worst Depression of her Life." *Glamour.com*, October 19, 2016. https://www.glamour.com/story/how-crazy-ex-girlfriend-rachel-bloom-survived-depression.

Marcus, Sharon. *Between Women: Friendship, Desire, and Marriage in Victorian England*. Princeton: Princeton Univ. Press, 2007.

Matejskova, Tatiana. "Straights in a Gay Bar: Negotiation Boundaries through Time-Spaces." In *Geographies of Sexualities*, edited by Kath Browne, Jason Lim, and Gavin Brown, 137–50. Burlington, VT: Ashgate, 2007.

McGill, Mary. "#Obsessed: *Ingrid Goes West* and Instagram's Toxic Gaze." *Another Gaze*, no. 2 (2018): 69–71.

McKee, Alan. "The Fans of Cultural Theory." In *Fandom: Identities and Communities in a Mediated World*, edited by Jonathan Gray, C. Lee Harrington, and Cornel Sandvoss, 88–97. New York: New York Univ. Press, 2007.

McNamara, Mary. "And They All Live Sardonically Ever After on the Intoxicating, Daffy *Crazy Ex-Girlfriend*." *Los Angeles Times*, October 12, 2015.

https://www.latimes.com/entertainment/tv/la-et-st-crazy-ex-girlfriend-2015
1012-column.html.

McRuer, Robert. *Crip Theory: Cultural Signs of Queerness and Disability*. New
York: New York Univ. Press, 2006.

Menzies, Robert, Brenda LeFrancois, and Geoffrey Reaume. *Mad Matters: A
Critical Reader in Canadian Mad Studies*. Toronto: Canadian Scholars
Press, 2013.

Mera, Miguel. "Is Funny Music Funny?: Contexts and Case Studies of Film
Music Humor." *Journal of Popular Music Studies* 14 (2002): 91–113.

Meslow, Scott. "Rachel Bloom Has a Lot to Say." *GQ*, June 13, 2018. https://
www.gq.com/story/rachel-bloom-has-a-lot-to-sa.

Midkiff, Sarah. "*Crazy Ex-Girlfriend* Broke a Major Taboo on Primetime TV."
*Refinery 29*, no. 21 (October 2017). https://www.refinery29.com/en-us/2017
/10/177612/crazy-ex-girlfriend-clitoris-rachel-bloom.

Millard, Drew. "'Crazy Ex-Girlfriend' Is the Funniest Show on TV You're Not
Watching," *Vice*, October 27, 2015. http://www.vice.com/read/crazy-ex-girl
friend-is-like-if-broad-city-and-seinfeld-combined-to-create-a-musical-1027.

Miller, Korin. "'13 Reasons Why' Is Not the Force for Mental Health Awareness People Say It Is." *Self.Com*, April 13, 2017. https://www.self.com/story/13
-reasons-why-suicide-and-mental-health.

Mills, Brett. "What Does It Mean to Call Television 'Cinematic'?" In *Television
Aesthetics and Style*, edited by Steven Peacock and Jason Jacobs, 57–66. London: Bloomsbury, 2013.

Mink, Casey. "*Crazy Ex-Girlfriend* Recap: Meet Rebecca, Who Is Totally Not
at All Crazy." *Hollywood Life*, October 12, 2015, https://gossipnow.net/crazy
-ex-girlfriend-recap-meet-rebecca-who-is-totally-not-at-all-crazy/.

Mitchell, David, and Sharon L. Snyder. *Narrative Prosthesis: Disability and the
Dependencies of Discourse*. Ann Arbor: Univ. of Michigan Press, 2014.

Mittell, Jason. *Complex TV: The Poetics of Contemporary Television Storytelling*.
New York: New York Univ. Press, 2015.

———. *Genre and Television*. New York: Routledge, 2004.

———. *Television and American Culture*. New York: Oxford Univ. Press, 2010.

Mizejewski, Linda. *Pretty/Funny: Women Comedians and Body Politics*. Austin:
Univ. of Texas Press, 2014.

Mizejewski, Linda, and Victoria Sturtevant. "Introduction." In *Hysterical!
Women in American Comedy*, edited by Linda Mizejewski and Victoria Sturtevant, 1–34. Austin: Univ. of Texas Press, 2017.

Mock, Erin Lee. "The Horror of 'Honey, I'm Home!': The Perils of Postwar Family Love in the Domestic Sitcom." *Film & History* 41, no. 2 (Fall 2011): 29–50.

Moe, John. *Hilarious World of Depression*. "Rachel Bloom Finds Her Voice, Then Uses It to Sing about Stealing Pets and Moving to West Covina, California." *American Public Media*, January 22, 2018.

Morimoto, Lori. "Ontological Security and the Politics of Transcultural Fandom." In *A Companion to Media Fandom and Fan Studies*, edited by Paul Booth, 257–75. Hoboken, NJ: Wiley-Blackwell, 2018.

Moskovitz, Richard A. *Lost in the Mirror: An Inside Look at Borderline Personality Disorder*. Lanham: Rowman & Littlefield, 2001.

Mulvey, Laura. *Citizen Kane*. London: Bloomsbury, 2017.

———. "Visual Pleasure and Narrative Cinema." In *Film Theory and Criticism*, edited by Leo Braudy and Marshall Cohen, 837–48. Oxford: Oxford Univ. Press, 2004.

———. "Visual Pleasure and Narrative Cinema." *Screen* 16, no. 3 (1975): 57–68.

Murphy, Caryn. "The CW: Media Conglomerates in Partnership." In *From Networks to Netflix: A Guide to Changing Channels*, edited by Derek Johnson, 35–44. New York: Routledge, 2018.

Newcomb, Horace M., and Paul M. Hirsch. "Television as a Cultural Forum: Implications for Research." *Quarterly Review of Film Studies* 8, no. 3 (1983): 45–55.

Newman, Michael Z., and Elana Levine. *Legitimating Television: Media Convergence and Cultural Status*. New York: Routledge, 2012.

Nguyen, Hanh. "*Crazy Ex-Girlfriend* Finally Went to Its Darkest Place Yet on Friday's Pivotal Episode." *IndieWire*, November 10, 2017. https://www.indie wire.com/2017/11/crazy-ex-girlfriend-i-never-want-to-see-josh-again-suicide -cw-1201896470/.

Niemiec, Ryan M., and Danny Wedding. *Positive Psychology at the Movies: Using Films to Build Virtues and Character Strengths*. Ashland: Hogrefe, 2013.

Nussbaum, Emily. "Glee Club: Fresh Starts on *Crazy Ex-Girlfriend* and *Younger*." *New Yorker*, January 18, 2016. https://www.newyorker.com/magazine/2016 /01/25/glee-club?source=search_google_dsa_paid&gclid=CjwKCAiA57D _BRAZEiwAZcfCxeca_dQSRcZamhGKOADPIJntf1b-rAqLFMw0aeAe hqG_UEQ3y-mI2BoCsNwQAvD_BwE

Offman, Hilary. "The Princess and the Penis: A Post Postmodern Queer-y Tale." *Psychoanalytic Dialogues* 24, no. 1 (2014): 72–87.

Owen, Rob. "Tuned In: Crazy for *Crazy Ex-Girlfriend*." *Pittsburgh Post-Gazette*, October 8, 2015. https://www.post-gazette.com/ae/tv-radio/2015/10/09/Tuned -In-Crazy-for-Crazy-Ex-Girlfriend/stories/201510090106.

Paskin, Willa. "*Crazy Ex-Girlfriend* Is Peak #PeakTV." *Slate*, October 8, 2015. https://slate.com/culture/2015/10/crazy-ex-girlfriend-on-cw-reviewed-this -show-is-peak-peaktv.html.

———. "What Does 'Peak TV' *Really* Mean?" *Slate*, December 23, 2015. https:// slate.com/culture/2015/12/what-does-peak-tv-really-mean.html.

Petronzio, Matt. "A Storied Glossary of Iconic LGBT Flags and Symbols." *Mashable*, June 13, 2014. https://mashable.com/2014/06/13/lgbt-pride-symbols/#d IkoP7vwmgqJ.

Pierce, Scott D. "*Crazy Ex-Girlfriend* Is Daft. You'll Love It!" *Salt Lake Tribune*, October 9, 2015. https://archive.sltrib.com/article.php?id=3040138&itype =CMSID.

Poniewozik, James. "Review: *Crazy Ex-Girlfriend*, a Musical with Twisted Songs." *New York Times*, October 11, 2015. https://www.nytimes.com/2015/10/12/arts /television/review-crazy-ex-girlfriend-a-musical-with-twisted-songs.html.

Press, Joy. *Stealing the Show: How Women Are Revolutionizing Television*. New York: Atria Books, 2018.

Press Release. January 24, 2006. https://cwtvpr.com/the-cw/releases/view?id =12625.

Price, Margaret. "The Bodymind Problem and the Possibilities of Pain." *Hypatia* 30, no. 1 (2015): 268–84.

Raitt, Jill. "The *Vagina Dentata* and the *Immaculatus Uterus Divini Fontis*." *Journal of the American Academy of Religion* 48, no. 3 (September 1980): 415–31.

Ravetto-Biagioli, Kriss. *Digital Uncanny*. Oxford: Oxford Univ. Press, 2019.

Richter, Nicole. "Bisexual Erasure in 'Lesbian Vampire' Film Theory." *Journal of Bisexuality* 13 (2013): 274–75.

Rodman, Ron. "'Coperettas,' 'Detecterns,' and Space Operas: Music and Genre Hybridization in American Television." In *Music in Television: Channels of Listening*, edited by James Deaville, 35–56. New York: Routledge, 2011.

Rodman, Sarah. "CW's *Crazy Ex-Girlfriend* Could Be a Winner." *Boston Globe*, October 12, 2015. https://www.bostonglobe.com/lifestyle/names/2015/10/11 /crazy-show-could-winner/LVZI58ovGKFfRgvoojc2hK/story.html.

Rollins, Samantha. "'Crazy Ex-Girlfriend' Proves That On-Screen Diversity Is Actually Really Easy to Achieve." *Bustle*. March 5, 2018. https://www.bustle

.com/p/crazy-ex-girlfriend-proves-that-on-screen-diversity-is-actually-really
-easy-to-achieve-8389564.

Rustad, Gry. "Metamodernism, Quirky and Feminism*." *Notes on Metamodernism*. Last modified February 29, 2012. http://www.metamodernism.com /2012/02/29/metamodernism-quirky-and-feminism/.

Ryan, Maureen. "'Crazy Ex-Girlfriend' Plans 'Our Version of a Happy Ending.'" *New York Times*, October 10, 2018. https://www.nytimes.com/2018/10/10/arts /television/crazy-ex-girlfriend-rachel-bloom-aline-brosh-mckenna-interview .html.

———. "For Women, the CW Is Still the Gold Standard." *Variety*, October 21, 2016, 28.

———. "From 'Supergirl' to 'Crazy Ex-Girlfriend,' Women Are the Real Heroes of the CW." *Variety*, October 12, 2016. https://variety.com/2016/voices /columns/cw-gilmore-girls-crazy-ex-girlfriend-1201885544/.

Sandvoss, Cornell. *Fans: The Mirror of Consumption*. Cambridge: Polity Press, 2005.

Scarlet, Janina. *Superhero Therapy: Mindfulness Guide to Help Teens and Young Adults Deal with Anxiety, Depression and Trauma*. Oakland: New Harbinger, 2017.

Schaffstall, Katherine. "'Crazy Ex-Girlfriend' Star Rachel Bloom on Writing about Mental Illness and Upcoming Musical Numbers." *Hollywood Reporter*. November 30, 2017. https://www.hollywoodreporter.com/news/crazy -girlfriend-star-rachel-bloom-writing-mental-illness-upcoming-musical -numbers-1063004.

Schantz, Ned. *Gossip, Letters, Phones: The Scandal of Female Networks in Film and Literature*. Oxford: Oxford Univ. Press, 2008.

Schneider, Michael. "The CW Looks to the Future as Its Parent Companies Evolve." *Variety*, August 7, 2019. https://variety.com/2019/tv/news/cw-cbs -warnermedia-1203294203/.

Sconce, Jeffrey. "Irony, Nihilism and the New American 'Smart' Film." *Screen* 43, no. 4 (2002): 349–69.

Sedgwick, Eve Kosofsky. *Between Men: English Literature and Male Homosocial Desire*. New York: Columbia Univ. Press, 1985.

———. *Epistemology of the Closet*. Berkeley: Univ. of California Press, 1990.

Segal, Judy Z. "Breast Cancer Narratives as Public Rhetoric: Genre Itself and the Maintenance of Ignorance." *Linguistics and Human Sciences* 3, no. 1 (2007): 3–23.

Shaviro, Steven. *Digital Music Videos.* New Brunswick, NJ: Rutgers Univ. Press, 2017.

———. "Post-Continuity." *The Pinocchio Theory,* March 26, 2012. http://www .shaviro.com/Blog/?p=1034.

Seitz, Matt Zoller. "*Crazy Ex-Girlfriend* Season 4 Beats the Odds." *TV Review,* October 10, 2018. https://www.vulture.com/2018/10/crazy-ex-girlfriend-season -4-review.html.

Sher, Ben. "Fraught Pleasures: Domestic Trauma and Cinephilia in American Culture." PhD diss., University of California, Los Angeles, 2015.

Shoemaker, Allison. "A Hard-to-Watch 'Crazy Ex-Girlfriend' Is Imperfect, Honest, and Remarkable." *AV Club,* November 11, 2017. https://www.avclub.com /a-hard-to-watch-crazy-ex-girlfriend-is-imperfect-hones-1820355727.

Skolnick, Arlene. "Beyond the 'M' Word: The Tangled Web of Politics and Marriage." *Dissent* 53, no. 4 (Fall 2006): 81–87.

———. "Talking about Family Values after 'Family Values." *Dissent* 57, no. 4 (Fall 2010): 96–102.

Sloane, Robert. "Who Wants Candy? Disenchantment in *The Simpsons.*" In *Leaving Springfield: The Simpsons and the Possibility of Oppositional Culture,* edited by John Alberti, 137–71. Detroit: Wayne State Univ. Press, 2004.

Slopen, Natalie, Amy Watson, Gabriela Gracia, and Patrick Corrigan. "Age Analysis of Newspaper Coverage of Mental Illness." *Journal of Health Communication,* no. 12 (2017): 3–15.

Somerville, Siobhan B. "Queer." In *Keywords for American Culture Studies,* edited by Bruce Burgett and Glenn Hendler, 203–7. New York: New York Univ. Press, 2014.

Spring, Katherine. *Saying It with Songs.* Oxford: Oxford Univ. Press, 2013.

Stahler, Kelsea. "'Crazy Ex-Girlfriend' Star Rachel Bloom Is Living Proof That Fangirling Is a Radical Act." *Bustle,* July 24, 2018. https://www.bustle.com /p/crazy-ex-girlfriend-star-rachel-bloom-is-living-proof-that-fangirling-is-a -radical-act-9844149.

Stevens, Maurice E. "Trauma Is as Trauma Does." In *Critical Trauma Studies: Understanding Violence, Conflict and Memory in Everyday Life,* edited by Monica J. Casper and Eric Wertheimer, 19–36. New York: New York Univ. Press, 2016.

Storr, Merl. *Bisexuality: A Critical Reader.* London: Routledge, 1999.

Stout, Patricia A., Jorge Villegas, and Nancy A. Jennings. "Images of Mental Illness in the Media: Identifying Gaps in the Research." *Schizophrenia Bulletin* 30, no. 3 (2004): 543–61.

Strouther, Danielle. "Quality and Risk in Contemporary U.S. Television." MRes thesis, University of Nottingham, 2017. http://eprints.nottingham.ac.uk/47419/.

Stuart, Heather. "Violence and Mental Illness: An Overview." *World Psychiatry* 2 (2003): 121–24. https://www.ncbi.nlm.nih.gov/pmc/articles/PMC1525086/.

Sullivan, John. *Media Audiences: Effects, Users, Institutions, and Power.* Thousand Oaks, CA: SAGE, 2012.

Summers, Anthony. *Goddess: The Secret Lives of Marilyn Monroe.* New York: Hachette, 2013.

Tan, Ed S. *Emotion and the Structure of Narrative Film: Film as an Emotion Machine.* Mahwah: Erlbaum, 1996.

Telotte, J. P. "The Call of Desire and the Film Noir." *Literature/Film Quarterly* 17, no. 1 (1989): 50–58. https://search-proquest-com.ucc.idm.oclc.org/docview/226986994?accountid=14504.

Thomas, Douglas. *Hacker Culture.* Minneapolis: Univ. of Minnesota Press, 2002.

Thomas, Kaitlin. "The CW Boss Defends Renewing *Crazy Ex-Girlfriend.*" *TV Guide,* January 8, 2017. https://www.tvguide.com/news/crazy-exgirlfriend-renewed-season-3-mark-pedowitz-cw/.

———. "How Crazy Ex-Girlfriend Embraced the Crazy and Became Must-See TV." *TV.com,* March 5, 2016.

Thompson, Robert J. *Television's Second Golden Age: From Hill Street Blues to ER.* Syracuse: Syracuse Univ. Press, 1997.

Tolentino, Jia. "How 'Empowerment' Became Something for Women to Buy." *New York Times,* April 17, 2016. https://www.nytimes.com/2016/04/17/magazine/how-empowerment-became-something-for-women-to-buy.html.

Tolentino, Jia. *Trick Mirror: Reflections on Self-Delusion.* New York: Random House, 2019.

Trites, Roberta. *Disturbing the Universe: Power and Repression in Adolescent Literature.* Iowa City: Univ. of Iowa Press, 2000.

Turchiano, Danielle. "Rachel Bloom Reflects on Emotional 'Crazy Ex-Girlfriend' Season and Plans for Final Year." *Variety,* May 17, 2018. https://variety.com/2018/tv/features/rachel-bloom-crazy-ex-girlfriend-final-season-interview-1202793228/.

United States Census Bureau. "Nearly 1 in 5 People Have a Disability in the U.S., Census Bureau Reports." https://www.census.gov/newsroom/releases/archives/miscellaneous/cb12-134.html.

Vandenberg, Kathleen M. "René Girard and the Rhetoric of Consumption." *Contagion: Journal of Violence, Mimesis & Culture* 12/13, no. 1 (2006): 259–72.

VanDerWerff, Todd. "Crazy Ex-Girlfriend's Unexpected Season 3 Renewal Shows How TV's Rules Are Changing." *Vox*, January 10, 2017. https://www.vox.com/culture/2017/1/10/14206016/crazy-ex-girlfriend-season-3-renewal.

Vaneijk, Maggy. "How Crazy Ex-Girlfriend Is Having the Smartest, Most Empathetic Conversations about Mental Health." *Pool.com*, November 22, 2017. https://www.the-pool.com/health/mind/2017/47/Maggy-Vaneijk-on-Crazy-Ex-Girlfriend-and-mental-health.

Vermeulen, Timotheus, and Robin Van den Akker. "Notes on Metamodernism." *Journal of Aesthetics and Culture* 2, no. 1 (2010): 1–14.

Vicari, Justin. *Male Bisexuality in Current Cinema: Images of Growth, Rebellion and Survival*. Jefferson, NC: McFarland, 2011.

Villareal, Yvonne. "Crazy Ex-Girlfriend' Creators Weigh in on the Exploration of Rebecca's Mental Health." *LA Times.com*, December 8, 2017. http://www.latimes.com/entertainment/tv/la-et-st-rachel-bloom-crazy-ex-girlfriend-20171208-htmlstory.html#.

Vines, Christine. "The Damage of "Crazy Ex-Girlfriend." March 22, 2017. https://electricliterature.com/the-damage-of-crazy-ex-girlfriend-be86d9d2b10.

Walker, Janet. *Trauma Cinema: Documenting Incest and the Holocaust*. Berkeley: Univ. of California Press, 2005.

Wallenstein, Andrew. "CW Courts Digital Auds with Original Content." *Variety*, May 17, 2012. https://variety.com/2012/tv/news/cw-courts-digital-auds-with-original-content-1118054214/.

Watts, Jay. "I'm a Psychologist, and This Is the Truth about Whether You Can Tell If Someone Is a 'Psychopath' or Not." *The Independent*, July 5, 2017. https://www.independent.co.uk/Voices/personality-disorder-mental-health-girl-interrupted-fatal-attraction-misdiagnosis-a7825066.html.

Weber, Brenda R., and Joselyn K. Leimbach. "Ellen Degeneres's Incorporate Body: The Politics of Authenticity." In *Hysterical! Women in American Comedy*, edited by Linda Mizejewski and Victoria Sturtevant, 303–23. Austin: Univ. of Texas Press, 2017.

Weldon, Glen. "The Top 27 Songs of 'Crazy Ex-Girlfriend,' Ranked, Ruthlessly and Dispassionately." *NPR*, April 8, 2019. https://www.npr.org/2019/04/08/709062466/the-top-27-songs-of-crazy-ex-girlfriend-ranked-ruthlessly-and-dispassionately.

Williams, Rebecca. "'Anyone Who Calls Muse a *Twilight* Band Will be Shot on Sight': Music, Distinction, and the 'Interloping Fan' in the *Twilight* Franchise." *Popular Music and Society* 36, no. 3 (2013): 327–42.

———. *Post-Object Fandom: Television, Identity and Self-Narrative*. New York: Bloomsbury Academic, 2015.

Williams, Zoe. "Lady Gaga, Miley Cyrus and the Rape Generation." *The Guardian*, June 24, 2014. https://www.theguardian.com/music/womens-blog/2014/jun/24/lady-gaga-do-what-u-want-rape-generation.

Wilson, Carl. "Crazy Exegesis." *Slate*, January 4, 2018. https://slate.com/arts/2018/01/crazy-ex-girlfriend-deconstructs-pop-music-and-destigmatizes-mental-illness.html.

Wilson, Stephen. *Information Arts: Intersections of Art, Science, and Technology*. Cambridge, MA: MIT Press, 2002.

Winch, Alison. *Girlfriends and Postfeminist Sisterhood*. Hampshire: Palgrave Macmillan, 2013.

Wisse, Ruth R. *No Joke: Making Jewish Humor*. Princeton, NJ: Princeton Univ. Press, 2013.

Woolf, Virginia. *A Room of One's Own*. 1928; reprint ed., London: Penguin, 2000.

Yahr, Emily. "'Crazy Ex-Girlfriend's' Raunchy, Hilarious Concert Tour Proves Low TV Ratings May Not Matter." *Washington Post*, April 9, 2018. https://www.washingtonpost.com/news/soloish/wp/2018/04/09/crazy-ex-girlfriends-tv-ratings-are-low-but-its-fans-are-loyal/?noredirect=on&utm_term=.44e2b418b2d8.

Younger, Beth. *Learning Curves: Body Image and Female Sexuality in Young Adult Literature*. Lanham, MD: Scarecrow Press, Inc: 2009.

Zacharias, Ramona. "Crazy Ex-Girlfriend Showrunner, Aline Brosh McKenna on Creating a Hit TV Show." June 20, 2018. https://creativescreenwriting.com/crazy-ex-girlfriend-showrunner-aline-brosh-mckenna-creating-hit-tv-show/.

Žižek, Slavoj. *The Sublime Object of Ideology*. London: Verso, 1989.

Zoller Seitz, Matt. "The Best Show on TV Is *Crazy Ex-Girlfriend*," *Vulture*, June 29, 2016.

———. *Mad Men Carousel: The Complete Critical Companion*. New York: Harry N. Abrams, 2015.

Zoller Seitz, Matt, and Alan Sepinwall. *The Sopranos Sessions*. New York: Harry N. Abrams, 2019.

# Contributors

**Lauren Boumaroun** is a PhD candidate in cinema and media studies at the University of California, Los Angeles. Her dissertation, "Everyday Cosplay: Engaging with Film and Television through Costume and Clothing," combines production studies and fan studies in an examination of everyday cosplay and the adaptation of screen costumes for the retail fashion market. She also researches audience psychology, representations of mental illness, and the therapeutic benefits of film and television viewing.

**Bibi Burger** is a lecturer at the University of Pretoria, South Africa. She lectures on Afrikaans literature as well as on the relationship between gender and literature. Her research interests include gender studies, ecocriticism, and South African comparative literature. She is a 2018/2019 African Humanities Program postdoctoral fellow.

**Charles Burnetts** teaches film in the Department of Philosophy and Religious Studies at Kings University College, the University of Western Ontario. His book is titled *Improving Passions: Sentimental Aesthetics and American Film* (Oxford Univ. Press, 2017). He has published articles in *Journal of Film and Video, New Review of Film and Television Studies*, and *Scope*.

**Christi Cook** received her BS in Psychology and her BA in Spanish from Abilene Christian University in 1999. In 2007, she was awarded an MA degree in women's spirituality at New College of California, and in 2013 she received her PhD in English from the University of Texas at Arlington. Her dissertation explores the portrayal of sexuality and gender in Anglo and Chicana YA literature. She has served as an assistant professor of English at Tarrant County College and at Southwestern Oklahoma State University, where she taught a variety of literature courses utilizing pop culture. She moved closer to home in Fort Worth, Texas, to be a professor of English at Weatherford College this year. Cook's other publications include "Holiness and Heresy: Viramontes, la Virgen, and the Mother-Daughter Bond" in *Critical Insights: Literature of Protest, Sacred Sex: Integrating Our Bodies and Our Spirituality*; "Home Is Where the Heart Is: The Parallel Construction of 'Home' and Cultural Hybridity in Chicana and Vampyre Adolescent Bodies" in *Race in the Vampire Narrative*; and "Bite Me: The Allure of Vampires and Dark Magic in Chicana Young Adult Literature" in *Nerds, Goths, Geeks, and Freaks: Outsiders in Chicanx and Latinx Young Adult Literature*.

**David Scott Diffrient** is professor of film and media studies in the Department of Communication Studies at Colorado State University. His articles have been published in *Cinema Journal, Historical Journal of Film, Radio, and Television, Journal of Fandom Studies, Journal of Film and Video, Journal of Popular Television, Journal of Popular Film and Television, New Review of Film and Television Studies, Quarterly Review of Film and Video, Post Script*, and *Velvet Light Trap*, as well as in several edited collections about film and television topics. He is the coeditor of *Screwball Television: Critical Perspectives on Gilmore Girls* (Syracuse Univ. Press, 2010) and the author of three books: *M\*A\*S\*H* (Wayne State Univ. Press, 2008), *Omnibus Films: Theorizing Transauthorial Cinema* (Edinburgh Univ. Press, 2014), and *Movie Migrations: Transnational Genre Flows and South Korean Cinema* (Rutgers Univ. Press, 2015). He is currently completing a book on the comic construction of "bad behavior" on American television.

**Kathleen W. Taylor Kollman** recently completed a PhD in American culture studies at Bowling Green State University. She served as a lecturer in English and women's studies at Wright State University for nearly a decade. Her scholarship focuses on feminist criticism of popular fiction and media. Kollman has two novels published. In addition to her PhD, she holds an MFA in writing popular fiction from Seton Hill University and an MA in literature from Wright State University. Her dissertation is on fictional representations of female US presidents in film, television, and literature produced during the twentieth century. Kollman is currently serving as a lecturer in English at the Wooster campus of the Ohio State University.

**Amanda Konkle** is an assistant professor of film studies and English at Georgia Southern University's Armstrong Campus in Savannah, Georgia. She is the author of *Some Kind of Mirror: Creating Marilyn Monroe* (Rutgers Univ. Press,

2019), focused on Marilyn Monroe's films and star persona, and of articles in *Quarterly Review of Film and Video, Teaching Media Quarterly,* and *Feminist Encounters.*

**Marija Laugalyte** recently completed a PhD in reception and cultural studies at University College Cork. Her doctoral research has focused on reparative feminist readings of female-centered television series, and her overall research interests span forms of reception, feminism and popular culture, adaptation, and fan reception. She holds an MA in Film Studies and a BA in English and French from University College Cork. She has been published in *Aigne* journal.

**Hazel Mackenzie** is lecturer and research lead for English Literature at the University of Buckingham. Her specialty is Victorian periodical studies. She has published essays on the journalism of Charles Dickens, William Makepeace Thackeray, Anthony Trollope, and George Eliot. She is currently working on a research companion to Dickens's *The Old Curiosity Shop* for Liverpool Univ. Press.

**Chelsea McCracken** is an assistant professor of media studies at the State University of New York at Oneonta. She received her PhD from the University of Wisconsin–Madison's Communication Arts Department. She has published articles in *Screen, Media History,* and *Asian Cinema.* Her areas of research include histories of global media industries, feminist and LGBTQ media studies, and American independent film.

**Christine Prevas** is a PhD candidate in the Department of English and Comparative Literature at Columbia University, and received their MPhil in English from the University of Cambridge. Their research focuses on queer affect and architectures of horror, particularly within the troubled domestic space of the haunted house. Their work has been published in *Journal of Dracula Studies* as well as in various outlets online.

**Caitlin E. Ray** is a PhD candidate in rhetoric and composition at the University of Louisville Department of English. Her research focuses on the intersection of disability studies and medical rhetoric, and she is currently studying the rhetoric and representation of rare illnesses. She has been published in *Pedagogy and Theatre of the Oppressed Journal, Kairos: A Journal of Rhetoric, Technology* *and Pedagogy*, and the edited collection *Making Future Matters* (Computers & Composition Digital Press). She is currently a graduate writing consultant at the University of Nebraska at Omaha Writing Center.

**Carel van Rooyen** completed his BA degree in language and culture at Stellenbosch University in 2014, majoring in visual studies, applied English language studies, and Afrikaans and Dutch. He continued his studies by doing an honors degree in Afrikaans and Dutch, writing his thesis on metamodern Dutch poetry. Now working in the education sector, he maintains and sustains an interest in pop culture, gender constructs, and identity politics.

**Stephanie Salerno** received her PhD in American culture studies from Bowling Green State University in 2016. Her research interests span affect and trauma studies, gender performativity and persona in popular music performance, and representations of difference in television and film. Her writing has been published in *Popular Culture Studies Journal*, *Performance Matters*, and *Journal of Popular Culture*. She can be reached at salernosas@gmail.com.

**Billy Stevenson** completed his PhD at the University of Sydney in 2014. His thesis focused on the role that cinematic infrastructure plays in a postcinematic media ecology. Since then he has published on postcinematic affect and contemporary film and television. He is currently completing a manuscript on the aesthetics of *Twin Peaks: The Return*.

**Margaret Tally** is full professor of social and public policy at the School for Graduate Studies of the State University of New York, Empire State College. She is the author of *Television Culture and Women's Lives: Thirtysomething and the Contradictions of Gender* (1995). She has also edited three book collections with Betty Kaklamanidou: *HBO's Girls: Questions of Gender, Politics, and Millennial Angst* (2014), *The Millennials on Film and Television: Essays on the Politics of Popular Culture* (2014), and *Politics and Politicians in Contemporary US Television* (2016). She has authored several articles and book chapters in the area of gender and popular culture. Her most recent book is *The Rise of the Anti-Heroine in TV's Third Golden Age* (2016).

# Index